Also by Hugh Fordin

The World of Entertainment! Hollywood's Greatest Musicals
   (The Freed Unit at MGM)
Jerome Kern: The Man and His Music
Vocal Selections from That's Entertainment!
Film TV Daily Yearbook of Motion Pictures and Television (52nd edition)

GETTING TO KNOW HIM

A Biography of
Oscar Hammerstein II

Hugh Fordin

GETTING
TO KNOW HIM

Random House / New York

Library of Congress Cataloging in Publication Data
Fordin, Hugh, 1935–
    Getting to know him.
    Bibliography: p.
    Includes index.
    1. Hammerstein, Oscar, 1895–1960. 2. Librettists
United States—Biography. I. Title.
ML423.H24F7   782.8'1'0924 [B]   77–6021
ISBN 0–394–49441–5

Manufactured in the United States of America
9 8 7 6 5 4 3 2
First Edition

Design by Anne Lian

Author's Note

When I started to work on this book, people wanted to know why I wanted to write the story of a man who didn't have a mean bone in his body, who was loved by everyone, revered by both his friends and his fans. There was nothing controversial about him; his character didn't seem to be particularly complex—but, of course, this is far from the truth.

Although I believed it important to provide a record of Oscar Hammerstein's forty-year contribution to the American musical theater, I didn't want to write just an "and then he wrote" book. I wanted to gain some understanding of the man himself who did so much not only for the theater but for many people who were lucky enough to know him.

Help in getting to know him came from many sources. I must first of all express my gratitude to Mrs. Oscar Hammerstein II, who granted me permission to use her late husband's archives, without which this book could not have been written. Dorothy Hammerstein was generous with her time and unfailingly patient, gracious and helpful. The children—William Hammerstein, James Hammerstein, Alice Hammerstein Mathias, Susan Jacobson Ades and Henry Jacobson

—were enormously cooperative and, at every step, friendly, open and frank (even when the tape recorder was rolling).

To list all others who aided me in many ways, providing letters and other documents, vivid memories and vague recollections, fresh leads and confirmation of facts, would be impossible, but I am deeply grateful to them all.

There are several that I am obligated to single out because of the extensive time and help they gave me:

Irving Berlin, Agnes deMille, Joshua Logan, Max Gordon, Stephen Sondheim, Mary Martin, Ruth Mitchell, Leighton Brill, Audrey Wood Liebling, Elaine Steinbeck, William O. Harbach and Fred Zinnemann shared with me the part of their lives that Oscar touched.

Arnold Michaelis; Alfred Simon; Stanley Green; Miles Kreuger; Betty Emery; Edward Waters, of the Library of Congress; Mildred Simpson, of the Academy of Motion Pictures Arts and Sciences; Professor Robert Knutson, of the University of Southern California; and Sylvia Shulman were of invaluable help to me in my research.

And Robin Chase, my collaborator, who helped to shape the material of this book, provided unfailing support.

Introduction

by Stephen Sondheim

I didn't know him well, but he saved my life. He and Dorothy. I was only ten at the time, the remnant of a divorce, and they took me in. My perceptions must surely have been even more distorted than those of the usual ten-year-old, but I remember being overwhelmed by the extraordinary serenity of their house in Pennsylvania. The huge living room was dark and cool and chic, the atmosphere was unhurried. Not reverent—there were too many children for that—but unhurried, promising that every wound would be healed and that boredom would be dispensed with forever.

They referred to it as The Farm, which seemed a very modest thing to call it. True, it was on top of a hill and it had acres of meadow and farmland in undulating Pennsylvania style and you could stand on the porch of the house and hear the sounds of lowing, mooing, squawking and cackling fill the air. But it was the distant air, and although the cattle were standing like statues, they were just beyond the tennis court. (To be fair, the tennis court was built a few years later; we used the one at The Farm across the road.) It was a place of material as well as spiritual comfort.

Oscar was elegant, which may surprise those who associate him with the homespun quality of his work. That elegance lay beyond his courtliness and in spite of the crassness, to my ears, of a New York accent which allowed "girl" to be pronounced halfway to "goil." (I learned only recently that the pronunciation had been considered elegant at the turn of the century, when Oscar was growing up.) It even lay beyond his nattiness—not that he was a dandy, he just always looked perfect, patrolling that delicate territory between the casual and the formal, whether on the court or at the bridge table; in fact, I think he was nattier *out* of doors—the sweatier, the nattier.

He chuckled a lot. Certainly he was capable of guffaws and even occasionally a roar, but I think he preferred to chuckle. Sometimes, again on the court, the only sign we would have that we'd amused him (or that he'd amused himself) was that the waistband of his tennis shorts would be jiggling up and down. His own humor was dry and restrained, distanced. I suspect he preferred to chuckle because it was a moderate action, and I think of him as a moderate man. But the moderation was a decision, not a convenience. In his work he was often daring—even, as in *Allegro*, shocking. He chose to use parts of himself at certain times and not at others. That makes for elegance, but it also makes for opacity, and as you read this book, you'll discover that no one knew him well—or at least no one *thinks* so.

When, at twenty-eight, I first went into analysis, he became inordinately curious. Each time we'd meet he'd ask pointed, if considerately impersonal, questions. Was it painful? Did childhood experiences really leave scars? Did I feel any change? I don't think he was considering therapy for himself, but I think he was looking for insights through osmosis; he hoped that my fumbling attempts at self-exploration would help to explain things about himself that he had never understood. Among them were his conflicted feelings about his collaborator and the relationship between work and sex—he had never been so intimate with me, and it wasn't merely the result of my having grown to personal and professional manhood that made it possible; the analysis was a bond between us, almost a secret.

That kind of curiosity prevented the moderation from becoming stodgy. Early on in our acquaintance, for example, he confessed to being baffled by "modern" music, music that wasn't tuneful in the traditional sense. Because he was curious, I gave him for his birthday a recording of the Ravel trio (I wanted to start him off as tunefully as possible), and I followed it each year with slightly more contemporary-sounding pieces. I never got him quite as far as *Wozzeck,* but by the time he died seventeen years later, I'd led him through the marshes of Prokofiev and into the thickets of Stravinsky. He didn't like everything I presented to him, but he never hesitated to say what he felt. Many people might have, for fear of being thought narrow-minded or philistine, but not Oscar. He was often conservative, but never reactionary. Moderate.

He was judgmental, a true moralist. Moralists tend to make better giants than they do fathers. His expectations were high, never higher than where his children were concerned, and so, given his moralism, he wasn't always a tolerant parent. He didn't understand children until they were of a rational age. Perhaps he felt a bit threatened by their whimsicality and impulsiveness, by their illogic, and his best defense was irony. Sometimes the irony lurched into sarcasm, and when it did, the victims were more likely to be his flesh-and-blood children than we outsiders (as you will see, the Hammerstein house during the years of World War II was virtually an orphanage as well as a home). He was the best surrogate father one could have wished for: always encouraging, always understanding, always gentle. Favored outsiders were easy for him to deal with. His own children fared less well, though, and I doubt if he ever connected the scars he left with the ones he asked about so many years later.

The point, of course, is that he *was* a giant. He changed the texture of the American musical theater forever, first with Kern, then with Rodgers. And to change that means not only to change musical theater all over the world, but to change all American theater as well, because musical theater has affected playwriting profoundly and permanently. There may be librettists and lyricists (very few) whose work is admired more, but there are none greater. That would be reason enough for this book, but there is a better reason, the best reason for all biographies of recent lives: to record the facts correctly before the peripheral figures forget and distort too much. To be alive at the same time as Oscar Hammerstein II was an enormous privilege, and the memories of those who knew him should be fixed and displayed immediately, before ripeness and rot set in.

He saved my life with his counsel and his presence. He taught me not everything I know but everything I needed to know in order to write for myself and not for him. But then, he taught everybody: he sang for us all. He understood everything about teaching because that's what he was, a teacher, and what he liked best about it was that "by your pupils you are taught" (verse, "Getting to Know You," *The King and I,* 1951).

Two months before he died, Dorothy had a birthday for him with his immediate children, their families, and us orphans from the old days. Whether he knew he was dying I have no idea, but he had had his picture taken by a fashionable New York portrait photographer in three poses, each grayer, more benign and less human than the other; they were gifts for all of us and were spread out in three piles on the piano. Facing for the first time the imminent death of someone who mattered to me, I suddenly felt the anguished need to have his autograph. I wanted permanent proof that he had existed. I looked at the three cream-matted poses and chose a humorously contemplative one, looking East. I asked him if he'd sign it. He stared at me as if I'd lost my mind: nineteen years of knowing each other, and I was asking for an autograph? Dinner was announced. Everyone headed for the dining room, leaving Oscar and me alone. He gave me a glittering and mischievous glance, and with a quick look of triumph he grabbed a pen and scribbled across the border at the bottom of the picture. Then, capping the pen briskly, he walked out of the room, clearly satisfied. I went to the piano and read what he'd written, what the man who had tutored and nurtured and argued with and tolerated me for nineteen years had written: "For Steve, my friend and teacher."

I saw him once more: a week later he asked me to lunch. In all the time we'd known each other, he'd never formally asked me for lunch; fathers don't ask sons for lunch. He took me to his club—I didn't even know he had one. I figured he must have something of particular importance to tell me and kept waiting for him to reveal it. Among other things, we talked about analysis, *The Sound of Music,* my parents, his children, the show I was writing. After lunch, I walked him back to 63rd Street, and we embraced and parted. All the walk home, I tried to figure out the reason for the lunch. To this day I don't know why I was so slow, but I finally got it. It was the elegant and moderate thing to do, and he'd done it. He'd never come close to saying goodbye, but he'd been saying goodbye.

GETTING TO KNOW HIM

One

Oscar Greeley Clendenning Hammerstein

Leaning out the living-room window of his parents' apartment on East 116th Street, Oscar Hammerstein II could see his father coming home from work on the Madison Avenue streetcar. When he got off at the corner diagonally opposite, Willie looked up, as he always did, to see if any of his family was there and waved at Ockie before crossing the street. This ceremony occurred each evening and when he left the house in the morning.

The Hammerstein family—Willie, his wife Alice, and their children, Oscar, born on July 12, 1895, and Reginald, nineteen months younger —lived as well-regulated a life as any of their middle-class neighbors in upper Manhattan. The young couple seldom entertained and had few visitors who were not members of the family. One would hardly have guessed that the job Willie Hammerstein went off to and came home from with such regularity was that of one of America's most successful theatrical managers, at Hammerstein's Victoria Theatre, the most colorful vaudeville house in New York.

Watching the tall, quiet, conservatively dressed family man walking home from the streetcar, one would have been even more surprised to learn that he was the son of Oscar Hammerstein I, the flamboyant showman whose name and face were continually in the public eye as he made and lost fortunes, built twelve theaters, ran several opera companies and conducted well-publicized feuds. With his passion for litigation, the short, stocky figure with a Vandyke beard was always involved in some lawsuit—once in forty separate but simultaneous ones.

Young Oscar knew little of all this while growing up in a comfortable sheltered environment far from theaters and show people, but he grew up to become a theatrical figure whose fame eclipsed the considerable fame of his grandfather, his father and his uncle. Not only did he contribute to the musical heritage of several generations with such songs as "Ol Man River," "Indian Love Call," "Who?" "You'll Never Walk Alone," "Some Enchanted Evening" and "The Sound of Music," but he radically altered the American musical with his *Show Boat, Oklahoma! Carousel* and *South Pacific.*

"The Hammerstein family is to the American theater what the Adams family is to American politics, and is equally worth the study," Clifton Fadiman once wrote. Seeing what effect this family had on its most famous member will help to illuminate the character of Oscar Hammerstein II; he would later write, "['Grandfather] was a strange man and so perhaps am I." In some ways Oscar II seemed the least strange of men, leading a quiet, orderly private life for most of his life. By temperament he was calm and steady; he accepted success with the same equanimity with which he accepted failure. Professionally he became a solid craftsman, a lyricist and librettist who knew all the rules and used them carefully to construct lyrics and books. Yet it was the ability of this conservative man to defy theatrical convention, discard the rules and take risks which lifted him above the ordinary run of craftsmen. He was described as "a careful dreamer," a phrase that suggests the curious combination of traits that runs through the Hammerstein family.

The Hammerstein story begins in Germany, where the lyricist's grandfather was born. Oscar Hammerstein, the first child of Abraham Hammerstein, a prosperous young contractor in Stettin, and his wife Berthe, was born on May 8, 1847. When he was eight, the family, which by now included four more children, was living in Berlin where Abraham was a trader on the stock exchange. When Oscar was twelve, he entered a music conservatory, where he worked reasonably hard on the violin, but it became plain that he was not destined to be a great performer. Instead, the shift in his education opened the door to what would become his life's passion: opera. All students at the conservatory were required to attend performances at the opera house. Once he had discovered opera, nothing excited him more. He discussed it as other boys discussed sports. He went as often as he could, with his class or with his mother. Every opera he saw was an overwhelming experience, and when he came home, his words tumbled out almost unintelligibly as he tried to communicate his thoughts and feelings. His father laughed at his exhilaration, but his mother listened encouragingly, even when the boy made reckless assertions of what he would have done had he been producing this or that work.

Two years after he entered the conservatory, all that was warm and tender went out of his life when his mother died. Accompanying the domestic tragedy were the rumblings of a broader crisis. The new Kaiser recalled Bismarck from his post in Paris, and together they embarked on their policy of blood and iron. Abraham Hammerstein would vehemently avow at the dinner table that at last Prussia was coming into her own. At night sixteen-year-old Oscar would lie in bed envisioning the army life that was sure to come, with nowhere to go on furloughs but the house ruled by his father and his new stepmother, an austere, heavy blonde whom the children called the Dutch Widow.

One sunny afternoon in the winter of 1865 young Oscar skipped the daily violin practice demanded by his father to skate on a lake near his home. When he returned to the house with flushed cheeks and the incriminating skates strapped over his shoulder, his father was waiting for him. A violent tirade was followed by an equally violent beating administered with a strap of the very skates that had caused the trouble. The next day Oscar left home. He sold his violin and, with this money, went to Hamburg and then to Dover, where he found a ship on which he could work his way to New York. He arrived with two assets: his freedom and a determination as strong as his father's to show *him* that he could do whatever he wanted to do.

His first job was cigar making, at two dollars a week. Within a year, he produced the first of his many inventions, a wooden mold that would ensure the uniformity of cigars. After selling the invention for $6,000, he went on to invent a machine that stripped tobacco by air suction, a device that was a forerunner of the modern vacuum cleaner.

Before he was twenty, he met and married a beautiful, gentle woman, Rose Blau. Although there were to be a good many women in his life, none would have the same hold on his love. During their court-ship they liked to attend the theater and the opera whenever he could afford to buy tickets. With his wife's approval, Oscar used the money from his inventions to invest in theaters, beginning with the Thalia. He combined his practical and artistic interests by writing music and one-act comedies for the program of the theaters he had invested in. Within five years, he was part owner of two and impresario of another.

After having given birth to four sons—Harry, Arthur, William and Abraham—Rose died. Oscar was so grief-stricken that his life came to a halt while his sister Anna looked after his household. He brooded and took long walks by himself, leaving his business affairs unattended. After a while, his resilient spirit exerted itself and he was once more able to invest, plan, and build.

In the early 1880's the homes on 125th Street were wooden shacks; to the north of that street not more than two hundred private houses existed on the West Side. Oscar saw an opportunity and, as usual, grabbed it. He built twenty-four apartment buildings and over fifty private dwellings. Deciding that a theater in Harlem might help at-tract people to the neighborhood, he built the Harlem Opera House, which still stands as the Apollo Theatre. Because the singers were hesi-tant about going so far uptown, he guaranteed them 90 percent of the gross receipts. Not surprisingly, he initially lost money on this venture; his first opera, the American premiere of Mascagni's *Cavalleria Rusti-cana,* was a flop.

Oscar chose this unpropitious moment to launch his first season of grand opera. Calling on Edmund Stanton, general director of the Metropolitan Opera Company, he proposed an arrangement by which artists from the Met might come to Harlem for brief periods. Stanton, outraged at the audacity of his new competitor, showed him the door. Undaunted, Oscar went ahead with his plan. Lilli Lehmann, then prima donna at the Met, was so charmed by him that she agreed to perform for a week. Walter Damrosch, who served as conductor for the engagement, remembered that it was not a financial success. "But that didn't faze the indomitable Oscar. He ran his hand deep into his trouser pocket, made up the deficit without a murmur, and when everything had been settled, he said to me, 'Someday I will be an im-presario.'" His fortunes foundering, Oscar reached the curious con-clusion that Harlem needed not one theater, but two, and built the

Columbus Theater on the East Side. This time he was right, and the theater's immediate profits revived the Harlem Opera House as well.

His next venture was the erection of a theater at 34th Street (on the present site of Macy's), a long building surrounded by tall grass and empty lots. With his instinct for signing talent, the theater prospered, as did the others he was soon to build. In them he presented variety programs that outdid all competitors in lavishness and originality. The news of his flamboyant feats both entertained and enraged New York. Once he wagered a hundred dollars that he could write the score, book and lyrics of an operetta in forty-eight hours. He closeted himself in a room at the Gilsey House, and while other guests complained that a wild man was howling and thumping a piano, he succeeded in completing *Kohinoor*. He won the hundred dollars but lost ten thousand when he insisted on producing the show and keeping it running for a week. The Hammerstein legend grew as Oscar engaged in fistfights outside his theaters, hissed his own performers, ran well-publicized legal feuds with ex-partners and pulled off coup after coup in his theatrical presentations.

With all his success, a restless spirit drove him on to new projects and new risks. Noticing that the intersection of Broadway, Seventh Avenue and 42nd, 43rd and 44th streets at Longacre Square (now Times Square) was a busy transfer point for streetcar passengers, he bought the entire block front on the east side of Broadway between 44th and 45th streets and sank his entire resources into building a theater there, again miles away from any competition. His new theater, the Olympia, would present comic opera, burlesque and vaudeville in three auditoriums which would accommodate six thousand people. There would also be a roof garden (unheard of in the United States), a restaurant, a promenade. Ground was broken in January 1895 with the opening scheduled for November. Although he used his sons as aides and did virtually everything himself—including inventing architectural details (he took out thirty-eight patents that year) that would ensure acoustical perfection and aesthetic splendor—he still found the costs staggering.

The opening was a mob scene—thousands of hopeful customers stormed the doors after the first ten thousand had been admitted. For the first year, the theaters were filled to capacity every night. Oscar was habitually to be found in a corner lobby of one of his theaters, impeccably dressed in a Prince Albert suit and a shiny topper. When a woman asked him to explain why he wore a hat indoors, he said, "Madam, I sleep in it!"

In 1898, three years after a second Oscar Hammerstein was born, his autocratic handling of stars and competitors, his passion for dispute and his expensive whims had led him again to financial collapse, despite the efforts of his sons, Willie and Arthur, who had joined the Hammerstein enterprises. The president of New York Life, which had foreclosed the mortgage on the Olympia, wrote him a note to tell him that a company representative would run the theater. The Old Man, as his family referred to him, wrote back, "I am in receipt of your letter, which is now before me, and in a few minutes will be behind me. Respectfully yours, Oscar Hammerstein." As usual, Oscar was not down for long. A year later, when his next theater opened, he announced to reporters, "I have named my theater the Victoria because I have been victorious over mine enemies—those dirty bloodsuckers at New York Life."

After the success of the Victoria, built at the corner of Seventh Avenue and 42nd Street, Oscar finally fulfilled the dream of a lifetime by pouring most of the profits into building and operating the mammoth new Manhattan and Philadelphia opera houses. For four years he engaged in ferocious competition with the Metropolitan, while introducing modern French and Italian works and making innovations in his productions which would change the face of opera in America. (The Met eventually bought him out for over a million dollars.) His life was almost totally consumed by work and his obsessive desire for presenting grand opera. Though he married again and had two daughters, he preferred to live not at home but in two small dusty rooms in the Victoria furnished with a bed, a piano and a few torn armchairs. There, among piles of music, scripts, legal briefs, he puttered with his inventions and dreamed his dreams.

The twinkle in his eye, his inscrutable calm in the presence of general excitement, his bluff which no one appreciated more than himself—even when circumstances were going hard against him—and the kindness and spirit of camaraderie which lay beneath his flashy, gruff exterior led one of his biographers, Carl Van Vechten, to the conclusion that he played a comedy with himself. "Surely no adventurer, however gifted or successful, gets half the fun out of his adventuring unless he is able to watch himself all the time and smile and marvel at the tricks and turns of destiny. Hammerstein had this quality."

Nowhere was the oddness of this man more apparent than in his relations with his family. Despite the fact that he worked every day with Willie, the Old Man never met his grandson and namesake until Oscar II was seven years old. The boy was taken to the lobby where the Old Man was standing. They shook hands, but Oscar II remembered no conversation or comment—only that he did not have the courage to meet his grandfather's eyes and that he was relieved when the meeting was over. Although Oscar I's second wife, Malvina, occasionally visited the younger Hammerstein, Oscar saw the Old Man only once or twice a year thereafter, and always during brief, silent encounters in theater lobbies.

All in all, the famous grandfather was an embarrassment to Oscar, his celebrity casting a broad shadow that he could not elude. "I couldn't understand," said Oscar, "why he wasn't a pain in the neck to everyone as he was to me." Though the relationship of Oscar I with Oscar II was odd, impersonal and anything but direct, and although in many ways they were totally unlike, qualities of the grandfather appeared in the grandson. Oscar I had been described as a "cheerful fatalist"; the same could be said of his grandson. In each, romanticism and idealism were combined with steady determination. Both had magnetic charm. And both were in love with the theater.

Oscar's father, Willie, did not share this love. His attitude toward the theater was that of a man forced into a business to make a living for his family. It was not that he was a failure. In fact, he was an astute and successful showman. Will Rogers attributed to him his decision to talk to audiences—an act that led to fame. Willie was known as a wonder worker who turned ordinary variety acts into the sensational features that made playing at Hammerstein's Victoria the goal of every American and European performer. But he didn't like "going to the theater." Plays bored him; operas bored him even more, and later they enraged him. He didn't approve of his wife Allie seeing his own stepsister Stella, who was by then acting on the Broadway stage. It all seemed too "fast."

Kissing his father hello in the evening and good-bye in the morning was nearly the whole of Oscar's experience with him throughout his childhood. Willie never punished him and seldom scolded him, the extent of his rebukes being to ask "Is that nice?" if he disapproved of something the child had done or said. He also didn't show much affection, though Oscar sensed that his father loved him. Like many other Hammersteins, Willie did not express affection or deep feelings openly, but resorted to a certain gruffness and clumsy humor in his shyness. Although words failed him in speech, he expressed his thoughts rather eloquently and movingly in writing, as this letter to his wife attests:

August 2, 1894

Dear Allie,

The day we met you told me everything that was in your heart. When you believe in something you've got to run with it. You trust. You trust yourself and you trust others. You trust and you commit; you lay yourself on the line. It has never been in my nature to trust, really, and consequently, when it comes to my feelings, I find it equally difficult and painful, may I add, to commit. In other words, I am an escapist.

I have been incapable of putting myself on the line because it inevitably ends up with my getting hurt. Perhaps this is all due to some strange, deep-seated insecurity.

As a child growing up, I never really had the feeling of belonging. My mother, as you know, died when I was all of four years old, and, although I grew very dependent on my Aunt Anna, she too left to be married very shortly thereafter. When "my shadow of a father" remarried, I always felt that my step-mother would pay more attention to her own daughters: Rose and Stella, than any of us [referring to the boys]. I, for one, retreated into myself. More and more I became a loner.

But regardless, as I admit these things about me, to you, I am also saying that I need and love you with all my heart!

Yours forever,
Will

It was Allie, his mother, who was the major figure in Oscar's early years. Without ever seeming stern or hard, she firmly directed his life. "I did not fear her," he wrote, "but somehow I couldn't have borne the thought of displeasing her. I adored her with all my heart." A pretty woman with fair hair and blue eyes, she had a full figure that met the aesthetic standards of the time. Although she was devoted to her husband, her sons, and to a home life bounded by Victorian propriety, she was nevertheless strong-willed, impulsive and atypically modern in her active support of such causes as the woman-suffrage movement and family planning. Unlike her husband, she adored the theater and attended a matinée every week. Once she wrote a letter to *Town Topics* deploring the ridicule that had greeted her father-in-law's "really fine endeavors," and the scandalmongering among newsmen that had "ruined him." Through a mutual friend, she was instrumental in getting Marie Dressler to sponsor a rally for the Old Man, which was a great success.

Allie developed an unusual hobby, perhaps because her energy was not sufficiently employed by her circumscribed middle-class life. She moved. Nine times in the twelve years between Oscar's third birthday and his fifteenth, the Hammersteins moved from one house or apartment to another in upper Manhattan. "It was never discovered which she enjoyed most," recalled Oscar, "dismantling an apartment preparatory to transfer, or the setting up of a new home." Enjoy it she did, plunging with zest into the business of reupholstering, repainting and furnishing each time they moved.

Her parents, James and Janet Nimmo, were an important part of Oscar's world. James Hunt Nimmo was born in 1836, in Glasgow, to firm, upstanding, middle-class Presbyterian parents. One day a young woman named Janet Smeeton delivered to Mrs. Nimmo a corset that her mother had made. Eighteen-year-old James was immediately attracted to her. Knowing that it was no use to ask his parents for permission to marry the daughter of a lowly corset maker, he scraped up what money he could so that they could marry and go to the United States. He got a job with an uncle who held an important position in the Sun Life Insurance Company in New Orleans. The Nimmos moved to New York when James was transferred there, and ultimately had five children, the youngest of whom was Allie.

Just before Allie and Willie Hammerstein were married, a crisis occurred that brought long-lasting changes to the family. Having made several business trips alone to Europe, James finally agreed to take Janet with him. At a London furrier where her husband had sent her to be measured for a fur coat, Janet discovered through a saleswoman's slip that James had bought a coat for another woman during a previous trip.

"My poor little grandmother got on a boat and came back alone, vowing never to speak to my grandfather again. When she arrived in New York, she told his firm what he had done, and when he returned he was out of a job," Oscar wrote. He added, "In those days they mixed up social and family scandals with business." In time his "poor little grandmother" broke her silence, but never again did her husband share her bed or hold another job. It ultimately fell to Willie to support his in-laws.

In a move that the Hammersteins made when Oscar was five and his brother Reggie—whose early inability to say "Oscar" resulted in "Ockie," the nickname that became permanent—was three, Willie took two apartments for the family in a house on West 112th Street. Reggie lived upstairs with his parents, while Oscar slept downstairs in the same bed as his grandmother. His grandfather remained in another room, which was devoted to his oil and watercolor paintings. James was not a very good painter, but it seemed to be a solace for him. "I suppose that he and my grandmother were much more unhappy together than they allowed me to see," Oscar reflected.

Every morning James would prepare a milk punch of milk, whiskey and egg to start the day. After he and his grandson consumed it, they began their daily routine: a stop at the neighborhood candy store on Madison Avenue, where Ockie helped himself to half a dozen sourballs, and then on to Mt. Morris Park (today Marcus Garvey Park), where each spent time sketching.

Despite their morning routine, and the bottle of Guinness's stout that Grandpa and the boy shared before bedtime each night, it was Grandma Nimmo who held a stronger place in his emotional life. "If I had been asked which of the two I loved more, my mother or my grandmother, I would have been deeply embarrassed. I think I loved my mother more, but I would not have had the heart to say so for fear of hurting my grandmother."

Grandma Nimmo also enjoyed walks with her grandson. When her emphysema caused her to sit down on the stoop of a brownstone to catch her breath, Oscar was "dreadfully ashamed" at being part of such a scene on a public street. While he felt very sorry for her, at the same time he hoped that she would soon recover, because people passing by would begin to stop and look at them. Feeling that it would be "silly and useless" to try to help by patting her on the shoulder, he would wait silently until she recovered.

Because of the financial burdens placed on Willie by the free-spending Oscar I, there was not a great deal of material luxury in the family. Oscar was always aware that things cost money and that one had to do without. But Mama, Grandma and Aunt Mousie, whom Oscar called a "second mother," seemed constantly at his beck and call, doing things for him, and always with the attitude that he was worth it. Oscar could do almost anything except go outside the house. His overseers impressed on him the idea that he was a little too good to play with any of the ordinary children on the street.

It was also established early on that he was a "delicate boy." Allie would say to him: "You look heavy under the eyes." Then, with concern on her face, she would turn to Mousie. "I always know when he's sick. He gets bilious attacks." Oscar was skinny and pale and he slipped quite easily into the role of "delicate boy," enjoying the days at home when he read one book after another.

The assumption that his health was delicate seemed to make no lasting impression on Oscar, who was almost never ill as an adult. The theory that he was accident-prone—constructed on two incidents, on his fourth and fifth birthdays, in which he fell off a toy wagon—had more lasting effects. Although he later became a good athlete, in other ways he remained physically cautious, unwilling to take unnecessary risks in his friends' daredevil games. When he read stories about physical derring-do, he became "bored or impatient." He never learned to drive a car or work any other kind of mechanical device.

It is not hard to imagine what damaging effects the coddling matriarchy might have had on Oscar. He always sensed that things were too "good" at home and would be tougher outside. But when the time came to face the outside world, he found that somehow he was prepared to meet these greater demands. "I might have run from the task in the light of a very bad upbringing, and yet the bad upbringing seems to have been good for me in many ways," he later reflected. The bad upbringing must have left Oscar with an inner security, a sense of his own worth, that would serve him well all his life.

His family also gave Oscar the impression that he was very bright and very talented. Unfortunately for Reggie, who his mother had wished would be a girl, Allie had decided, "Oscar's the genius— Reggie's the clown." The others supported the notion. Oscar loved to sit and listen to the grownups talk, and was often asked to perform for visitors. The *pièce de résistance* of his repertoire was a recitation about a little boy who died, "Little Boy Black." Oscar could perform this with heartbreaking effect. He was convinced that he would become a great actor and hold much larger audiences in the palm of his hand one day, a prospect that pleased him enormously. His ambition was fired by the matinées at the Hammerstein uptown theaters that his mother occasionally took him to now. The most memorable were *The Little Minister*, with Maude Adams; *Becky Sharp*, starring Mrs. Fiske and Maurice Barrymore; and the tryout of *Floradora*, featuring the famous Floradora Sextette, singing "Tell Me, Pretty Maiden."

At a performance of *A Romance of Althone*, which Oscar attended with both his parents, the tenor Chauncey Alcott looked up at their box and seemed to be singing to Oscar's mother. There was hell to pay once they returned home. Willie was extremely jealous of Allie. He used every excuse he could to keep her home, and when they did go out, there was often a violent argument afterwards because some man had been looking and Willie contended that he wouldn't have looked if she hadn't looked back. Once, at the roof garden atop the Victoria Theatre, Allie and Willie were sitting in one box with brother Arthur and his first wife, and a man in a Panama hat was sitting in a box nearby. Allie later reported to Mousie that he was quite good-looking and very well dressed. When the man looked over at their box once too often, Willie went into his box and punched him in the nose. Oscar often witnessed his father's jealous outbursts and even saw his parents, as well as his mother and her sister, in physical conflict. The fights never lasted very long, but Oscar found out that if he started to cry they would stop immediately, and he learned to cry deliberately at such times. It wasn't difficult to do because he was genuinely shaken by the fights. Still, his impression was that the relationship between his parents was "a big love affair."

During the winter of 1901, when Oscar was six, the family moved down to the north side of Central Park West at 87th Street, adjacent to an empty plot of land. Oscar and Reggie could step out of their first-floor windows to this private playground that they shared with only a few cats and dogs. What Oscar would remember about this spot of land was a vivid experience he had that first Christmas Eve.

As Oscar and his brother lay trying to fall asleep, Allie and Mousie tiptoed into the room and whispered that Santa Claus was coming. Presently Willie entered, disguised not in the conventional red suit but in a long, black sealskin coat and tam-o'-shanter. He had a white beard and carried on his back a bag filled with toys. After announcing that he was Santa Claus, he asked the boys what they wanted for Christmas. Oscar had a moment of doubt when he suspected that this was not really Santa, but he reeled off his list of hoped-for gifts. Performance over, Santa and his entourage left the room. Then while lying in his bed next to the window, Oscar suddenly saw Santa Claus, in his sleigh drawn by reindeer, soar above the fence and fly away over Central Park.

This night made a deep impression upon Oscar. His first published piece of writing, in the *Hamilton Echo*, in 1908, was a remembrance of the visit and the subsequent vision. Years later, in 1953, he wrote of it again. "I am not quite certain whether he continued to fool me or whether half way through my requests I began to suspect he was my father. If I did, I didn't let on. I wouldn't have spoiled his fun for anything. I was striking a fine balance between a kind of half skepticism and a half faith. This seems to have been a pattern which has followed me through life or perhaps which I have followed through life. I have felt the capacity to be either a religious zealot or a complete cynic, and I have rejected both extremes and seem to have fallen somewhere in the middle. I am, let us say, one-third realist and two-thirds mystic."

The 87th Street apartment was also the scene for what Oscar would later refer to as "one of the black marks on my history." He and his brother were in the lot playing football when Oscar threw the ball so far that it landed in the street. Reggie started out for it when Oscar called to him, warning that he was not supposed to go into the road. (Both boys were forbidden to cross the street alone, or indeed to step off the pavement.) "He did anyway and he retrieved the ball. Later I told on him to my mother. She let him off with a mild rebuke for breaking the rule, but at the same time she let me know that she did not admire me for having told on my brother, especially since it was my ball he had rescued." Ashamed of his behavior in this incident, Oscar often tried to analyze his motive for acting in such a manner. "I myself never had any urge to break a rule. This desire to show independence and to be as unshackled as possible, which almost all human beings have, is something which I never had." When Ernst Toller, the German playwright, told him that the Germans had a "lust to obey," Oscar commented that he must have been born with some of this.

He was indeed a good boy, a fact that was verified when he began school at P.S. 9 on 81st Street and West End Avenue. At the end of each week, the school principal, Miss Bernholz, a thick, gray-haired woman who always wore stiffly starched white shirtwaists, handed out cards to those who had been good during the week. Oscar received many, some of which hung framed in his study when he was an adult.

By the time he started school the Hammersteins had moved again, this time to the Endicott on Columbus Avenue between 81st and 82nd streets. Grandma Nimmo had taken it upon herself to teach Ockie the alphabet and some rudimentary arithmetic before he entered school. He was a good student and skipped two classes within the next three years. Reading came easy to him and he would often go

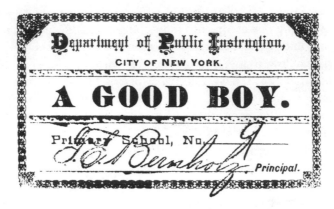

through two books a day. Oscar was a good speller and found that writing wasn't difficult, either. But later, in his professional work, he claimed that writing cost him a good deal of effort.

While Oscar was being promoted, Reggie was being left back, until there was a big distance between them. The family thought it "cute" that Reggie didn't like school and in his presence told stories of how he fell asleep in class. He had already decided, at six, that if he couldn't distinguish himself as a scholar, he would distinguish himself as a comedian. Oscar heard his mother remark to his first teacher, Miss Grant, that Reggie never told lies. Oscar wrote later that the reason Reggie didn't tell lies was not moral resolve but the desire to be praised by his mother for such virtues. He wrote, too, that the worst thing an adult can do is to ridicule a child's deficiencies, for then "he has nothing to live up to." The futures of the two Hammerstein brothers would give validity to this observation; unfortunately, Oscar did not always follow his own advice when he became a father.

Allie was brought up an Episcopalian and had her sons baptized in this faith. Although she seldom attended services, she saw that the boys followed some religious observances. They fasted on Good Friday and ate fish on Fridays, but their religious training was not strict. Neither Willie nor his family were practicing Jews; they entered a temple only when someone had died. Later in life Oscar was a "religious" man in a sense, but he never joined a formal religious group or attended weekly services.

One day, when a doctor visited the school to examine all the students, an older girl was told to take Oscar and Reggie home immediately. When Allie came to the door, Oscar burst through, grabbed his mother around the hips and bellowed. Even though he had been dismissed because he had chicken pox, and was never punished at home anyway, he felt so guilty that he thought he would be given some dreadful punishment, which he hoped to forestall by his dramatic outburst. Once he was tucked into bed, he asked his mother if Dr. Bilhoefer would be coming.

"Of course not," she replied. "Dr. Humphrey attends our family now. Why do you ask?"

As a sly smile came over his face Oscar replied, "Oh, I was just curious." The fact was that he had developed a crush on Dr. Bilhoefer's wife. He loved not only her big brown eyes and soft blond hair, but her short, petite frame. "She didn't tower over me the way my tall mother and Mousie did." His own height was of concern to Oscar at that time. When Grandma Nimmo admonished him at night to lie very straight in bed so that he would grow tall, he made every effort to do so.

The 1902 Christmas entertainment at P.S. 9 was the scene of Oscar's public debut as an actor. His interest in the theater was growing as he began to wonder about that mysteriously exciting place called the Victoria which took his father away every morning. When he demanded to be taken to it, the immediate and emphatic reaction was always "No!" Willie was vehement in his opinion that three members of the family in this raffish profession were enough. "No son of mine . . ."

But Oscar's persistence eventually won out, and on a certain Saturday afternoon Oscar and Reggie were taken to a matinée at the Victoria. In the lobby they caught their first glimpse of their famous, remote grandfather. Willie placed them in a stage box and left to attend to other business. The house lights dimmed and the curtain rose on a new comic opera, *The Fisher Maiden.* Oscar's recollections of the enchanted afternoon were dim in the particulars, but he retained a vivid image of the magnificent blue that seemed to fuse together the actors, the music and the dancing. In the years that followed, he and Reggie attended matinées at many playhouses, always sitting in boxes provided as a courtesy to the Hammersteins. They loved the theater, but felt the superiority of "insiders," though that was no proof against the glamour of it all. They were always excited after the show and came home to practice the songs they had heard, which they never hesitated to perform. They specialized in imitations, too, the most famous being Reggie's version of George Arliss in Ferenc Molnár's *The Devil,* which he accomplished with squinted eyes and a sinister manner. Oscar noted and remembered not only the performances, but the theaters themselves, many of which would one day run his own shows.

Every summer the Hammersteins went to the country to escape the sweltering heat of the city. As with their apartments, they never stayed anywhere as long as they had originally planned. At any given moment Willie and Allie might exchange "the look" that signaled the family to begin packing. An hour or so later they would be on their way home. Short as they were, the trips were memorable for Oscar. A favorite place was Saugerties in the Catskill Mountains, another Arverne, near Far Rockaway on Long Island, where they stayed in the turreted, shingled Hotel La Grange. He remembered another seaside visit to Staten Island because of an incident there that made a lasting impression on him. One day his mother and Mousie went out in a sailboat with a married couple whom Oscar didn't know. When it grew late and they hadn't returned, he became so panicky and furious that he said to himself, "I hope they're drowned!" When they returned and told of being becalmed, Oscar made an angry confession of his wish. His mother was hurt and deeply impressed by his anger, he recalled. When he heard that the boating strangers were fine swimmers who did the "Australian crawl," he vowed never to learn that stroke. "I'm afraid I never did," he later confessed, "although it is a vow I wish I had been able to break."

Grandma Nimmo became terminally ill with acute emphysema in late July of 1903. Tanks of oxygen were brought in and the adults whispered of "coma"; the whole thing was terrifying for the boy. After he was taken into a dark room to see her, he cried for a long time.

In the fall the Hammersteins moved again, this time with a special reason: none of the family would have thought of occupying an apartment that someone had died in, for they considered it bad luck. This time, Grandpa Nimmo and Mousie took their own apartment in Brooklyn, and the Hammersteins an apartment in the Aylsmere at Columbus Avenue and 76th Street. This move into a more luxurious building in a nicer neighborhood represented a step up for the family. To Oscar it represented a new era in his life, with a new school and, for the first time, the society of neighborhood friends.

Oscar's new friend, LeRoy Harding, lived in a brownstone that served as a recreation hall for the neighborhood kids, with a pool table in the basement and a wigwam they had erected for their Indian game on the fourth floor. At their new church, this time of the Universalist sect, a crude gymnasium was built in the basement. The place was dusty and ill-equipped, but Oscar loved it and learned to play basketball there.

When he was nine, Oscar started piano lessons, which he enjoyed. He learned pieces quickly by imitating his teacher Miss Helen White's rendition and learned to read music well. He felt that he bluffed his family into thinking he was a virtuoso by playing with dramatic expression. Weekly music-lesson time was also used for Allie to have a professional manicure done by Miss White's sister, Libby. One day Libby suggested that Oscar have a manicure; he put up no protest, but fainted for the first and only time in his life.

Associated in Oscar's mind with living in the Aylsmere was the circumcision that Dr. Humphrey thought he and Reggie should have "for sanitary reasons." Anxious about the operation, Oscar made up his mind that they were not going to fool him or "put him out." When they pulled the ether mask over his face, he decided to concentrate on one thing to keep his mind from wandering into sleep. Over and over he silently spelled his name, O-S-C-A-R, concentrating on each letter. The doctor marveled at how much ether it had taken to put a child of nine to sleep.

It was in the same year that old Oscar began to devote all his time to grand opera and left the running of the Victoria entirely to Willie. Until then, the relationship between them had been that of an absolute sovereign to a prime minister. The relief that his father's removal from the Victoria brought Willie soon turned to bitterness as Oscar I cleaned out the Victoria's coffers to finance his dream. A newspaper cartoon showed a truck drawing up to the box office at the Victoria every evening to load up with currency and the same truck arriving at the Manhattan Opera House to disgorge the lot.

After two years of planning and building, the Old Man opened his New Manhattan Opera House (now the Manhattan Center) on December 3, 1906. When a friend asked what he was opening with, he replied, "With debts."

The Metropolitan, just four blocks away, was firmly entrenched, with a stable of stars and socialites willing to subsidize it; Oscar's attempt to compete with it seemed doomed to failure from the beginning. He knew the odds, but obstinately and recklessly believed that he could do the impossible.

During four seasons his citadel flourished despite the fact that he started on a shoestring. He attracted stars by his impetuosity and magnetic charm,* took risks on lesser-known names, experimented with new ways of production and introduced more new operas (such as *Tales of Hoffmann, Salome* and *Elektra*) in this country than anyone else had ever done in any similar period.

German-born Oscar took to the American creed of competition with zest; he scheduled his operas on the same nights that The Met performed ,and enjoyed every minute of the fight. With only a meager $52,000 advance subscription sale, against the Metropolitan's $400,000, his one-man effort came out $750,000 ahead the first season. He introduced his own stars, a long list that included Melba, Tetrazzini, Bonci, McCormack, Trentini and Calvé. But he always emphasized the composer, the production itself, with stars integrated into the cast and the work itself. His importation of Mary Garden was controversial and innovative, for she was thought to be "unsuitable" for New York, performing as she did in the new French manner.

For four years the battle raged, with the Met booking Caruso three times a week in opposition to the upstart Hammerstein house. Many felt that it was the spirit and presence of the man himself, who sat through every performance on a kitchen chair in the downstage right wing, invariably in his peculiar top hat and smoking a long black cigar, that gave the performances their élan and vitality. He was a severe critic of his performers and a ruthless manager. The opera was the thing, and he dealt harshly with anyone who did not contribute to his conception of the work.

The success with which he carried out his dream not only caused the Met to make greater efforts on its own behalf to attract customers, but also educated the public's taste and stimulated its receptivity to new forms of opera.

At one point in the battle, the Metropolitan Opera House seriously considered merging with the Manhattan, with Hammerstein coming

---

* When Nellie Melba turned Hammerstein down, he returned to her Paris apartment the following day and literally carpeted her floor with hundreds of thousand-franc notes. His bizarre gesture caused her to change her mind and they soon became close friends.

in as their general manager. When the directors asked to meet him for lunch, Hammerstein sent a note: "Gentlemen, I am not hungry."

Eventually both his financial condition and his own personality caused his opera house to close. Hammerstein quarreled with his most ardent and important supporters, the Clarence Mackays (the future in-laws of Irving Berlin), over a trivial incident and arrogantly ordered them never to enter his opera house again.

He had little respect for tradition and less for the trappings of wealth and social position. Fiercely independent and vastly arrogant, when a rich socialite offered, through an intermediary, to provide whatever money he needed to finance an opera, Hammerstein said to the messenger, "Tell him to go to hell." In London he greeted His Majesty George V with "Pleased to meet you, King."

In 1910, with disaster facing both the Met and Hammerstein's opera house as it became apparent that the city could not support two such institutions, the Met's board, not realizing that Hammerstein had no more money to continue, offered him $1,250,000 to cease his opposition and withdraw from producing grand opera in New York and Philadelphia (where he had also built an opera house) for a period of ten years.

He was defeated—for the moment—but not discouraged. The Old Man quipped that he didn't blow his brains out because he couldn't find a bullet hard enough to penetrate his skull. He said more seriously, "I am never discouraged. I don't believe in discouragement. I was not cast down. I merely discovered my inability to do what I had thought I could do. That discovery did not fill my heart with tears or regrets, neither did it destroy my self-esteem. To do anything in this world, a man must have full confidence in his own ability. If I haven't confidence in myself, others will not have confidence in me." He set off for England to build the London Opera House.

Despite the Old Man's draining of the Victoria's profits to finance his opera, the theater under Willie Hammerstein was so successful that his competitors (Keith, Proctor and Tony Pastor) drew up an agreement surrendering the mid-Manhattan area north of 30th Street and south of 96th Street to Willie in order to forestall his combining with any other chain and overwhelming all other vaudeville business. A brilliant talent broker, Willie signed such stars as Australian swimmer Annette Kellerman for her New York debut as "the million-dollar mermaid," the Dolly Sisters, Al Jolson, Fanny Brice, Weber and Fields,

Buster Keaton, Will Rogers and Houdini. In addition, he introduced famous prize fighters and was the first to use motion pictures between acts. His recognition of the public's desire to see persons of notoriety for whatever reason led him to book record-breakers and oddities of every kind, giving the Victoria a reputation as "the great nut vaudeville house of New York." But a huge audience thronged to the theater and kept it running profitably every week of the year.

Willie had an uncanny talent for digging up acts that cost him little and effectively publicizing them. A large prize was offered to anyone who could make "Sober Sue" laugh. Celebrated comedians tried and failed—for the simple reason that her facial muscles were paralyzed. Willie paid the girl twenty dollars a week and took in thousands as the public flocked to see the contest. His attitude toward the novelty attractions showed some contempt for the performers. When a woman who had just been acquitted of murdering her husband begged to appear a second week, Willie answered, "No, madam, not unless you shoot another man."

Meanwhile Oscar's fascination with the theater grew stronger. The boy was finally allowed to see evening performances; he was thrilled and awestruck by the famous vaudevillians, the singers and dancers. He once declared himself "the luckiest mortal alive" just to be under the same roof with one of his favorites. In 1905 Oscar saw his Grandfather Hammerstein tread the boards of the Victoria. The appearance arose from a casual joke. When minstrel-showman Lew Dockstader complained how hard it was to find a good end man, Hammerstein asked if he would do. It was only for one night, but Willie saw to it that Broadway was saturated with the news, with handbills proclaiming "Debut Extraordinary." Oscar I came out to tremendous applause, sang a song, recited a monologue and told a few jokes. The audience clapped and stamped for fifteen minutes afterwards.

In 1908, when Oscar was thirteen, his parents entered him as a day pupil in Hamilton Institute, on 81st Street near Central Park West. Hamilton Institute made a slight pretense of military training, and Oscar, a gangly six foot one and a half inches, would sometimes drill in an ill-fitting uniform at the 22nd Regiment Armory at 68th Street and Broadway.

During these years, summers were spent exclusively at the Brighton Beach Hotel on the boardwalk in Brooklyn, New York. It was a very large hotel, with yellow clapboard, a green roof and a porch a city-block long. The front of the hotel faced the Atlantic Ocean and right behind it was the Brighton Beach Race Track. Oscar loved his "second home," * especially in the evenings, when he would lie in his bed looking out over the moonlit ocean and listen to Slater's Brass Band playing on the porch. The band would play not only military marches but all the scores of Victor Herbert, Leslie Stuart and the various Viennese composers who were popular at the time.

Oscar also became a bookmaker at Brighton. From the back porch of the hotel he could see the horses start across the field and run along the back stretch. He would lose them coming down the home stretch, because the grandstand was in the way, but between the grandstand and the clubhouse turn he could see the finish. Oscar, Reggie and LeRoy Harding used to sit on the back porch every day with Allie, Mousie and some of the other ladies who lived at the hotel. He began by making ten-cent bets, but then became more systematic. After studying the form sheets in the *New York Telegraph* he would make up a chart of what he thought the proper odds would be. The ladies would bet with him or, as he said, "I would make book."

One summer, Oscar and Reggie became totally mesmerized by *Major Gordon ("Pawnee Bill") Lillie and William F. ("Buffalo Bill") Cody's Combined Wild West Show.* Their favorite was an episode where a stagecoach came out, drove around the arena and was then beset by a tribe of wild Indians. "Reggie and I, after seeing the show, made contact with the company manager and for the rest of the engagement we were allowed to see the show free by being the two children in the stagecoach." They were delighted with this form of paying for their admission even more than with seeing the rest of the show.

At the end of the summer of 1910, Oscar's comfortable, happy childhood ended when his mother died in her thirty-fifth year. Allie had been a strong, early advocate of birth control, but with preventive methods still unsophisticated, her death was due to abortion complicated by acute peritonitis. Oscar refused to believe that his mother was going to die, even though he saw sadness and resignation on the faces of his father and Mousie. He couldn't imagine living without her, so he concluded that she was not going to die. When she did die on August 20, Oscar felt the necessity to steel himself and not give way to grief. He walked to the corner store and bought a scrapbook.

---

* The Hammersteins were by then living at the Barnard, 106 Central Park West.

Returning to his room, he began pasting in it pictures of famous athletes that he had been clipping and saving for a long time.

"Then I went for long walks and thought it all over, and began to adjust myself. All by myself. I never felt like going to anybody for help," Oscar wrote years later. "And while I don't quite understand this, I know this is what happened. I also know it crystallized an attitude toward death I have had ever since. I never feel shaken by death, as I would have been if this had not happened to me when I was fifteen. I received the shock and took it, and sort of resisted, as an enemy, the grief that comes after death, rather than giving way to it. I get stubborn and say this is not going to lick me, because it didn't then."

Oscar continued to work hard at Hamilton Institute that winter. In the summer, he and Reggie went to Weingart's Institute, a boys' camp in Highmount, New York, where he made many friends he was to keep all his life. Among them were: Harold Hyman, later Oscar's doctor and a noted author of medical books; Lorenz Hart, his future classmate at Columbia and Richard Rodgers' first collaborator; David and Myron Selznick; Leighton K. Brill, who was Oscar's assistant for over twenty years; Milton Cohen and Milton Kadison, who remained close lifelong friends.

Weingart's was noted not only for being the first summer camp, but for its excellence in sports, particularly baseball. Oscar played first base, acted as editor of the camp newspaper and performed in the annual entertainment, *The Minstrel Show*. The camp's natural setting gave him his first real taste of the country. On summer evenings he would lie on the grass, listening to crickets chirp and the wind blow, feeling "wonderment and deep appreciation" of the world around him.

While Oscar and Reggie were at camp Willie married Mousie. Although her sister had been just as strong and impulsive as she, Mousie had a much rougher exterior. Both her appearance and her speech were somewhat coarse; "Hiya, Tootsie" was her usual greeting. She was a humorous, active and affectionate woman. In a letter on the eve of their marriage, Willie wrote:

> Only God knew that, in the mutual loss we alone suffered, a sympathetic feeling was planted in each other. In the last eleven months, those two seeds continued to grow, steadily ripening, until today, we find ourselves in the full bloom of love. . . . I hope to have many years before me to prove my sincerity and the trust I have in you. But, if God, in his wisdom, should decide death can-

cel this love, I pray that I will go first—I would dread any further life if I were the one chosen to remain. For in this world there will never be a substitute for you. On the name of my dear dead wife I swear this.

Yours always as a husband,
Will

Mousie proved perfectly suited to her new position. She managed to run the family apartment in a seemingly effortless way, accepting occasional crises casually, often using them to her own advantage. And, at the same time, with an almost uncanny instinct, she was able to handle any difficult situation diplomatically and with humor. She not only was a devoted wife but, as a stepmother, she encouraged a closer relationshp between Willie and his sons.

In September of 1912, Oscar entered Columbia University. The English department at Columbia in those days was a brilliant one; headed by Brander Matthews, it included John Erskine and Carl Van Doren. The roster of undergraduates of that era contained many names—besides Oscar's—destined to become famous, names such as Howard Dietz, Bennett Cerf, Morrie Ryskind, Herman Mankiewicz, M. Lincoln Schuster, Richard L. Simon and Lorenz Hart.

In the same month, Willie suddenly resigned from the Victoria as a public protest against his father. It was Mousie who suggested that he ask his elder son to draft the statement that the press was clamoring for. As they worked together, Oscar began to know Willie for the first time, and they found common ground for communication. The facts that Oscar helped his father write were summarized by the first sentence of the statement: "I left the Victoria Theatre because I hoped that by so doing I could save my father from himself." The last straw for Willie was his father's secret negotiation to sell the Victoria's vaudeville franchise to the Shubert brothers and use the money to build a chain of opera houses across the country, now that the Metropolitan had banished him from New York. The last few years had been a financial nightmare for Willie as he built up the "Victoria Goose" only to see the golden egg go to Oscar I's hopeless operatic ventures. Now his father had gone too far.

He stayed away from the theater for months, and he and his son spent more and more time together. Oscar felt deep compassion for him and was finally able to overcome his filial reticence and feel comfortable with his father. In one of their talks, Willie said openly what he had felt for so long. "Ockie, you must promise me you will never

do anything so foolish as to consider making the theater your livelihood. Become a lawyer. You'd be great at it and it's also one of the
more secure professions I know of." It never occurred to Oscar to do
anything but please his father; he gave him his word of honor. After
three months, with Arthur acting as peace negotiator, Willie and his
father reconciled their differences, and the Old Man was back at his
old stand in the Victoria's lobby.

Columbia University was a stimulating, exciting place for Oscar.
He maintained high grades while becoming an avid participant in
extracurricular activities. He played first base on the freshman baseball team,* became a member of Pi Lambda Phi fraternity and attended Friday beer celebrations at the Lion Bar.

Back at Weingart's for the 1914 season, the Hammerstein boys
received word to hurry home: their father was dead. Two years
earlier, Willie had been stricken with what was diagnosed as a mild
case of scarlet fever. When he recovered, he continued to complain
of severe neurological headaches. Eventually, at Arthur's insistence, he
entered a hospital and, on June 10, succumbed to Bright's Disease.

As they were about to board the train for the ride home, Oscar
picked up the New York newspapers, thinking that they might help
to take their minds off what lay ahead. Unfortunately, they only made
things worse. The *New York Herald's* headline read: HAMMERSTEIN'S
DEATH A SHOCK TO THEATER CIRCLE. The *New York Times* reported:
HAMMERSTEIN, THE BARNUM OF VAUDEVILLE, DEAD AT FORTY.

Arthur met the boys at the station. Driving up to their Central
Park West apartment, he began briefing them on the funeral arrangements. Arriving at the corner of 91st Street, he noticed a group of
newspaper reporters gathered in a circle. In the center stood the Old
Man, who was saying, "What can I say?—I'm stunned. Two of my
boys gone within three months—Abie died only a little while ago,
you know. Another of my boys, Harry, has a terminal illness. I tell
you, I'm stunned."

With his head bowed low, he said, "In my life, I have experienced
every great joy, every triumph, every success, every honor that can
be won by a man, single-handed; and I also have experienced every

* During one game, Oscar had an accident that resulted in his losing the knuckle
on the second finger of his left hand.

sorrow, every disappointment, every grief, and every tragedy. But this . . ." He stepped away, took hold of his son's arm and slowly walked into the house.

Later, Oscar II walked into one of the bedrooms in the apartment and found his grandfather alone, crumpled up in a chair, his face inexpressibly sad. "He looked small and beaten. This made me feel strong. Surprising myself with an unnatural valor, I walked right over to him and said: 'How do you do, Grandfather?' He shook my hand limply. I sat down near him. Nothing more was said by either of us. The continued silence gave me the strange feeling that I had not come into the room at all. He seemed still to be alone." Presently Arthur entered and the ordeal was over.

Willie was accorded a funeral that was more like one given to a prominent world figure than a publicity-shy theatrical producer. Arthur had at first intended to hold the services in his late brother's home, but when the rooms began to overflow with floral tributes and word came that numerous organizations would be sending their representatives, he quickly made arrangements with Temple Israel.

More than a thousand people congregated at the Harlem synagogue on Sunday morning, June 14, 1914. In accordance with Willie's disapproval of ostentation, the temple was not decorated. The only flowers were those brought in on the casket, which was rolled down the aisle in the Jewish tradition. The service was brief and simple.

Two hours later, as Willie was laid to rest beside Allie in Woodlawn Cemetery, taps was sounded over Broadway as it would be sounded forty-six years later for his son Oscar.

Willie's death did not affect Oscar as deeply as his mother's had, although he was now without parents at the age of nineteen. Interestingly enough, since he had promised his father that he would stay out of the theater, one of the first things he did that fall, as soon as school started, was to join the Columbia University Players. Mousie was thrilled, but Arthur voiced his displeasure. "Ockie, don't! I promised your father that I would never permit it."

Oscar assured his uncle that these theatrical ventures were merely extracurricular and that it was still his intention to enter law school at the end of the year.

The annual Columbia varsity show was a major social event, put on in the Grand Ballroom of the Hotel Astor for a week's run each spring. Though acted by students, and produced by recent graduates, they were noted for their near-professional quality and were reviewed by the New York newspapers.

Oscar's first appearance was in the 1915 musical, *On Your Way.* After Herman Axelrod, '15, opened the show as narrator, Oscar came on as Clarence Montegue, a poet, and sang "Looking for a Dear Old Lady." His debut did not go unnoticed. The New York *Evening World's* critic stated: "Oscar Hammerstein II, the consumptive looking poet, was fun without trying to be. Maybe he wasn't intended to be funny but he was light as a feather on his head and his feet. He danced like Al Jolson and had some original steps and faces of his own. Oscar is a comedian and as a fun-maker he was a la carte, meaning all to the mustard."

That same year, Carl Van Doren, who was Oscar's faculty adviser, sent for him and asked what he planned to do after graduation. Oscar again announced that he was going to be a lawyer. Van Doren made a face. "Oh . . . well . . . I thought you were going to be a writer."

"This," Oscar later said, "is precisely what I was dying to hear somebody say. I left his office in Hamilton Hall and floated down Morningside Heights."

Whatever his true inclination, he enrolled in Columbia Law School in what would have been his senior year. (He received his B.A. at the end of the first year of law school.) The outstanding event of the year, however, was his major part in *The Peace Pirates,* the 1916 varsity show. For the first time in four years, undergraduates were the authors. The book and lyrics were written by Herman J. Mankiewicz,* '17. Oscar wrote a few routines for his friend "Mank's" libretto in addition to playing a black-faced comedian.

Lorenz Hart, '18, was at the time both a member of the cast and drama critic for the school's *Daily Spectator.* Of Oscar's performance he wrote: "He proved to be thoroughly original and distinctly funny, and demonstrated his ability to 'put over' a song. He also wrote the Shakespeare burlesque in Act II, and contributed humor far above the level of horseplay in his impersonation of Nijinsky."

Oscar later wrote of Hart's performance as Mary Pickford: "There was nothing subtle about Varsity Show satire in those days. Imitating

---

* Mankiewicz was a successful screenwriter most noted for his Academy Award–winning screenplay for *Citizen Kane.*

the way movie ingenues were chased around trees by playful but purehearted heroes, Larry skipped and bounced around the stage like an electrified gnome. I think of him always as skipping and bouncing. In all the time I knew him, I never saw him walk slowly. I never saw his face in repose. I never heard him chuckle quietly. He laughed loudly and easily at other people's jokes and at his own too. His large eyes danced, and his head would wag. He was alert and dynamic and fun to be with."

This same varsity show was the scene of Oscar's introduction to the man who would collaborate first with Larry Hart and then with him: Richard Rodgers. Only, he wasn't a man then, but a small, dark-haired fourteen-year-old, who appeared backstage after the Saturday matinée with his older brother, Morty, a member of Oscar's fraternity. Morty told Oscar that Dick had asked to meet the worldly college man whose performance he had admired. Young Hammerstein and young Rodgers shook hands and talked for a few minutes. Rodgers later described Oscar at this meeting as a "very tall, skinny fellow with a sweet smile, clear blue eyes and an unfortunately mottled complexion." He made young Dick feel that his approval was the greatest compliment he could receive. That afternoon Dick made an irrevocable decision: to go to Columbia in order to write varsity shows.

If it was necessary to endure Columbia Law School in order to remain true to his father and his uncle, Oscar was prepared to do so, but his enthusiasm remained with the Players. Even before finishing his first year of law, he was commissioned by the play committee to write their next varsity show with Herman Axelrod.

In the winter of 1917, Oc and Ax began to apply themselves to the task of creating the annual show. In describing *Home, James,* his first book for a musical, Oscar said: "Our method was simple. I wanted to be the leading comedian as I had been the year before. So we wrote a waiter part for me. We knew a joke about a waiter and considered this a good start toward the development of a comedy character. Knowing that we would need love songs, we invented a less than light romance with complications that pleased us very much."

They chose as their composer Robert Lippmann, known as "the loudest piano player in the fraternity house." Lippmann played his tunes for them and they fished for titles and ideas. They wanted to write songs that were entertaining, with good rhymes and jokes in them, and if they didn't seem to fit the story, the authors twisted the story around a little to fit them. Hammerstein and Axelrod, both students of the theater, knew all the lines that were getting big laughs on Broadway, and they brightened the dialogue of their own play by calmly appropriating them.

When the varsity show was presented on March 28, 1917, Oscar was again singled out for his acting ability. The *New York Herald*, in fact, used a two-column headline: OSCAR HAMMERSTEIN, 2D, COMEDIAN IN COLUMBIA SHOW, "HOME, JAMES!" Their critic went on to say that "as Armand Dubonnet, maitre d'hotel, he gave a skillful interpretation of a part which could easily have been mediocre in other hands. His performance would have done credit to the best of the Broadway comedians, and shamed not a few."

Still, there are no hints of Oscar's later style in either the book or the lyrics. For the most part the songs are pedestrian and have little to set them apart from those found in run-of-the-mill college shows. Years later he said in his book *Lyrics:* "About my own seamy past. I intend to quote some of my early efforts, the main motive being to reassure younger writers. Knowing how bad I was at one time, I hope that they will be encouraged."

Oscar's lyric for the show-stopping number, "Annie McGinnis Pavlova," in *Home, James,* according to the *Alumni News,* began:

> Clancey was fond of a show,
> From opera to movies he'd go.
> On dancin' and prancin' Clancey was keen,
> But the Ballet Russe he never had seen.
> For five dollars a throw he decided to go
> And he bought him a seat in the very first row.
> Annie came out. Clancey yelled, "Stop her!
> She ain't no Roosian, for I knew her poppa."

> Annie McGinnis Pavlova,
> I'll stop you from puttin' one over,
> 'Twas in Hogan's back alley,
> You learned the bacchanale
> And now you're the pride of the Ballet Russe.
> They call you a zephyr, a fairy, an elf,
> Put on your flannels, take care of yourself!
> For the costume you're wearin's a shame to old Erin,
> Oh Annie, you'd better go home. . . .

He was fond of reciting these lyrics, pointing out whenever he did that the blame had to be shared with his collaborator, who later turned to real estate. "Like him, I expected to make my living at another calling."

Oscar remained vitally involved in the Players, even after he left Columbia. In 1918 he wrote and directed *Ten For Five*, "the War show," and the following year Dick Rodgers came back into his life. Actually, since their first meeting Oscar had seen Dick several times when he came with his brother to the Pi Lambda Phi house and played on their old piano. It was in 1919, under the auspices of the Akron Club, a social-athletic group, that Oscar and Dick wrote their first two songs together. The show was *Up Stage and Down;* the songs, "Can It" and "Weaknesses." The following year, when Oscar was a dominant force on Columbia's play selection committee, he decided that Rodgers and Hart were ready to write the year's varsity show. Once again, Oscar collaborated with Dick, this time on a song called "Only Room For One More." For the 1921 varsity show, Oscar was chairman of the play committee, co-author with Axelrod and director of Rodgers and Hart's *You'll Never Know.*

During his second year at Columbia Law, thinking that the schoolwork he found so dreary would be easier if he had some practical experience, he took a job with the firm of Blumenstiel & Blumenstiel. Willie had left him some securities, which gave him an income of approximately fifty dollars a week, and Blumenstiel & Blumenstiel paid him five dollars a week for his legal efforts. He began by filling out supplementary proceedings blanks, looking up precedents—which he enjoyed very much—and doing odd jobs around the office. When the spring term ended he remained with the Blumenstiels, who thought this tall young man might be a suitable summons server. His first assignment took him to Jersey City, where, in response to his ring, a man came to the door of a run-down building and, saying "The fellow you're looking for is out," slammed the door in his face. His second assignment took him to a bar on Third Avenue. Nobody there had ever heard of the proprietor, the person to whom the summons was addressed, and once again Oscar quietly departed. Blumenstiel & Blumenstiel shifted him back to indoor work.

In April 1917 the United States entered World War I, starting the draft on June 5. On that day nearly ten million men, filled with patriotic fervor, registered for the draft. Oscar, along with Axelrod and Mankiewicz, was among the first in line. Warned that he might be classified "4 F" by the Army because he was so thin, Oscar had stuffed himself with bananas and consumed gallons of water. Nevertheless, while both his friends were inducted, Oscar was turned down as underweight.

Disappointed by his rejection, unhappy with his five-dollar-a-week law job and dreading his return to law school, Oscar went with a group of friends to the New Jersey shore for the weekend. On Saturday night the young men were invited to a party in Deal Beach. Another guest at the party was Myra Finn, a distant cousin of Richard Rodgers'. Oscar had met her years before when he was at Weingart's and she was spending the summer with her family in a cottage nearby. Living within blocks of each other in Manhattan and being part of the same social milieu, they had seen each other from time to time through the years. Now he took another look at Myra, kissed her hand during a game of spin-the-bottle, and came away from the weekend determined to marry her. She was twenty, almost two years younger than Oscar. A very small woman, four feet eleven, who was often described as "cute," she was not a great beauty, but she had a quality of gaiety and liveliness that attracted men throughout her life.

When Oscar went to ask her father's permission for the marriage, Willy Finn inquired whether Oscar was a virgin and Oscar replied that he was. "You mean you're going to practice on my daughter?!" Though fond of Oscar, Finn was not at all enthusiastic about the marriage. He hoped that Myra would find someone of more substantial means and expectations. Finn himself had made and lost a great deal of money in various real estate speculations.

Brazen and opinionated, Willy Finn was an abrasive but rather charming man. Although he and his wife, Florence, always lived together during the twenty-eight years of their marriage, Willy was a far from faithful husband. His life style was as mercurial as his temperament; the family would have a luxurious boat one month and not enough money for dinner the next. Despite the lack of financial stability, Myra and her brother Frank enjoyed the amenities of private schools, music lessons and summer houses.

Florence Finn was a quiet but rather obstinate and complaining woman, in the words of a family acquaintance, a "quiet shrew." When "Mike," as Myra was called, stayed home, her mother would say to her, "Why are you staying home every night? Go out . . . have some fun." Then, when she did go out, Florence would berate her with "Stay home once in a while."

Myra herself had a disposition that ran hot and cold. While

lively and witty at times, she was negative, stubborn and demanding at others. Like Oscar's own mother, she was opinionated, but unlike Alice, her convictions were expressed with an air of superiority. She also shared her own mother's illogical, contrary nature and was later described as the kind of woman who, if a window was open, wanted it closed and, if it was closed, wanted it open. Despite her father's opposition to the marriage, Myra was determined to marry Oscar, and Willy had no choice but to agree with her decision.

Now on the threshold of marriage, dissatisfied with his law career, living in a time disjointed by the World War, Oscar arrived at a turning point. He had been prepared to leave law school to join the Army and, disappointed when the Army turned him down, was ready to question the career he was pursuing to satisfy his father's wishes. Carl Van Doren's words came to him again: "I thought you were going to be a writer." Oscar decided to quit law school before his third year and to make the theater his career. At the end of June he went to Uncle Arthur's office to apply for a job.

Arthur Hammerstein was a successful producer of musical comedies. After years of managing his father's opera affairs, in 1910 Arthur was finally allowed to put together his first Broadway production—Victor Herbert's *Naughty Marietta*. For his next show, he commissioned Herbert to create a new musical for *Marietta's* star, Emma Trentini. When the temperamental composer walked out on his contract, Arthur promptly signed Otto Harbach and newcomer Rudolf Friml. To engage an unknown, inexperienced composed for a major Broadway operetta starring an established actress represented a bold, even reckless gamble. How well that gamble paid off can be measured by the result: the score Friml wrote for Hammerstein was *The Firefly*, one of the greatest successes American operetta has known.

Oscar made it clear to his uncle that he was not looking for temporary employment but that he wanted to be a Broadway playwright. Arthur was reluctant to accede to his nephew's request, partly because of Oscar's promise to Willie, and partly because he agreed with his late brother that two generations of Hammersteins in show business were enough.

"It's in my blood," Oscar declared, "and, furthermore, I need the money now that I'm getting married."

"But how can I face the memory of your father?" Arthur replied.

Oscar argued that it would be criminal if he, a Hammerstein, were to be denied entrance to the profession that was his heritage and which was now the compelling interest of his life. Why not give him a chance to prove his ability? Arthur mumbled something more about the solemn necessity of keeping one's word, but it was evident that he had weakened, and the interview ended with Oscar's being hired at twenty dollars a week, as an assistant stage manager on Arthur's current Broadway hit musical, *You're In Love*. Still hoping to discourage his nephew, Arthur predicated his agreement on the understanding that Oscar would not undertake to write for a year.

A few days after the long-running show closed in August, convinced by now of his nephew's ability, Arthur made him a member of the permanent staff as his production stage manager. The same week Oscar and Myra Finn took out a marriage license. They were married in her parents' apartment on West End Avenue on August 22, 1917. After a simple ceremony and a wedding breakfast, they hurried to catch the train for Lake George, New York, where they were stopping en route to Canada.

The following evening, from the Fort William Henry Hotel at Lake George, Oscar wrote a letter * to Mousie that provides some insight into his state of mind at the time, and into his affection for her. Like his father, Oscar could more easily express in writing the feelings that he had difficulty communicating verbally.

Thursday nite,

Mrs. William Hammerstein
302 Central Park West
New York City, New York

Dear Mousie:
. . . boys are an unappreciative lot, and I suppose it has been only on unusual occasions that Reg and I have realized all that you have been, and are to us—and all that we have meant to you.
I imagined for myself just what thots [sic] passed thru your mind as you saw me start on my honeymoon. To you it was just the latest of a long series of developments which you have watched take place thru out my whole life. You have seen and known everything of any importance—every experience that I had for the past twenty-two years. The significance of that close and dear relationship has never been borne upon me so keenly as it has in these two days. Perhaps I am already getting older. All this discus-

---

* This is the only letter from Oscar that was found among Mousie's private letters when she died.

sion is merely an explanatory preface to a text which I want to recite to you, and that is that I haven't broken away from you; that this new step I have taken will result in our living in different houses—but will not draw us any further apart than we have ever been.

As for married life, Mouse, I am sure that I was cut out for it. I am very, very happy. You can write to me, if you wish, to Chateau Frontenac, Quebec, Canada. I'd love to hear from you. Do not mail the letter later than Saturday. I'll try to write to Reggie later, and you'll hear from me again in a day or two.

Lovingly,
Oscar

After a weekend in Canada, he was back in New York involved in the hectic preparation for Arthur's next five Broadway productions. Oscar describes how he operated: "I was an office boy and playreader by day, stage manager by night, and an eager kibbitzer at the rehearsals of the new shows."

Despite Arthur's stipulation that Oscar not write for a year, in just three months a situation arose to alter the arrangement. During the out-of-town tryout of *Furs and Frills,* there were the usual minor crises, both on the stage and within the script, and the authors, Edward Clark and Silvio Hein, pressed for time, assigned Oscar, with Arthur's consent, to write a song for their second act. "This was my first professional work. I was writing a lyric for a hostess to greet her guests shortly after the curtain rose." Oscar titled his song "Make Yourselves at Home." He wrote only the opening chorus, which was intended merely to raise the Act II curtain and to be drowned out by the hoofing of the chorus and the clatter of late arrivals:

> Make yourselves at home,
> Neath our spacious dome.
> Do just as you please
> In twos or threes if you'd rather
> But rest assured you'll be no bother . . .

He later commented wryly on these lyrics: "How did she know they would be no bother? As I remember, a bizarre assemblage came on the stage, carrying tennis racquets, wearing riding clothes and gold costumes in the rather styled designs of a theatrical costumer of the period. They were almost certain to raise hell at her house before the weekend was over." He quoted his early lyrics with a frequency bordering on masochism, and each time added, "Boy, does that stink!"

The only salve to his conscience was that since it was considered one of his apprenticeship chores, he didn't get paid for it.

In the summer of 1918 Arthur put a new musical, *Sometime*, into production. Rudolf Friml was again his composer and Rida Johnson Young was the librettist, basing her book on Oscar's original scenario about the loves and adventures of a theatrical company. Oscar assumed an interesting double role for this production: he stage-managed the production while playing the part of the stage manager in the show. But in the course of extensive revisions, his part was written out.

Ed Wynn was brought in to headline the show during its pre-Broadway engagement in Washington. Oscar remembered the great comedian's preliminary reading of the book as his first lesson in comedy writing. Wynn was playing the principal comedy role, a character named Loney. The opening scene, designed to build up his entrance, was studded with references to "dear old Loney," "sweet old Loney," "darling old Loney," and the like. Wynn listened with increasing exasperation, and finally burst forth irritably, "Want me to be funny? Then for God's sake say: 'Where is that louse Loney, that stinker Loney, that crook Loney?' Then, when I come on, they'll laugh."

Mae West, who had been spotted originally by Arthur while she was making a brief appearance at the Victoria, made a big step toward stardom with her performance in this show. She took a fancy to Oscar and proclaimed him her mascot, insisting that he be in the wings whenever she went on. One day she took him aside and said, "Listen, get out of this crazy business and go back to your law career. The theater ain't for you, kid. You got too much class!"

Class or no class, Oscar had no intention of going back to the law. His world was the theater; there was no question about that. The only question was, What part of the theater? Despite his cavorting in varsity shows, he had no serious ambition to be an actor, and certainly didn't want to be a stage manager all his life. He was now, more than ever, convinced that Van Doren was right: he wanted to write for the theater.

Arthur read a story about a girl whose escape from a tyrannical family and a drunkard lover leads her to an engagement with a man she doesn't love and to employment in a gambling house, but eventually she is happily united in marriage with her reformed true love. Arthur suggested that Oscar try his hand at making a play out of it—

if he liked. Liked! "I would have liked the telephone book," he said, "if it would get me a production."

A dress rehearsal of this play, *The Light*, was held at the Casino Theatre on West 39th Street, on May 15, 1919. Oscar I, making a rare public and even rarer family appearance, attended the performance of his grandson's first play. In the five years since the triple blow of his three sons' deaths in 1914, the Old Man's life had begun to darken. Plagued by illness, he now suffered from increasingly severe bouts of melancholia. He had always had temporary fits of depression which lasted a day or two, usually at some lull in his work, and then disappeared the moment something interested him, but now they became frequent and prolonged. He drifted in and out of public notice, his energy declining as he battled the Metropolitan Opera and his chronic diabetes. At the play's conclusion, he patted young Oscar on the back and assured him that he had written a good play, but added that he was the better cigar maker.

The Light opened a split week engagement in Springfield, Massachusetts, on Monday evening, May 19. It appears that the elder Oscar was being either kind or a bit short-sighted in his remark because the verdict of the local critic was cataclysmic. Under the headline "THE LIGHT" IS NOT DESTINED TO SHINE VERY BRILLIANTLY: CRUDE PRODUCTION OF A MODERN DRAMA BY OSCAR HAMMERSTEIN, 2D, FAILS TO INTEREST was the comment: "Back to the darkness from whence it emerged for cradling at the Court Square theater last evening will soon go 'The Light,' a play by Oscar Hammerstein, 2d, produced by Uncle Arthur. Its christening robe may well suffice as a shroud for a deadly dull play. Its serious moments are absurd, and of comedy there is none except such as results from scenes and incidents which the author did not intend to be comic."

From Springfield the play traveled to New Haven, where reviewers found it old-fashioned, but said that though the author had done nothing new, he had "accomplished one thing exceedingly well, he has pictured some types that are alarmingly true to life." The one accomplishment was not enough; *The Light* folded after seven performances, without coming into New York. Oscar always referred to his first play as "The light that failed."

While the play was weak, the way Oscar handled his first failure was not. "When I went into the Saturday matinée, I knew I had a big flop. There must have been about twenty people in the Shubert theatre that day. When the ingenue came on, one of her lines was, 'Everything is falling down around me . . .' and at that precise moment her petticoat started falling down. I didn't wait for the yell that followed. I just ran out of the theatre, went into the park, and sat on a bench. While I was sitting there, an idea came to me for a new show. So I started writing it."

Years before, Oscar I had said, "I am never discouraged. I don't believe in discouragement. When I had failure, I refused to be cast down." Oscar II said, just a few years after *The Light* failed, "The inability of that show to go over did not discourage me." Like his grandfather, he refused to be cast down, and immediately plunged into his next effort.

The last meeting of the two Oscars occurred just two months later in Lenox Hill Hospital, where Oscar I lay in a coma, the disease he was incapable of conquering now in its final stage. Oscar II remained in the Old Man's room for five minutes, watching him and listening to his tired breathing. He reflected that this was the longest time he had ever spent alone with his grandfather. As he waited for the elevator in the corridor, a handsome, big-boned woman came up to him and said, "Aren't you Oscar Hammerstein's grandson?"

"Yes, I am," Oscar replied.

"I'm his wife."

"How do you do," Oscar said, as they shook hands and smiled politely. The elevator arrived, relieving his embarrassment, and he left the hospital.

"I walked down Park Avenue feeling lost and unclassified. My grandfather was dying and I didn't know how I felt about it. I had no deep sorrow to give way to or to resist stoically. I had no resentful memories of a domination from which I could now feel free. I could make no crass speculations concerning my probable inheritance in his will—I knew he was broke. I had none of the conventional thoughts or emotions of a bereaved grandson. It was an uncomfortable feeling, the more uncomfortable because in some vague way my heart had been touched, and I didn't know why."

That same day, August 1, 1919, at 7:30 P.M. Oscar Hammerstein I died. His funeral service was held at Temple Emanu-El, the synagogue filled to capacity with people who had come to pay their last respects. The honorary pallbearers were the principal theater owners and managers of the day: Belasco, Cohan and Harris, the two Shubert brothers, Al Woods, Klaw and Erlanger, Morris Gest and Percy Williams. John McCormack, whom Hammerstein had brought to America, representing the many performers who owed their fame and fortune to the Old Man, sang "The Lost Chord."

The announcement of Oscar I's death at seventy-two was carried on every newspaper's front page as well as in editorials. *The New York Times* editorial said:

> In the popular mind Hammerstein's fame rests on the minor aspects of his greatness . . . His name will always recall the eccentric silk hat of his prime, with a black cigar tilted up beneath it. It will recall his tireless energy, his fertility of resource, his amazing faculty of enlisting the support of men and money, his building of gigantic theater after theater—most of which failed through being located according to ideas of real estate values which were true in themselves but too far ahead of his time. It will recall his cheerful courage in failure and his quick turns of speech at all times. It will recall the amazing publicity expert who used his own eccentricities to their limit for public effect. One sentence reveals vividly the intense workings of his mind. 'Nature's greatest mistake is her failure to equip us with a switch to turn off our thought.' The restless energy of his mind and his inexhaustible fertility of invention made him, during one brief period, the regenerator of our musical life; but first and always he was a character of almost titanic force and picturesqueness.

Oscar II did not skim the tributes, but read them all very carefully. He was astonished to realize how little he knew of his grandfather and equally astonished to realize that suddenly he wanted to know him. Feeling that he was "a posthumous victim of [his grandfather's] charm," he now began to seek out information about Oscar I from eager storytellers who thrust their reminiscences upon him, and years later would seek more as he began a biography of the Old Man. "Perhaps for the first time it seemed safe to try. He couldn't hurt me now. He couldn't humiliate me. The fears and resentments of this remote 'old man,' developed in my childhood, were no longer a block to our union. It is ironic and sad and strange that I did not begin to understand or like my grandfather until the day of his death. But he was a strange man and so, perhaps, am I."

Oscar and Myra had begun married life, in 1917, in a small apartment at 509 West 121st Street. From there they moved the following year to 122nd Street and West End Avenue, and their first son, William, named for Willie Hammerstein, was born on October 26. A second child, Alice, named for Oscar's mother, would be born on May 17, 1921. (Both children, incidentally, were delivered by Dick Rodgers' father, who was an obstetrician.) Oscar was a typical Hammerstein father in having no affinity for small children "below the age of seven."

Many of the people who formed their social circle in the early days of their marriage remained Oscar's lifelong friends. Milton "Kaddy" Kadison had been Oscar's friend since summer camp and had dated Myra before she fell in love with Oscar. Others were Milton and Rose Heller, who was Myra's childhood friend; Betty and Herman Axelrod and Ellie and Howard Reinheimer. Reinheimer had also gone to Columbia Law School and was now Oscar's lawyer. Though not overtly shy, Oscar had a reticent quality, a softness and humility that attracted people to him. Says Rose Heller, "Who could resist those warm blue eyes, that loving smile, that gentleness!"

Myra helped Oscar by typing scripts, but when her efforts to demand more of his attention failed, she turned more and more to her own social activities as he remained engrossed in his work. A moody and complex woman, she seemed dissatisfied much of the time. Their marriage was not particularly satisfying to Oscar, either, but good Victorian boy that he was, he interpreted marriage not as something to be judged bad or good, but as a reality to be accepted. In any case, he was preoccupied by the theater. Supervising productions in his job with Arthur, working with the Columbia University Players and writing plays, he also saw every show that opened on Broadway and took extensive notes on plots, actors, production details and his own critical evaluations which eventually filled a 280-page scrapbook. He was observing, absorbing information, studying the curriculum of the theater with an interest and intensity that he had not been able to bring to law school courses. He was preparing.

It is easy to imagine that Oscar might simply have trusted to luck at this point in his career, playing his famous name and connections for all they were worth, as did so many second- and third-generation theatrical offspring. For those who have done so, the famous name has more often proved to be more a curse than a blessing. The Hammersteins' fame and influence did not make Oscar spoiled or opportunistic, did not cause him to doubt his own part in the success that began to come to him. He accepted the "luck" that circumstances brought him, and by hard work, perseverance and talent, made it work for him.

Two

One Foot in the Door

Oscar began his career as a librettist in a decade in which Broadway reflected and satisfied the country's postwar mood. Eager to forget the ugliness and deprivation of war, heady with life in a booming economy, easily earning and spending money, the American public, seeking pleasure and escape, enthusiastically supported a decade of musical theater that gave them just what they wanted. The theatergoer neither wanted nor expected real life at eight-thirty. An evening at the theater provided the audience with fast, easy pleasures that asked no commitment or mental energy in return. With the popular revues—*The Follies, Vanities, Scandals, Frolics, Gaieties, Hitchy-Koos* —the theatergoer's senses were stimulated with the opulence of lavish productions, easy laughs, beautiful and provocative girls, sophisticated and risqué material, the upbeat jazz sound, spectacles and novelties, and star turns by favorite performers.

Alternately the tired businessman might seek his entertainment and escape in the musical comedies, with their orthodox form and sugar-coated, optimistic plots, that employed the expected element at the expected time, characters of romance and derring-do, lyrical music and lush settings, familiar routines from popular performers.

The musical theater had not found its form in the twenties, but was still a mélange of disparate elements, a hodgepodge of operetta, musical comedy, star vehicle, farce, melodrama, snazzy show, romantic show. There was little unity to the musical, as producers and writers gave the public what it expected and wanted: a formula of songs, dances, favorite stars, comedy, romance, pretty girls, production numbers, novelty numbers and grand finales. The story existed as a string to hang these elements on and had little relation to them or to reality and real emotion. The pattern was a bit of story, song cue, a bit of story, song cue.

As Oscar practiced his craft in the early years, he stayed in touch, as he always would, with popular taste and interest. But even as he mastered the existing structure of the musical, a determination grew in him to bring the elements together in a relationship that would make songs an integral part of the story and make both express something more real and more expressive of human life and emotion. This determination, shown only haltingly and infrequently at first, would eventually change the structure of the American musical.

In his early years, Oscar worked with a great number of collaborators. It is difficult to know what causes the kind of chemistry between collaborators that brings out the best in both men, but unparalleled in the annals of collaboration was Oscar's ability to work with so many composers, of such varying styles, and create shows that for each composer were artistic successes, and often the greatest successes of their careers. In his first decade in the theater he worked with Herbert Stothart, Rudolf Friml, Vincent Youmans, Sigmund Romberg and Jerome Kern.

The show that Oscar began writing on a New Haven park bench when his first effort failed was still undeveloped as its author led a hectic life during the late spring and summer of 1919. Arthur had several new Broadway musicals lined up and was sending out six road companies of his three current New York hits. His position as production manager meant that Oscar was responsible for supervising all his uncle's attractions. When not working, he attended every Broadway play.

On August 6 all of this activity stopped when Actors Equity went out on strike. The association was only six years old at the time, having been organized for the express purpose of getting the producers to sign a standard contract with minimum pay and basic safeguards against the exploitation of actors. Now, with the contract up for revision and renewal, the managers amiably agreed to everything except the one issue that seems most indefensible now: they would not agree to pay the actors for extra matinées on legal holidays and other special occasions or to limit the number of paid performances to eight a week. The reason for the refusal was that the managers did not want to recognize Equity as the sole bargaining agent for the actors because Equity's contemplated joining of the A.F.L. was seen as a threat to the autonomy of the producers. Since actors were thought to be living in a world of fantasy, the notion of an actors' strike was considered unbelievable. However, it happened, not only on Broadway but across the nation as well.

Though the strike caused chaos in the theatrical world, it was indirectly a boon to Oscar. Now he could devote all his time to that show he wanted to write. Working in a summer cottage in Far Rockaway, Long Island, that he had rented for Myra and one-year-old Billy, he decided that it would be a musical. By the end of the month-long strike, he had the book but no music for his would-be lyrics.

He found his collaborator in Herbert Stothart, who had been Arthur's resident musical director for the past five seasons. Stothart had proven brilliant at his job, able to sense when a show was lagging and to lift it with the music. A former member of the University of Wisconsin's music faculty, he was eager to become a Broadway composer, and so far his only opportunity had been two interpolated songs (with lyrics by Arthur Hammerstein) in *Somebody's Sweetheart*. Working together on Arthur's productions, Oscar had become a close friend of the tall, strikingly handsome man with magnetic black eyes who was ten years his senior.

Anxious as Stothart was to collaborate with Oscar, he was worried about the practicality of their efforts. "How can we be sure that Arthur will want to produce it?"

Oscar thought for a while and came up with one of the few cons of his life. "Herb, I want you to sit in when I read it to him and every time I look up for his reaction, I want *you* to laugh."

When Arthur heard Stothart's uproarious laughter, he fell into Oscar's trap: he thought that if Oscar's script was that funny to Herb, it must be a good one. He instructed the two men to work fast in writing the songs and getting the show ready for production.

With the book in hand, the two began working in the manner that was standard with American collaborators at that time: Stothart first wrote the music and Oscar then set lyrics to it. When Oscar reversed this process after he began collaborating with Rodgers in 1942, he realized that writing the words first was a more logical procedure, music being the more flexible and less specific of the two mediums. Grand-opera scores are usually set to texts already written by librettists, and Gilbert always wrote the lyrics before Sullivan composed the music, but for a long time none of the American teams worked this way.

The traditional American system of putting words to music was probably accounted for by several factors. One was that in the first decade of this century the best musical plays were being created in Vienna, so that American librettists had to write translations of lyrics for existing tunes. Also influential in determining the order in which songs were put together was the deviation from orthodox meter in the distinctly American ragtime and jazz, which was so difficult to work with that composers needed a free hand without worrying about lyrics. Also, the craze for dancing in the second decade of the century meant that the most important consideration for a song was that it be a good dance melody, and the lyrics had to be fitted to a refrain written mainly to be danced to. In any case, Oscar continued to follow the custom of writing lyrics to fit melodies through the next twenty-four years of collaborating with Stothart, Rudolf Friml, Jerome Kern, George Gershwin, Sigmund Romberg, Vincent Youmans, Richard Whiting and others.

The finished show, *Joan of Arkansaw* (*sic*), began tryouts in Boston on December 1, 1919. The plot, which had certain overtones of *Madame Butterfly*, dealt with an American soldier who is torn between his love for two women, Toinette in France and Joan in his hometown in Arkansas. Although the Majestic Theatre's opening-night audience unhesitatingly expressed its approval and delight, the response from the critics was mixed: one rave, two qualified nods and one pan. On the plus side was Brooks Atkinson, writing for the *Boston Evening Transcript,* who thought that Oscar had displayed good taste and the "necessary skill" with the plot for this "passingly agreeable" entertainment but commented that it was a good thing that the plot of a 1919 musical comedy did not matter a great deal, "and an especially good thing for this particular production."

During the Boston run, Arthur, trying to improve the show, peremptorily brought in the veteran comedian, Ralph Herz, and ordered a large part to be written for him. When Oscar learned of his uncle's decision, he went back to his room at the Crown Hotel and cried, but the next day he and Stothart began rewriting the show in order to accommodate Herz. When the production moved on to Washington, Arthur's move proved to be astute, for all three critics gave the show their heartfelt endorsement, singling out Herz for his unique contribution.

On January 5, 1920, Oscar's first musical opened on Broadway at the Central Theatre. The newspapers made much of his name and his position as the third generation of Hammersteins. In the *Evening World,* under the headline OSCAR II MAKES HIT AS MUSICAL COMEDY AUTHOR—GRANDSON OF LATE HAMMERSTEIN WINS WITH "ALWAYS YOU," Heywood Broun began his review with: "If the late Oscar Hammerstein could have been present at the premiere he would have been filled with pride, for his grandson and second of his illustrious name provided the book and lyrics of this charming musical comedy, one of the daintiest and most refreshing that Broadway has seen in many a day." Another noted that the younger Oscar had perhaps unconsciously absorbed a certain amount of "gag and hoak." Every critic referred to Oscar's family; they were also unanimous in endorsing the show for its freshness and "its touch of originality which went beyond the elimination of much of the customary ingredients to be found in ordinary musical concoctions."

More important than the recognition was the vivid lesson that Oscar learned from watching the audience react to his first musical. While working as a stage manager for Arthur, he had been impatient with all the talk devoted to motivation, situation, character. Convinced that the jokes, songs, dances and pretty chorus girls were all that mattered to an audience, he thought the librettists were kidding themselves to think the plot mattered at all.

Now, as he sat in the Central Theatre watching the opening night of *Always You,* he was at first disappointed with the feeble laughter that some of his favorite jokes received and then startled when a joke that he hadn't expected the audience to react to caused a big laugh. Analyzing that unexpected laugh, Oscar realized that it depended on a line that had been spoken in a previous scene. This discovery became one of his basic axioms: Playgoers follow the plot. He soon discovered that all the beautiful songs, talented casts, gags and expensive production details could come tumbling down in an inglorious heap if they were not supported by a shrewdly constructed book.

The score of the show was published by Harms & Company,

which was to publish the score of every show that Oscar wrote, and a lifelong connection was established between him and Harms's head, Max Dreyfus. An astute musician and perceptive judge of talent, Dreyfus was more than a music publisher; he was a powerful figure in the music world. His office was always filled with composers and writers; everyone from established names to untried hands used it as their daily meeting place, and many composers were under contract to Dreyfus. Every day Victor Herbert would walk through the outer office where the apprentice composers and musicians were gathered and offer such advice as: "Listen, boys, don't let a day go by without writing a bar of music. Even if it's only one bar, write every day."

Dreyfus knew everyone in the theatrical world, was in touch with everything that was happening on Broadway and Tin Pan Alley, and had the power and respect that allowed him to put into effect his sure instinct for knowing the right man for the right spot. When Victor Herbert walked out on *The Firefly* it was Dreyfus who brought Rudolf Friml to the attention of Arthur Hammerstein; Dreyfus was instrumental in launching and establishing the careers of Jerome Kern, George Gershwin and Vincent Youmans, among others.

Just as *Always You* was leaving New York for an extended road tour, Oscar learned that Arthur was planning a new musical, *Tickle Me*, which would star Frank Tinney, the famous vaudeville entertainer. Naturally, he wanted to write it. Arthur, confident of his nephew's ability but aware that he needed to learn more about his craft, brought in Otto Harbach to collaborate on the book and lyrics. Oscar would later say that this union was the first important force in his creative career.

Otto Harbach, born Hauerbach, in Salt Lake City, Utah, in 1873, had written unsuccessful play scripts at night as he worked on a New York newspaper as a copywriter for several years. In 1908 he joined forces with composer Karl Hoschna; in a three-year period they wrote three dire failures and two hits, whose songs include: "Cuddle Up a Little Closer" and "Every Little Movement Has a Meaning All Its Own." After Hoschna's death in 1911, Arthur Hammerstein hired Harbach to work on *The Firefly* with Victor Herbert, and when he walked out on the show, Rudolf Friml took on the assignment. This show began a sixteen-year, fourteen-show association between Harbach and Arthur, to whom he expressed deep gratitude and respect: "He had courage, and the money he risked was always his own. He was willing to open doors for me—an unestablished writer." He wrote twelve shows for Arthur before his first meeting with Oscar; in one of them, *High Jinks*, Arthur's daughter Elaine, Oscar's childhood play-mate, played her first acting role.

Harbach, twenty-two years Oscar's senior, was a practical and clear-thinking man with a calm, disciplined temperament. The two men were complementary; Otto had experience and Oscar had youth, industry and raw talent. From the very start their relationship was that of two collaborators on an equal footing, with Harbach dividing credits and royalties equally despite his collaborator's youth and in-experience. Oscar often said that he was born into the theatrical world with two gold spoons in his mouth, referring to Otto Harbach as the second. Not only was Harbach one of the kindest, most tolerant and wisest men he knew, but he was the best play analyst that Oscar ever met, and a born teacher. Like most young writers, Oscar was eager to get words down on paper; Otto taught him to think a long time be-fore actually writing. Along with other important precepts, he taught Oscar never to stop work on anything if he could think of one small improvement to make.

Otto made two rules when they began to work. The first was that the story must have interest. The second was that all the elements must be integrated in the show; neither songs nor jokes could be put in unless they were germane to the plot. In explaining the construction of a show, Harbach compared the elements of a musical play to the ingredients that go to make a fire—logs, kindling, matches, a good fireplace.

Arthur recruited a third member for the *Tickle Me* writing team, an expert in situation comedy named Frank Mandel, who had worked previously with Otto. Born in San Francisco, eleven years older than Oscar, Mandel had received a law degree after graduating from the University of California. As uninterested in the law as Oscar, he had shown one of his early plays to Henry Miller, the famous Broadway producer, which led to a collaboration with David Belasco. Mandel went on to write shows on his own, as well as with Lew Fields, Victor Herbert and Guy Bolton. He would later be associated with Laurence Schwab in producing several of Oscar's shows. Red-haired Mandel, an intense, nervous man with a noted sense of humor, was also a brilliant manipulator of stocks and bonds and made a fortune on Wall Street.

The story that Hammerstein-Harbach-Mandel conjured up concerned Frank Tinney who, in the role of Frank Tinney, accompanied a motion picture company to Tibet. He played several parts before the cameras and several more before the footlights, while the scenery was being changed. One feature of the production was a "ground glass" effect devised by Arthur, an arrangement of successive glass curtains through which the actors walked into a fade-out. It was an ingenious idea, its only flaw being that it didn't work. On the opening night of the tryout in Stamford, Connecticut, Tinney, dressed in his second act finale costume, came before the footlights and said, "This next scene won't work, so you won't see it. I just wanted you to know that the boy and girl do get together. So now you can go home."

Which they did, happily: it was 12:15 A.M. After some frenzied carpentering, including writing a whole new second act during the remaining out-of-town engagements, *Tickle Me* opened at the Selwyn Theatre in New York on August 17, 1920.

Arthur not only saw to it that his glass-curtain setup worked, but added two other gimmicks reminiscent of Willie and the Old Man. The first act closed on a production number entitled "The Ceremony of the Sacred Bath," revealing a horseshoe falls of glistening soapsuds. Colored lights played on the millions of bubbles, from the size of those blown out of a clay pipe to those as big as footballs, as pretty girls stepped out of the falls. The effect, on that hot August night, brought the house down.

The Arthur Hammerstein touch was an opulent but not always tasteful one. In this same show Oscar and Otto's song "We've Got Something" was accompanied by an ensemble of girls marching down into the aisles with baskets on their arms and distributing to the men in the audience little flasks labeled "Compliments of Arthur Hammerstein, a Tickle from *Tickle Me*—Carstair's Whiskey." Not amused, agents of the Federal Prohibition Enforcement Bureau appeared at Arthur's office the following day with a court order, only to learn that the bottles had really contained the standard stage "booze"—tea.

Although the critics made minor complaints that the libretto and lyrics suffered from too many inside jokes, and that the plot was "no better than it should be," all but one of the daily reviewers approved of the production. The show had no trouble competing at the box office with Marilyn Miller in *Sally*, W. C. Fields and Fanny Brice in *Ziegfeld Follies*, George White's *Scandals* or Eugene O'Neill's *The Emperor Jones*.

On the heels of *Tickle Me* came Oscar's second musical, *Jimmie*, which began its life on November 17, 1920, as the opening attraction of Selwyn's new Apollo Theatre. For the first time Oscar had the thrill of seeing two of his shows not only running in New York at the same time, but playing side by side at adjoining theaters on West 42nd Street. The plot was an uninventive Cinderella story designed to show off the talents of the star, dancer Frances White.

The reviewers described the new Apollo at some length, finding it comfortable and attractive, As for *Jimmie,* they thought the story and songs sufficiently consistent and interesting, but saved most of their praise for the chorus line, the costumes and particularly the star. Oscar and his collaborators had obviously given Frances White the good vehicle that they were meant to provide, permitting her to do all the things that had caused her admirers to be her admirers.

During 1921 and 1922, Oscar continued to work on shows that were primarily vehicles for established stars: *Pop* was a comedy, without songs, starring stage—and, later, screen—personality, O. P. Heggie; *Daffy Dill* again starred Frank Tinney; and *Queen O' Hearts* was written for Nora Bayes.

The first of these, *Pop,* written in collaboration with Frank Mandel, opened and closed in Atlantic City in the fall of 1921. Decided failure that it was, the show reinforced the axiom that Oscar had learned from the audience at his first show. He and Mandel sat in a box counting the laughs. The show got more than two hundred, or better than one a minute; the audience laughed but they didn't believe the story or the characters, and the play was a flop.

Arthur's instructions for the next opus, to star Frank Tinney, must have been that he wanted a scene in a Chinese garden and one on a pirate ship and that Tinney must have a scene with a horse. *Daffy Dill,* with songs by Oscar and Stothart, opened at the Apollo Theatre in August 1922; it fulfilled Arthur's requirements and allowed Tinney to do his most popular routines, from a blackface number to a juggling scene. Apparently the lowest common denominator of the musical show patron would not have felt insulted by subtlety, wit or by anything he might have thought "high brow" in this show. Oscar later remembered one song in particular, "My Little Redskin," as "a real horror." Wearing bathing suits, the female chorus came out with deep sunburned make-up, and the lyric featured the double meaning of "redskin."

Guy Bolton, who collaborated on *Daffy Dill,* was a busy and successful musical book writer who worked only this one time with

Oscar, but remained a friend for years. An Englishman who had started out as an architect, Bolton was a deft writer who had worked with P. G. Wodehouse and Jerome Kern on the intimate musical comedies for the Princess Theatre which had made some strides toward integration of songs and plot.

The day of the *Daffy Dill* dress rehearsal, Myra expressed fear at being left alone in the Hammersteins' house in Douglaston, Long Island, where they had moved with Billy and Alice the year before, after the success of *Tickle Me*. It was arranged that Bolton should stay with her, since he didn't want to go to the rehearsal anyway; the night marked the beginning of an affair between Myra and Bolton, who was not married at the time. This was not Myra's first affair, nor was extramarital dalliance uncommon among the people they knew. It was not something they discussed or faced up to; it was simply part of their lives and their routine of working hard and playing hard. Years later, in notes he scribbled for an autobiography, Oscar wrote of this period: "Great need—False values—my fault as well as hers. I am an idiot but work hard."

While *Daffy Dill* was playing its seventy-four performances, Oscar began work on a musical for producer Max Spiegel. *Queen O' Hearts* was written for the popular Nora Bayes, who had first become a vaudeville star under the auspices of Willie Hammerstein. Miss Bayes took young composer Lewis Gensler to Max Dreyfus, who approved of the tunes he heard and suggested that Oscar write the lyrics.

Again he collaborated with Frank Mandel on the book, about a successful marriage broker, and several songs, one of which, "Tom-Tom," became a big hit. The show lasted only five weeks in New York before going on the road, even though reviewers had predicted a long run for the "sparkling, jingling," if conventional, musical.

These early shows in which Oscar was involved were being written and produced according to a "formula" for musicals of the day. The ironic comment on this formula method in a song from *Always You* shows that Oscar was already dissatisfied with the limitations that it imposed on his creative integrity. As Arthur threw in stars, extra comics, girls with little flasks and glass curtains, Oscar wrote (in "The Tired Business Man"):

> Start with a little plot,
> Cook it but not too hot,
> Throw in a heroine,
> Maiden so simple and ingenuous.

Then let your tenor shine,
With his high C;
Write in a well known joke,
Use all the old time "hoke"
For this is the surest plan
To entertain the tired business man.

One of the set pieces in the formula was the "icebreaker," a number performed as the first-act curtain went up, with lots of action and the actors singing something that was not very intelligible. Its purpose was to keep the audience interested enough while late-comers were banging down their seats without giving them any valuable part of the plot or wasting a good song. Oscar felt that the very existence of the icebreaker—in this case "IloveyouIloveyou" [*sic*]— illustrated a kind of insincerity about musical comedy writing in general in that period. The composer and lyric writer concentrated mainly on a few major efforts: a big dance number, a love ballad, a light comedy duet, one or two songs for the comedians (never the composer's best music, for he didn't want to waste it on a comedy song). In the rather shoddy medium of the musical comedy, neither public nor critics expected much of a show, generally taking it to be a display of girls, jokes and tunes.

As for the librettist, he was a kind of stableboy: if the race was won he was seldom mentioned; if the race was lost he was blamed for giving the horse the wrong feed. Typical of critics' comments about the book for a musical was: "But when did a musical comedy ever have good libretto and what does it matter anyhow?" Oscar felt that this widespread attitude was not conducive to an author's integrity or self-respect, though he was the first to admit that the field of libretto writing was full of hacks and gagmen who earned the ignominy attached to musical comedy books. The pity was that the few patient men, such as Otto Harbach, who kept on writing well-constructed musical plays, most of which were successful, had very little chance of being recognized for their effort.

Oscar's next show, *Wildflower*, starring Edith Day, again provided no exceptions to the formula of the day. "The task of the reviewer," said Woollcott in his *Herald* column, "is to sit down before the musical comedies as they pass along and make known next day how each one differs from those that have preceded it. But *Wildflower* simply doesn't." It had, however, an extraordinarily long run—four hundred and seventy-seven performances—in 1923. Perhaps the reason was that Vincent Youmans had written a varied and colorful score or perhaps it was that Oscar, Otto and Arthur had turned out what one critic called "an adroit and workmanlike example of the genus musical comedy."

Youmans had written only one middling-successful Broadway show—with Ira Gershwin—before Max Dreyfus, for whom he was plugging songs, recommended him to Arthur. Badly in need of a hit, Arthur had asked Rudolf Friml to write the score for his projected show; when Friml pulled out because he didn't want to work with Stothart on the music, Arthur was again willing to take a chance with a newcomer.*

Small and dark, the handsome twenty-four-year-old Vincent Youmans was introverted and shy, but had a brilliant mind and lofty ambitions. He was never satisfied with merely composing for the musical theater. Like George Gershwin, his goal was to be a serious composer, though unlike Gershwin, he never succeeded in this.

Oscar wrote two songs, one with Youmans, that appeared in *Hammerstein's Nine O'Clock Revue*, a late-evening entertainment of songs and sketches imported from the Little Theatre in London. The back of the program was an advertisement for Arthur Hammerstein Attractions: *Wildflower* in its second season; *Plain Jane*, a musical by Oscar Hammerstein II, William Carey Duncan, Herbert Stothart and Vincent Youmans scheduled for December; and *Gypsy Jim*, a "unique play" by Oscar Hammerstein II and Milton Gropper opening in January. As if he weren't busy enough, at about this time Richard Rodgers, Larry Hart and Herb Fields asked Oscar to help them with the book of a show they were working on, *Winkle Town*. Oscar agreed but had little time to spend with them and, in fact, the show was never produced.

Plain Jane, on which Oscar again collaborated with Youmans, had become *Mary Jane McKane* by the time it began its 151-performance run on Christmas Day 1923 as the premiere attraction of the Imperial, the Shubert's newest theater on West 45th Street. With antic heroine, unhackneyed melodies † and production numbers free of tasteless

---

* Reporting on the Broadway opening, the *New York Times* critic said, " 'Wildflower' contains the most tuneful score that Rudolf Friml has written in a number of seasons." It is hard to know who was more surprised by this comment—Friml or Youmans.

† Youmans used some of the melodies again. "Come on and Pet Me" later became a big hit as "Sometimes I'm Happy."

gimmicks, the musical made an impression on the critics and the audience by the way it "capsized many of the current notions of musical comedy . . . with winning grace." They also noted that the plot—about a girl who disguises her good looks in order to achieve business success—was well defined and the whole production a "masterpiece of pruning." This was the first evidence of what later emerged as one of Oscar's greatest gifts.

Oscar missed the premiere because that night he was in Springfield, Massachusetts, attending the first performance of *Gypsy Jim.* It was his third stab at writing a straight play, this time with Milton Herbert Gropper. Gropper had attended Columbia with Oscar and had then started a career as a newspaper reporter. Soon he was writing one-act plays for a newspaper syndicate and in 1919 he sold David Belasco *The Charwoman,* which was well received on Broadway. A short man with a round, gnomish head and an unctuous voice, Gropper was always in and out of Oscar's life.

Gypsy Jim starred Leo Carrillo and was about an eccentric millionaire who went about restoring people's faith in themselves; it opened in New York on January 14, 1924, at the 49th Street Theatre. The flowery dialogue caused Alexander Woollcott to remark in the *New York Herald:* "This lyric speech became so contagious that the authors were in grave danger of seeing the newspapers break out this morning in a rash of notices such as this:

> "Oscar Hammerstein 2d and Milton Gropper
> Wrote a comedy that came an awful cropper."

Not much, that, as poetry, but fairly prophetic. After a run of thirty-nine performances *Gypsy Jim* passed quietly away on Saturday, February 16, 1924. Oscar's comment at the time: "I learned then what my grandfather often told me, that there is just no limit to the number of people who stay away from a bad show."

There was not much time to brood about the play's demise; two days later, on Monday, February 18, *New Toys,* another Hammerstein-Gropper effort, which dealt with the second year of marriage, was presented at the Fulton Theatre (now the Helen Hayes) by Sam H. Harris. The play was trailed by a lengthy subtitle, "A comic tragedy of married life after the baby arrives." Woollcott went at it again: "The process of disintegration proceeds so far that the final scene reaches a level below any explored, even by *Gypsy Jim.*" *New Toys* lasted as long as many new toys: three weeks. Oddly enough, although this was Oscar's worst Broadway failure, it was his first work to be made into a motion picture. First National released it in 1925 with a cast that included Richard Barthelmess, Mary Hay, and Clifton Webb.

The frenetic activity of this year illuminates Oscar's scribbled note: "I am an idiot but work hard." The Hammersteins had moved the year before from Douglaston to Great Neck, where Guy Bolton lent them his house for nine months while they looked for a house to buy. Great Neck at that time was a popular and smart show-business colony, with such residents as Scott and Zelda Fitzgerald, Leslie and Ruth Howard, Eddie and Ida Cantor, and "Plum" and Ethel Wodehouse. Oscar, Myra, five-year-old Billy and three-year-old Alice, along with two cats, Mary and Marjorie, began living in their own small house at 13 Grace Avenue in the summer of 1924.

This house represented to Billy his first recollections of a rift between his father and his mother. He remembered that his father often slept in the other twin bed in Billy's room. He enjoyed waking up to find his father in the next bed and recalls that Oscar would raise his knees so that son could slide down them onto his stomach. "He wasn't there every night but it was always with eagerness that I'd wake up in the morning to see if he was in the bed so I could play with him."

Rose-Marie, Oscar's third show in 1924, had its inception in a story that Arthur had heard about an annual ice carnival in Quebec, which featured an ice palace high on the hill overlooking the city. According to Arthur's information, at the close of the week's festivities, the celebrants would climb the hill on snowshoes and, torches in hand, melt down the palace. "What an idea for a musical!" exclaimed Arthur. "What a finish!" He sent Oscar and Otto to Montreal in April to research the matter. They found out immediately that the story was nonsense. Oscar wondered how you would melt down a palace on stage every night anyway, but mused that if anyone could do it, Uncle Arthur could.

He and Otto stayed at the Chateau Frontenac where they tried skiing until Oscar fell down and couldn't get up, much to his partner's amusement. They heard about an Indian moccasin factory to which they traveled on a very cold day only to find that the Indians were taking a half-day off. The whole trip yielded one scene in *Rose-Marie*.

When Rudolf Friml heard from Otto that Arthur was planning a new musical, he called him to say he would like to do the music for it. Arthur said, "Rudy, I'd love you to do it but you wouldn't agree the last time to work with Stothart and that's the only way it will work." Friml's last show, *Cinders,* for which he turned down *Wildflower,* having lasted only thirty-one performances, he agreed to work with Stothart.

The evening before the *Rose-Marie* Long Branch premiere, Arthur, his wife Dorothy Dalton, former stage and screen star, and Oscar were having dinner at the nearby home of his cousin, Walter Reade.* Soon after they arrived Arthur was called to the telephone. Eduardo Ciannelli, a member of the cast who was also Stothart's brother-in-law, was calling to tell Arthur that he and Oscar should come to the hotel in Long Branch immediately. Stothart's wife had arrived to surprise Herb—she had indeed surprised him in bed with her sister and had thrown open the window and jumped to her death.

The next day, while everyone was still in shock from Dorothy Stothart's death, trouble developed with the stagehands and Oscar and Arthur had to move the scenery and prepare for the first performance. Arthur's anxiety was increased by the fact that he had used $85,000 of his own money to finance the entire production. Despite all the difficulties, the opening night sailed along smoothly at the Imperial Theatre on September 2, 1924.

Where *Wildflower* showed Oscar using his taste and talent to produce the best of the formula musical comedy and *Mary Jane McKane* showed him beginning to break away from some of the conventions, *Rose-Marie* marked some more serious departures from the orthodoxy of musical comedy. Oscar recalled that people laughed at him when he said he was going to try a musical with a murder in it, for such a thing was unheard of in the treacle sea of the usual musical comedy plots. *Rose-Marie* ended with only two people on the stage, instead of the usual crowd of elaborately dressed actors. The program listed no songs, but included this note:

> The musical numbers of this play are such an integral part of the
> action that we do not think we should list them as separate

---

* Reade, who owned the Broadway Theatre, where *Rose-Marie* was to open, was the son of Anna, Oscar I's sister, who had first come to this country to raise Arthur, Willie et al., and who had then married Henry Rosenberg. They had three children, one of whom was Walter, who started his career as Willie's box-office treasurer and later changed his name to Reade when he began his chain of theaters during World War I when German names were unpopular.

episodes. The songs which stand out, independent of their dramatic associations, are "Rosemarie," "Indian Love Call," "Totem Tom-Tom" and "Why Shouldn't We" in the first act, and "The Door of My Dreams" in the second act.

This represents wishful thinking more than full realization of the goal of integration, since the musical still followed the story-song-cue-story-song-cue pattern in some measure. However, the book and score blended to an extent unusual in those days; *Theatre Magazine's* Arthur Hornblow pronounced it "head, shoulders and waist above the customary drivel about Prohibition and Brooklyn."

Oscar never set out consciously to break conventions, and in fact distrusted discussions of trends and schools of musical theater. He sat down to write a play because he liked the subject matter or the characters or some other aspect of it and then did as well as he could to write a good show. "I don't think very often of trying to create any new tendency or revolution. Sometimes the revolution comes but it is incidental to the main aim of trying to write something that's good."

Brilliantly mounted and well performed by a cast headed by Dennis King, *Rose-Marie* was a great hit, and it remained on Broadway for one year, four months and seven days, a record-breaking run for its time; *Show Boat*, three years later, ran longer, but only by fifteen days. Five road tours ran concurrently for three years, with one company returning to New York to resume the second of many Broadway engagements in January 1927. The property had similar success in the English, French and Australian stage presentations. In addition, MGM produced three motion picture versions.

With *Rose-Marie*, Oscar reached financial success. Over the years the show grossed $21 million, with a sizable portion of that amount plus ASCAP royalties going to Oscar.

This show marked not only a departure from the formula musical, but more assurance on Oscar's part not only about his knowledge of his craft, but about his growing conception of the "musical play." In fact, his assurance might well have been called chutzpa when the young man, who had been writing shows for only four and a half years, sent a note to all the drama critics in the principal cities on the play's tour urging them not to review *Rose-Marie* because as drama critics they were not qualified to criticize musicals. They exhibited their ignorance, he explained, when they so often said that the book of a musical doesn't matter, when in fact there was never a successful musical show which did not have a solid libretto as a foundation. "The critics' problem is that they do not recognize what a good libretto is, and do not realize that a good musical comedy must not necessarily be a good play." The forms are so different, Oscar said, that there is only one point on which they may be criticized similarly on a legitimate basis: in both a libretto and a dramatic play there must be a plot containing characters which hold the interest and sympathies of the audience and meet in significant climaxes; in the ideal musical the plot would be told through music.

Oscar's major complaint against the drama critics was that their criticism of musicals had degenerated to a formula because they had little liking for or knowledge of musical shows. "Since musical shows, good or bad, are constructed with painstaking attention to detail, great consumption of energy and carefully analyzed scientific principles of showmanship, it is unfair not to accord sincere and expert criticism to them."

His lengthy note to the critics was one of the early skirmishes in a battle of sorts that he waged against them all his life, sometimes with justification, sometimes not. Later in his career, Oscar was so acclaimed by critics that his broadsides at them sometimes seemed to have a petulant and self-righteous tone. Although he did have a tendency to "preach," the tone can be better understood in the light of the many early years in which he suffered abuse or neglect at the hands of drama reviewers who were, as he accurately pointed out, ignorant about the musical theater in general and the work of a librettist in particular.

The amount of work he produced is clear evidence that Oscar did not have a great many leisure hours at home. Although he was a "family man" in orientation, he did few household tasks, was notoriously inept at repairs and never felt comfortable with children under seven. However, he did play with Billy, throwing crumpled paper into a chandelier in an indoor version of basketball, or sledding with him in the snow. Both children would skate on a spot on the front lawn of 13 Grace Avenue that filled with water and froze. Billy has recollections of his father with a cane, often carried in those days for fashion rather than utility, going out to watch the children skating. Oscar would teasingly put the cane under his skates to trip him and then poke him with the cane as he tried to get up, laughing all the time.

Reggie was always around the house in Great Neck in those days. Since he left Columbia University he had been in California in the film business with the Selznick organization and was now back East in his first Broadway job, as stage manager of *Rose-Marie*. The years spent at opposite ends of the country had in no way diminished the strong bond of love and affection that had always existed between the brothers. Both Oscar and Reggie felt that Reggie had "gotten the short end of the stick" from their mother, and Oscar seemed to spend the rest of his life trying to make up for it, always giving him support and encouragement. Their lives were already very different. Oscar was a family man industriously pursuing a career; Reggie was a carefree playboy who treated his work as a means to finance his pleasurable social life. Reggie worked on Oscar's shows as both stage manager and "director of book" for the next several years, and then began producing shows on his own, though he would return to Oscar's productions from time to time throughout the next three decades.

On January 15, 1925, Oscar, Myra, Billy and Alice sailed for London on the *Majestic*. This was Oscar's first trip to Europe since his "Grand Tour" with Kaddy and another friend in the summer of 1913. The Hammersteins took a flat in St. James's Court, Buckingham Gate, where they lived for three months while Oscar supervised the London production of *Rose-Marie*, which at his suggestion starred Edith Day.

Every morning when Billy awoke he would find that his father had left for him during the night a lead soldier of the kind he himself had played with by the hour as a child. A small French, British or African Zouave soldier would be standing on the sink, on the toilet seat, on the floor near his bed—in a different place each morning.

Before he came to London, Oscar had thought that he, Stothart and Arthur would pop in at rehearsals, make a few suggestions and pop out again, but after seeing several English musical productions, they thought they'd better take advantage of the producers' willingness to hand over control to them.

During auditions for the understudy to Edith Day, Oscar got a kick out of the way one of the English girls rendered the first line of "Indian Love Call." She looked at the sheet music, which read "When I'm calling you—oo-oo—oo-oo-oo," and then sweetly trilled, "When I'm calling you, double o, double o . . ."

The night before the Manchester Palace Theatre tryout, an assistant stage manager came to Oscar and told him that a little old lady was sitting on a campstool in front of the theater, in the rainy, foggy night. "Bring her in and let her see the dress rehearsal" was his answer. The man went outside to invite the old lady in, but she said, "Oh, I couldn't do *that*. It would spoil things for me!" Oscar was delighted by this "charmingly British reaction." In fact, he enjoyed London and most things British, including teatime, which came at four-thirty, come hell or high water, rehearsal or no rehearsal.

Though he loved the English, he didn't entirely understand them. At the London opening he felt that the show was dying before his eyes as he sat in a box with Arthur and noted that the audience remained strangely silent. "Wait until the Mounties come on. They'll love the Mounties," he whispered to Arthur. There was no sign of enthusiasm when the Mounties came on. "Wait for the totem-pole dance," he whispered to Arthur. They had outfitted forty girls in lavish totem-pole costumes, which created quite an effect, since they fell down on the stage one by one like a row of wooden soldiers. But the totem-pole dance came and went with no audible response from the audience. However, the musical ran for two years at the Drury Lane Theatre, breaking every record until *Oklahoma!* opened at the same house.

When Myra and the children returned home, Oscar went on to Paris, where he took an apartment alone on Avenue George V. For six weeks he had a love affair with Paris and the French people that he was always to remember. He worked on their forthcoming production of *Rose-Marie* and completed the outline for a new Broadway show.

Back in New York, his first call was to Otto Harbach to ask him to collaborate on the project. Otto was amenable but asked him to collaborate first on *Sunny*, to which he was already committed. The chance for Oscar to work on *Sunny* was a serendipitous one, for it brought about his long-lasting friendship and collaboration with Jerome Kern at a time when the musical theater was ripe for their contribution. Hammerstein and Kern proved to be perfectly suited not only by talent and temperament, but by the creative directions that had been developing in each. And the theater and its audiences were ready in the late twenties, as they might not have been before, for the productions of this partnership.

Jerome Kern had a fifteen-year head start on Oscar in the business. From 1905 to 1915 he had been a rehearsal pianist and an adapter of European musicals; such songs as "They Didn't Believe Me" had been interpolated into many shows. In 1915 he wrote his first full score, with

Guy Bolton and P. G. Wodehouse, for *Nobody Home,* beginning a series of ten musicals that they would write for the 250-seat Princess Theatre on West 39th Street.*

In the three and a half years of Princess Theater shows, the collaborators became the darlings of the critics as well as of New York audiences, and the shows had an invigorating effect on the musical theater. The fresh and even startlingly new quality of the shows stemmed not only from the talent of their authors but partly from necessity. The Princess was so small that there was no room on the stage for large choruses, and thus the shows had no choruses at all except for ensemble quartets and sextets. A revolutionary orchestra was devised by Kern for the small pit that would hold only about eleven musicians. These small shows had an intimate quality and a finesse that could not be matched in the larger houses on Broadway, then and for many years.

In 1920 Kern, with the same collaborators, turned to a more elaborate format with Florenz Ziegfeld's *Sally,* starring Marilyn Miller. This smash show contained a jewel called "Look For The Silver Lining." In the next five years Kern wrote an equal number of shows, trying out different collaborators with each.

Jerome Kern had met Oscar only once or twice, but he had been introduced to the Hammerstein family in 1902. On a Friday in late August, returning to his family's summer cottage in Arverne, New York, for the weekend, Willie Hammerstein sat beside a young man on the Long Island Railroad. The young man, Jerome Kern, asked Willie if he knew the Arverne station, for he was going there to visit friends. As the men chatted on the train, Kern told Willie that although he was working at a summer job in his father's merchandising store in Newark, he hoped to be a songwriter and was entering the New York College of Music in the fall. When they arrived at the station, Willie asked Kern back to his house. Although the Hammersteins did not have a piano, their next-door neighbor, Edward B. Marks, the music publisher, did, and Willie took Kern there to play some of his tunes. Marks was so intrigued with this young man's ability that he hired him. Allie Hammerstein was the chairwoman of a benefit that weekend at the village casino. Kern provided her with a tune for the occasion, to express his appreciation. Entitled "At The Casino," it became his first published song, printed that fall by Marks' Lyceum Publishing Company.

* Another of them, *Very Good Eddie,* enjoyed a successful Broadway revival during the 1976 season.

In 1905 Willie called Max Dreyfus to ask him to suggest a replacement for Marie Dressler's accompanist, who had just quit. Dreyfus sent Kern over, who remained at the Victoria for four months. He never forgot Willie's kind encouragement and help, and he watched the career of Willie's son with interest.

When Oscar joined him to write *Sunny*, Kern was under exclusive contract to Charles Dillingham to write three musicals. A producer as important as Ziegfeld and Arthur Hammerstein, Dillingham had begun his theatrical career as Oscar I's press agent at the Olympia and declared he was delighted to have his "talented grandson" working for him.

The first conference was held at the Kern home in Bronxville, New York. Although Kern was reputed to be hard to get along with, he didn't seem so to Oscar. A short man with keen blue eyes and a quick smile, he bounced nimbly from one subject to another, giving Oscar the impression that he would have to remain alert to keep pace with him. They discussed a plot that had already been decided upon before Oscar's entrance into the collaboration. Oscar remembered that Jerry stuck to the high spots of the show, leaving what came in between to Oscar and Otto; he wanted to talk only about the "big stuff" and his talk developed it and made it bigger. The composer didn't play any music that day; he was all story and showmanship, and it was evident that he knew something about everything. Oscar was stimulated and dazzled.

Oscar and Jerry quickly became close friends, working together as if born for this collaboration, temperaments and creative strengths dovetailing perfectly. However, Oscar did find out later why people had warned him that Jerry was a "tough guy" to work with. "He has abnormal impatience with incompetent fakers and when they cross his path he comes down on them like a blockbuster." Although Oscar was never on the receiving end of one of these blasts, he did see others "get it" and felt sympathy for them.

His impression of Jerry must also be attributed to Oscar's own disposition, which so often focused on the best side of other people's natures. In discussing the warnings about Kern, Oscar said, "I have come across that in several instances. I think it's better not to believe anything you hear about people that's bad until they prove it to you because you don't know what the source of the difficulty was in the other cases."

It was characteristic of Kern that he didn't go to the piano that first day. He didn't think a score was important unless it was linked with a good libretto; he was, oddly enough, more intense about story and characterization than about music. This was one of the factors that made Kern and Hammerstein so well suited to work together. Like Oscar, Jerry had been striving for better-integrated musical comedies.

However, they were not to make much further progress toward this particular goal until a few years later. *Sunny* was one of those tailor-made affairs in which Kern, Hammerstein and Harbach had to contrive to fit together a collection of important theatrical talents. Their job was to build a show around a cast that had already been assembled as if for a revue. Dillingham had signed Cliff Edwards, known as Ukulele Ike.* Oscar recalled that "his contract required that he do his specialty between ten o'clock and ten-fifteen! So, we had to construct our story in such a way that Ukulele Ike could come out and perform during that time and still not interfere with the continuity." Also signed for the cast were Jack Donahue, a famous dancing comedian; Clifton Webb and Mary Hay, who were a leading comedy dance team at the time; Paul Frawley, the juvenile lead; plus an entire onstage musical ensemble, George Olsen's Dance Band, in addition to the orchestra in the pit.

Dillingham had signed Ziegfeld's star, Marilyn Miller, hoping that she would match her success in *Sally*. One day in July 1925 he called Oscar into his office, where Marilyn and her husband, Jack Pickford (Mary's brother), sat, and said, "Now tell Marilyn the story of the show."

Oscar launched into the plot that Otto and Jerry had conceived. Sunny, a bareback rider in an English circus who is in love with one man is loved by another, and eventually marries a third man after stowing away on a ship bound for America in order to follow man number one. In the end all is sorted out. Oscar outlined the whole show, every step of the way. Marilyn didn't open her mouth throughout the exposition. Oscar gave her dialogue, acted out scenes, ran through tentative lyrics, and when he was through she looked at him and said, "Mr. Hammerstein, when do I do my tap specialty?" †

---

* Later in the run, Borrah Minnevitch, the harmonica rascal, replaced Edwards.
† Fred Astaire, a Dillingham star at the time, devised some of Marilyn Miller's dance routines.

"No problem," Dillingham interjected. "Oscar, just work it into the book."

Work it into the book! Oscar said to himself. You think Charles Dillingham cares about the book? He'll throw in the kitchen sink for *Sunny*.

In fact, it wasn't as great a problem as it might seem because the script wasn't entirely committed to paper. In those days it was almost never finished before the cast began to work; when *Sunny* went into rehearsal, the dialogue and numbers for the first act weren't set, and the second act didn't materialize until the run-through before the opening out-of-town. This was not at all unusual; in fact, George M. Cohan said that it was much better not to write a second act beforehand because after you heard the cast read the first act, you got to know them better and could write a better second act for them!

As Oscar was sitting on his front porch one Sunday, Jack Donahue drove up. Joining Oscar, he said, "I've got a dance I'd like to cue into the show if you could." Oscar asked him what it was like.

"It's a drum dance. I'll show you." And he began to dance on the wooden porch, which clicked with his taps. Engrossed, Oscar watched him as he went through the whole routine. When he finally looked out toward the street, he saw a huge crowd that had gathered in front of the house, also watching, fascinated.

One day while still at work on the songs, Oscar was with Jerry at the Bronxville house. They were at the piano, where most of Jerry's work was done—a piano with a working desk attached to the keyboard to facilitate writing, the desk and piano covered with sheets of music. Jerry often scribbled his melodies with pen and ink on the reverse side of manuscripts that happened to be at hand. He played Oscar his latest tune. It was a catchy one, but right from the start it posed what seemed a hopeless problem for the lyric writer. Oscar stared in dismay at the first note, a B natural held for two and a quarter bars, or nine beats. What could fit that extraordinarily sustained note? He knew that it couldn't be a long, awkward word, because that would kill the song immediately. Nor could a phrase be used. It had to be a word which could be repeated again and again, progressing the song each time without becoming inane or monotonous because Jerry posed practically the same problem five times. Moreover, it had to be a word ending with an open vowel so that a singer could hold it for these long counts.

Oscar's answer was "who." Jerry credited this word with saving his tune, and other professionals, after one look at the music to which Oscar had to fit it, uttered exclamations and whistles of respect. To the layman, Oscar's solution may seem an obvious one, and the fuss made over him for finding it just another example of theatrical exaggeration. But the professionals knew that even "why" would have killed the song because "why" sounded too nasal and whiny when a singer tried to hold it for nine beats; and that while "you" might have been passable, it would not have stood up under the five-time repetition. Understanding all the technical problems involved and admiring the way he handled them, the professionals began to watch Oscar Hammerstein II.

Though he worked alone on the lyrics for "Who," Oscar worked with Otto on the ten other songs, among which were "Sunny" and "D' Ye Love Me?"

The Philadelphia tryouts were a nightmare. Reviews noted that it was disappointing in book, score, dancing and in general staging; seldom did a show have so much potential or so much need of fixing and alteration. Otto was on the road with *No, No, Nanette*, but Jerry and Oscar worked with director Hassard Short completely revamping the second act in an attempt to make it less a revue, even with all the specialty numbers that had to remain. The changes were successful; the show opened to good reviews and audience acclaim on September 23, 1925, and ran for a year and a half at the New Amsterdam Theatre. It was the most expensive musical produced up to that time, but it earned back its investment easily. *Sunny* played in London for eleven months and was filmed twice. Despite all the success Oscar never liked it.

With *Sunny* out of the way, Oscar was now able to return to *Song of the Flame*, the story that he had begun in Paris earlier in the year. Set at the time of the Russian Revolution, it was the story of a White Russian peasant girl who becomes a revolutionary leader and a nobleman who falls in love with her. Arthur was producing and had arranged for Oscar, Otto and Rudolf Friml to collaborate. When Friml pulled out once again because of the contract, Arthur asked George Gershwin to share the composing with Stothart.

This was the only time that Oscar worked with Gershwin. While writing the show, the composer was also composing his "Concerto in F," as well as a Broadway musical, *Tip-Toes*, with his brother Ira. Gershwin was conceited and cocky, but he was also extraordinarily talented and rather sweet. He was not difficult to work with, and preparations for the show went smoothly.

Song of the Flame, which opened on December 30, 1926, at the Forty-fourth Street Theatre, was an opulent "romantic opera." It was reported that on opening night Otto Kahn said to the producer, "Arthur, you have made a mistake. Move your show down to the Metropolitan; that is the place for it. I will give you the house." Arthur did not accept the offer.

The show was a popular success: 219 performances on Broadway, a healthy road tour and a Warner Brothers picture in 1930. It was, however, distinguished more by the spirit and style of its production, the Russian choir, the "gay-colored, variegated settings," and "the beauty of bizarre costumes and backdrops" that swept the stage in ensemble numbers than by the score and the libretto, though some critics noted that the show could lay claim to "real music" and a "genuine" plot.

The Oscar Hammersteins wanted to remain in Great Neck but were ready for a bigger establishment. The summer before, they had bought from Larry Schwab one third of an acre in Kenilworth, one of the new "developments" entered through private gates. The pie-shaped lot was on a strip of land abutting Long Island Sound. That summer the family celebrated the Fourth of July on their new property with fireworks more spectacular than the pinwheels and Roman candles that Oscar had provided for the children; at the end of the day, the Sands Point Yacht Club, just three-quarters of a mile away across the narrow channel, burst into flames.

After months of construction made difficult and far more expensive than planned—increasing the cost from $95,000 to $145,000—by the problems of excavating in sand, the house was finally ready. It reflected Oscar's financial success. A large Tudor-style mansion,* it was entered through great oak doors; in the hall was a dark-banistered staircase with a huge portrait of Oscar I at the first landing. The living room had lead-glass bay windows on the left, French doors overlooking the Sound on the right and a mammoth stone fireplace at the far end.

Though the living room was used for frequent parties for old friends, as well as the Great Neck theatrical crowd, the family spent

* The Hammersteins' Kenilworth house is now owned by Alan King. It was used in the motion picture *The Anderson Tapes*.

more time in the bright room beyond, a solarium with a fireplace backing the one in the living room. It had flagstone floors, and its wall space was completely windowed to provide a sweeping view of the Sound. A big dining room on the other side of the hall also overlooked the water.

Upstairs, Myra's bedroom was above the solarium and Oscar's room was next to hers. He and Billy shared the bathroom between their rooms which had a huge stall shower. Billy, who was eight when they moved into the house, set his oversized Philco radio to go off at seven each morning with an exercise program. He and his father would do the exercises together and then run out to swim in the bay. (Later, Oscar would write of Billy Bigelow and his imagined son in the "Soliloquy" from *Carousel:* "When we go in the mornin's for our swim.") Alice's room was on the other side of the stairway, near the room of the governess—sometimes "Mademoiselle" and sometimes "Fräulein"—with servants' rooms beyond.

Upstairs was an attic filled with small rooms, with a large space in the center that served as the children's playroom. Below the center stairs was a stairway leading down to a wine cellar and a "Rathskeller" that was large enough to have a ping-pong table. This, along with the living room, was the scene of many parties.

During the summer months of 1926, Oscar signed to collaborate on two shows with Otto. One, produced by Arthur and Sam Harris, was *The Wild Rose,* with music by Friml; the other was *The Desert Song,* with music by Sigmund Romberg, produced by Schwab and Mandel. The almost simultaneous opening dates of the two shows caused Otto and Oscar to agree at the outset to share the credit but to split the tasks—Otto would work almost exclusively with Friml and Oscar with Romberg.

The Wild Rose underwent drastic revisions during tryouts, so that little of Oscar's work remained in the show by the time it arrived in New York, though he was credited with the book and lyrics. Arthur had hoped to duplicate the success of *Rose-Marie* by signing three of its collaborators for this show, but *The Wild Rose* was neither a critical nor a popular success and it closed after sixty-one performances.

Such standards as "Lover, Come Back to Me," "When I Grow Too Old to Dream," "One Kiss" and "Stouthearted Men" grew out of the association between Oscar and Sigmund Romberg which began with *The Desert Song* and continued through 1941, with five shows and three movies. It was an important association for Oscar, for many of the hallmarks of his later work took form in the book and lyrics of this first show with Romberg: romanticism, a musical play rather than a comedy with music, a topical or universal theme woven into the libretto.

Oscar gave credit to Romberg for helping him develop his habit of working hard. The first day that he brought him a finished lyric, Romberg led him to another room, handed him a pad and pencil and persuaded him to write another. Afraid to come out empty-handed, he finished another song that afternoon. Oscar later joked that Rommy tried to keep him "under lock and key" to get as many lyrics as he could for his seemingly inexhaustible supply of melodies.

When Oscar submitted a lyric, Rommy would play the song and say, "It fits." Disappointed at first with such limited approval, Oscar later realized that Romberg meant not only that the words fit the music, but that they fit the spirit and mood of the music and therefore were absolutely right.

Born in Hungary in 1887, Sigmund Romberg was a violin prodigy whose parents wanted him to become an engineer. He completed an engineering course at Bucharest University but found, upon his arrival in America, that engineers were a dime a dozen, and worked for a time in a pencil factory for seven dollars a week. Turning to his avocation, music, to earn a livelihood, he wound up as a pianist at a gypsy café on New York's Lower East Side for fifteen dollars a week and all the goulash he could eat. He spent five years in the atmosphere of red-checkered tablecloths and pungent kitchen odors until he was rescued by the Shuberts in 1914. Hard-pressed for composers on their Broadway production line and impressed with his talent, they commissioned him to write the music for the Winter Garden show *The Whirl of the World*. For the next ten years, under exclusive contract to these theater magnates, he turned out some forty shows, among which were *Maytime, Blossom Time* and *The Student Prince*.

Rommy was never ashamed of his extreme sentimentality. Shortly before he first began working with Oscar he returned to Hungary to visit his father and mother. When they asked him to play some of his music for them, he begged off, saying he was too tired, not in the mood, or offering various other excuses. This went on for several days. Then one afternoon a carriage arrived at the door and he invited his parents to accompany him to the town's Concert Hall. His parents were met at the entrance by the manager, who escorted them to the theater's center box. On the stage they saw a sixty-piece orchestra. They were the only people in the entire house. A fanfare brought their son out of the wings. Baton in hand, he bowed to his father and mother, faced the orchestra and conducted a two-hour concert of his American successes. As the last notes faded away he bowed to his audience of two and left the stage with tears streaming down his face.

Rommy was very funny, with his own brand of endearing malapropisms or Rommyisms. At Belmont Park, he told Jerry Kern, who was wearing a yachting cap, "You look like a race trout." At an ASCAP meeting he said: "If anyone here has an opinion, this is a democracy, they can express it," but when lyricist Irving Caesar started to say something, Rommy interjected, "Irving, one word from you and you're out the window!"

Oscar noted that it is not invariably true that an artist's work is a reflection of personal character, for some men sublimate their good qualities in their art and have little goodness left over to distribute among friends and relatives. In Rommy's case, however, Oscar felt that his music was Rommy himself: romantic, exuberant, positive.

Interestingly, since the show shared the exotic locale of *The Sheik* films, which made Rudolph Valentino an international idol, one day while Oscar was working with Rommy at the Hotel Marie Antoinette, across the street from Campbell's Funeral Parlor, he could see a triple line of people waiting to get inside to view Valentino's body.

Along with capitalizing on the public's fascination with the romantic desert, Oscar also seized on the notoriety of silent film star Clara Bow for one of the show's twenty-two musical numbers. Called "It," the song begins:

> There was a time when sex appeal
> Had quite the most complex appeal
> Mister Freud
> Then employed
> Words we never had heard of . . .
> But the seed of sin,
> Now at last has been
> Found by Elinor Glynn
> In one word
> She defines
> The indefinable thing . . .
> She calls it "It" . . .

Earlier in the year the newspapers were full of the revolt of Abd-el-Krim and his army of Riffs against the French in Morocco, and drawing rooms were full of talk about T. E. Lawrence, his adventures in Arabia and his book *The Seven Pillars of Wisdom.*

The Desert Song revolves around the son of a general, a young French officer named Pierre Birabeau. Sickened by the cruelty of the French troops toward the Moorish people, he has gone over to the enemy and, as "the Red Shadow," leads the Riffs in their battle against French domination of their country. The story of mistaken identity and derring-do seems contrived and trite today, but critics in 1926 felt that the plot and the well-developed characters could stand on their own without music.

Out of town the show was called *Lady Fair*, a title which Oscar was not at all happy with. While making the train ride back from Boston for the Broadway opening, after scanning some of Rommy's unused melodies he took his long yellow pad, thought for a while, and started to write the song that would produce the title:

> Blue Heaven and you and I
> And sand kissing a moonlit sky . . .
> Oh, give me that night divine
> And let my arms in yours entwine.
> The desert song . . .

The Desert Song opened at the Casino Theatre (Oscar's lucky house) on November 30, 1926. It was declared a "sure winner" and ran 471 performances. The show was a financial bonanza not only for Schwab and Mandel, but also for Oscar, who had invested heavily in it. The darling of summer stock, local light opera repertory and recording companies, it has had countless Broadway revivals over the years, one as recent as 1974; in addition, there have been three Warner Brothers films.

Oscar said the London production taught him a valuable lesson. When he first wrote the opening chorus, or "ice breaker," he was not very careful about the lyrics to the "Feasting Song." Knowing that it was to be sung by a male chorus that would be required merely to bellow while latecomers were seated, he wrote words that could be sung comfortably without any particular attention to shades of meaning. Sitting in the Drury Lane, to his dismay he heard the English male chorus clipping their consonants so sharply that every word could be distinguished, ringing out over the audience clear as a bell. "I felt like a cornered criminal. I had been caught writing words with not very interesting meanings and here, lo and behold, they were being sung so that they could be understood!"

Thereafter, he always assumed that someday somebody might sing even an opening chorus in an intelligible way and therefore the words had better be good. Oscar found a parallel to this in a photograph of the top of the Statue of Liberty's head taken from a helicopter. He was amazed at the detail there, since the artist must have been sure that only the sea gulls would ever see it. "Bartholdi was artist enough, however, to finish off this part of the statue with as much care as he had devoted to her face and her arms and the torch and everything that people can see as they sail up the bay. He was right. When you are creating a work of art, or any other kind of work, finish the job off perfectly. You never know when a helicopter, or some other instrument not at the moment invented, may come along and find you out."

One of Oscar's favorite Rommy anecdotes has a connection with *The Desert Song*. One night, years after the show was produced, Jerry Kern and Rommy were partners in a bridge game. Playing in hearts, Rommy paused, frowned, muttered, "Eleven, twelve, thirteen," obviously counting trump. Jerry remembered that one trump was still out and nonchalantly began to hum "One Alone." Rommy played a card, and when Marc Connelly trumped it, lost the lead and went down six on the hand. Jerry pounded his fist on the table and fumed: "You dumb Dutchman. What the hell do you think I was humming?"

"One of my songs," replied Rommy.

"Yes, but which one?"

"Who knows from lyrics?" said Rommy blandly.

One day in the fall of 1926, Jerry called Oscar at home and said, "Oc, I've read half of a book and I think it would be great for us to make a show of."

"What book is that?" inquired Oscar.

"Edna Ferber's *Show Boat*. It's got a million-dollar title to begin with, and I think it's wonderful. I've only read half and I'd like to do it." Oscar bought a copy of the book, read it and agreed wholeheartedly with Jerry. After independently making layouts of the story, they found that they had both picked the same scenes from the novel to construct the musical.

Now they had to acquire the rights from the Pulitzer Prize—

winning author.* At the opening of Jerry's *Criss-Cross* on October 12, 1926, at the intermission as the audience drifted out to the lobby, Jerry spotted Alexander Woollcott. He fought his way through the crowded lobby, grabbed Woollcott's arm and interrupted his conversation with a woman to say impetuously, "Look, Aleck. I hear you are a friend of Edna Ferber. I wonder if you'll kind of fit it in for me to meet her. I want to talk to her about letting me make a musical from her *Show Boat*. Can you arrange an introduction or a meeting or something?"

Woollcott, with his usual relish for the dramatic, said musingly, "Mmm, well, it might just possibly be arranged, if you'll have patience and let me do things in my own way. I think I can just do it if I play my cards right."

"Oh, thanks," said Jerry. "Thanks awfully, Aleck. I'll be waiting."

Now Woollcott pounced on his dramatic moment. Turning to the woman beside him, he said, "Ferber, this is Jerome Kern. Jerry, Edna Ferber."

The next day a meeting was held in Florenz Ziegfeld's office with Jerry, Oscar and Edna Ferber. Within an hour *Show Boat* was born.

As Miss Ferber left, Ziegfeld turned to the two men and said, "Listen, boys, I want this show to open my new theater in February, so you've got to work fast."

Oscar and Jerry heard of a real showboat just finishing its trip on Chesapeake Bay at the end of its season, and hoping to get some local color, they went to Baltimore and then took a little train to the small dock where the boat was tied up.

They arrived at about four or five in the afternoon. The men in the company were on shore shooting birds, but they met the women, who were very welcoming and gracious. When the men came back, they cooked the birds and Oscar and Jerry joined them for a lovely dinner on board. They fell in love with them all. In a glow of friendship Oscar remarked to Jerry, "These are real people, these are show people, these are our kind of people."

After supper, they went upstairs to the auditorium and attended the performance. Watching the show progress, Oscar began to hate his new-found friends. It wasn't that they were bad actors, but that they didn't care. They ran through their lines mechanically and had no

* Edna Ferber was given the award the previous year for her novel *So Big*.

feeling for the theater at all. The two men sneaked away before it was over, without saying good-bye. Oscar was ashamed of his reaction because they were such nice people, but it was impossible to overcome his distaste.

While Oscar and Jerry worked on the show, Ziegfeld told another set of collaborators to hurry up with their play because he wanted it to open his new theater in February. *Rio Rita* was finished first and Ziegfeld announced that *Show Boat* would play another house, but he was vague about the production plans.

One Sunday afternoon, as they sat in Jerry's house worrying about rumors that Ziegfeld had overshot his costs on the new theater and *Rio Rita,* the partners decided to confront Ziegfeld and pin him down about his plans for their show. A few minutes later they were in a car bound for his house at Hastings-on-Hudson, planning how they would go right in and say, "Have you got the money to put on *Show Boat?* Tell us: yes or no." They were greeted at the sumptuous Ziegfeld mansion by a butler who looked to them like a bank president. Surrounded by priceless *objets d'art,* they waited; a very Ziegfeldian maid in a black dress with white lace and an apron and cap came in and asked them to wait a little longer. Then the assistant butler, looking like a bank president's son, asked them to follow him. They were ushered upstairs to the west wing and into the bedroom suite of the pauper who couldn't put on their show. Looking past the imposing fourposter bed and beautiful furnishings, they could see into the bathroom, which was as big as most drawing rooms, where Ziegfeld was being shaved by a man with a long white beard who looked like King Leopold of Belgium. Oscar remembers it as being the most impressive production he had ever seen, on or off the stage. Ziegfeld said, "Wait a minute, boys." Then he came out in a brocade dressing gown and started to tell them about the wonderful business that *Rio Rita* was doing up in Boston.

He asked them to stay for a "pot luck" lunch, which was another elaborate production. Footmen stood behind every chair as they ate course after course. At about three-thirty or four, Jerry and Oscar, in a kind of misty contentment, waddled out of the house, never having dared to ask if he had enough money to put on *Show Boat!* "We had had turtles imported up from Florida. We had had all the delicacies in the world. How could you ask a man like that if he had money enough to put on a show?"

On February 2, 1927, *Rio Rita* opened at Ziegfeld's new theater.

In the ten minutes required to read the eight reviews, whatever interest Ziegfeld had for *Show Boat* faded. His new theater was successfully launched and what he wanted most was a few months on the soft, warm sands of Florida. Oscar and Jerry were "damn sore" but there was nothing they could do about it.

Oscar decided to use the waiting time by going to London and supervising the Drury Lane production of *The Desert Song*. When he discussed this plan with Myra, she was negative about the trip but finally agreed to follow him on a later boat.

His stateroom on the *Berengaria* engaged, and his bags more or less packed, Oscar devoted a part of his farewell week at his Great Neck home to a neighborly game of touch football. His team stuck to the American football rules whereas the opposing team, headed by Leslie Howard and Philip Merivale, insisted on playing the English soccer rules. Under the circumstances, it was hardly surprising that Oscar managed to sprain both his ankles and further aggravate his chronic back ailment, and that he was obliged to cancel his reservation and take the next boat, the *Olympic*.

The schedule changes of the two boats, *Show Boat* and the liner to Europe, were blessings in more ways than Oscar could know.

Three

One Foot, Other Foot

The scene aboard the S.S. *Olympic* before its midnight sailing on March 2, 1927, was a festive one. The sleek ocean liner blazed with lights as well-dressed passengers and the friends who had come to wish them bon voyage drank champagne and milled about the ship. For Oscar it was a nostalgic occasion as well, for this was the very ship that he had taken when, at seventeen, he had set off with two friends to see Europe for the first time. In his "strictly confidential" diary that summer of 1913, he had recorded the boyish hijinks and fun of three adolescents wandering about foreign countries, his innocent enjoyment of all he saw and did and his constant quest for "a pretty girl." The thirty-one-year-old man who boarded the *Olympic* in 1927 was going to London to work. A successful man with two children and a promising career, he was working almost constantly now and had accommodated himself to a marriage that brought him little enjoyment or satisfaction.

Oscar was traveling alone, since Larry Schwab and others in *The Desert Song* entourage had left as planned on the *Berengaria* and Myra was staying behind. As he walked through one of the ship's salons with Howard Reinheimer, the boyhood friend who had become Oscar's lawyer and was now seeing him off, Howard said, "There are Dorothy and Henry. Let me introduce you to them so you'll know somebody on the ship." Henry Jacobson was a diamond merchant; his wife, the former Dorothy Blanchard, was a tall, slim young woman with auburn hair and clear blue eyes, her face strikingly beautiful with a strong bone structure, her athletic body characterized by an unusually upright and graceful carriage. The introduction was brief; Dorothy didn't really look at Oscar as she hurried through the amenities with the air of someone who didn't want to be "stuck" with a stranger on a six-day voyage.

The following morning she rose early and went to the deck alone. As she was walking around and around, Oscar was circling in the opposite direction. Each time they passed, he said "Good morning" and she said "Good morning." When Dorothy finally sat down in a deck chair to avoid the awkwardness of the repeated greetings, Oscar came over and asked if he might sit on the end of her chair. For the first time she really looked at him—and "that was it! It was like the rivers rushing down to the sea." She was twenty-seven, had been married for two years and had a son, but this was the first time in her life that she had felt this way, as it was for Oscar.

Despite their immediate attraction to each other, the first conversation, as they sat on the deck chair, was not auspicious. When Oscar told Dorothy what his work was, that he was going to London to direct one of his shows, *The Desert Song*, she said, "Oh, dear."

"Why?" asked Oscar.

"Well, I don't like that sort of show. I always think it's silly when people are singing down each other's tonsils."

They continued to see each other on the ship, walking, talking, having meals together. Dorothy told Oscar that his face reminded her of the conformations on mountains which are shaped like faces. He talked about his career, telling her that he felt his work up to then was not really very good. He expressed the sense of unreality he had in trying to write musicals, explaining that real life seemed much better than anything he could write about.

They discussed their marriages. Oscar said that he was neither happily nor unhappily married, but that was the way marriage was supposed to be. Dorothy knew that she wasn't very happy in her marriage. She realized now how immature she had been when she married; she wouldn't have given Oscar a second look a few years before because he would have seemed too serious. Caught up in the fun and excitement of New York, she had blithely married an attractive, nice man because he was so "sweet." She knew now that it had been wrong to marry without love. As for Oscar, he realized for the first time what that deep love he had sensed between his father and mother had been all about. By the time the boat docked both were certain that this wasn't a passing fling. Earlier Oscar had said to her, "If I were a schoolboy, I'd carry your books home from school." One day, after they arrived in London, he said, "If we weren't both married, I'd ask you to marry me."

They often met in the Green Park. If it started to rain they went into the Piccadilly Hotel to sit in the lobby and laugh—somehow, everything made them laugh. In the hours they spent together, Dorothy told Oscar about her life and her family. Her Scottish mother, Marion, had gone to New Zealand as a child and had later married an English sea captain. Educated at Winchester, Henry James Blanchard had run away to sea when he was fifteen but had been brought back with the promise that he could go to sea as a gentleman when the time came. He trained as a cadet-midshipman and got his first command on June 7, 1899, the day that Dorothy was born in Launceston, Tasmania, the island off the southeast coast of Australia. The family soon moved to Melbourne, where Dorothy was brought up with four sisters, two half brothers and a half sister. This glamorous and sophisticated woman always retained a homey quality that had its roots in her childhood home.

As a young woman, Dorothy was leading a pleasant enough life in Melbourne. She was busy with parties and charity work, had even played a small part in a professional play. However, when she was twenty-two, she decided she wanted to leave Australia. Her parents begged her not to go, but she reminded her father of his own adventurous spirit that had caused him to run away to sea when he was much younger than she. They finally agreed that she could go to England, where her mother had relatives.

In London she got modeling jobs and even a second-lead role in a silent movie starring Betty Compson. One afternoon she was telling a friend how fed up she was with life, since she had become disillusioned with a man to whom she was very attached. When the friend suggested, "Why don't you go to America?" Dorothy impulsively went to book passage on a ship sailing for New York in two weeks. She cabled home for money and asked her agent to arrange work for her, which he did by sending Dorothy's picture to Ziegfeld, who cabled back word that she had a job in the *Follies*.

On the ship going to America, Sir Arthur and Lady Duckham, who were to become lifelong friends, took Dorothy under their wing. A wire service had sent a photograph of her sailing for America to be a Follies girl to the Australian papers. In New York she was greeted with a cable from her mother: PLEASE DENY THAT YOU'RE GOING IN FOLLIES. The Duckhams shared her mother's apprehensions about Dorothy becoming a Follies girl, with all that the term implied, and begged her not to take the job with Ziegfeld but to come back to England with them. Dorothy agreed to drop out of the show but was determined to stay in America, though she needed a job to do so.

Coming out of New York's Algonquin Hotel, where she was staying, Dorothy ran into a friend who told her of an opening in the cast of *André Charlot's Revue of 1924*, a bright English import starring Beatrice Lillie, Gertrude Lawrence and Jack Buchanan. Dorothy went to the Times Square Theatre, met with Charlot and left with a contract as both understudy to Miss Lillie and show girl. Dressed in gray chiffon, she played the part of smoke on an ashtray while Buchanan sang and blew smoke rings!

Jill Williams, another member of the company (who later became one of Dorothy's close friends and even later, as Mrs. Hugh Willoughby, her private secretary) remembers that they all thought "that Australian girl" a little batty. One day Jill came offstage with another player whose name was Louise Arms, to find Dorothy sitting cross-legged in the wings saying, "Arms! Arms! Arms! for the love of Allah!"

As Dorothy recounted her life for Oscar she told him how exciting she had thought going on the stage would be, and how soon she had realized that it wasn't. "It wasn't nearly as wicked as I thought it would be." A few days after this conversation he showed her some lyrics he had just written for *Show Boat*—"Life Upon the Wicked Stage."

> Life upon the wicked stage ain't ever what a girl supposes;
> Stage door Johnnies aren't raging over you with gems and roses.
> If some gentleman would talk with reason,
> I would cancel all next season.
> Life upon the wicked stage ain't nothin' for a girl.

When Myra arrived in London, Dorothy met her for the first time in the lobby of the Carlton hotel, where she picked up the Hammersteins to take them to a friend of hers who bred Kerry blue terriers, which they wanted to buy. Dorothy told Oscar how cold it was in the country and he went upstairs to get a coat.

"Oh, I hate London! Don't you?" said Myra.

"No, I love it," replied Dorothy.

"Do you have a lover here?" asked Myra.

Dorothy, startled, replied, "No, why?"

"Well, I've just left one in New York. He's divine," Myra said, and continued to discuss the subject at some length and in some detail. Listening to her, Dorothy had the feeling that Myra didn't love Oscar. When Oscar came downstairs, Dorothy walked over to the florist in the lobby and bought him a red carnation.

Back in New York, Oscar and Dorothy returned to their separate lives but tried to see each other whenever they could. Sophisticated New Yorkers though they might have seemed, their relationship was tinged with romanticism. Oscar would tell Dorothy the precise time he would look at the moon that night and ask her to look at it then, too. Despite their deep feelings for one another, Oscar made no move to change his life. As usual, he plunged into work, continuing the preparation of *Show Boat* that he and Jerry had begun months before.

Ziegfeld prolonged the postponement of the show with one delaying tactic after another. Not only was *Rio Rita* a smash hit, but he had little faith in the Kern-Hammerstein property. It was not the sort of show Ziegfeld was accustomed to; there was to be no chorus line, no spectacles, no burlesque humor routines. The plot involved unhappy marriages, miscegenation, tragedy. "Hammerstein's book is too serious," he told Jerry. "In its present shape, it hasn't got a chance except with the critics and I'm not producing for critics and empty houses." The very thing that had made Edna Ferber grant the rights of her novel to Oscar and Jerry made Ziegfeld less than enthusiastic about the venture.

Weeks went by without word from him. From time to time he reported complications, such as: "I've offered the leading role to Gertie Lawrence, but she's busy and I'll have to wait until she's available." He didn't drop the option altogether because he hated to hand over to another producer the composer who had given him such a big hit with *Sally*. Oscar and Jerry were irritated by the delays, but they used those months to work carefully and thoroughly on the show. They spent

many hours, usually at Jerry's house in Bronxville, discussing the characters and scenes, plotting how the songs would grow naturally from
the play's structure. "We had fallen hopelessly in love with it," said
Oscar. "We couldn't keep our hands off it. We acted out the scenes
together and planned the actual direction. We sang to each other. We
had ourselves swooning."

Collaboration has often been compared to marriage; the two kinds
of union are probably most alike in the way that they resist precise
analysis, particularly when they are "good." Oscar was easy to work
with and highly adaptable to a diversity of composing styles and personalities. Many people found Kern a difficult man, but he had worked
with a variety of lyricists. Successful as each had been with other partners, there was something special about the Kern-Hammerstein collaboration that consistently brought out the best in each.

The union was happy in part because of deep similarities of style
and character. Oscar's almost-son and pupil, Stephen Sondheim, describes Kern's music in terms that could be applied to Oscar's lyrics:
"Hard-won simplicity is the keynote." His explanation of why Jerry's
music stands up so well under countless rehearings, surviving the
moods of popular taste, is as apt an explanation for the durability of
Oscar's lyrics as it is for Kern's melodies. "[They] deal with the
essentials, not the decoration. And the essentials are timeless."

Kern and Hammerstein shared, too, a profoundly American quality of style and outlook. Though their music was rooted in the fertile
Middle European and English school of operetta writing, the form
and spirit were purely American.

Different as their personalities were, Oscar and Jerry enjoyed
working together and relaxing together with their families and ac-
quaintances. They formed a deep friendship in the course of their
collaboration. After Jerry's death, Oscar said that he "had a greater grip
on my whole being than anyone else I have known." Unlike many of
their colleagues in the theater, neither was basically a sad or tormented man. Their work seemed to spring from joy and optimism.

Whatever the reasons, through working together each consistently
reached beyond his good to his best. Certainly Jerry helped Oscar to
be more careful in his work and to combat his tendency to spread his
time and talent too thin. In his early days Oscar often knocked off a
lyric overnight or on a train ride to Long Island. He was talented
enough to get away with it. However, when he worked in a slower,
more painstaking way, the effect on his writing was pronounced. Both

lyrics and libretti began to shine with the sincerity and integrity that came to characterize his work.

Adapting proved to be a much better *modus operandi* for Oscar than creating an original story. Edna Ferber's novel, rich in atmosphere and large in scope, followed the complex lives of a Mississippi River showboat family over the course of a half-century. The sprawling narrative took the characters from New Orleans to Chicago to New York and back to the Mississippi. It contained material that had never been seen on the musical stage: unhappy marriages, family friction, gambling addiction and racial bigotry.

To transform this intricate, many-charactered story into a play with songs and dances was a formidable task. Oscar's libretto retained the scope and richness of the novel, captured the essence of Ferber's characters and remained true to the novel's themes. And thirteen solid songs, six of them among the greatest hit songs in theatrical history, emerged as integral parts of the story.* It was quite a feat.

Oscar made many changes, of course, but he selected his material wisely. He began the libretto with life on the river when Magnolia, or Nola, is eighteen, incorporating the important relationships and incidents of her childhood into the first scenes and songs of the play while bringing riverboat gambler Gaylord Ravenal into her life at the same time. For many of his Act I scenes, such as the *Cotton Blossom* theatricals and Julie's confrontation with the sheriff charging her husband with miscegenation, he used dialogue from the novel. The first act contains small plot deviations, but the nature of the characters and the strains of their relationships are preserved. Rather than the usual misunderstanding at the end of Act I, this couple marries, a major departure from the conventions of musical shows.

As the scene shifts to Chicago in Act II, Oscar altered the book's plot and setting more extensively. The life led by Nola and Ravenal in the city is revealed through scenes Oscar placed at the Chicago World's Fair and their rooming house. Julie Dozier, the half-Negro woman who befriended the young Nola, plays a larger part in Oscar's play, reappearing years after she has been forced to leave the showboat because of her marriage to a white man and making Nola's singing career possible. The survival of Cap'n Andy and Ravenal, who appear in the final scene of the play, somewhat diminishes the strength of both Parthy

---

* *Show Boat* is the only Broadway score to contain as many as six standards: "Can't Help Lovin' Dat Man," "Make Believe," "Why Do I Love You?" "Bill," "You Are Love" and "Ol' Man River."

and Nola, though their qualities of endurance and determination so important to the theme of the novel are clear. Though some of the harsher aspects of the story were modified, in Oscar's libretto the novel's characters remained full, their lives a plausible mixture of joy and sorrow.

Oscar took the story up to 1927, reducing Nola's daughter's role to one scene at the end of the play, and leaving out the New York–based section of the novel, one of the weakest parts of Ferber's work in any case. It must have been tempting to include it, jazzy New York settings being so popular with audiences in the twenties. Perhaps Oscar knew that it would impair the tone of the play, or perhaps he was just following his own inclination to stay away from "slick urban" settings. Asked once why he never wrote the kind of sophisticated musical that Cole Porter, the Gershwins, and Rodgers and Hart were turning out, Oscar replied, "You mean one that takes place in a New York penthouse? Mostly because it doesn't interest me."

Oscar and Jerry were determined to give their show dramatic continuity, to make every song an integral part of the story. "Can't Help Lovin' Dat Man," an important and oft-repeated song in the show, illustrates the kind of integration they achieved. "Can't Help Lovin'" is first sung in the *Cotton Blossom*'s pantry, capturing the spirit of the many hours spent in the kitchen by Magnolia in her childhood. Nola tells Julie that she is in love and Julie warns her, "Love's a funny thing—there's no sense to it—that's why you got to be so careful when it comes creeping up on you—" and begins to sing:

> Fish gotta' swim birds gotta fly
> I gotta love one man 'til I die
> Can't help lovin' dat man of mine . . .

This expresses one of the major themes of *Show Boat* and foreshadows Nola's lifelong love for Ravenal. The song serves as exposition about Julie's background and prepares the audience for her confrontation with the sheriff when Queenie, the black cook, looks puzzled and asks Julie how she knows the song. Queenie makes it clear that this is a Negro folk song that she has heard only black people sing. Julie, who is "passing" as white, responds with a swift look of terror before going on with the song, her character and experience illuminated by the way she sings.

In Act II the song serves as a plot device when Julie recognizes Nola in Chicago by hearing her sing it.

Oscar was aware that the novel he admired was a sprawling book and that a play requires tightness. Troubled with the play's lack of cohesiveness, he realized that Ferber had used the Mississippi River as a unifying focal point and decided to write a river song which would do for the play what Ferber had made the river do for the novel. When he first told Jerry of this idea, Kern said that he had too much to do at the moment and couldn't contemplate writing another tune right then. Oscar studied the score as it existed and suggested to Jerry that he take some of the banjo music he was using to introduce the showboat and merely slow down the tempo. Jerry did just that. He slowed down and inverted the bright, gay notes of the "Cotton Blossom" song to produce the powerful "Ol' Man River." Oscar later said that he had no intention of writing a "protest" song, or a tribute to the underdog, but that making "Ol' Man River" the song of a simple black man who labors ceaselessly on the banks of the Mississippi made the river and its eternal flow symbolize the hardships not only of his life but of all human beings, black and white. He did not deny that his rugged lyrics could be interpreted as a protest song, "but I wasn't conscious of writing that at the time."

The lyrics of "Ol' Man River" illustrate Oscar's belief that rhyme should be unassertive, used only when it is absolutely demanded by the pattern of the music. Too many rhymes lead the listener to anticipate the next rhyme, particularly if it is a familiar one dictated by the concentration on sound rather than meaning; if the listener is kept waiting for a rhyme, he is more likely to listen to the meaning of the words. Oscar used "Ol' Man River" to illustrate his point that if one has fundamental things to say in a song, the rhyming becomes a question of deft balancing.

> Ol' Man River
> Dat Ol' Man River
> He mus' know somethin'
> But don' say nothin'
> He keeps on rollin'
> He jes' keeps rollin' along.
> He don' plant 'taters
> He don' plant cotton
> And dem dat plants 'em
> Is soon forgotten . . .

Edna Ferber recalls in her autobiography that as the writing of the play progressed she heard bits and pieces of the score, listened to

"Can't Help Lovin' Dat Man" with its bemused lyrics, and "melted under the bewitching strains of 'Only Make Believe' and Gaylord Ravenal's insolent, careless gambler's song." Jerry appeared in her apartment late one afternoon with a look of quiet exultation in his eyes. He said he wanted her to hear a song that he and Oscar had just finished, to know what she thought of it. Kern, who did not play the piano particularly well, and whose voice, though true, was not memorable, started to play and sing "Ol' Man River." Ferber reports: "The music mounted and mounted and mounted and I give you my word, my hair stood on end, tears came to my eyes. I knew that this wasn't just a musical comedy number. This was a great song. This was a song that would outlast Kern and Hammerstein's day and my day and your day."

With the score, lyrics and book finished and Ziegfeld still putting off a definite production date, Oscar continued to revise and polish the libretto, but accepted two other assignments as well. He started *The New Moon* with Romberg. Arthur wanted to inaugurate the huge, neo-Gothic Hammerstein's Theatre, which he had just built with profits from *Rose-Marie*, with a big operatic show and he commissioned Oscar, Otto and Viennese composer Emmerich Kalman to create a musical that would star Metropolitan Opera singer Louise Hunter. They came up with *Golden Dawn*, a sumptuous, rather ponderous operetta about a European girl who is forced to become the taboo wife of an African tribal god but is eventually saved by an English Army officer. The most memorable features of the presentation were the first topless girl to be seen on a Broadway stage and the American debut of Cary Grant. Reggie had met Grant, then Archie Leach, when he was a stilt-walker advertising Coney Island and introduced him to Arthur, who offered him a two-year contract. His debut in *Golden Dawn* consisted of one line of dialogue.

Arthur's theater received more attention and favorable notice than the play. A bronze statue of Oscar I was set in the vaulted, domed lobby decorated with mosaics. Stained-glass windows depicting the Old Man's important operas were flooded with light to produce an effect that was "simply paralyzingly admirable," according to drama critic Alan Dale. The play had a respectable run, but Walter Winchell called it *The Golden Yawn*.

When Oscar found time to be at home, the Hammerstein household was not a peaceful one. He was short with Myra and, by all reports, she was an extremely difficult woman. Even friends who enjoyed her energy and sharp wit found her domineering and insensitive to the feelings of others. She was aggressively outspoken and irritable. "Don't throw your clothes down the chute," she would shout at Reggie. "I don't want your filthy clothes touching mine." Myra's manner took the edge off her good qualities. She was very generous, but usually managed to offend even people she helped.

Henry Jacobson knew about Dorothy's relationship with Oscar. In the summer of 1927 he suggested renting a house near the Hammersteins on the North Shore. Despite Dorothy's warnings that it was not a good idea, Henry insisted, perhaps to force the issue in the hope that her "infatuation" would run its course. The two couples saw each other often at the parties of mutual friends and even visited each other occasionally.

Dorothy and Oscar tried to be discreet about their meetings when they walked or went for long rides on horseback. Late in the summer, however, Dorothy asked Henry for a divorce. He refused, still convinced that the attraction would pass. In fact, he conceived of a scheme to make Dorothy so jealous that she would "come to her senses." He carried out his plan, having an obvious flirtation with another woman, but it had no effect at all on Dorothy.

Oscar was unable to face the thought of divorce. Always unwilling to face unpleasantness, he was particularly reluctant in this case. He knew that he hadn't put his whole heart into the marriage and felt guilty about his part in its failure. The idea of divorce was at odds with his background and his nature. Though Myra's infidelities were common knowledge, Oscar refused to recognize them. He went on working, seeing Dorothy, living with a wife he didn't love, putting off doing something constructive about his unhappy situation.

Finally Ziegfeld set *Show Boat* rehearsals for September 8, 1927. He was no more enthusiastic about the show, but an attempt by Arthur to obtain the rights propelled him into action. Irritated as he was by the long delay, Oscar knew that it had given them time to make the show better.

It is generally assumed that the original cast had four or five stars. As a matter of fact it had none. No one was billed above the title and no one was given any special featuring, but because of their fine performances many of them became stars. Those first to be signed were Norma Terris (previously seen in Oscar's *Queen O' Hearts*) in the role of Magnolia; Edna May Oliver and Charles

Winninger as her parents, Parthy and Andy Hawks; Sammy White and Eva Puck, as Frank and Ellie May; and Howard Marsh, Jules Bledsoe and Tess Gardella as Gaylord Ravenal, Joe and Queenie, respectively. Neither Jerry nor Oscar was satisfied with the actresses who auditioned for the complex character of Julie La Verne. One night Jerry attended a minor revue called *Americana* and heard a small, tousled-haired singer sit on a piano and sing "Nobody Wants Me" in a sweet, clear voice ranging from plaintive high to throaty low, each word calling out honest emotion to an enthralled audience. He promptly informed Oscar and Ziegfeld that they had their Julie— Helen Morgan.

At the beginning of rehearsals, because no actor had yet been cast to play the role of Steve opposite Helen Morgan's Julie, Oscar read the lines. No one told her that the polite man who said "Thank you" and "I beg your pardon" to everyone, including chorus girls and porters, was the author and director of the show. The big-hearted Helen later took Jerry aside and, pointing to Oscar, said, "Why not give him a break? He seems to understand the part."

Helen couldn't keep her eyes off Oscar, that "soft-voiced, self-effacing, blunt-featured fellow with dark, long-lashed eyes and gentle face." He in turn watched in amazement the steadily growing characterization of Julie in the hands of a woman who had never played a dramatic role before. He saw that everything she did was exactly right, that her instincts were sure. Nobody had to tell her how to move, gesture or put over a song. She behaved like a veteran.

Oscar and Jerry worked feverishly to pull the huge production together. To one who didn't know that they were equals, recalls a cast member, the pair gave the appearance of a huge, patient Newfoundland watching over a small crown prince at a public reception. Oscar reminded others of a left guard on a football team, a prize fighter, or Babe Ruth, though Oscar's nose was smaller and more delicately shaped.

During a rehearsal, seeing trouble in the second act, Oscar and Jerry decided to make a radical change, with a new song and change of scene. Oscar felt that Ziegfeld had better be told and so he went to sit with him in the fifth row while some numbers continued rehearsal and started to describe the change. Oscar noticed a faraway look in his producer's eye and wasn't quite sure he was listening. In the middle of a sentence, Ziegfeld called to one of the girls onstage. "I like the way you had your hair done yesterday." Oscar stopped in the middle of his explanation and said to himself, Well, that's the end. I am going to go on and write what I want to write and not bother him any more. Let him take care of the girls' coiffures.

This was the only show that Oscar ever did with Ziegfeld. He found the producer unequaled when it came to the production of purely visual effects: the beauty of girls, the beauty of scenery and costumes. But Ziegfeld was uninterested in what the audience heard, probably because he didn't know much about it.

The night of the Washington opening, November 15, 1927, Ziegfeld was discouraged and nervous. Overwhelmed by his conviction that the show was a flop, he began to cry when there was little applause for the big numbers. When the elaborate Chicago World's Fair scene didn't bring cheers, he sobbed. "They don't like it. Goddam it, I knew they wouldn't." After reading the ecstatic reviews, Ziegfeld was still pessimistic. "Maybe the critics did like it, but the public won't." It wasn't until he arrived at the National Theatre the next morning to be greeted by the sight of thousands of people lined up outside, standing in the drizzling rain in a line that extended from the box office down the block, around the block and back again, that he grudgingly conceded, "I guess we made it."

Fortunately, Ziegfeld could not give much more attention to the production. With his *Rosalie* in Boston, he was acting as referee in a "boxing match" between the Gershwins and Romberg-Wodehouse. In addition, *The Three Musketeers* was in rehearsal with the ever volatile Rudolf Friml providing the score.

Whatever his deficiencies, Ziegfeld was probably the ideal producer for this musical play that Oscar felt was "born big and wants to stay that way." It overflowed with production opportunities that beckoned showmanship on a grand scale. Oscar later felt that Ziegfeld's opulent production was as essential to the play as the words and music and that any new production must be equally lavish.

The play ran one hour and forty minutes overtime on its first night in Washington. Working through the night at the Willard Hotel, Oscar and Jerry cut fifty minutes. The cast rehearsed the cuts and put them in at the matinée. There was another rehearsal which followed, with more cuts going in that very evening. Forty more minutes had to be cut, and through the eight weeks in Pittsburgh, Cleveland and Philadelphia, they whittled and juggled. They ate so many meals in their hotel rooms that it became their practice to run out and buy a bottle of Worcestershire sauce the minute they checked in a hotel. Jerry would stick it in the piano so that it was always available for the many steaks they ate as they worked. Oscar was never able to reduce the show to the time span of other musicals; the curtain never fell before 11:27. On the nights that the play spilled over past 11:30, Ziegfeld had to pay the crew for an extra hour, and he begged Oscar to cut more dialogue. Oscar couldn't find a word he didn't think necessary and suggested that Ziegfeld cut an entertaining dance number that was not crucial to the show. Ziegfeld wouldn't, and the deadlock remained. There seemed to be no way of cutting down this stubborn big musical.

As they cut and shaped night after night, Oscar was forced to stay up much later than his usual bedtime, a notoriously early one by theatrical standards. All his life he was to keep more regular hours than most theater people, continuing the pattern that his father had long ago established. When he left, Jerry, who would happily work until morning, vigorously objected to his early departure. Finally Oscar developed a routine that he followed most of their collaborative years. Inconspicuously edging slowly toward the door, he would disappear with a "good night" over his shoulder. Jerry christened this "the Hammerstein Glide." According to Oscar, Jerry delighted in exerting his ingenuity in keeping him up. Just as he was sneaking off unobtrusively Jerry would think of some topic to keep him up. "All he has to say is: 'About that reprise in the second act . . .' and he's got me."

When the show got to Pittsburgh, Oscar and Jerry realized that they needed a song for Magnolia and Ravenal in the second act. After Jerry composed a simple little tune, Oscar retired to his hotel suite to fit words to it. The composer, with his usual enthusiasm, waited breathlessly for the result.

Jerry had a blind hatred of the word "cupid." It was a symbol to him of all the operetta lyrics of the twenties, all that was corny and old-fashioned in the Viennese school of musical theater. Oscar worked out a song titled "Why Do I Love You?," but perversely dashed off another lyric. He handed the second lyric to Jerry, who eagerly grabbed it, propped it on the piano and started to sing with his usual wild, impassioned screech:

> "Cupid knows the way
> He's the naked boy
> Who can make you prey
> To love's own joy.
> When he shoots his little arrow

> He can thrill you to the marrow.
> Hurry and depart
> When you hear his name
> Once you feel his dart
> You are his game
> Till you fall, your heart he'll harrow
> Cupid always knows the way."

After a few bars, he slammed his fists down angrily on the keyboard. Then he saw the joke and burst into raucous laughter. Later he framed the original copy and hung it in his study.

Oscar wrote the lyrics for "Make Believe" in an unconventional way. While Jerry played a melody for him, he found some words to fit the middle part: "Couldn't you, couldn't I, couldn't we." He had no idea what "you" and "I" "couldn't do" because he wasn't thinking of the situation or the people who were going to sing it, but was simply listening to the tune and thinking of what would go with it. He wrote the rest of the lyric around that single line. He told younger lyricists that while he wouldn't recommend this method, it illustrated an important point about songwriting: "inspiration" comes to you when you are active, not when you passively wait for it.

By the time they reached Philadelphia, three scenes and eight songs had been cut, and the show was finally frozen. Word had seeped into New York from *Show Boat*'s successful out-of-town run, and theatergoers were grabbing up tickets, even at the unusually high price, $5.50. On Tuesday evening, December 27, 1927, the production opened at the Ziegfeld Theater. When the second-act curtain came down, there was a five-second silence and then thunderous applause erupted from the audience. An hour later, Arthur Hammerstein excitedly entered the home of a friend.

"What's wrong, Arthur?" the friend asked. "Show no good?"

"Tonight I've seen the perfect show," replied Arthur. "My decision to take Oscar into show business has been justified. Tonight I knew that I did right by Willie after all, even though I broke my word. I'm a happy man!"

The critical reaction was unusual in its unqualified praise. Brooks Atkinson of the *New York Times* had missed opening night to cover Barry's *Paris Bound*, but two weeks later he wrote: "Shortly after the opening of *Show Boat*, other henchmen of the press were privately and publicly acclaiming it as 'the best musical show ever written.' . . . [and] this superlative praise of 'Show Boat' does not seem excessive.

Faithfully adapted from Edna Ferber's picturesque novel, set to an enchanting score by Jerome Kern, staged with the sort of artistry we eulogize in Reinhardt, *Show Boat* becomes one of those epochal works about which garrulous old men gabble for twenty-five years after the scenery has rattled off to the storehouse."

The show was so popular that Ziegfeld planned a second production to run simultaneously on Broadway, signing Libby Holman as Julie and Paul Robeson as Joe. Ziegfeld later abandoned this plan, but he kept the original running for 572 performances. It was subsequently revived five times on Broadway and a countless number of times all over this country and abroad. In the fifty years since the show opened, it has grossed over thirty million dollars.

Both of its time and ahead of it, *Show Boat* would prove to be a milestone, a turning point in musical theater. It marked the beginning of a fresh and distinctively American form that rose from the ashes of Viennese operetta, vaudeville and revue. The change was not immediately apparent; chorus lines, comedy turns and silly stories continued to fill the Broadway stages of the late twenties and thirties, but gradually the form took hold, with Hammerstein and Kern, as well as the Gershwins, Rodgers and Hart, Lerner and Loewe, Stephen Sondheim and others, contributing to its further development.

Just one week after *Show Boat*'s debut, the opening of *The New Moon* in Philadelphia provided a dramatic example of the way Oscar could take in stride the juxtaposition of success and failure. With the rapturous acclaim of the New York critics for the "best musical ever written" ringing in his ears, he rushed to Philadelphia to face disaster. After five days of rehearsals made chaotic by cast replacements, drastic revisions, technical problems and a dispute with the union which made it necessary to change nearly the entire crew, the opening night had proved catastrophic. Oscar had put up a quarter of the money for the show, which was being produced by Larry Schwab and Frank Mandel, and at the end of the week he persuaded them to close "for revisions," which usually means forever.

Still, life should have looked pretty bright to the thirty-two-year-old author of a respected smash hit who had seen a creative dream come true in *Show Boat*. It didn't. Dorothy, pregnant with her second child and wanting to give her marriage another try, told Oscar that she couldn't see him again.

Oscar, Myra and the Kerns sailed for England in March to oversee the London production of *Show Boat*. The first song rehearsal was a memorable moment for Oscar. The principals met in a small dingy rehearsal hall over Manzie's restaurant in Chandos Street. Paul Robeson, who was to play Joe, sat on a little cane chair in the middle of the creaky varnished floor. There was a fog outside and the room was dimly lit by a single wall bracket. Jerry sat at an old upright piano and played while Robeson sang "Ol' Man River." The others were transfixed as they watched and listened. Oscar felt for five minutes that there was no other place in the world, no other time.

With Robeson, Edith Day as Magnolia and Cedric Hardwicke as Cap'n Andy, the show was as great a success in London as it had been in New York. When he returned home, Oscar decided to revive *The New Moon* and, with Frank Mandel, began to rewrite the entire book. Based on an historical incident, it was the story of an eighteenth-century French nobleman who fled France and became an indentured servant in New Orleans before leading a band of renegades to a battle for equality on an island in the West Indies.

Perhaps one of the reasons that Oscar decided to try *The New Moon* again was to provide occupational therapy not only for himself but for Romberg, who was badly shaken by the recent death of his old friend and collaborator, Dorothy Donnelly. Oscar spent hours listening to the melancholy composer pour out his unhappiness. He often had to force him gently to the piano or write lyrics first in an effort to stimulate the usually prolific Romberg. (Early lyrics for "Lover, Come Back to Me" suggest that Oscar wrote them before the melody was composed.) Of the fourteen original songs, they retained only three—"Stouthearted Men" among them—as they rewrote the score.

Dorothy's second child, Susan, had been born in March and she still refused to see Oscar. He was at home very little. When he wasn't working with Romberg or Mandel, he spent most of his time at the apartment of his assistant, Leighton Brill. A friend since the Weingart days, "Goofy" Brill was an amusing, happy-go-lucky character, a charming loser. Always ready with a sure-fire scheme to find the gold at the end of the rainbow, he would invariably fail and just as invariably bounce back with enthusiastic plans for the next scheme. Oscar was fond of him, and found his humor and optimism attractive. Brill was a loyal and devoted friend and served as Oscar's assistant until the mid-forties.

He also saw his brother even more frequently than usual. In addition to giving help on Oscar's shows, Reggie was a partner in a midtown speakeasy. During the production of *Show Boat* Reggie had begun his long affair with Helen Morgan, who had an apartment in the same building as Brill.

Oscar seldom talked about the way he was feeling, but his lyrics for *The New Moon* suggest his uneasy emotional state at the time. In an unused song he wrote of lying alone, gazing at the sky, "wondering how and why I lost a world I used to own." It was not only Dorothy's refusal to see him but his own indecision that plagued him. The world he used to own was the ordered life that was so important to him. His love for Dorothy had forced him to face uncharted emotional areas and profoundly disturbing conflicts.

Interestingly enough, a show he began that summer with Harbach, Stothart, Bert Kalmar and Harry Ruby was called *Good Boy.* It was the tale of a stage-struck country boy who leaves for New York with his mother's admonishment in mind to resist the temptations of the big city and remain a "good boy." He does. Oscar was much less sure of his own "good boy" status as he confronted the thought of divorce and abandoning his wife and children.

In the summer Dorothy had begun to see him again, but the situation was as muddled and unresolved as ever. By August Oscar had added intense professional pressures to his personal ones. He was hurriedly finishing *Good Boy,* for a September 5 premiere, and was solely responsible for *The New Moon,* scheduled to open on September 19. He had begun *Rainbow* with Vincent Youmans, slated for a November debut, and was being pressured by Jerry for a commitment on a show that Arthur and Ziegfeld were vying for.

The New Moon went back on the road. Oscar took long walks all over Cleveland and Pittsburgh, disappearing for hours at a time. When Goofy discovered him crying one night in the hotel and asked if he could help, Oscar replied, "Goofy, you can't help me. Nobody can."

A Cleveland *Plain Dealer* reporter, writing a feature article because he "always wondered just how the makers of such a show do comport themselves on an opening night," inadvertently provided a picture of Oscar's emotional state in a column in which he believed he was just describing the usual backstage nerves. Unaware that Oscar was usually extraordinarily calm under pressure, the reporter wrote that he "looked more like a battle-scarred halfback than a writing man" and that he "jumped if you looked at him." Hammerstein, he reported, jabbed at his nose, rubbed off a fly that wasn't there and jerked out his pocket watch while saying very definitely that he wasn't nervous. During the play he paced, stopped, held his breath, took notes, whispered, paced some more, appeared, disappeared. His face was a thundercloud, only his eyes showing pleasure and displeasure.

The New Moon was a success in its second incarnation, both out-of-town and on Broadway, where it opened at the Imperial Theatre on September 19 and subsequently chalked up 509 performances. In fact, the score contained more standards than any other Hammerstein-Romberg operetta: "One Kiss," "Stouthearted Men," "Softly, as in a Morning Sunrise," "Wanting You," and "Lover, Come Back to Me." *
New York critics unanimously agreed that it was a delightful show with taste and distinction, beautifully produced, acted and sung. Oscar did not attend the New York premiere.

Sensing his friend's indecision and despair the previous week, Goofy had finally told Oscar about Myra's many affairs with other men. Stunned, Oscar went to Larry Schwab for verification. Schwab told him honestly that her infidelity was common knowledge.

Oscar finally had to recognize what he had refused to see before. Now he felt there was no reason for him not to divorce Myra, even though it would mean breaking up his family in a selfish desire to achieve his own happiness with Dorothy. He asked Myra for a divorce and she flatly refused. If he tried to divorce her on the grounds of her infidelity, she promised to create a front-page scandal. After issuing this threat, Myra withdrew to her room and locked the door. Oscar pleaded with her to discuss it with him, but she refused.

Oscar snapped. He couldn't eat or sleep. He worked all night after working all day in the theater. A few days after his confrontation with Myra, he voluntarily entered Leroy Sanitarium, a small private hospital on Manhattan's Upper East Side. Wrapped in sheets, he was given cold baths to calm him and wheeled back to his room, shaking, crying, muttering the names of baseball players. He cried himself to sleep, repeating, "It's not going to lick me" over and over to himself.

---

* Romberg was always accused of "borrowing" by people in the business. The middle section of "Lover, Come Back to Me" is said to come from Tchaikovsky. During the thirties, while Larry Hart and Dick Rodgers were in the bungalow next to Rommy's at the Beverly Hills Hotel, they heard Rommy playing a Tchaikovsky piano concerto over and over again. Larry said to Dick, "Listen, Rommy's busy on another score."

Lunching with Oscar, when an instrumentalist began to play in the restaurant, Dorothy Fields said, "Oc, that's 'One Alone,'" to which Oscar replied, "You mean 'Liebestraum.'"

He had no psychiatric treatment, discussed his problems with no one. Within two weeks he was functioning again, leaving the hospital on occasion in white tie and tails to dance with Dorothy. The next week he checked out of Leroy and returned to work on *Rainbow*.

Oscar never spoke, publicly or privately, about his "breakdown," but he suggested its importance years later in *Allegro*, the show he called "more autobiographical" than anything else he ever wrote. The play's turning point occurs when the central character, Joe, discovering that his wife is having an affair, realizes that his life has been an empty pursuit of false goals. Joe drops his head on his arms while his parents appear behind gauze and speak to him about his youthful ideals. Then a chorus reminds him that *"a boy mustn't let a girl see him cry/You said that to yourself a long time ago/When Grandma died . . ."* and he raises his head, saying to his nurse, who asks if he is feeling better: *"Yes . . . I'm sorry . . . I went kind of haywire I guess."* After this episode, Joe leaves his wife and the life that was contradicting his values and ideals and leading him in the wrong direction. The chorus sings "One foot, other foot," the song that accompanied his learning to walk as a baby, as he metaphorically learns to walk again, this time in the right direction.

Although Oscar cried profusely at plays and weddings, he never let anyone "see him cry" when he was in real emotional pain. The weeks at the Leroy Sanitarium were the only time in his life that he was unable to deal quietly and privately with confusion or sorrow. His muttering of the names of baseball players recalls the hours he spent pasting pictures of baseball stars into a scrapbook as he coped with his mother's death. All evidence suggests that this was the most profound inner crisis in Oscar's adult life.

Soon after he left the hospital, Myra agreed to a divorce, perhaps because Oscar was less ambivalent after his crisis, more resolute about the need for a divorce. She stipulated that she must be allowed to bring the suit charging Oscar with adultery, the only grounds for divorce in New York State. He learned from his lawyer that it was possible to "set up"—with a girl and a hotel room—the proof required by the court without involving Dorothy, and agreed to Myra's terms.

Oscar resumed work on *Rainbow* as calm and controlled as ever. He needed all the control he could muster for this promising but beleaguered show, whose lack of success mystified not only its authors but thoughtful reviewers, such as Brooks Atkinson, who said he was unwilling to believe that a musical play with such a spacious historical theme, produced with so much artistic integrity, could fail. But fail it did.

Rainbow was clearly intended to follow the direction of *Show Boat* with integration of the musical's elements in a colorful, realistic plot, this one set in the rough West of the '49 Gold Rush. Laurence Stallings, who with Maxwell Anderson had written *What Price Glory?* in 1924, suggested to Oscar that they write a musical together based on his story of love, death and the Army in the West. Vincent Youmans agreed to collaborate with Oscar on the songs.

Rehearsals had begun in September, with the score incomplete, the book rough and Oscar absent, still in Leroy Sanitarium. Stallings made a stab at writing some songs and Gus Kahn was brought in to furnish lyrics but there were continuous battles between Youmans, director John Harwood and Philip Goodman, the producer. Youmans was temperamental and Goodman, who had previously owned an advertising agency, was notoriously difficult. Jerry Kern once arrived in his office to discuss another project and introduced himself with: "Good morning, Mr. Goodman. I'm Kern. I hear you're a son-of-a-bitch. So am I!"

Harwood was fired just as Oscar returned and he took over the directing, making major cast changes as well as revising the book, eliminating songs that were too difficult to sing and adding new ones.

When they left for tryouts in Philadelphia and Baltimore, the show was still unwieldy and rough but critics in both cities referred to it as another *Show Boat*, with Charles Ruggles scoring a personal triumph as the mule driver and Libby Holman attracting notice as the seductive camp follower.

Libby Holman, then unknown, had originally auditioned for the part of Lotta and been rejected by Goodman because her voice was too low. When she heard that they were recasting the role out of town, she auditioned once more, this time for Oscar, and was accepted. He and Youmans asked her to come to their suite in the Bellevue-Stratford in Philadelphia. "Hum something," Youmans said. She did. He started playing around with a melody at the keyboard. "Keep humming." She hummed, her voice swooping around to give them an idea of her range and style, both unusual in those days of sweet-sounding sopranos, as Oscar and Youmans busily worked. By the end of the night they had finished the song tailored to her voice requirements, "I Want a Man."

I want a man, a man I'll keep wanting until I die.
I want to find the kind that keeps wanting, the same as I.
Don't want a butterfly lover,
Stopping to pass the time,
If I am true to my lover,
He too
Has to
Be true.

Say it's a dream,
Say I'm a fool,
Tell me I don't belong.
Say it's a scheme,
That breaks the rule.
Tell me that I'm all wrong . . .

The Broadway premiere was a disaster. Ruggles' mule relieved himself copiously down front center stage just before Brian Donlevy's tender love scene. One set change took over half an hour, and as Max Steiner's orchestra played the score over and over the audience began to count the number of crosstown El trains rumbling past the backstage of the Gallo Theatre, which was just around the corner from Hammerstein's. The audience was anxious to be pleased and responded as well as it could, but playgoers' limits were tested by the second act, which started after eleven o'clock and rambled on uncertainly.

The reviewers thought that the show could be saved by cutting and revising; they all recognized elements of a great musical in the realistic action and dialogue, the integrated musical numbers and the originality that made few concessions to the conventional musical comedy pattern. However, for all its strength, the script is marked by some fatal flaws: characters who are basically unsympathetic, weak motivation, some corny, obvious humor and some dialogue that was too raw for audiences in 1928. The show closed after twenty-nine performances, a flop. Usually Oscar felt no loyalty to plays that failed, even his own; he said he respected audiences enough to think that if a show ran only a few weeks there must be something very wrong with it. However, he and Youmans called *Rainbow* their "gorgeous flop," proud that although it failed, it had tried to break ground with realistic, earthy subject matter.

When the opening-night curtain finally came down on the debacle, Oscar left the theater as quickly as he could. He and Dorothy walked through the chilly night to the Gotham Hotel, where they had so often talked over lunch or dinner in the year and a half since they met. Oscar sat quietly, his body tight from the frantic hours and weeks behind him. Dorothy put her hand on his. "Ockie, I've decided! I'll leave for Reno as soon as I can get ready."

As Oscar looked at her his whole body seemed to sigh, to relax.

She told him about the resolution that she and Henry had come to. They would not tell his sick mother about the divorce and Dorothy would continue to visit her as her daughter-in-law. The decision to divorce had been extremely painful for Dorothy, not only because she hated to hurt Henry, but because she had had to agree to let him bring up their son Henry, while Susan went with her. As difficult as it was for her, she knew that the situation as it stood was not good for any of them.

"Dorothy," said Oscar, "once all this is done, we will never be apart for even one day. We will promise ourselves that."

On a wet, cold day in mid-December, Henry Jacobson helped Dorothy, eight-month-old Susan and her nurse into a cab for Grand Central to catch the train West. As the taxi moved down 57th Street, it stopped frequently in the traffic, and each time Henry drew abreast of the car as he walked down the street. Dorothy sat with tears streaming down her face, feeling pain anew each time she saw him. She knew she must be with Oscar, but what was she doing to this dear sweet man and to her children?

Oscar talked to her in Reno almost daily. Early in the new year, he, his lawyers and Myra's lawyers gathered in a West Side hotel room to stage the farce that the divorce demanded. Someone arranged for a girl to meet them at the hotel. She and Oscar took off just enough clothing to set the stage; the hotel manager knocked at the door, then entered saying, "You're not going to do this in my hotel!" Oscar and the girl put on their shoes and coats and the whole troupe moved on to Goofy's apartment.

He saw Dorothy once in Reno and then stayed with the Kerns in Palm Beach to await her return after the necessary period of residence in Nevada. Oscar loved life with the Kerns on their boat, named *Show Boat*. He wrote Dorothy that he was enchanted with deep-sea fishing and the small nautical ceremonies, such as the hoisting of the flag to show that the owner is aboard. He loved, too, the easy, funny hours when Jerry, Eva and eleven-year-old Betty gathered friends to play games.

The Kerns' life centered on Jerry. It wasn't that he was domineering; it was just that he had a way of expecting to have what he wanted with such childlike honesty that no one thought of disappointing him. Oscar found that everyone around Jerry seemed to be in a conspiracy, with Eva as its spearhead, to let him have his own way.

Eva Leale Kern was the naïve, protected, seventeen-year-old daughter of an English innkeeper when she first met and was captivated by twenty-three-year-old Jerry. After a two-year courtship by letters heavily censored by her stern father, Eva and Jerry married and settled in New York, where Jerry had been born and raised. Though shy with people she didn't know, Eva loved to laugh with Jerry and with the close friends they entertained. She shunned the theatrical world and parties away from home, preferring to focus her life on taking care of Jerry, with his whims and unpredictable hours.

Jerry worked when he felt like working. One day he might start at nine in the morning and work until three the next morning, and the next day spend the afternoon at a telephone making bets on the races. He might wake up at nine or at two, want eggs or baked beans or shad roe for breakfast. The conspirators saw to it that he had what he wanted.

However Jerry might indulge his whims, the score he was working on was always done on time, and always done well. Although he had no desire to write "serious music" (a phrase he hated), Jerry was intensely serious about his music. He had high standards, taste and a strong degree of detachment in judging his own work. He might wrestle with a modulation for hours, with his shirt off and his undershirt drenched with sweat. He wouldn't let go of a musical problem until he solved it. Successful as he was, Kern found no magic formula for producing hits. As he and Oscar sat on the *Show Boat*'s deck one day with their rods, Jerry said, "You know, Oc, composing is like fishing. You get a nibble, but you don't know whether it's a minnow or a marlin until you reel it in. You write twenty tunes to get two good ones—and the wastebasket yearns for music."

Jerry was an avid collector of books, stamps, silver and antique furniture. An insomniac, he often spent the night studying to improve his knowledge of the items he collected. He was a prudent buyer, but spent a great deal for important items; he paid $2,000 for one page to complete his original edition of *The Pickwick Papers*. He told Oscar that his 1,482-piece book collection had become so valuable that he worried about leaving it in Bronxville when he went on vacation and he was finding it a chore to maintain, less a hobby than a career. Oscar advised him to sell it and later arranged a meeting between him and the auctioneer who had handled Oscar I's estate.

The day after the sale began at the Anderson Gallery he sent a wire to the management: "My God, what's going on?" What went on was a ten-session auction that brought Jerry $1,729,462.50, the highest figure ever brought by a book collection anywhere in the world. *The Pickwick Papers* in original parts sold for $28,000; a Robert Burns manuscript, purchased by Kern for $6,500, sold for $23,500. The day Jerry collected his check he passed the Argosy bookstore around the corner from the gallery, saw a rare volume and bought it.

When they weren't fishing or playing games, Oscar and Jerry worked on *Sweet Adeline,* which Arthur was to produce in the fall. As usual, they had such fun working together that Oscar felt the perfect career would be to write unproduced shows with Jerry and never have them get into the hands of mere actors and singers.

The Kerns provided the perfect tonic for Oscar as he waited out the last few weeks before his marriage to Dorothy. In his final letter to her from Florida, Oscar wrote: "You will get this letter Saturday, so I believe it will be my last letter—maybe forever, if we can keep our promise to ourselves, as I believe we shall. Sometimes, perhaps, I shall write to you even when I am with you—just for the fun of it."

On Monday, May 13, 1929, Oscar, Dorothy, Howard Reinheimer, Herman and Betty Axelrod, Harold Lion, Jill Williams and Leighton Brill took a floor at the Belvedere Hotel in Baltimore where Oscar and Dorothy were to be married the following day. (Legal matters in connection with Oscar's divorce made Howard suggest a wedding in a state other than New York.)

The next morning, Oscar and Dorothy stood in front of their friends in the bridal suite of the Belvedere and promised to love, honor and cherish one another until death parted them, vows that they would happily keep for the next thirty-one years. As they sat at the wedding breakfast that followed the ceremony, they showed no signs of the strains that had marked the last year of their relationship. Dorothy, in a gray dress and cape trimmed with fox fur, looked serenely happy; beside her, Oscar chatted and joked easily, the picture of a contented man.

Reggie had not been able to attend the wedding for a rather bizarre reason: he went to see a girl friend off, and failing to leave the ship in time, he was caught on board until it docked in Le Havre. Upon his return, he was able to have dinner with Dorothy and Oscar in Boston before they sailed—with Susan and her nurse—on the *Olympic* for their honeymoon trip to London and Paris.

When they returned, Oscar, Dorothy and Susan lived in an apartment in the Weylin Hotel on East 54th Street. During the summer Myra moved out of the Great Neck house and into the Dorset Hotel on West 54th Street. Billy and Alice had been sent off to summer camp without being told of their parents' divorce, and they were shocked to return from camp and find themselves living with their mother in Manhattan. Oscar came to their apartment often for breakfast, in an effort to provide some stability and continuity, but the children were confused by his being at breakfast when he hadn't been there the night before. Eleven-year-old Billy was very troubled, anxious and beset by frightening nightmares. Harold Hyman, now the family doctor, diagnosed him as "suffering a psychic insult." Concerned about his son, Oscar followed Dorothy's suggestion that he take Billy on a trip to reassure him of his father's interest and love. They sailed to Bermuda and back, spending their days tossing quoits, talking and walking the ship's decks. Billy enjoyed the cruise, but remained unhappy about the family's separation and hostile to Dorothy.

During the July 4th weekend, when Oscar and Dorothy were aboard the Kerns' *Show Boat* anchored off New London, Connecticut, Jerry played a new melody he had just completed for *Sweet Adeline*, which they were preparing for mid-July rehearsals. Oscar was touched by its beauty and worked out a lyric titled "Don't Ever Leave Me," which he dedicated to Dorothy.

The easy fun that they had writing the show in Florida continued through rehearsals and into production. The show's leading lady, Helen Morgan, who had just left *Show Boat*, characterized the backstage atmosphere as "cheerful harmony," and Jerry called it the pleasantest company he had ever been associated with. Many familiar faces filled the rehearsal hall. Arthur was producing; Russell Bennett was again providing the orchestrations; Len Mence and Charlie Butterworth from *Good Boy* were in the cast and Reggie and Goofy were again on hand.

Jerry entered into the production with his usual enthusiasm and attention to detail. During one rehearsal he leaped up from his seat and went rushing down the aisle yelling, "No, no, no, that's not right." Oscar, directing onstage at the time, assumed something was seriously wrong with the way the cast was performing. Jerry rushed up and said, "That spittoon has no rubber mat. All spittoons have rubber mats under them. Somebody get a rubber mat!"

During another rehearsal, when Len Mence was running through his part as theatrical manager Sam Herzig, using stereotyped "Jewish" gestures, Jerry again came hurtling onto the stage saying, "Cut that out."

Mence said, "But Arthur told me . . ."

"I don't give a damn what Arthur says," yelled Jerry. "I won't have any stuff like that on my stage for any musical that I write!" Mence played the role straight.

Helen Morgan had been involved in the show from its inception, for stories she told Oscar and Jerry about her days as a singing waitress in a German beer garden called Adeline's suggested to them the locale and title for the musical. Oscar had long wanted to write a play about the idea of the sacrifices made by one sister for another, and Jerry wanted to do a show about the Gay Nineties.

One night Jerry called Oscar and said, "I see bicycles flitting by on Riverside Drive." Since Jerry lived in Bronxville, Oscar knew he was referring to a sight in his head. Jerry went on, "I see bicycles with Chinese lanterns going through the night and I hear their bells— a merry symphony of bells . . ."

That vision, or memory, along with Helen's beer garden, gave them the atmosphere of the play, always their first step in creating a show. Both felt that the ultimate success of a show depended on the soundness and innate interest of the original mental image and mood, which was referred to as a "bicycle" ever after. Next they began to think of characters. In this case they started with the two sisters and their father, talked about them, got to know them well and blocked out a plot.

While Oscar wrote a full draft of the dialogue, Jerry worked on the music. They then worked literally together, assembling the material and deciding where the songs should go, after which Oscar wrote the lyrics. Before they finished, they liked to have every detail worked out, even the stage business, which is why they preferred not to have an outside director for their shows.

Although the original vision of bicycles on Riverside Drive had to be dropped from the production because the staging proved to be too difficult, Jerry's atmosphere, Helen's beer garden and Oscar's two sisters remained its foundation.

For *Sweet Adeline* Oscar and Jerry wrote thirteen songs, among which was "Why Was I Born?," a perfect lament for Helen Morgan's mournful style as she perched on a piano. Her short, plump body, plain features, protruding eyes and small soprano voice seemed to belie her reputation as a singer of torch songs. But without question she was a powerful presence—her sad eyes and small hesitant gestures, along with the wistful undertones of melancholy in her voice, expressed emotion in a way that audiences found riveting.

The tragedy hinted at by her eyes was the tragedy of events thrust upon her not by fate but by her own tormented and self-abusing nature. She was a naïve, rather ordinary person who was terrified of being alone and clung to her mother and friends with a childlike intensity. Helen suffered several brushes with the law because of her involvement with speakeasies. Her life was filled with troubled romances and marriages and she died of cirrhosis of the liver at forty-one. Burns Mantle's reaction to her singing "Why Was I Born?" in a "brave little voice" was that he didn't know why she was born unless it was to sing such songs.

Oscar felt that the first two lines of the song's refrain asked life's basic questions and that the third and fourth questions implied the answer:

> Why was I born?
> Why am I living?
> What do I get?
> What am I giving?

Sweet Adeline opened at Hammerstein's Theatre on September 2, 1929, to glowing reviews and an enthusiastic public. It was proclaimed the successor to the "epochal *Show Boat*" by Brooks Atkinson. Time has proved otherwise, but Hammerstein and Kern did use some of the same kind of devices and elements of that show. Again they picked a colorful American time and peopled it with three-dimensional characters with problems. The heroine of *Sweet Adeline* gets drunk, not for farcical effect, or because of a villain's machinations, but for the reason that she is a human being subject to human frailties. Again the libretto was well-knit, and the songs expressed emotion with simple honesty.

Another interesting similarity which was picked up by one critic was the ability of the authors to simulate the quality of an authentic folk song. Just as "Ol' Man River" had the ring of a black laborer's song, so "Es Was Schon Damals So," subsequently sung as " 'Twas Not So Long Ago," was reminiscent of a German folk ballad. (Thirty years later "Edelweiss" was widely believed to be an old Austrian song, though Oscar and Dick Rodgers composed it for *The Sound of Music*.)

Oscar spent the last weeks of autumn in 1929 preparing for a move to California. He had signed a remarkable contract with Warner Brothers–First National Pictures: he would write four operettas over a two-year period at $100,000 per film against 25 percent of the profits, with final approval of each film.

If he and Romberg had been writing an operetta about his life, Oscar might have stopped right here. In the story, the son and grandson of famous theatrical impresarios would go through years of learning his craft, and enduring a marriage to the wrong woman, until he overcame the hardships of life to marry his true love and become a successful, respected writer. The last scene would show him departing for Hollywood to conquer new worlds.

Real life, of course, is not that simple. The effects of the economic depression would be felt by the theater and the film industry. Not only fortune but his own shortcomings would bring Oscar a long period of failure in which it seemed that there was no place for him in Hollywood or on Broadway. But that was in the future. The present was very bright indeed as he, Dorothy and Susan boarded the Santa Fe Chief for California in early December.

The Hammersteins were not the only emigrants from Broadway in 1930. With the advent of sound, movie studios needed experienced writers, composers and actors from the legitimate stage; they lured Kern, the Gershwins, Rodgers and Hart and many others. Those who accepted the studios' lucrative offers had no thought of giving up Broadway. They continued to write shows, but welcomed the challenge of the new medium—and its financial rewards.

Oscar was heady with his future in films; in newspaper interviews he expressed his excitement at the endless experiments in form that the new medium offered. He jestingly told Dorothy that as soon as they were millionaires, he would buy her the yacht she had recently admired, Mrs. Harrison Williams' *The Warrior.* He and Romberg went right to work at Warners on *Viennese Nights,* an operetta about an Austrian shoemaker's daughter (Vivienne Segal), a wealthy officer (Walter Pidgeon) and a penniless young composer (Alexander Gray). With the advent of sound, operettas were thought to be ideal for the new talkies because of the popularity of musicals and the continuing appeal of the escapist romanticism that had been so popular on the silent screen.

Oscar inscribed the completed screenplay: *Dearest Dorothy, this book and its author are yours, forever and ever—Oscar.* Dorothy made an appearance in the film as a woman sitting in a symphony box alongside Vivienne Segal. Though Miss Segal offered no competition to Dorothy in terms of beauty, the cameraman was so smitten by Dorothy's looks that he spent more than the usual time in seeing that the lighting on her was perfect.

The elaborate, nearly two-hour-long Technicolor production, complete with elaborate sets and lavish costumes, took only twenty-four days to shoot. Oscar was avidly learning the technical aspects of the new medium. His first experience with the techniques of motion picture production made him enthusiastic about the possibilities for film musicals. He saw that the screen helped librettists enormously. Not limited by time and space as the stage was, film could take characters anywhere, compress the plot, do away with encumbrances of entrances and exits.

Direction of movie musicals had been diffuse and haphazard in the past; Oscar saw his own position as author-supervisor as an innovation that would help unify the elements, and he asked Warner's for a strong director. Alan Crosland had been in motion pictures since 1912 and had recently directed *The Jazz Singer.*

One day during the filming, the studio buzzed with excitement when former President Calvin Coolidge, his wife and her mother came to see how movies were made. Unfortunately, the Coolidges had picked a day to visit when small technical details were being attended to and no big scene was scheduled to be shot.

The *Viennese Nights* cast was hastily assembled, with orders to reenact a sequence that had already been photographed. When the former President's party arrived on the set, they found everyone apparently at work, orchestra playing, cameras in their soundproof booths rolling, the director giving orders. The actors sat at tables in a beer garden set, drinking steins of beer. Although prohibition was still in effect, Gene Lockhart and Walter Pidgeon had brought in a case of real beer from Canada. The waiters served real beer to them and near beer to the others.

Coolidge watched the scene with his usual serious air. After a few minutes he asked Alan Crosland, "What is it they are drinking?"

"Beer," replied Crosland.

"Near beer?"

"Of course, Mr. Coolidge. Near beer."

The former President said he would like some and Crosland told an assistant to bring Mr. Coolidge a glass of beer. When he returned, Mr. Coolidge took a large draft and remarked, "Best near beer I ever tasted."

Crosland investigated. "Oscar," he whispered, "they made a mistake. They gave him the real stuff!"

The night before he was to see the rough cut of the film, Oscar had the dream that he always had before each of his plays opened. In the dream he is sitting in the audience watching the first performance and realizing that things aren't going too well. The rest of the audience seems to realize this, too, and soon there is a rustle and stir as people look at each other and nod understandingly. Two or three get up to leave the theater, then five more, then ten, twenty—hundreds stampede up the aisles until the theater is completely empty except for Oscar and the actors onstage. The dream would become so painful at this point that Oscar would awake, lying for several minutes in a cold sweat.

No one could predict whether it would be a popular success, but both Oscar and Warner's had high expectations. William Koenig, head of studio operation, sounded him out about supervising all musical productions. Oscar was noncommittal. He wanted to continue in motion pictures but was doubtful about giving all his time to the studio administration. He was determined to keep his identity as an author. In addition, he hated to relinquish the chance of making more money than any set salary that they could offer.

On March 10, 1930, Oscar, Dorothy and Susan left from San Francisco aboard the S.S. *Ventura* to visit Dorothy's parents in Australia. Oscar had never met them or any other member of Dorothy's large family, and although Dorothy had seen her father in England, she had not been home since she left for London eight years before.

On board ship, Oscar began the story for his next film and took rolls and rolls of movies on his 16-mm camera. The films reflected a typical amateur effort, with an abundance of footage of water, but the fact that he manipulated the camera at all was something of a feat for Oscar, who was unable to do anything with his hands and regarded all mechanical devices as instruments of the devil. He photographed Susan's second birthday party and Dorothy patiently trying to teach her to swim in the ship's pool.

On March 26 they arrived in Sydney. As the ship docked Dorothy began to shout, "Dubby! Doody! Here we are!" Two women on the pier waved madly and shouted back, "Dots! Dots!" This was Oscar's first introduction to the other members of the Three Destroying Angels. So dubbed during childhood by their mother, the three sisters— Dots, Dubs and Doodles (Dorothy, Florence and Eleanor)—were famous for their escapades, usually instigated by Dots.

They all traveled together to Melbourne and the Blanchard family residence on Alma Road in the comfortable suburban section of St. Kilda. The house, "Sandhurst," was a large stucco structure with wood and tile trim set in nearly an acre of lawns, gardens and palm trees. Marion Blanchard, a stately, beautiful woman of sixty-three, took an instant liking to Oscar and insisted that he call her Mother. She was a gifted painter but confined her efforts to paintings for the family and used the decoration of her home as the primary outlet for her artistic talents. Though a rather proper woman, she admired Oscar not only for his talent and sense of responsibility, but for his "wandering," as she put it, his desire to squeeze everything he could out of life.

Henry James Blanchard, a distinguished sixty-five-year-old with a strong, handsome face and penetrating eyes, was not as taken with his new son-in-law. He had liked Henry Jacobson enormously when he met him years before in England and was angry at his daughter for divorcing him, though he was pleasant enough to Oscar. When Dorothy came to the house alone once during the visit, Captain Blanchard growled, "How'd you get off the chain?"

The Australian press produced long articles, radio broadcasts and interviews with the "celebrated playwright" and his Australian bride. Certainly the Hammersteins were glamorous subjects for the "down under" newspapers. Rich and successful, Oscar was tall and attractive, his shock of dark hair brushed straight back, his voice soft and musical. His wife, tall, blue-eyed and beautiful with classic features, a hometown girl and beauty-contest winner, was now a well-traveled, charming woman. She spoke easily to the reporters about her travels and modestly attributed her own distinctive manner and style to being Australian. The gold pocket watch that Oscar always carried was a reminder of the attraction of other Hammerstein men to Australian women. Inscribed "To Oscar with love from Nellie," the watch had been given to his grandfather by Nellie Melba, with whom Oscar I had had a long artistic, personal and possibly romantic association.

The Hammersteins left Australia on April 17, bringing Doody back with them on the S.S. *Tahiti*. From the ship Oscar radioed Romberg parts of the scenario for their forthcoming film so the composer could start working on themes for the songs.

Back at their rented house in Beverly Hills, they gave a dinner party to celebrate their homecoming and to welcome some good friends from New York: Jerry and Eva Kern, Otto and Ella Harbach, and Howard and Ellie Reinheimer. With the Jack Warners and Alan Croslands also invited, Dorothy knew that the men would go into a corner to talk business while the women were left to their own devices. She decided to try the English method of leaving the men in the dining room after dinner so they could get all the business talk out of their system. Her plan backfired. The men stayed in the dining room until after one in the morning while Dorothy, sitting with the other women, fumed in the living room.

During production on Oscar's second movie, *Children of Dreams*, Billy came to California. In New York, Oscar had seen the children often at breakfast or at lunch at the Sherry-Netherland or the Casino, followed by a matinée, but he had not seen them since he came to California. Alice was at camp, but Billy accompanied his grandparents, Willy and Florence Finn, on a trip West.

He loved to go to the studio with his father, and Oscar gave him a movie camera with which he shot many scenes from *Children of Dreams*. His visit to the house in Beverly Hills did not go as well. Deeply affected by the divorce and by his mother's oft-expressed resentment of "that woman who stole my husband away," Billy glowered and was hostile to Dorothy. Dorothy did not know how to deal with the young terror, and Oscar stepped in to tell Billy that if he continued to act this way he didn't want to see him anymore. The situation remained unresolved when Billy left with his grandparents to return to New York.

Children of Dreams was a romantic story that again involved two poor young people (Margaret Schilling and Paul Gregory), this time itinerant farm workers who are picking apples in a California orchard when they meet. Both of Oscar's first motion pictures dealt with poor young people who become involved in the big-time music world but ultimately realize that true happiness lies in their love for each other, not in success or material rewards.

The two-picture commitment for that year finished, Oscar and Dorothy returned with Susan and Doody to New York on September 6, 1930, and took a furnished apartment at 1067 Fifth Avenue.

In November *Viennese Nights* began its first-run release. During the year, four film versions of Oscar's plays had been produced and distributed: *Song of the West* (*Rainbow*), *Golden Dawn, Sunny* and *The New Moon.* The film studios had gone overboard in their first burst of enthusiasm for musical films and had plunged into production without sufficient study of the problems involved in filming such shows. In 1929 they produced fifty-seven musicals and ninety films with songs; in 1930, seventy-four musicals and sixty-two with songs. Most of them were bad and the public soon began to equate music in pictures with boredom. As the public became sated with movie musicals and the pinch of the Depression became more acute, Hollywood had to respond.

Retrenchment was the order of the day as once-prodigal spenders started nursing nickels and dimes. The California Gold Rush of 1929–30, like the one in 1849, passed into history. Costly musicals were dropped from production schedules and Hollywood concentrated on low-budget pictures made with casts of players under long-term studio contracts to keep the 12,000-odd projection machines grinding in half-empty theaters across the country. The top brass in Hollywood lost all interest in music during 1931, except for those already in the cans, and looked to stark drama to lift the talkies out of the Depression pit.

Although the theory had been that audiences would welcome light fare to escape from the economic burdens of their lives, in fact the national mood was serious and people flocked to *All Quiet on the Western Front* and to films by Von Stroheim and Von Sternberg. The situation arrived at the point where movie houses were hanging out signs saying "No music in this picture" as a bait for the public.* With the reversal, the Broadway librettists and composers, who had re-

---

* *Children of Dreams,* released in July 1931, with unremovable musical sequences, could not even obtain booking at a first-run house.

ceived huge sums to come to Hollywood, retreated. Oscar said they fled the Brown Derby and rushed back to the soft sour-cream arms of Lindy's.

Viennese Nights, with newspaper advertisements featuring the names and photographs of Hammerstein and Romberg instead of those of the stars, received good notices. It was a hit in England, but not in this country, where it suffered from the surfeit of musical films and did not run long.

A few weeks after *Viennese Nights* was released, Oscar received a phone call from Jack Warner. He had sent his studio boss the scenario for his third picture, entitled *Heart Interest.* After the basic amenities, Warner said, "Oscar, do you and Rommy really insist on making two more pictures?"

Oscar had been expecting this and replied warily, "What do you propose?"

Warner said, "I'm not sure. Let me take it up with Reinheimer."

A settlement was reached whereby Oscar and Romberg each received a hundred thousand dollars to cancel the contract. "The most money I ever got for *not* making two pictures," Oscar remarked.

Arthur had also gone back to New York, announcing that he would devote all his time to stage activities and that because of the public's lack of interest in musical movies, his contract to produce operettas for United Artists had been canceled. (What he didn't announce was that his first and only film, *The Lottery Bride,* with a Friml score and starring Jeanette MacDonald, had been rejected by both the critics and the public.)

Arthur was in financial trouble. His last show, *Luana,* a Friml operetta that played the season before, had been a total disaster and the theater had been vacant ever since. The Hammerstein Theatre's fourteen-story office building that he had built along with the theater in 1927 had never been fully rented because of its location at Broadway and 53rd where the El thunderously ran by.

Soon he made another announcement. In a sink-or-swim effort to survive, Arthur had made definite commitments on four shows, all involving Oscar. The first would be *Ballyhoo,* starring W. C. Fields and directed by Oscar, with book and lyrics by Harry Ruskin and Leighton "Goofy" Brill and a score by Lewis Alter. The second would be *Camille,* with Helen Morgan starring, Oscar providing the libretto and Jerry Kern the music. The third, *YMCA,* was to be written by Goofy; and the fourth, a drama, to be written by Oscar.

Oscar was already working on a musical with Romberg to be produced by Schwab and Mandel and had committed himself to work with Jerry on a new musical for Ziegfeld. His pace, as he planned to work on one show after another, was as frenetic as it had been in his earliest years in the theater. His judgment obviously did not run a straight course. The seasoned professional who believed strongly in the integrated musical play, agreed to direct a show created solely for a star, written by an old friend who was not a writer and produced by an uncle whose taste and approach were outmoded. The man who knew that *Show Boat* was good because he and Jerry had over a year to work on it had set himself a schedule in which such care was not possible. With an annual income that exceeded that of any other librettist at the time, he was in a position to pick his own projects, but Oscar felt insecure about money and worried about his financial obligations to his two families and growing children.

Emotional need, too, led him to agree to work on artistically questionable shows, to spread himself so thin that the result would inevitably be haphazard. Part of that need was the desire to keep busy, to be involved in the theater all the time. There was also the need to protect, encourage and help the people who came into his orbit through family ties or long-term friendships. It was Oscar who urged Arthur to let Goofy, who had expressed his ambition to do something on his own, "try his wings" at writing. It was clear to everyone who knew him that Oscar had protected his brother, Reggie, for years and would continue to do so. Also, he would stand by his uncle to the end, even at the expense of his own work, long after Arthur's shows demanded a more modern producer's touch. The loyalty, sense of obligation and optimism that made Oscar so admired and loved as a man worked against a steady artistic development as personal considerations often took precedence over professional judgment and his sense of integrity about his work. Oscar continued an inner battle with the "false values" he so often referred to in his autobiographical notes.

And so he set to work on the aptly titled *Ballyhoo*. Louis Alter, who had written some songs for Fanny Brice and had garnered some success in Hollywood, was recommended as a composer to Arthur. Harry Ruskin had been signed to collaborate with Goofy on the libretto. When rehearsals started, the book was a mishmash, though it really didn't matter because W. C. Fields wanted only one thing onstage—to get a laugh—and would annihilate any material in his efforts to do so. Fields had worked for Willie at the Victoria and always called Oscar "Sonny" and got along well with him, but he knew what his public wanted to see and he was going to give it to them.

Fields wasn't the only member of the cast who got along well with Oscar. All actors loved him and enjoyed working with him. He knew how to talk to actors, didn't scare them and was exceedingly patient with them. As a result, they would try anything that he suggested they do.

Reggie was, as usual, stage manager for the production (though again Oscar opted to give him his billing for staging the book). He didn't have the same kind of relationship with actors that Oscar had. Theater people found him to be a nice guy to sit and have a few drinks with, a gentle dreamer, but he didn't command the same respect.

Ballyhoo was in no way ready to be frozen by the Philadelphia tryout on December 1. Oscar wrote lyrics for "No Wonder I'm Blue" and had to put up with the gag "Oc must have lived in a zoo" because again he used animals in such lines as *"A doe with no stag, that's me . . . A bud with no bee . . ."* Certain songs had come to be known as a "real Oscar Hammerstein type of lyric" for other reasons as well. One was the repetition he used to make a song "flow," as in "No Wonder I'm Blue," with its repeated phrases: *"What's the trouble with me? The trouble with me is plain as day; I'm in need of a mate, In need of a mate who'll come to stay."*

At Ford's Theatre, in Baltimore, one week before the New York opening, Oscar realized that the second act was dying and, recognizing the spot where death began, told Alter that they needed to throw out the song and replace it with a stronger one. The inexperienced Alter couldn't believe that Oscar would take this risk so close to the opening date, but he went back to the hotel and worked all day and all evening. He came up with a torch song with an odd and striking tune. Alter worried that it would be too difficult to put lyrics to it because it had strange chords in addition to a syncopated beat. He gave it to Oscar at eleven-thirty that night. At seven the next morning Oscar handed him the completed lyric, verse and chorus, for the song entitled, "I'm One of God's Children (Who Hasn't Got Wings)." Alter was thrilled, though not surprised, because he was so in awe of Oscar that he thought he could do anything.

Oscar called a rehearsal for ten that morning. While Janet Reed was rehearsing the number with Oscar for that evening's performance,

Oscar said, "You mustn't shake your shoulders. Forget your body. I'm going to try an experiment and have a fixed baby spot set just on your face. You'll be leaning against the proscenium and if you move your head you'll be out of the frame of light. That's all there is to it. So, just sing the hell out of it!"

When Reed introduced the song to the Forrest Theatre audience that night, it stopped the show. The song started quietly with a jungle beat, the balcony rail pin spot on Reed while the other girls moved in the semidark background. With the playgoers intrigued by the effect, the beat grew more insistent and the odd melody with its offbeat words began to build to a resounding climax. The song was the strongest spot in the show and, except for W.C. Fields, one of its few redeeming features.

> 'Cause I got no man to mess me around
> I'm a lonesome weed that grows in the ground.
> I'm one of God's children who hasn't got wings.
> When the bats fly low and night's in the sky
> And there's no one home except me and I,
> I'm one of God's children who hasn't got wings.
> I just want a sweet accommodatin' man to have a sip o' gin with.
> Then we'd have some lovin',
> 'Cause the gin would just be somethin' to begin with.
> But I got no man to mess me around,
> I'm a poor lost mare a pawin' the ground.
> I'm one of God's children who hasn't got wings.*

The production never was buttoned up and after every evening performance there were always late rewrites and conferences deep into the night. Alter remembers Dorothy as being the "den mother," seeing that there were stacks of sandwiches, coffee and lots of pads and pencils in the "Ballyhoo Suite."

Ballyhoo opened at the Hammerstein on December 22, 1930, to reviews that were less than enthusiastic. Both critics and audiences were happy to welcome Fields back to Broadway, from which he had

---

* One night in 1955, Oscar's son Jimmy came home from an off-Broadway revue he had just seen, raving about one of the numbers, a song he had never heard before. Oscar asked him the name of the song. "'I'm One of God's Children,'" replied Jimmy.

His father went into his study and returned a few minutes later with an enigmatic smile on his face and piece of sheet music in his hand. "You mean this song?" he said, dropping it on the table beside Jimmy. Jimmy's jaw dropped open.

been absent since the *Vanities*, two years before, but the book was termed "rather dreadful in an amateurish way," with only a couple of songs, a talented dance chorus and the wondrous Mr. Fields to recommend the affair.

Although he had written only "the couple of songs" singled out for praise (either by choice or by a printing error, he received no program credit as lyricist), Oscar dashed off letters the next day to the three reviewers who had called the score imitative saying that he thought the tunes were "exceptionally strong," and that he was "quite taken off [his feet]" by their remarks. He quibbled with details of their criticism, asked Alison Smith (the *New York World*) to write and explain what she "considered the points of similarity" to others, and requested from Atkinson (the *Times*) a list of the earlier songs recalled to him by those in *Ballyhoo*. "Choosing melodies is an important part of my work and I do not like to think I am getting a tin ear."

Gilbert Gabriel printed a retraction in the *New York American*. Atkinson replied, and on December 27, Oscar wrote him again, thanking him for his letter in a more conciliatory tone: "I don't agree with any part of it but that is beside the point. I have a vaguely pleasant feeling of coming closer to a critical mind—a type of mind, which God knows, seems pathetically far away on mornings after New York opening nights." He asked Atkinson to lunch with him, but had to get the last word in by saying that perhaps the critic's impression of having heard the music before was due to the repetition of orchestral effects used in shows, cabarets and radio. "I believe that you can take ten distinct melodies and, ironing them out under the proper combination of saxophone, clarinet and drum, make them all sound alike."

Oscar's initial letters have a petulant and self-righteous tone, perhaps caused in part by his own unresolved conflicts between personal and professional needs, which led him into the mess of *Ballyhoo*. His professional judgment having turned out to be so poor, Oscar might have been trying to convince himself of the show's worth as he railed at the critics. In any case, he couldn't argue with the public and its lack of response to the expensive production. After two weeks, Arthur, now at the end of his rope, had to close the show.*

* W.C. Fields and the company took over the venture and attempted to run it cooperatively, but gave up after a few weeks.

For Arthur Hammerstein 1930 was a bad year. On January 30 the Manufacturers Trust Company sued him for $1,253,652, the amount of his two mortgages. In order to keep his Broadway and 53rd Street theater building operating, he had sold his family's lavish home in Beechhurst, Long Island, and the ownership of the Republic Theatre that had been left to him by his father, and had put every penny into the Hammerstein Theatre that represented his career as a producer.

This was a difficult time for all the old-time producers, who had invested only their own money in their shows. When the giant Bank of the United States was forced to close on December 11, 1930, Broadway was finally convinced of the depth and duration of the economic collapse. Managers now were forced to trim production schedules, costs and ticket prices, and actors began to take voluntary salary cuts. The Shuberts, who had made over a million dollars' profit the year before, showed a net loss for 1930. In 1931, musical comedies declined to fourteen from the previous year's twenty-one (there would be four in 1935).

Arthur had the additional problem of maintaining an office building. He filed a petition of voluntary bankruptcy, listing his liabilities at $1,649,130, his assets at $53,083 and his cash at $5.77. Standing handsome and dapper as ever outside the Brooklyn Federal Court after filing, fifty-nine-year-old Arthur said, "When Mayor Walker comes back into the city I will ask him to take the statue of my father and put it in some public place—possibly around Times Square. It is a curious thing that when he was exactly my age, my father went through the same thing. In 1897 he lost under foreclosure the Olympia Theatre. . . . In a couple of years, when conditions improve, I'll be back again, bigger than ever."

Before filing for bankruptcy, he had transferred the rights to all his shows to his wife, Dorothy, her father (John H. Dalton), and his business manager, Hugh Grady. Arthur and his principal competitors, the Shuberts, had always been at each other's throats. Now, smelling a rat, the Shuberts set their lawyers to work and found that the transferrals of rights had all been made on the same date, the same paper and the same typewriter. They forced Arthur to offer the properties at public auction. Except for one bidder present, no one seemed to have heard of the auction in Mineola, the auction that would dispose of the producing rights and writers' royalties in perpetuity to thirty-one shows, which included *The Firefly, Naughty Marietta, Wildflower, Rose-Marie* and *Sweet Adeline.* The one bidder was Lee Shubert; the bid by which he acquired this gold mine, $684. Arthur had met his match in devious operators.

Arthur was finished, but the next year Howard Reinheimer filed a suit on behalf of his clients—Oscar Hammerstein, Otto Harbach and Herbert Stothart—"in the matter of rights and royalties" in the property *Rose-Marie,* which the Shuberts had been licensing all over the world at great profit. Since in those days there was no standard Dramatists Guild contract, there was some question about the rights, and Reinheimer wanted it clarified. In a second suit on the royalties due his clients, he flatly accused the Shuberts of theft, claiming that their statements were fraudulent and that they had cheated his clients. The suits were settled out of court, and they turned out to be very costly for the Shuberts as other authors began to file suit against them.

When the Dillingham-Ziegfeld estates were to be auctioned, Lee Shubert again drove up to the auction, confident that he could grab another plum. When he arrived he found Howard Reinheimer there. Alerted to the sale, Reinheimer had pooled resources of Oscar, Jerry, Irving Berlin and others, which amounted to $25,000, to bid against the Shuberts because they feared clouding of the rights and loss of royalties. J. Robert Rubin, the chief MGM attorney, joined the pool and pledged up to $50,000 because his studio had purchased film rights to many of the properties coming up for auction. The Shuberts stopped bidding at $40,000 and the valuable estate went to the group.

A few weeks after *Ballyhoo* folded, Oscar received a call from Lewis Gensler, his former collaborator on *Queen O' Hearts.* His latest show, *The Gang's All Here,* was in serious trouble in Philadelphia. This "musical comedy revue," with a score by Gensler, who was also doubling as co-producer, had a book by Marc Connelly and Russel Crouse, and lyrics by Owen Murphy and Robert A. Simon. Connelly had walked out and Gensler and Crouse wanted Oscar's help. There were only two weeks in which miracles had to be performed, but Oscar could not resist helping old friends and he began doctoring the book and direction. He again ran into the problem of a comedian, in this case Ted Healy, who was determined to use his own jokes even at the cost of destroying the other material in the show. Crouse

The first Oscar Hammerstein, as depicted in Vanity Fair's *"Men of the Day" series. The fashionable magazine described him as "a man of superb self-confidence, genial, real, astonishingly able, and versatile."*

"The two people who ran my life during my childhood," Oscar later said, "and perhaps influenced me even more than my mother were her father and mother, my grandparents, James and Janet Nimmo."

Willie Hammerstein when Oscar was a child.

A portrait study and the only extant picture of Oscar's mother, Allie.

Oscar Greeley Clendenning Hammerstein at the age of six months.

Anna Nimmo, Oscar's aunt and subsequently stepmother, whom he called Mousie. "I have no idea why I called her Mousie. Maybe she prompted it. Maybe she liked the idea. Mousie was like a second mother to me even while my mother was alive."

Hammerstein's Victoria and Roof Garden built by Oscar I and operated by Willie at the corner of 42nd Street and Seventh Avenue. Sam S. Shubert said later, "Just as the Hammersteins are entitled to the credit for making 125th Street, so are they entitled to having started 42nd and Broadway as the center of theater and night life in New York City."

Oscar at the age of twelve.

Oscar (far right) with the varsity baseball team of Hamilton Institute.

Reggie, age ten and a half.

WHEN OSCAR MAKES HIS DEBUT

What Might Happen If the Indomitable Theatre Builder and Resourceful Inventor Should Try His Luck As an Exponent of Minstrelsy.

Mr. Hammerstein Hastily Dashes Off a Few Dozen Encore Songs.

[Editor's Note—If an apology be deemed necessary for any fantastic act of the enterprising Oscar Hammerstein, the following extract from a day's news last week may answer the purpose: "In the lobby of the Victoria Theatre yesterday afternoon Lew Dockstader remarked that good end men were scarce. Oscar Hammerstein, who was standing near by, asked if he might be considered a candidate for this position, and without a moment's hesitation Dockstader told the manager to name his own terms."]

YOU could hardly blame the people of New York for forsaking the opera, neglecting dinner parties, and in many instances forgetting business appointments, for this was the date of Oscar Hammerstein's debut in minstrelsy.

Mr. Hammerstein had bolstered up waning seasons before. Frequently he accomplished this feat by erecting a new playhouse; sometimes he provided the needed impetus with an especially imported artist of sensational accomplishments; when he could find the time he dashed off a lively opera or an entertaining musical comedy—but whatever he did the New York public had come to regard as novel, and they intended to make the present occasion a first night of first nights.

The seating capacity of the Victoria Theatre had been disposed of six hours after the announcement of Mr. Hammerstein's engagement. It was now a fight for standing-room with the privilege of peeping through the fire exits being hawked by the speculators on the sidewalk. The playbills read this way:

```
DEBUT EXTRAORDINARY!!

The One, The Only, The Original

OSCAR HAMMERSTEIN,

Broadway's Favorite Comedian,

Will positively appear in a Budget of Songs, Jokes and
Funny Sayings, fresh from his own pen,

In Conjunction with Lew Dockstader's Minstrels.

If you don't like the first part, Mr. Hammerstein will
write a new one during intermission.

Remember the place—One of the 57 that Oscar built.
```

So, as chronicled before, you could hardly blame the public this night for forgetting everything but their love of country and family. "Parsifal" was the bill at the Metropolitan, but at eight o'clock Herr Conried counted the audience on the fingers of one hand and announced that the second section of the opera would not be sung. Three blocks up the street William Gillette had been facing crowds nightly, but the grim possibility of giving a performance to the janitor and the latter's personal friend now seemed a certainty. Henrietta Crosman next door laid claim to the season's success, but even she grew nervous with such opposition right under her very nose.

It was a Hammerstein night. Lew Dockstader would be present, Carroll Johnson would contribute a few fancy steps, and Neil O'Brien would conscientiously endeavor to earn the salary which Manager James H. Decker paid him, but the sentiment was all Hammerstein.

The audience—or as much of it as could squeeze in without straining the Victoria's walls—was now in.

In the foyer Joe Ullman had placed a tiny blackboard, on which the betting was registered as follows:

```
10 to 1 that Oscar makes a hit.
 1 to 2 that the Syndicate offers to star him.
15 to 1 that he forgets his lines.
11 to 5 that he won't stick to the music.
```

A few tarried to learn the closing odds, then hastened to their seats as the strains of the orchestra informed them that the first part had begun.

"Gentlemen, be seated."

William H. Hallett had given the stereotyped command, and fifty dusky "gentlemen" obeyed. Mr. Hammerstein was not of the fifty. Neither was Lew Dockstader. Following the regular minstrel tradition, their entrance was reserved for a more dramatic situation.

"'When the Sunset Turns the Ocean's Blue to Gold' will be rendered by Manuel Romain."

Again the voice of the haughty interlocutor.

The ocean's blue was vocally and artistically gilded when——

"Say, Mistah Hallett, did you heah that a wife is the most valuable jewel in the crown of matrimony?"

In traditional falsetto Carroll Johnson had asked the question.

"Yes, Mr. Johnson," replied the haughty interlocutor, "a wife is the most valuable jewel in the crown of matrimony."

"Huh?" retorted Johnson, "and uneasy lies de head that wears a crown."

"'Asleep in the Deep' will be rendered by William H. McDonald."

Again had the interlocutor spoken, and Mr. McDonald obliged. In fact, he was obliged to respond to an encore, for the audience was good-natured; it did not wish to interfere with the plans of the stage management and Mr. Hammerstein. They relied on the latter to give a good account of himself when his time came.

"Say-y, Mistah Hallet, did you all ever see a dog that chewed tobacco?"

"Absurd," replied the interlocutor. "A dog chew tobacco! Really,

A Faithful Copy of the Poster.

The Only Oscar Makes His Entry Amid Thunders of Applause.

The last public appearance of Oscar I. It was an evening organized at the Hippodrome, on March 26, 1916, for and by a considerable number of American composers. Gathered around "the Old Man," seated at the piano, are (left to right): Jerome Kern, Louis Hirsch, A. Baldwin Sloane, Rudolf Friml, Hammerstein, Gustave A. Kerker, Hugo Felix, Sousa, Lesley Stewart, Raymond Hubbell, John Golden, Silvio Hein and Irving Berlin.

Making his debut with the Columbia University Varsity Players, Oscar (far left) in his costume for The Peace Pirates. *The little lady next to Oscar is Larry Hart.*

In London, on the Thames, with Henry Rockermaker during their 1913 trip abroad.

Playing the comedy lead, a part he wrote for himself in the Varsity Players production of Home, James.

With his first collaborator, Herbert Stothart, at a rehearsal of their first Broadway musical, Always You.

Posing for a rather Edwardian photograph, Oscar (seated center) and (left to right) Herman "Ax" Axelrod, Bunny Frankel, Milton "Kaddy" Kadison and Myra Finn, Oscar's soon-to-be first wife.

Columbia University yearbook, Class of 1918.

Uncle Arthur, the man responsible for launching Oscar's theatrical career. The inscription reads: "To Mr. Bernard Shaw Hammerstein from his uncle, Arthur Hammerstein, October, 1923."

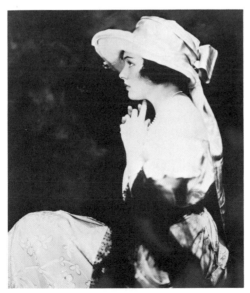

Elaine Hammerstein, Arthur's daughter, when she was under contract to Selznick Studios, Hollywood.

The Hammerstein Theatre, located on Broadway between 53rd and 54th Streets. Built by Arthur Hammerstein in 1927 as a memorial to his father. (The theater is now known as CBS-TV's Ed Sullivan Theatre.)

Helen Morgan, who rocketed to stardom as a result of her brilliant performance in Show Boat, *here re-creating her role of Julie in Universal's film version (1936).*

Paul Robeson, who played Joe in the 1928 London production and the Broadway revival in 1932, also appeared in the same film.

Dorothy Blanchard Jacobson, taken at the time of her marriage to Oscar.

Oscar at the same time.

Charlie Butterworth posed for Edward Steichen in his costume for Sweet Adeline.

The Blanchard family on the occasion of Oscar and Dorothy's first trip to Australia in 1930. (Left to right): Marjorie, Frederick Love (Mona's husband), Dubby, Mona, Oscar, Dorothy, Henry and Marion Blanchard, Doodie, Rosamund, Loraine, Margaret (Dubby's daughter) and Susan Jacobson.

Jerry Kern and Otto Harbach in Hollywood (1930).

Arthur on the set for his film The Lottery Bride *(United Artists 1930) with composer Rudolf Friml and Jeannette MacDonald, who later starred in several film versions of Oscar's operettas.*

Dorothy (far right) making a brief appearance in Viennese Nights. *The others are Vivienne Segal, Bela Lugosi and Alexander Gray.*

With Rommy (Sigmund Romberg), during the ill-fated East Wind.

Jerry, Dorothy Fields and George Gershwin in Hollywood a short time before Gershwin's death.

always remembered how much he had learned from watching Oscar work, but valuable as Oscar's contribution was, it was not enough, and the show quietly departed three weeks after its New York premiere.

A happy family event took place during this period: Dorothy and Oscar's son was born on March 23, 1931. He was named James after Dorothy's father, who had died two months earlier, and Oscar's maternal grandfather, James Nimmo. Oscar's first words when he saw Jimmy at Harbor Hospital, on Madison Avenue and 60th Street, were "He looks like an angry Jew." He had food sent up to Dorothy's room from the corner "deli," the Colony Restaurant. During her hospital stay, Oscar and Dorothy spent hours reading aloud *The Good Earth* by Pearl Buck, crying copiously at the sad parts, enjoying the book enormously.

The day Jimmy was born he received his first telegram.

WELCOME OLD MAN IN CASE YOU GROW UP ANYTHING LIKE YOUR FATHER HOW ABOUT HOLDING THE SEASON OF NINETEEN FORTY SEVEN OPEN AND YOU AND I WILL DO A SHOW FOR ZIEGFELD CHEERIO JEROME KERN

Oscar wrote back: "Yes, his name really is Jimmie. Do you want to make anything out of it? . . . Jimmie is flattered by your offer to do a show for Ziegfeld when he is only sixteen years old. Still perhaps that might be the right age to do a show for Ziegfeld."

Back at 1067 Fifth Avenue Oscar was reading as many as four novels a day trying to find a good vehicle for adaptation while Ziegfeld pressed him and Jerry to come up with another *Show Boat*, to do a revival and/or to prepare a sequel for *Show Boat* using Jerry's idea of following Kim's life and bringing in Paul Robeson as the son of Joe and Queenie who goes on to a successful concert career. Neither man was very enthusiastic about the sequel and, to Ziegfeld's dismay, the matter was dropped.

At the same time, Oscar was negotiating a partnership with Larry Schwab and Frank Mandel in which he would invest $100,000 and join them in taking a two-year lease on Arthur's former theater, where they would produce their own musical attractions. Oscar (though remaining a silent partner) would share in all their enterprises and would write exclusively for the partnership except for one show a year for Arthur. Ziegfeld was "terrifically shocked" by this news and told Oscar that if he "had any idea of your being willing to make a tie-up such as you did with Schwab and Mandel, I would have been flattered to have such a chance offered to me."

The first production under the partnership, *Free for All*, officially opened the Broadway season at the Hammerstein, now renamed the Manhattan, on September 8, 1931. Richard Whiting wrote the music and Oscar the lyrics and book, which was about a group of college students who are so enamored of communism that they set up a commune in Nevada. Oscar tried several innovations in his writing and staging of the show: no singing/dancing ensemble, a hero who doesn't make good, the absence of more than ten consecutive minutes of moonlight and romance, and lovers who do not get parted during the proceedings.

The musical received negative notices. The absence of a chorus line thrust the book into a prominence it couldn't survive, slow-paced and labored as it was. Audiences of the Depression years were looking for more modern fare in playwriting—something serious or satirical —but the young communists were indistinguishable from any other radically minded college group, the psychoanalyst scene a "hokum howl" that was more suitable to the low comedy of vaudeville than a sophisticated Broadway stage and whatever irony there was, was pale and obvious. *Free for All*, termed by the critics as "innocuously forgettable," closed after fifteen performances.

Oscar, Schwab and Mandel immediately turned to their second production, which would open in Pittsburgh on October 5. They took out of their trunk a recently discarded Hammerstein-Romberg-Mandel operetta, *Beauty Be with Me* and retitled it *East Wind*. The order of the day was retrenchment; there were no current events or innovations in the story about a girl reared in a convent who is sent for by her father in Indochina and falls in love with a young man who goes to the dogs when he becomes infatuated with a Chinese hooch dancer.

Though Pittsburgh, Cleveland and Baltimore drama critics found merit in the show and felt that it could be successfully tightened to put it into the hit category, New York critics were unanimous in blasting the show when it opened on October 27. Burns Mantle's headline read: "EAST WIND" BLOWS UP AT THE HAMMERSTEIN. Although Gilbert Gabriel apologetically wrote, "Maybe you'll like it much better than I did . . . it simply can't be as dumb and duddy and devoid of the seven cardinal virtues of musical comedy as I thought it last night," apparently it was. The second Schwab-Mandel-Hammerstein production lasted only a week longer than the first one did; twenty-three performances.

In the thirteen months since his return from California, Oscar had written the books and lyrics for two complete shows, directed and written songs for a third and doctored a fourth. All were resounding flops. Oscar said he "took a deep breath and started all over again." He decided to leave theater management and production to others and to concentrate on writing just one play the following year. He called slipshod work without depth "insincere" and attributed to it much of his failure. The tendency to ignore the fundamental things and to deal only with the superficial, he once said, "is man's great tragedy." Certainly it was a tendency he had to fight often in his own life. He had already learned from *Show Boat* that his writing was markedly better when he devoted his time and attention to it for a long period without distraction. Although he learned the lesson once again when the Kern-Hammerstein *Music in the Air* was successful and satisfying, the problem did not disappear.

However, in 1931 he stuck to his resolution to spend a full year on one play, and it turned out to be a particular favorite, his "own special darling," he called it. *Music in the Air,* produced by Peggy Fears, began with Oscar's desire to write about a music publisher's office. Jerry suggested moving the publisher from the blare of Tin Pan Alley to a more mellow and romantic atmosphere, and they chose Munich. By the mid-thirties Oscar would be deeply involved in a political group fighting Nazism, but there was no hint of conflict in the peaceful Germany of this play. (When he revived it two decades later, the setting seemed so unrealistic that he moved the action to Switzerland!)

As Oscar worked with Jerry the Hammersteins moved out of the Fifth Avenue apartment they had rented and back into the Great Neck house. The change was brought about by Mousie, who came to see Dorothy one day and said, "Would you do a wonderful thing for Ockie? The house in Kenilworth hasn't been rented and it would take a great load off his mind." Dorothy had not wanted to live there because she didn't like its neo-Tudor style and, of course, its associations with Oscar's first marriage. With his usual reluctance to face embarrassing or unpleasant subjects, he had said nothing to Dorothy, but had apparently expressed financial worries to Mousie, whom he saw often. (He regularly took the children to visit her in the apartment in

Flatbush to which she had moved after Willie died and the boys went off on their own. The youngsters hated these visits. They cringed as she shouted "Tootsie!" and swooped down to kiss them and embrace them in her tattooed arms—King George was on one and the Prince of Wales on the other. They suffered the kisses out of duty and greed, for she always rewarded them with a five-dollar bill.) Dorothy agreed to the move. She planned and executed the redecoration with the same sort of skill that Oscar's mother, Alice, had always shown in her frequent moves. She changed the atmosphere of the house with bright Scottish tartans, but it remained a "Manderly" for her, a constant reminder of the woman for whom it had been built.

Her feelings about Myra were exacerbated by the visits that Billy and Alice paid them in the Kenilworth house. Oscar's older children were immediately fond of Jimmy, but their relationship with Dorothy was still strained and difficult, their natural feelings of friend-liness poisoned by their mother's continual references to "that woman" and what she had done to destroy them all. As Alice and Billy approached their former home, Alice asked her brother what she should call Dorothy. "I can't call her mother and I can't call her Mrs. Ham-merstein."

"I don't know what you should call her," snapped Billy. For a long time Alice called her nothing.

Billy continued to be uncomfortable and hostile, though that summer he began to be involved more deeply in Oscar's new house-hold. Dorothy enlisted him to help her paint the bath-house walls in an effort to build common bonds with him, and while they worked she talked to him about his father, telling him what a good and honor-able man he was. Billy also painted the stones along the roadways and even dabbled in coast surveying, putting up cork buoys near the rocks around the point that the house was built on so that at high tide mariners would be warned of their danger. For his birthday in October, Dorothy suggested to Mousie that she give Billy a motor-boat. He was delighted with the boat, which he christened *The Mouse*.

The children spent more and more time with Oscar and Dorothy as Myra began to travel frequently, leaving Billy and Alice with them during her European trips or weekends away. During the winter she moved to California with the children. Billy had attended Blair Academy, a boarding school in New Jersey, the previous year, but now he and Alice were enrolled in private schools in Beverly Hills. A few months later Myra moved, with her mother and Alice, to Vienna. Billy came to live with Oscar and Dorothy and attended Great Neck High School.

Oscar wrote often to eleven-year-old Alice and encouraged her interest in poetry. He ended a letter in the fall with:

> Do you like your new school any better?
> Tell me all in your very next letter!
> I'll not wait very long to receive it,
> But whatever you write—I'll believe it.
> My luncheon is waiting—it's creamed finanhaddie,
> I'd better go eat it—best love
> From your
> Daddy

In other letters he commented on poems she had sent to him, such as in this excerpt:

> The first verse of *"The Brook"* is by all odds the best because it is smooth and simple and seems to catch the swift laughing spirit of a brook. I should perfect the other verses and use this first verse rather as a refrain recurring after each verse. That is, you'll write a verse then you'll go into "Here I go! Here I go!" etc. Now, in what you call your second verse I like the first two lines *very very* much.
>
>> When the night begins to fall
>> Sleepy men walk by my side . . .

Oscar sent her *The Oxford Book of Verse,* advising her to read it slowly and in small doses, no more than one or two poems at a time, and to try to understand each line. He told her that she wouldn't find Tennyson's "The Brook" in the Oxford book but that he would find her a copy of it. Quoting the last lines of the poem, "Men may come and men may go/But I go on forever," Oscar admitted, "I became a little self-conscious as I wrote it down just now because the philosophy is strangely like 'Ol' Man River, he jus' keeps rollin' along.' The young man who wrote this song was not consciously imitating Tennyson, but there you are—The ideas *are* similar, aren't they?"

Oscar always wrote many letters each month, to his children, colleagues and old friends. On occasion he used letters to perpetrate practical jokes, such as the elaborate one he started in 1932 with his close friend and neighbor, Sandy Stronach. Using stationery that he had had imprinted *Emil Haasenfreud/President of the Douglas Manor Citizen's Association,* Oscar told Stronach that he had received repeated complaints about the Stronachs' parties. He made a few veiled threats and reminded him that "Douglas Manor has no desire to compete with Hollywood." For weeks Stronach worried about his eviction from the community. It wasn't until years later that he got his revenge. When Oscar was living in California, he showed his family a "sweet letter" from a farmer in West Virginia who went on for pages about how great Oscar's songs were and how much they had done for his family and sick sister. Touched by the fan letter, Oscar wrote back and a correspondence started which caused discomfort when pleas for money began, and he had to answer with great tact. The "poor farmer" was eventually discovered to be Sandy Stronach, who had a summer house in West Virginia.

Music in the Air was shaping up well for its scheduled November opening. In the libretto, Oscar explored the nature of the theater and of professionalism. An old music professor in a small Bavarian village, with his daughter and her beau, takes a tune he has written to an old school chum who is now a leading music publisher in Munich. The young rustics become involved in flirtations with a sophisticated leading lady and her lover, a theatrical composer. The young country girl, who has a lovely singing voice, is offered the lead in a play, but proves at the first rehearsal to be terrible onstage. Oscar put into the mouths of the characters some of his strong feelings about professionalism. Accused of being unfair and breaking the poor girl's heart by firing her, the director says, "Do you want us to throw away the chance of seventy-odd people making a living just because . . . a beginner wants a little adventure in the theater? . . . You think I'm awful? Wait until you come against an audience. I'm sparing you that!" He asks what is unfair about giving the part to a woman who has spent years preparing for it. Oscar's treatment of the characters reflects his reaction to the charming but inept performers on the Maryland showboat. The villagers are portrayed more sympathetically than the cynical theatrical people—as long as they stay on the other side of the footlights.

The melody for "I've Told Ev'ry Little Star," one of the songs from the score, was suggested to Jerry by a sparrow. He often listened to bird calls and kept notations of the calls. This one was "6 A.M. bird song from the willow outside the east window." Jerry didn't reproduce the calls literally, but used them as a basis for working out a theme. The tune proved such a stubborn one for Oscar that he said, "There were times during those hot August days when I wished the sparrow had kept his big mouth shut!"

Another song from *Music in the Air,* "The Song Is You," was one of Jerry's favorites. He was so pleased with it when he finished that he called Oscar in Great Neck, placed the phone near the keyboard and played it for him. (When he had doubts about a composition, he turned the bust of Richard Wagner on his piano away from him.) "The Song Is You" has been cited as a masterpiece of theater songwriting because it combines a romantic mood with a comic one. The song itself is highly romantic, but it is set in a scene of adult comedy. The two worldly lovers, the actress and the composer, show their unblinking understanding of each other as they acknowledge it is the song he uses to seduce other women at the same time that they express their love for each other.

The word "dream" appears in five songs from the score. The word bothered Oscar for years; he claimed it turned up uninvited in his lyrics and he wasn't sure what this meant precisely:

> I hear music when I look at you
> A beautiful theme of ev'ry dream I ever knew.
> —"The Song Is You"

> When lights along the shore go out,
> My man looks my way:
> Then we let one light more go out,*
> And while soft breezes bless us,
> And moonbeams caress us,
> We dream in Egern on the Tegern See.
> —"In Egern on the Tegern See"

> Night flies by
> Dawn breaks through
> I'm awake and I'm lonely,
> My lover is only a dream of you.
> —"One More Dance"

* When Oscar was preparing the 1951 revival of *Music in the Air,* he noticed that his secretary, Shirley Potash, had made a typing error making "one light more" into "one *more* light." Oscar returned the page with the following notation, which he put in large capital letters: "Don't ever kill that rhyme again, as long as you live! My secretary in 1932 did that and the mistake was printed in the published copy. Is there no progress in this civilization?"

I'm alone
And the night is all my own
To dream of love
To love my dreams
To lose them all in shadows.

—"I'm Alone"

There's a dream beyond a dream
Beyond a dream beyond a dream,
—"There's a Hill Beyond a Hill"

The last, "There's a Hill Beyond a Hill," an inspirational marching song performed by the ensemble, also contained two lines that suggest a song in *The Sound of Music* twenty-seven years later:

Climb the highest mountain
To ford the deepest river

The collaborators used two new devices to reinforce the integration of book and score. They mapped out the staging so that when one actor began to sing, others continued actions onstage and life would not seem to stop on the downbeat. Oscar also wrote dialogue in the rhythms of the song it led into, to provide smoother transitions from talking to singing.

As usual, the Kern-Hammerstein team wanted no outside director. Oscar directed the book and Jerry was everywhere at once. They had written detailed stage directions into the script, down to the smallest production detail. Joseph Urban created the sets and Joseph Harkrider the costumes, as they had for *Show Boat*. The cast included Walter Slezak as the young man from the village, Al Shean (of Gallagher and Shean), Marjorie Main and Tullio Carminati.

When *Music in the Air* began its Philadelphia tryouts in October, the only work that was required before it was ready for Broadway was technical polishing. It opened in New York on Election Night, November 8, 1932, and instantly became a "special darling" to both the audience and the critics, who gave full credit to Oscar and Jerry for book and score of the "organic work of art." The show ran for a year and a half in New York, toured the country, and was made into a film starring Gloria Swanson and John Boles in 1934.

After the hectic period that had produced flop after flop, Oscar's year of careful work had paid off with a big hit. He was not to have another for eleven years.

Four

Troubles and
Hopes and Fears

Oscar's period of failure could not have been predicted in 1932. For a thirty-seven-year-old who had already earned financial, popular and critical success, knew his craft, worked well with collaborators, and understood public taste and the theater, what could go wrong? In fact, it was difficult at the time to see that something *was* going wrong. In the best of times flops had been interspersed with hits. In the worst times there were near successes, enthusiastic beginnings, good offers. Oscar's daily life was the same in the bad years as in the good: he was active, kept up a heavy correspondence, approached his current work with optimism. However, by 1942 they were saying in Hollywood, "He can't write his hat"; and in New York, "Poor Oscar, the parade has passed him by." Even he thought his career might be finished.

It wasn't, of course. The bad years were followed by a second period of success that surpassed the first, not only in fame and fortune, but in work of far greater artistic merit. What, then, caused the failure in the first period? Economic conditions were a factor, as were social changes that transformed audiences and the theater. Oscar worked for many of the years in film, a medium that clearly did not suit his talents. However, not all the causes were external. Why did he remain in Hollywood? Why did he exercise bad judgment, lose touch with the public, produce work so inept? He had much to learn, about himself and his profession, in the next eleven years.

There was no hint of a downslide in early 1933, with *Music in the Air* selling out and *Show Boat* launched on a successful Broadway revival just five years after its original debut. In March the Hammersteins sailed for England—with Billy, Susan, Jimmy, a nursemaid and many steamer trunks—to live there for a while. Their reasons were partly personal; Oscar and Dorothy found exciting the prospect of settling in a country they both loved. In addition, neither England nor its theater seemed to be suffering from the economic depression that was making the future of the American theater look so uncertain. London seemed the right place to be as the Hammersteins moved into a comfortable house just outside the city, in Weybridge, Surrey.

Oscar's move to London had been suggested by his friend Louis Dreyfus, Max's brother, who asked him to write some musicals for the Drury Lane Theatre. A larger, more aggressive version of his brother, Louis Dreyfus had worked for a few years as an itinerant merchant after emigrating to the United States soon after Max did. On a visit to his family in Germany, he used his first savings, two hundred dollars, to acquire all rights to *The Chocolate Soldier*, which had flopped there. After arranging for its production in London, he took the music to Chappell, a small English publisher. When no one there would see him, Dreyfus printed the score himself. The show was an enormous success and he made the money that helped him buy Chappell's. In time, Dreyfus built it into one of the most important music publishing firms in the country and became a powerful figure on the West End and a member of the board of directors of the Drury Lane Theater.

Before writing anything new, Oscar directed *Music in the Air* for English producer Charles Cochran. It opened in May to restrained critical notices but to popular acclaim, and had a seven-month run at His Majesty's Theatre and an extensive tour.

At Louis Dreyfus' recommendation, Oscar went to Berlin to see the newest operetta by Central Europe's most popular composer, Paul Abraham, and agreed to adapt it for London. *Ball at the Savoy*'s light conventional plot about the near infidelities of Marquis and Marquise de Daubles at a fancy-dress ball makes it difficult to see what interested Oscar in the project. The show was given a sumptuous production at the Drury Lane, "a feast for . . . the senses," according to one reviewer. Critics were not kind about the book and score. "The music is exactly what we have been hearing for years," said *The Observer*, "and the plot would have bored to tears even our great-grandmothers." Maurice Evans, who played the Marquis, was advised by the same critic "not to throw himself away on such nonsense." A bit of chauvinism crept into the press comment: "I would visit Drury Lane no matter what the entertainment offered. But I am sure that our national theatre could find a much better play, and English at that, to fill it." The public viewed *Ball at the Savoy* almost as dimly as the first-night judges; it had a respectable but unprofitable 184-performance run.

Billy Hammerstein, who was fourteen, worked as a "go-for" on the show during his vacation from the Swiss boarding school he was now attending. At home, his relationship with Dorothy was as strained as ever. One night soon after his arrival, he heard Oscar and Dorothy discussing him in the next room. She was crying as she said, "He's hopeless, Oscar, so indifferent and difficult. I'll never get anywhere with those kids!" They felt that Myra was responsible for Billy's negative attitude, but Oscar reassured Dorothy that someday the children would "catch on" to her and everything would be all right. The next day he took Billy for a long walk on the Surrey countryside. "Billy, did you ever know me to tell lies?" he asked.

"No."

For the first time, Oscar discussed the problem forthrightly, explaining that one woman doesn't "steal" another's husband, unless something is wrong with the marriage. His more honest, adult approach obviously helped, because Billy settled down to family life with no more than the usual adolescent strains.

The Hammersteins had many English friends. They joined St. George's Hill Tennis Club and enjoyed an active social life. A racing buff since his childhood, Oscar endured seven fittings for the suit of tails that he had made for the races at Ascot. Jerry Kern, who also loved horse racing, and Eva had come to visit by the time the Derby was held at Epsom in late summer.

Jerry had just finished *Roberta;* he and Oscar tossed around ideas for their next show together. A book that they talked and corresponded about for years was Donn Byrne's *Messer Marco Polo*, a slight tale of the adventurer's growing love for Golden Bells, a Chinese girl with whom he had naïve philosophical discussions. At one of their first conferences Oscar said to Jerry, "Here is a story laid in China about an Italian and told by an Irishman. What kind of music are you going to write?"

"It'll be good Jewish music," replied Jerry.

Oscar wrote a libretto entitled *Golden Bells*; they completed three songs and continued to renew their option on the Byrne novel for the next few years. As much as they liked the story, they discovered that it was too limited for a full-length musical and they abandoned the project.*

Another "bicycle," or idea for a show, was *Fluffy Ruffles*, Oscar's story of a theatrical family. He wrote a detailed treatment stressing the notion that nothing is so ludicrously old-fashioned as that which is extremely "up to date" in its time. "The good and the simple and the true are alone eternal." Again, he and Jerry discussed the play for years, but never wrote it.

They had been approached by the Theatre Guild about adapting DuBose Heyward's play *Porgy*. Jerry and Oscar met with the Guild and Al Jolson, who wanted to play the lead, but when they found that George Gershwin had already contacted Heyward about turning the property into an opera, they withdrew from the project.

The show that they finally decided to write was suggested by their visit to the Derby, which is as much a fair as a horse race. The night before the event, the downs around the grandstand were studded with the caravans and tents of gypsies and itinerant carnival buskers gathered there to entertain the large crowds who came down from London. Fascinated by the atmosphere, Jerry and Oscar decided to write about the peripatetic English fair people.

Their choice may have been influenced by the troubles Louis Dreyfus was having with his fellow colleagues at the Drury Lane, which had produced all but two of Oscar's shows † in London. Under

---

* Oscar and Jerry were not the only ones attracted by the property. Max Gordon later commissioned Richard Rodgers and Lorenz Hart to write the score. Nothing materialized. In the late sixties it was announced that Robert Nathan and Sig Herzig (an old friend of Oscar's) would write the book, with a score by Robert Emmett Dolan and Johnny Mercer, and starring Shirley Yamaguchi. This was also shelved.

† After *Rose-Marie*'s 851 performances in 1926, Oscar had succeeded himself at the Drury Lane with *The Desert Song, Show Boat*, a revival of *Rose-Marie* and *The New Moon*. In 1947 an eight-year Hammerstein era would begin with 1,511 performances of *Oklahoma!*, followed by 506 of *Carousel*, 802 of *Show Boat* and 926 of *The King and I*.

attack from the British press for presenting foreign plays with foreign actors at what was thought of as the national theater, they were resistant to Dreyfus' plan for a Kern-Hammerstein original.

The collaborators may have chosen to write about an English traveling photographer and his three daughters in order to give a less alien cast to their musical. Though well-meant, this choice had adverse effects: it was partly their unfamiliarity with British customs that led to fatal weaknesses in the libretto of *Three Sisters*.

Reggie and Leighton Brill came to London to work on the production. Oscar even tried to interest Arthur in backing West End shows, but his uncle, anxious as he was to return to "the show game," was determined to do so only under his own name, not as a "money lender." After his bankruptcy Arthur was feeling humiliated by the reception given his attempts to get back into producing. He assured Oscar that there was nothing he could do to help and that he should let his conscience rest. "I know that I always could depend on you so why drag you down with me," he wrote.

During the preparations for *Three Sisters*, the Hammersteins gave up their country house, went back to New York for a while, and returned with the Kerns for the production. The two couples took adjoining suites at the Savoy Hotel, where working was heavily laced with hours of bridge playing, with food sent up from the grill. Dorothy had always liked Jerry, but thought him something of a bully, particularly toward his wife. At the hotel, Jerry was picking on Dorothy about one thing and another and one day she "let him have it." The spat cleared the air; the next day he bought her a George III silver pitkin and they became great friends, often shopping together for the antiques both so avidly collected.

Three Sisters opened on April 9, 1934. The first performance was three and a half hours long. The story of the loves of the three girls, one for a constable, another for an aristocrat and the third for a gypsy, was long, rambling and unrealistic. Although "I Won't Dance" and "Lonely Feet" were successful songs, the rest of the score was unoriginal, and the songs so long and heavy that the wryness of the mock-sentimentality evaporated before they were done.

The reviewers were a bit arch, but they all found some of the material attractive and thought the musical would have a healthy run once it was properly trimmed and pulled together. One critic noted that the "let's-be-British" regime at the Drury Lane had started with an American author, an American composer and an American leading lady (Charlotte Greenwood), but found the show satisfactorily British in flavor. Theatergoers were not as tolerant, and the show played for only six weeks.

One day Oscar said to Jerry, "Well, what next?"

Kern's reply was, "Hollywood. For good."

The 1934 Broadway theater season had produced only two book-musicals by midyear. New York writers, composers, actors, directors once again flocked to Hollywood, this time in earnest, with long-term contracts. They came with hope, ready to contribute their proven abilities to the booming medium. Renting lavish houses with swimming pools, tennis courts and palm trees, they set to work with enthusiasm.

By June Oscar had signed a one-year contract with Metro-Goldwyn-Mayer at $2,500 per week and had rented a house for the family at the top of La Brea Terrace, overlooking the Hollywood Valley. The London failures had shaken his self-confidence, and the country's uneasy financial condition and his relatively unsettled life in the past two years had churned up those needs for security and systematic living that were so important to Oscar. Although ASCAP royalties and offers from producers assured him a decent income on Broadway, the lucrative Metro salary and a chance to settle down were too attractive to refuse.

Despite his recent flops, Oscar's professional success had earned him a reputation that caused his arrival in Hollywood to be met with awe, which he soon dispelled with his easy manner. He became a participating member of the "writer's table" at MGM, a group which gathered either in the huge hangarlike studio commissary or at popular nearby restaurants. The lunches were a breath of New York in the foreign surroundings. Dorothy Parker could be sure of an appreciative audience for her description of Hollywood as a woman with white suede gloves holding a bagel with a bite out of it. The others told funny stories about their irreverent doings.

The New Yorkers' lives in Hollywood were once described as "the Algonquin Round Table gone West and childish." The Hammersteins lived a more settled life than many, but they were quickly caught up in the antics. Over lunch one day at the Brown Derby, Oscar, Robert Benchley, Harry Ruby, Marc Connelly, Charlie Butterworth, Nunnally Johnson, Charlie Lederer and one or two others began amusing themselves by discussing plans for an annual picnic of an athletic club that didn't exist. Committees were appointed to obtain baseball caps and to solicit local merchants for prizes for the athletic events. Butterworth made a proposal: if they would name the club after him, he would contribute a catcher's mitt, masks and fielders' gloves for the other players. Thus was born the "Butterworth A.C.," a joke that occupied them for months. Oscar wrote two songs for the organization, one a pep song:

> B-U-double-T-E-R-W-O-R-T-H!
> That spells many a happy day
> With companions brave and gay
> And when we play the Eagles
> Who gets left in the lurch?
> Not the B-U-double-T-E-R-W-O-R-T-Urch!

When Lederer criticized his song, a mock feud developed between them that was carried on for years. When they met at parties, they would speak only through an intermediary; their acting was so convincing that many thought they were serious. The playfulness was sustained for long periods. Once Oscar sent Lederer a cable from London: DEAR CHARLES ENGLAND IS ONE BIG BEAUTIFUL GARDEN. Lederer never acknowledged the cable, but two years later sent Oscar a cable from London saying, YES. ISN'T IT. Not to be outdone by his fellow club members, Connelly got into the act by sending them both a wire reading, WHICH PART?

Dorothy, upon learning of the B.A.C.'s existence, formed a Ladies Auxiliary. Connelly's impression was that she was the only member. She presented each of the men with a terrycloth scarf handsomely embroidered with the club's monogram.

Connelly, Ruby and others congregated at the Hammersteins' home for their almost daily badminton game. All the B.A.C. members were athletic and often played baseball, one of Oscar's favorite sports, as well as tennis on the Butterworths' grass court. Oscar seldom lost a game of any kind, and he played tennis particularly well. One morning he told Dorothy, "I had the most terrible nightmare last night."

"What was it?" she asked, expecting a traumatic tale.

"I dreamt I was playing tennis and the ball was coming toward me. I thought it would be out and let it go past. It was in and I lost the point."

"You call that a nightmare!" exclaimed Dorothy. "You're not even an adolescent."

Eventually the board of the club called a meeting at which it brought various charges against Butterworth and the name was changed to the Stay-As-Sweet-As-You-Are Athletic Club.

Although Oscar was seldom quoted in the anecdotes in which he figured, he was considered a witty man. His reputation was probably due to his appreciation of humor and wry comments which, though not memorable in themselves, added to the fun. One of the few stories to which he did contribute the punch line was about a party at Harry Ruby's house. Divorced at the time, Ruby invited the Hammersteins, Connellys, Butterworths, Benchley, Woollcott and others to a dinner prepared by his badly managed staff of servants. After the final course of a meager dinner, Ruby asked Oscar if he would like a brandy.

"No, thanks, Harry," he said. "I never drink on an empty stomach."

When Ruby asked the Hammersteins to dine on another occasion, just before leaving, Oscar told Billy, whose voice had just changed, to impersonate him and call his host to say brusquely, "Harry, this is Oc. Can't make it tonight," and then hang up. Billy called a few minutes too late. Ruby picked up the phone, Billy repeated his father's dialogue and Ruby said, "Not coming over, Oc? That's funny, because I can see you walking in the door!"

They played a great many games in Hollywood. Eddie and Mildred Knopf held spirited gambling sessions at their house, and charades was played everywhere. Jerry Kern, who had arrived in California in the fall of 1934, was, of course, mad about games. One night at the Hammersteins', Oscar and Hy Kraft took a deck of cards and began playing a game that made absolutely no sense. Obsessed with finding out the strategy of the game, Jerry hovered over them watching intently as they continued to bait him, until Oscar finally let on what they were doing.

There was an edge to the Hollywood humor. A guest at one of the frequent parties that Dorothy Parker and her husband, Alan Campbell, gave was greeted with "Come on in and meet the shits," and he realized that once he went inside, he would be one of them. Parker showed the bitterness that many of the Easterners felt. The elaborate fun disguised their growing dissatisfaction with movie work and its inevitable compromises, as studio heads maintained creative as well as financial control over the artists' products.

Oscar began happily enough. Metro was fast becoming the richest, biggest and most productive of all the studios; their films had a polish and technical skill that set them apart. His first assignment was to write several songs with Jerry, who was not under contract to any one studio, for a film, *Reckless,* to star Jean Harlow. Oscar's next task was to write a libretto for a film with Romberg, *The Night Is Young,* about Archduke Franz Otto. "When I Grow Too Old to Dream" from the score became one of the most enduring Romberg-Hammerstein songs. The first day that he worked on the eight-line refrain, the music suggested the line: "When I grow too old to dream." He was delighted with it at first, finding it smooth, easy to sing, in the mood of the music. The next line came very naturally, too: "I'll have you to remember." This was going to be so easy to write, he thought; he'd knock off for an hour or two. He stopped suddenly. What did it mean? "When I grow too old to dream"—when are you too old to dream? too old for what kind of dreams? As a matter of fact, when you're old, aren't you likely to dream about the past more than at any other time in your life? How did this silly line ever come into his head? Oscar threw it aside and worked on another title, then another and another. He finished several refrains based on other titles and didn't like any of them. In between he would return to "When I grow too old to dream" and try to convince himself that it did mean something. He would reject it, but regretfully, because it had a quality that appealed to him. It became so insistent that he began to wonder whether his instinct wasn't truer than his reason; if this line didn't mean anything, why was it so attractive to him?

The song and its use of the word "dream" plagued Oscar for weeks, as it had before, in another context. He decided that he must be giving "dream" a special meaning, the sense of a lover dreaming about the present and the future and that the lover was saying, "When I grow too old to love you and to dream about loving you, I will be remembering our love in the past." He felt that this interpretation might be supported by the rest of the refrain:

> When I grow too old to dream,
> I'll have you to remember,
> When I grow too old to dream,
> Your love will live in my heart.
> So kiss me, my sweet,
> And so let us part,
> And when I grow too old to dream,
> That kiss will live in my heart.

He liked it—adored it, in fact—and he walked up and down his study singing it, wishing it were not obscure but feeling that if he liked it so well, perhaps other people would, too, and would not be too analytical about its meaning. He submitted it to Rommy, who was delighted. Harry Rapf, his producer, and Dudley Murphy, the film's director, were delighted. Oscar kept his mouth shut and didn't mention his doubts about its semantic aspects.

The Night Is Young was a film that was easily forgotten, but "When I Grow Too Old to Dream" grew very popular. Several months after the film's release, Max Dreyfus asked Oscar exactly what the song meant. Oscar replied, "I'm not quite sure," and Dreyfus laughed very loudly; he had talked it over with some other songwriters, and though they loved the song they all wondered what it meant.

Later Oscar decided that the music had a great deal to do with establishing the legitimacy of the unclear lyrics: linked to the music, the lyrics lulled the listener into accepting them simply as music superimposed upon music. Oscar was forced to admit that there was something to be gained in the use of words with emphasis on sound rather than on meaning and clarity.

In making *The Night Is Young*, Oscar received a discouraging lesson in film-making procedures when the producer called in two screenwriters, who completely changed the story and characters, although they retained much of the score. So much for the organic musical, not one of Hollywood's priorities in the mid-thirties.

The dismay with which he viewed a rough cut of *The Night Is Young* in early December didn't help him face the horrendous family Christmas that year. He had wired Mousie that Reg would come to get her to bring her and little Henry, who was now eight, to California for Christmas.

Mousie arrived and immediately set everyone on edge. Susan dreaded sharing her room with her stepgrandmother, whom she found physically repulsive. She would watch in fascination as Mousie removed her wig, shaped like a cruller, to reveal a bald spot in the middle of her flaming red hair. Mousie blamed Dorothy for the fact that they didn't see much of her and didn't take her to enough parties. Fond as he was of her, Oscar was rather embarrassed by his loud, vulgar, tattooed stepmother. Mousie sensed the embarrassment but, unable to blame her "Tootsie," directed her anger at Dorothy, who was actually less ashamed of her than Oscar, since Mousie wasn't her kin. Things came to a head on Christmas morning, when Dorothy gave Mousie a radio and she said, "I don't want it. Goddammit! I don't want it!"

Dorothy said, "Well, Mousie, if you don't want it we can change it and get something else."

"You're goddamned right I will," said Mousie, and she hurled the radio at her.

By this time everyone was upset. Henry opened a present, a cap pistol with wooden bullets, that delighted him. Oscar insisted that he give up the bullets because they were dangerous.

Henry said, "They're only wooden, they're fake. Besides, you can't really fire the gun."

Oscar lost his temper and gave his stepson a clout on the head. The family tension slipped into hysteria. Henry screamed, the family's golden retrievers, Mike and Bruce, scampered around over the wrappings and unopened presents barking frantically; everyone reacted to the momentous event of Oscar losing his temper.

Dorothy, Susan and Henry repaired to a bedroom to cry. At dinner, Oscar, Jimmy and Mousie—the Hammersteins—sat at one end of the table, and Dorothy, Henry and Susan—the Jacobsons—at the other. The only piece of dialogue was Mousie saying, "Would you like some hard sauce, Jimmsy-boy?"

Dorothy and Oscar didn't speak to each other for several weeks afterwards. Both embarrassed and hurt, they didn't know what to say. Each would lie in bed wrapped in misery and silence.

When their lease expired, the Hammersteins moved to Brentwood, where they rented another house. Mousie returned East, and Billy arrived from New York, where his mother was again living, to stay with them and complete his school year.

Alice and Billy had spent the previous summer with Oscar in California. Both were getting along better with Dorothy now and they enjoyed the lively household. Jimmy was then four and Susan, or "Cookie," was six. Oscar was still uncomfortable with small children, but he told Jimmy stories and entertained him with *The Wizard of Oz* or the funnies, which he read by adopting different accents to act out each part. On his way to the studio, Oscar would drop Susan and Jimmy at school. In their chauffeur-driven Rolls-Royce, he would start a story that he made up, perhaps about a lima bean that rolled out of a pot and went down the street, and have the children continue the next chapter, forcing them to think up situations and ideas. He encouraged their artistic endeavors: Alice's poems and lyrics, the piano compositions of little Jimmy and Billy. He even went so far as to have a song entitled "Friendly Little Farm" commercially published, with music by William Hammerstein and words by Oscar Hammerstein II. When asked what he wanted for a birthday or Christmas gift, he would say to the children, "Don't buy me something; write something for me."

Susan considered "Ockie," always the name she used for Oscar, her father; though she saw Henry Jacobson for visits throughout her childhood, he seemed something of a stranger to her. Oscar was a figure of security to her and she trusted him completely. All of the children felt this security and trust, but to all of them he was an authoritarian figure, who was a bit remote. Oscar was someone they respected and even feared a little; for all the fun that the family had, he was never a chum.

Although Oscar's kindness was renowned outside the home, the children never found him particularly kind, because he often found it easier to communicate with them, particularly the boys, through teasing and urging them to be competitive. The teasing sometimes had a harsh edge to it. He would trip Billy on the ice and laugh as he struggled to his feet. He would invent a mythical friend of Jimmy's; no matter what Jimmy had done, "Sammy Goldstein" did it a little better. His verbal teasing and competitive verbal duels increased as they grew older.

Oscar said that the reason for this rough treatment was a desire to put the children in perspective with the world, to toughen them, to help them become independent and make their own way, He did, in fact, allow them to make their own mistakes and try things for themselves, and was never an overprotective father. Oscar gave his children stability, a sense of the ridiculous and a standard of reality about what was important, even as they lived in that most unreal and superficial of worlds, Hollywood. He gave them a sense of reality in the family too, and was not afraid to assert adult authority. Once, at a dinnertable discussion about a family decision, Dorothy said, "It's a democracy, so let's have a vote."

Oscar said, "The hell with it. It's not a democracy. I'm the head of the family."

He did not unburden himself or expose his weaknesses to his children. He may not always have seemed like a "real person" to them, but he was always a father. In his effort to guide them, he sometimes became a bit didactic. When Alice wrote about her disappointment in a trip she had taken through the Panama Canal en route to California with Myra and Billy, he responded with a long letter:

It seems to me you are both pretty severe critics of new things, new places and new experiences. I myself think that the mere fact of a thing being new and out of my ordinary course of daily living makes that interesting.

Maybe you don't agree with me. You have a perfect right not to. You are yourself, and you don't have to be like me, and if you don't find something exciting it is silly to make believe that you do. But remember this: if you *do* find something exciting, it is silly to make believe you *don't*. Lots of people think it is very smart to seem unconcerned by things that delight other people. They think it makes them superior and above the ordinary weaklings. People who say the world is a dull, flat place are very unlucky, because the world will always think that those kind of people are dull.

The best way to enjoy life is to be enthusiastic—and when you are enthusiastic don't be ashamed of it. Try to find things you like and don't waste too much time in telling people what you don't like. Nobody wants to hear it.

Love from your boring old father, known in his more frivolous moments as

Daddy

Although they respected and trusted their father and felt his love and concern, the children did not feel the kind of warmth from him that they felt from their Uncle Reggie, who was often around the house.

At this time Reggie was working for Hal Roach Studios, though by the following March both Oscar and Reggie were discouraged with the latter's prospects in Hollywood and thought he should try his hand in London, where "he clicked better than any place he has ever been." Oscar said that until Reggie got a job he would continue to carry him and instructed his lawyer to draw up a contract "whereby I employ him as London representative for a salary of $10,000 a year. . . . In other words, the thing can be made to look legitimate. . . . In drawing up the contract, state that it is his duty to be on the lookout for talent for me . . . in general, take care of whatever foreign interests accrue to me and any negotiations I may have with a British producing or film company."

Oscar could show Reggie the kindness and protectiveness that he couldn't or wouldn't show to his children. He took care of Reg, never blew up at him, never teased him or took advantage of him verbally, though he certainly could have. Perhaps Oscar's harshness with the children came partly from a desire, conscious or unconscious, to prevent them from becoming the kind of charming but weak and unsuccessful (unsuccessful, at any rate, in Hammerstein terms) man that Reggie was.

Years later, reflecting on his own childhood in a "strange, disorderly, unsystematic" family, Oscar said no matter what the circumstances of a family, the love a child most needed was a sense of security that "among millions of other atoms very like himself . . . he is something very special, worth promoting, worth perfecting, worth building up to that position of prominence and achievement where he can lie in his bed or stand on a hill or walk down the street and say to himself with conviction: 'What a good boy am I.'"

In regard to the world outside the family, Oscar maintained the same kind of detachment that characterized his relationship with his children. He was willing to give money, time and care not only to good causes but to needy individuals and was sensitive to human beings no matter what their status, but Oscar showed in all this a lack of emotional involvement. The sense of objectivity that made people love and respect him also kept him somewhat isolated from life.

His children sensed his discomfort with the actual world. Billy was walking on a sidewalk with him once when they were horrified to see a parked motorcycle topple to the ground, pinning under it a boy who had climbed up on the machine. As Oscar went over to lift the motorcycle and free the boy, Billy remembers feeling that his father was doing something foreign to him and was doing it only because there was no one else to do it and he couldn't ignore it or pretend it hadn't happened.

On another occasion Billy went with Oscar and Reggie into a restaurant where they were confronted with a bellicose drunk. Again, Billy felt uncomfortable that his father was being exposed to such a thing. He was grateful that Reggie was there because Reggie knew how to deal with anything that came up, whereas his father wasn't supposed to be part of the ordinary world.

When Billy told Oscar about the time he helped a blind man after overcoming a reluctance to touch him, Oscar said, "If that had happened to me, I would have crossed the street to the other side, so that I wouldn't have to know about it."

The same mechanism that caused Oscar to shove aside unpleasant thoughts operated to make him avoid seeing unpleasant realities. Yet it was clear that he fought this tendency all his life in whatever way he could. He supported the common man and his problems not only in the political area but also in his work. Although those close to him knew that Oscar preferred to ignore anything unpleasant, they also knew that if you presented him with a problem, no matter how terrible it was, he would deal with it.

In January Oscar began work with Jerry on *Champagne and Orchids.* Trying to buck the Hollywood system, he wrote Metro's musical production chief Sam Katz, "I know I am not writing this screen play in the orthodox manner. I know that before dialogue is written there is usually a treatment concocted by a producer and two or three writers in constant conferences—an elaborate scenario which contains all sorts of details, devices and indeed everything but dialogue, and a soul."

He and Jerry submitted the libretto with five completed songs. Katz gave the green light and told Oscar he could produce the film. A cast was assembled: Jeanette MacDonald, Nelson Eddy, Wallace Beery, Clifton Webb and Constance Collier. But the production was continually postponed and finally scrapped. Although abandoning a picture was not particularly unusual, Metro was apparently as dissatisfied as Oscar was with his "barren year" there and didn't pick up his option in May.

He signed a non-exclusive one-year deal with Paramount that would guarantee him $150,000. The studio also expressed interest in financing any Broadway ventures that he became involved with. Oscar wrote to Alice in New York that he would be there in the fall, promised her a Broadway opening night and said how much he was looking forward to working in the theater again. He enclosed a poem he had written for her:

To Alice On Her Birthday
(Set to her musical composition, dedicated to me last Christmas
. . . with love and best wishes from Daddy)

> Her eyes are brown
> And she's just fourteen
> (This is the seventeenth day of May)
> She looks her best
> When her face is clean
> (Women are funny that way)
> She's just too short to be tall
> And she's just too big to be small
> She's just fourteen

And she's "in between"
But quite serene with it all.
Her eyes are brown
And she's just fourteen
(This is the seventeenth day of May)
I'd love her eyes
Were they blue or green
(Fathers are funny that way)

The Hammersteins moved back to New York in September. Oscar planned to write a show with Jerry and another with Romberg, to be financed partly by Paramount. The "Princess Theatre" type of musical that he and Jerry had discussed was eventually abandoned when they both became too involved in other plays to meet the Christmas deadline. Oscar had resumed his association with Schwab and Mandel, both of whom had left Broadway for a few years after the *East Wind* disaster. Their new musical, *May Wine*, was an adaptation by Mandel of a recent novel, *The Happy Alienist*. This was the first non-operetta that Romberg had attempted and its setting was a very different Vienna from the one he was accustomed to. The play began with an Austrian psychoanalyst announcing to the police that he had killed his wife and flashed back to the events and psychological motives leading to the alleged murder. The final scene revealed the corpse as a dummy and saw the pair happily reunited.

The production opened in New York on December 5, 1935, to reviews that hailed its efforts to break convention and further integration, but the Romberg-Hammerstein score was not strong and none of the eleven songs became long-lasting hits. John Mason Brown called Oscar's lyrics "uncomfortably obvious," John Anderson termed them "deft and clever" and six other reviewers didn't mention them at all.

Audiences liked *May Wine* well enough to give it a seven-month run in a season that was unhealthy for musicals. Of the ten produced that year, Cole Porter and Moss Hart's *Jubilee* shuttered quickly; *Jumbo*, the Rodgers, Hart, Hecht-MacArthur extravaganza for Billy Rose, closed with a $200,000 loss and Gershwin's *Porgy and Bess* played only 121 performances. To be sure, the musical theater was still no place to make a living.

The Hammersteins returned to California to a house that Dorothy had bought with her "bauble," Oscar's gift the year before of his copyright ownership for "When I Grow Too Old to Dream." Located at 1100 Benedict Canyon Drive in Beverly Hills, the creamy-white

French provincial house was an unpretentious but large and comfortable residence surrounded by lawns, flower gardens and high hedges. Dorothy decorated it with the English and American antiques that she loved to collect. Although her mother said in a letter to Oscar that "from the description, it must seem like living in one of the palaces in the Arabian Nights," in fact Dorothy's decorating gave this house a friendly, cozy atmosphere.

Oscar had still done no work for Paramount and now became immersed at Universal in their new film version of *Show Boat,* for which he had written the screenplay. His old standby provided one of the two good work experiences that Oscar had in all his years in Hollywood. He said that director James Whale's wish to remain faithful to the original was "the boon all authors dream of—and almost never receive." The property had been filmed once before by Universal in 1929 as a silent film that was altered three-quarters of the way through production to become a semi-talkie, with a narrative and a synchronized score that included a few of the original songs. Carl Laemmle, Jr., whose father was founding head of Universal, wanted to make a proper sound version with Kern and Hammerstein.

Oscar opened up the book to include scenes depicting Magnolia's successful singing career and her daughter's Broadway debut. Laemmle and Whale made no changes in the screenplay, which he wrote in the East, and consulted him on all aspects of pre-production, including decisions on casting.

Paul Robeson was signed as Joe, whose part in the story was expanded with new scenes and songs. He proved to be as compelling on film as he was onstage.

Irene Dunne had been everyone's only choice for the role of Magnolia, a part she had played in a Washington, D.C., production and a subsequent road company. Raised in Kentucky and graduated from Chicago Musical College, she had a lovely lyric soprano voice and had begun her career in Broadway musicals. She got her job in *Show Boat* when Ziegfeld saw her in an elevator and sent his secretary scurrying around the building to find "the girl in the blue hat." A talent scout, spotting her in the tour during the Los Angeles engagement, offered her a Hollywood contract. She had since built a good reputation in films, starring not only in musicals (*Sweet Adeline* and *Roberta*) but also in nonmusicals, such as *Cimarron*. Although she was then thirty-one years old, she was able to bring a mischievous, girlish quality to Magnolia's early scenes.

The search for a proper Ravenal continued almost until the day shooting began. Robert Taylor, Paul Gregory, Walter Pidgeon, John Boles, Frederic March and Nelson Eddy were all candidates at one time or another, but Allan Jones was finally signed.

Oscar had only one objection to the rough cut he saw in March. He felt that Ravenal's well-dressed, self-assured appearance in the final scene took the drama out of his meeting with Magnolia. When Whale added a penultimate scene that firmly established Ravenal as a failure, Oscar was delighted. The film became a popular and critical smash hit when it was released in 1936.

Finally he began his first assignment for Paramount, writing lyrics to composer Erich Wolfgang Korngold's score for a light opera, *Give Us This Night*. Although he was not officially working on the screenplay, Oscar rearranged dialogue, set songs in the shooting script and suggested plot revisions in an effort to build the part of Metropolitan singer Gladys Swarthout.

Korngold had been attracted to the idea of the scenario as it had been described to him. He knew nothing of the Hollywood penchant for rewriting scripts during production but Oscar knew, and he formally asked studio production head William LeBaron to apprise him of any changes "because almost anything you do is sure to have an influence on my approach to the lyrics." He remarked to Korngold as the script went from hand to hand: "This thing gets worse from week to week—by the time they film it, it will be useless." He was right. Critics later noted that the story was anemic and that Miss Swarthout's talents were wasted, since she spent most of her time being sung at by a very hammy Jan Kiepura. Hammerstein and Korngold had devised the first original opera sequence on film, as well as ballads that *Time* magazine found "the most advanced light opera music yet composed for cinema," but the motion picture was not a success, chiefly because it was dominated by Kiepura's poor performance.

Shifting over to producer Arthur Hornblow, Jr.'s unit at the studio, Oscar began work on *The Count of Luxembourg*, based on Hungarian Franz Lehár's 1912 operetta. Hornblow was flattering in his comment on Oscar's adaptation and original lyrics and he promised to cast the picture as soon as he cleared up three other projects on his production schedule. He also promised to let Oscar co-direct one picture and have full director credit on a second.

As months passed, none of these promises was translated into reality. Instead, Hornblow and LeBaron asked Oscar to conjure up a vehicle for the "hot box-office" team of Carole Lombard and Fred MacMurray. He found it in *Burlesque,* the George Manker Watters–Arthur Hopkins play which had been filmed as *Dance of Life* by Paramount in 1929. Oscar wrote a treatment changing the burlesque comedian to a "sweet-hot trumpet player" who begins in a Panama honky-tonk and, with his wife's help, achieves success in an El Morocco–type New York nightclub. Oscar shared screen credit for the shooting script with Virginia Van Upp, a film writer who had spent her life in the industry. The film, *Swing High, Swing Low,* was a middling success for MacMurray and Lombard, but was nothing more than standard Hollywood fare.

Oscar had found financial security in Hollywood, and little else. The work was unsatisfying and the fun had begun to pall. He indicated his disillusionment in a short play, found in his files, about "a band or drones . . . [who] lack any real purpose in life but are beset with the idea of having a good time purely for themselves." In his dissatisfaction, he turned, for the first time, to something other than work or home for fulfillment. He became active in an organization devoted to a cause he believed worthwhile, the Hollywood Anti-Nazi League, of which he was a founding member in the summer of 1936.

His was not the only emerging political consciousness in Hollywood that year. In the twenties and early thirties, workers in the movie colony were so absorbed in their rapidly developing medium that they were not much concerned with the greater world. Even the intellectuals among them found that the collective responsibility of film-making tended to make the individuals involved less concerned about the substance of the product in terms of what really mattered or its relationship to truth. At the same time, the attitudes of the Hollywood moguls who ruled the studios were anti-intellectual and crudely anti-labor. Determined to keep total control in their kingdoms, they paid their personnel well and kept a firm grip on the reins, artistic as well as financial.

One of the first signs of unrest was the forming of the Screen Writers Guild in 1933. When profits took a nose dive that year, executives asked writers to agree to 50 percent reduction in salaries. The guild was established to protect employees against the pressures that caused their "unselfish volunteering." Political awareness in the film capital was sharpened by the California gubernatorial election of 1934, which divided the community into two camps. Alarmed by the radical measures advocated by Upton Sinclair, the Democratic candidate, the wealthy and conservative studio heads marshaled massive funds for his opponent, Frank Merriam, and began to pressure their employees. They told them not to make the mistake of supporting Sinclair and "asked" them to contribute a day's wages to Merriam's campaign. The contest was bitterly fought. Merriam won the election, but not before many serious political issues were raised and debated.

Many Hollywood intellectuals, mainly but not exclusively writers, found a sense of purpose and hope in their new political awareness. Perhaps not all felt, as Dorothy Parker did, that they were "living in Babylonian captivity working for cretins," but most shared Donald Ogden Stewart's feeling that in both work and play they had "reached a level upon which no further development of maturity was possible." At work the writers had little artistic control; they were well-paid carpenters, manipulators of material. They made the best of it, but they were disgusted with the films that they turned out, resentful of the men responsible for the system, and increasingly anti-Establishment. Hollywood had given these talented professionals financial success but no inner satisfaction. Their private lives were luxurious, their social lives fun, but they felt as rootless and adrift as the nation seemed to be.

The "liberal" group was one of the most attractive in Hollywood, filled with people who were generally more intelligent, more likable and more admirable than others. In the mid-thirties their talk turned from studio gossip and the recounting of silly antics to serious and important matters. As Stewart said, they had stepped off the pleasure cruise and were ready to go into action against Nazi fascism.

It was not surprising that Oscar joined the fight. Although he had been unaware of Nazism five years before, when he wrote *Music in the Air*, talks with Germans, as well as a trip to Berlin while he was living in England, had convinced him of its evil. The majority of Americans still felt that Hitler's hooligans were too outrageous to be taken seriously; the Hollywood League Against Nazism was established to change that attitude. The first meeting took place at Dorothy Parker and Alan Campbell's house in June 1936. Donald Ogden Stewart was named president, and Oscar, Parker, Florence Eldridge, Frederic March and nine others formed its executive council.

Oscar was active in the League for the next year. He attended frequent sessions of the executive council and played a prominent role in the many benefits, dinners and rallies to attract new members and provide a platform for anti-Nazi speakers, such as Thomas Mann. As chairman of the cultural commission, Oscar held regular meetings in his house, at which the group organized radio broadcasts, articles and short films about the threat to "cultural liberty" posed by the Nazis. The next spring, the commission was incorporated in a new interracial commission, with Oscar remaining as chairman. Its purpose was to "combat racial intolerance and thus combat Nazism, which uses intolerance as a weapon to attain power." The committee was Oscar's first affiliation with a cause that would remain one of his primary interests: understanding among people of all races.

The League was initially supported by many prominent people and achieved status and influence in the liberal community. Gradually studio executives and others withdrew their support because there was disagreement about whether it should become anti-communist as well as anti-fascist and doubts arose about the role played in the organization by members with questionable affiliations. Oscar was not active in the League after he left California in early 1938 and withdrew his membership the following year. However, when during the fifties the State Department cited his League membership as a doubtful activity, his answer was essentially the same as it had been when the Communist issue was raised at meetings in the thirties: "My interest now is to do all I can to stamp out Nazism, which I think is the greatest threat to our culture and our safety. If there are Communists in this organization, and if they are willing to help me do this, I can work with them without becoming a Communist myself. If there were a forest fire outside of Los Angeles and we all ran out with buckets to pour water on it, I would not ask the man at my shoulder what his philosophy was . . ."

Dorothy was active in the League but found her own special interest as well when she became a professional decorator. Her business started when Larry Schwab, who was finding it difficult to produce on Broadway, asked her to look for a furnished house in California. When she found that the only decent ones were unfurnished, she used money from her savings account to lease and decorate three houses; she used purchasing agents when she decorated houses for Norma Talmadge and the Pandro Bermans and then decided to set up her own headquarters. She found a shop at 9172 Santa Monica Boulevard in Beverly Hills and had a replica of her signature written across the window.

She was making a vocation out of something she had always been interested in—her "disease," as she called it. Even when she was a young girl she had surprised her mother upon her return from a trip by redecorating her bedroom, making curtains from damask table-cloths, staining floors and covering furniture. She was a "natural homemaker" with sure taste. Using English and American furniture with Chinese accents, she created a homey but smart look. She said herself that she liked a "slight dash of vulgarity" to avoid a sterile atmosphere. If she was looking for chairs to go around a small table, she would always ignore four matching Chippendales to pick nonmatching ones in order to create an interesting room.

The number of clients grew as Dorothy's natural flair and taste attracted attention. Dr. Jules C. Stein, president of the giant talent agency, Music Corporation of America, himself an authority on antique furniture, engaged Dorothy to supervise the entire installation of MCA's opulent new multimillion-dollar Beverly Hills building, designed by Paul Williams.

Dorothy had several assistants, including Betty Kern and Nella Howell, but her principal aide was twenty-two-year-old Louis Bowen. Now one of New York's leading fabric and wallpaper manufacturers, Bowen describes Dorothy's approach as spontaneous and decisive. If she wanted a picture hung in a client's house, she would grab a hammer and nail, take off her shoes and hang it immediately. If the grand piano was dusty, she wouldn't wait for a dustcloth but would pick up her fur coat and give it a wipe.

The store in Beverly Hills reflected not only Dorothy's taste but her style of living. In the back was a sort of salon where a cook-maid would prepare lunch for visiting clients and friends. Jerry Kern, who had taught her a great deal about antiques, would often come disguised as a sea captain or an old German. After poking around commenting on everything, he often stayed to lunch and regaled Dorothy with stories of his exploits as a collector. His favorite was about the time he bought a heavy silver serving tray from a supposedly reputable dealer; when he discovered it to be fraudulently hall-marked, he asserted the medieval privilege of a dissatisfied client and required the man to melt down the piece or face exposure.

An important decorating job for Dorothy, from both a professional and personal point of view, was Dorothy Fields' home on Arden Drive in Beverly Hills. Like Oscar, who had been a classmate at elementary school, Dorothy Fields came from a theatrical family and was a lyricist. She worked with many collaborators, often with Jerry.

Dorothy's father was Lew Fields, one half of the famous vaudeville comedy team of Weber and Fields, who later turned producer and launched his son Herb, as well as Rodgers and Hart and others. When Dorothy began writing lyrics, Lew put his foot down firmly and said, "Ladies don't write lyrics," an admonition she ignored throughout her sensational career. There has been only a handful of women lyricists on Broadway—notably Anne Caldwell, Dorothy Donnelly and Carolyn Leigh—and she was by far the most successful of them. Working with a wide range of composers,' from Fritz Kreisler to Jerry Kern to Cy Coleman, she had a great diversity of style which is apparent in her songs, some of which were: "Lovely to Look at," "Pick Yourself Up," "Make the Man Love Me," "I Can't Give You Anything but Love," "Big Spender" and "The Way You Look Tonight" (for which she and Jerry received the 1936 Academy Award).

A warm, vibrant and astute woman, Dorothy Fields became a lifelong friend of both Oscar and Dorothy. When Dorothy decorated her home she was not yet married, but the large house with many wings became the California residence of all the Fields—Lew and Rose, Herb, Joe and Frances, a "nonpro" sister.

Dorothy never took a job that required her to be out of the city because of her responsibilities to Oscar and the children. Billy and Alice were often around the house now, because their mother had moved back to California. She had remarried, but when she got a divorce after six months Oscar resumed alimony payments, though he was not obligated under law to do so. Myra was a constant irritation. She told friends that she was following her former husband from place to place because he "needed" her. Although Dorothy and Oscar never saw her, she would call often to complain about one thing or another, or to ask Oscar for a favor. Although she would berate him in front of the children, he was always very protective of her.

Broadway was again having a bad year, but Oscar continued to receive offers to do shows. Billy Rose wanted him to do a show for the Hippodrome, Erik Charrell wanted him to adapt *White Horse Inn*, an Austrian operetta, for the Rockefellers' Center Theatre, and working on Byrne's *Messer Marco Polo* with Jerry was still a possibility.

In March Oscar wrote to Arthur: "It is time I came to a decision in my own mind about these things so that if I sacrifice money to be made out here I will at least have some tangible reason for doing so and a good prospect, in my own opinion, of coming out ahead." He was tempted by the offers, but decided that there was no justification for leaving the "sure money" in Hollywood, especially since his next picture would be a big-budget original with Jerry. When *High, Wide and Handsome* opened, one New York film critic said, "Kern and Hammerstein haven't contributed anything special in California . . . but in this one composition they make up for all their lost time among the eucalyptus trees and swimming pools."

Paramount's Adolph Zukor, anxious to match Metro with a "class" musical, instructed Arthur Hornblow, Jr., to spare no expense in making a "big picture." With Hammerstein and Kern already committed to the screenplay and the score, Irene Dunne was borrowed from RKO and Randolph Scott, Dorothy Lamour, Charles Bickford, Akim Tamiroff, Elizabeth Patterson, William Frawley, Ben Blue and Alan Hale were signed. Rouben Mamoulian was to be the director.

Rouben Mamoulian, who would later direct two of Oscar's shows with Dick Rodgers, had reached Broadway and Hollywood by way of Moscow and London. He had staged many plays for New York's Theatre Guild, among them *Marco Millions, Wings Over Europe,* and *Porgy and Bess.* Mamoulian's screen record was equally impressive.

Paramount spent so much money on salaries and elaborate location sets and later marketed the picture so poorly that it never recouped its investment. However, it was a fine motion picture, a lusty adventure story about the birth of the oil industry deftly blended with fantasy, romance and score. *High, Wide and Handsome* was ahead of its time in many ways, one of the few integrated musicals made before the forties.

Hollywood was trailing behind Broadway in the development of the integrated musical partly because of the extraordinary complexity of the medium in terms of the collaborative efforts involved. In addition to all the elements that had to be fused in creating a musical play, the cinema introduced new components, such as the rhythms and melodic structure of a song in relation to the precise way it was shot, the speed and direction of camera movements, the planning of cuts and the quality of color and lighting. As Oscar had found on Broadway, the proper fusion of even the simplest elements of a stage production required a strong concept and a strong hand from beginning to end. There were few strong hands in the musical field to deal with the cumbrous technical aspects of the new monster medium. Although there were directors and dance directors skilled in one area or another, Ernst Lubitsch and Rouben Mamoulian were the only two who seemed to know what they wanted to do with the whole, and they were only sporadically given the chance to do it. An Astaire-Rogers musical or a Busby Berkeley production number had wonderful goodies, but they were self-contained, so little affected by the total environment of the film that they were as charming removed from the film as they were in it.

An integrated musical had popped up from time to time, since *Show Boat,* on the screen and on the stage, but it was not widely accepted as an example of what the musical ought to be until 1943, when *Oklahoma!* burst upon the scene. Arthur Freed, a successful lyricist who became the MGM producer virtually solely responsible for the Golden Age of the film musical (*Meet Me in St. Louis, Summer Holiday, An American in Paris, Singin' in the Rain* and *Gigi*), would later call Oscar Hammerstein II the man who made it all possible.* Ironically enough, the man who made it all possible created only one original film of quality during his Hollywood years.

Oscar devoted the bulk of his time throughout that fall and winter of 1936 to the *High, Wide and Handsome* screenplay and lyrics. He worked out with Jerry the integration of score and scenario and with Rouben a shooting script that would deal seriously with the historical events while keeping the charm of the personal relationships and adding some elements of fantasy. In the film's lively climax, circus performer Irene Dunne leads a bizarre group—thundering elephants, bearded lady, dwarves, strong men and acrobats—to aid her estranged husband, Randolph Scott, who is battling ruffians while trying to complete his oil line before a deadline set by the railroad-magnate villains.

The lyrics of the six songs in the film are succinct and gay. They range from the fetching bit of doggerel "Allegheny Al," which sounds

---

* Arthur Freed, a worshipful admirer and devoted friend, was, by his own admission, inspired by Oscar's concept of the organic musical and recognized that such integration must be essentially the work of one man. In film, this meant a strong director, and under Freed and his brilliant associate Roger Edens, such directors as Vincente Minnelli, Stanley Donen, Gene Kelly, Charles Walters and Mamoulian had full control of all the pieces.

as if it might have been sung on the Monongahela, to the lusty title song and the haunting "The Folks Who Live on the Hill."

Although Oscar didn't usually use tricky rhymes, this score contains two.* The lively "Will You Marry Me Tomorrow, Maria?" rhymes "bombazine" with "village green." And "The Folks Who Live on the Hill" uses "veranda" with "command a (view)." Oscar felt that there was some sort of curse on the word "veranda" in his lyrics which prevented songs containing it from becoming hits. While this song has a small band of ardent admirers, it never attained great popularity or a wide sale. Jerry scribbled on the top of his manuscript of this odd melody with an unusual six-bar release: "Oscar, this is to me a **** choice morsel. Maybe I'd better send you a recording because unless you play the figure in the accompaniment it loses everything."

The lyrics express one of Oscar's deeply felt sentiments in the pure, uncluttered style that characterizes so much of his best work. In the simple description of a scene that represents a deep love between a man and his wife, he was giving substance to his own dream.

> Many men with lofty aims, strive for lofty goals,
> Others play at smaller games being simpler souls.
> I am of the latter brand; all I want to do
> Is to find a spot of land, and live there with you.
> > Some day
> > We'll build a home on a hill top high, you and I,
> > Shiny and new
> > A cottage that two can fill.
> > And we'll be pleased to be called
> > "The folks who live on the hill."
> > Some day
> > We may be adding a thing or two, a wing or two,

---

* Oscar always found it a great help and timesaver to use a rhyming dictionary. His choice was *Loring's Rhymers Lexicon,* now out of print. He believed, however, that this source should be used only as a supplement to one's own ingenuity, and not a substitute for it. Oscar did not open the book until he had exhausted his own memory and invention of rhymes, knowing that attractive combinations of words to make double and triple rhymes are not found in rhyming dictionaries—nor are modern words or colloquialisms which can be used with humorous effect in a song. "A rhyming dictionary is of little use and may, in fact, be a handicap when one is writing a song which makes a feature of rhyming. If you would achieve the rhyming grace of W.S. Gilbert or Lorenz Hart," Oscar's advice was "never to open a rhyming dictionary. Don't even own one!"

We will make changes as any fam'ly will,
But we will always be called
"The folks who live on the hill."
Our veranda will command a view of meadows green,
The sort of view that seems to want to be seen.
And when the kids grow up and leave us,
We'll sit and look at that same old view,
Just we two,
Darby and Joan who used to be Jack and Jill,
The folks who like to be called
What they have always been called
"The folks who live on the hill."

When *High, Wide and Handsome* was released, it was acclaimed by New York film critics as "the best show in town," "magnificent entertainment," a "spectacular musical film which departs refreshingly from the banal pretty-pretty tradition of the films with music." Howard Barnes said it was a show best described by the adjectives of its title, and Gould Cassall said, "It sets its story against an authentic American background without ever cheapening that background, its history or its people."

Abel Green, *Variety*'s editor, sounded a practical, pessimistic note about the film's chances of recouping the high production costs, and proved to be correct. Paramount took New York's Astor Theatre and Los Angeles' Cathay Circle Theatre for expensive, reserved-seat, two-showings-a-day performances. Both theaters withdrew the attraction after six weeks, and Green noted: "It was a big mistake to have road-shown this high cost feature."

The night the film was first sneak-previewed Adolph Zukor walked across the polished floor of the Riviera Country Club in Hollywood to wring Oscar's hand and say, "That's the greatest picture we ever made!" A few months later, with the picture's road-show exhibition backfiring and producing less revenue than expected, Zukor walked past Oscar in a restaurant and stared through him as though he had never seen him before in his life.

Paramount did not renew his contract. Oscar moved to Columbia Pictures, often referred to as "that B picture studio on Gower Street." The lady with the torch was not noted for her musicals then, and in 1937 the studio produced only two, one of which was *When You're in Love*, which Jerry had written with Dorothy Fields. He did very little in his eight months at the studio. When William Perlberg asked him for his opinion of a script, Oscar warned him, "You may be falling into something which has a very limited chance of success," and referred to one scene as "so exactly like the scene in *One Night of Love* [Columbia 1934] that the least sophisticated member in any audience is sure to recognize it, label it a cheap imitation of the real thing, and immediately lose respect for the whole picture."

Oscar's only contribution at Columbia was the title song for a film starring Grace Moore and Melvyn Douglas. The lyric, written as a favor to producer Everett Riskin and Ben Oakland, was one of a very few that Oscar ever wrote simply as a song, not as part of an entire score. This song, unrelated to anything in the film except the words of the picture's title, was sung no less than three times within the movie, and went on to become a standard. The song: "I'll Take Romance."

Having second thoughts about his decision the year before to stick solely with movies, he began to talk to Max Gordon about some Broadway projects. Max was acting as consultant to RKO Pictures but remained an important Broadway producer. Originally a friend of Willie Hammerstein's, he and Oscar had been friends for years. Max had tried to get Oscar for *Roberta* and other shows, and now he wanted him, as well as Jerry, to join forces with him in producing for Broadway. Oscar agreed to do so, but still could not bring himself to leave Hollywood altogether. Max wrote to him in February 1937, "I believe as you do that you ought to be [in California] for six months of the year to protect families that are dependent on you. Of course, if we should come out with one of those knock-outs, you might be able to cut this down to three months and then finally cut it out altogether."

In March, Oscar and Dorothy went to London to scout properties. Through Louis Dreyfus he met and signed Gerald Savory, a young English actor who had written West End's current hit comedy, *George and Margaret*, to write an original book for a musical that he and Jerry would do on Broadway the next season.

After they had been in London for three weeks, Oscar returned after a matinée to their suite at the Berkeley to find a cablegram: DEAREST OSCAR JERRY GRAVELY ILL STOP HAD A MASSIVE CORONARY STOP WE NEED YOU PLEASE COME HOME SOON LOVE EVA.

The Hammersteins hastily made travel arrangements and left London for a long vigil that would consume most of Oscar's time and thoughts for months. Jerry's coronary attack was very severe. After three weeks, he suffered an embolism and was said to have "died" for a brief time. He could not be moved from his home and his condition remained extremely critical. The household tensely awaited some sign of recovery. After a few weeks it became apparent that he would pull through, but now the problem was to make the energetic Jerry stay in bed while he recuperated. Oscar was the only person outside the family who was allowed to see him, and he was told by Jerry's doctors not to discuss anything connected with work for six weeks. He would convey to Jerry the good wishes of friends and keep them posted on Jerry's progress. It was not until May 10 that Jerry was even allowed to sit up for a few minutes each day.

Fortunately, three months before the attack the Kerns had moved from the Beverly Wilshire Hotel to a large stucco house that they built at 917 Whittier Drive in Beverly Hills, so Jerry's months of confinement could be spent in his own home. The ambiance of the house was exactly like that of the Kerns' home in Bronxville. Jerry had supervised the decoration of the house, which was filled with the fine antique furniture, silver and china that he had been collecting for years. While working on *High, Wide and Handsome*, Oscar had complained to Jerry about working at a desk, which he found uncomfortable and confining. Jerry gave him a Victorian traveling desk which Dorothy mounted on legs tall enough for him to work standing up. Oscar used the desk for the rest of his life.

Although Jerry was allowed to return to the studio in July, there was still concern about how this intense and energetic man would adjust to life after a heart attack. When George Gershwin died of a brain tumor at Cedars of Lebanon Hospital on July 11, 1937, no one wanted to tell Jerry or to let him see the newspapers for fear of a relapse. The following day Jerry turned on his radio and heard Gershwin tunes being played on every station. He said, "George is dead, isn't he?"

Gershwin's early death saddened everyone who knew the man and his work. Oscar was asked to write a eulogy for the service in Hollywood which took place simultaneously with the funeral at Temple Emanu-El in New York. Oscar's long eulogy was read by actor Edward G. Robinson.

His contract with Columbia finished, in the fall Oscar worked on one picture at Metro and one at RKO. The making of MGM's *The Great Waltz*, a biographical film about Johann Strauss II, was marked by misunderstanding, strife and rancor. Eminent French director Julien

Duvivier arrived from France equipped with only a few words of English and little desire to learn more. So polylingual was the atmosphere that an assistant director appeared on the set with a sign on his back bearing the legend "English Spoken Here." When Duvivier fled, Victor Fleming did what he could to shape the picture into something presentable. When writer Gottfried Reinhardt was discussing the casting with the producer, Bernie Hyman, he brought a recording of Meliza Korjus singing a Mozart aria. Hyman was transported. "We'll put that in the picture," he said. To Reinhardt's protest that since the aria was by Mozart and the film was about Strauss, they couldn't use the song, Hyman said, "Who the hell is going to stop me?"

Oscar's lyrics to Dmitri Tiomkin's adaptation of Strauss's melodies were as banal and uninspired as the rest of the proceedings.

His next project was to write a screenplay for RKO, adapting two stories by Irene Castle about her husband, Vernon, for a Pandro Berman film to star Fred Astaire and Ginger Rogers. The Castles, who had been responsible for the phenomenal growth of ballroom dancing in their brief period of fame, had played the Victoria frequently and become good friends of Willie Hammerstein and Lew Fields. As he worked Oscar talked to Lew in order to bring authenticity and color to the screenplay, which ended with Vernon Castle's death, not the usual Astaire-Rogers finale. Oscar wrote to a friend, "I like it very much but then I always like them before some director gets hold of them and puts them on the screen in his own individual way." *Castles in the Air* remained on the shelf, going through numerous changes after Oscar turned in his completed screenplay in December 1937. The title was changed a couple of times, other writers were brought in, Berman lost interest and Irene Castle hated the idea of being portrayed by Ginger Rogers. The movie was eventually made and released in 1939 to mixed reviews. *The Story of Vernon and Irene Castle* marked the end of the Astaire-Rogers cycle of films. It marked an end for Oscar, too. He would not write another screenplay for many years.

In January 1938 he began to work on a musical play about West Point with Jerry and Otto Harbach, and committed himself to several other productions with Larry Schwab. Reporting to a friend, Oscar wrote: "Writing a play again makes me very homesick for the theatre and makes me realize again the futility of trying to get the same gratification out of screen writing."

Many of the powers-that-be in Hollywood had soured on Oscar as much as he had soured on them. Whereas the mention of his name had brought a respectful silence to the MGM writers' table in 1935, now in offices and conference rooms it brought an embarrassed silence. To some, Oscar was "the kiss of death," despite *Show Boat* and *High, Wide and Handsome.* A widely quoted remark of the time was: "Oscar is a dear friend but he can't write his hat." One night Lew Gensler came into a party at the Schwabs to find Oscar alone in the den. "Hi, Oc. Where is everybody?" he called out.

"Maybe they heard I was coming," replied Oscar.

Oscar later said that he "just didn't fit in" in Hollywood. He thought that writing for a weekly salary, with an obligation to produce something each week, was not the way he worked best, and in point of fact his best work had been done when he worked for many months and even years on a libretto and lyrics; his worst, even on Broadway, when he had rushed and spread himself too thin. In addition, in films, the words he wrote were neither his property nor his direct responsibility. The producer who bought them could do what he wanted with them and usually did. In the theater, Oscar felt, the words were his "child" and were directed immediately to the audience. Whether the public liked them or not, came to see the show or did not, was the direct responsibility of the creator of the show and would directly determine his fortunes. Writing the Hollywood way was more secure, bringing a high weekly salary with it, but for Oscar the work produced was not likely to be good.

In retrospect it is clear that the nature of film-making and the stage of evolution of the original screen musical in the thirties offered no opportunity for Oscar to contribute his best creative efforts. Oscar's skill lay not in isolated lyrics and dialogue, but in the conception and execution of an organic musical.

By April 1938 he knew that Hollywood was not for him, and was working on four legitimate shows, but with Dorothy's business thriving in California, it was difficult to leave. He wrote Reinheimer that even moving East for the summer "would mean a summary shutting down of Dorothy's business for six consecutive months which would be equivalent to shutting it down for good. This doesn't seem fair to her nor does it seem wholly wise since it is being operated on a profit." He told his lawyer that he realized this was essentially a "personal and domestic question of mine," and he struggled with the problem without mentioning it to Dorothy.

One night, two weeks later, Oscar and Dorothy returned home from a dinner party at the Knopfs'. Dorothy was quiet as she sat at her dressing table. Suddenly she said, "You know, Ockie, it's better to wear out than to rust out and we're rusting out."

Oscar hurried from the bedroom. Dorothy stood with her eyes closed, afraid that her words had hurt him deeply. A few minutes later he came back into the room and said, "Did you mean that?"

"Yes, I did."

"Then let's get the hell out—tomorrow."

Leaving "tomorrow" would actually take months, but the Hammersteins immediately began their preparations. Dorothy's assistant, Louis Bowen, agreed to help her set up the business in New York. Oscar arranged to produce several shows, two with Larry Schwab and two by himself, and to write one with Jerry and Otto Harbach. "I am coming back to the Broadway stage this season in a big way," he wrote to Louis Dreyfus. The Broadway he was returning to looked much healthier than it had for years. *Variety* reported 187 new plays, many of them musicals, and "Hollywood scripters back on the boards."

Oscar went to New York in April to attend shows and "absorb again the feeling of the pace and the people." His confidence and optimism were high as he plunged into his projects. The first, *Gentlemen Unafraid*, would renew the Kern-Hammerstein-Harbach team for the first time since *Sunny* in 1925. A story about Southern cadets at West Point torn between their loyalty to the South and their duty to the North during the Civil War, the musical was to be performed in celebration of the twentieth anniversary of the St. Louis Municipal Opera Association in June before a fall opening in New York.

One day as Oscar, Jerry and Harbach were working on *Gentlemen Unafraid* in the Benedict Canyon house, Larry Schwab phoned to ask if he could bring over a young girl to audition for a part.

"What's she done?" replied Oscar.

"Nothing, really," answered Larry. "She's been teaching dance at Franchon and Marco studios . . . but I caught her act the other night at the Little Troc and she's got one helluva voice!"

"In that case, sure, bring her over," Oscar said. "Oh, by the way —what's her name?"

"Mary Martin. But for Christ's sake, don't let on who you are or do any introducing when we come over or she'll be a basket case!"

"Don't worry," Oscar said, and hung up.

Mary Martin, from Weatherford, Texas, was twenty-five then,

and had been in Hollywood for several months but had never been to Beverly Hills. "I wasn't prepared for such grandeur, such taste," she remembered. "I was ushered into the drawing room where a lady and several gentlemen were having tea. The lady was elegant, attractive, cool, the personification of everything I ever dreamed of in a Noël Coward movie. The gentlemen were gentlemen."

Larry took Mary straight to the piano, without introducing Dorothy, Oscar or the others. Determined to give them a sample of everything she could do, Mary began with a fast rhythm number, sang a ballad, and then a low "Oh, Rock It for Me." Finally, she announced to her small audience that she would like to sing a semi-classical song. "You probably don't know it. It's called 'Indian Love Call.'"

When she had finished her last "You-oo-oo-oo-oo-oo-oo" there was a polite murmur. A "tall, craggy man who looked like a mountain" walked Mary to the door and thanked her for coming. He said: "Young lady, I think you have something. I would like to work with you, on lines and phrasing, if you could come to my house every day."

Mary said, "Oh, yes, yes, yes, thank you."

And then with that "twinkle in his eyes" that she learned to know so well, he added, "Oh, and by the way, I did know that song. I wrote it."

Oscar kept his word and worked with Mary. Within days of their first meeting he arranged for her to sing for Jerry and Richard Berger, who was in charge of the St. Louis operation. Mary's first impression of Jerry was that he was simply "adorable. The tiniest, most birdlike man I ever met. He was like a spirit, like a bird 'one day old,' as Sir James Barrie once described his own creation, Peter Pan."

Oscar had rented a studio for the audition. Mary was going through the process of having her teeth capped and she arrived straight from the dentist who had put temporary caps in that day. As she danced, putting her all into it with strenuous leaps and turns, suddenly a cap flew out of her mouth and landed on Oscar's thigh before bouncing to the floor. Oscar was so embarrassed that he sat perfectly still, not knowing what to do. Mary was upset, but she picked up the cap, put ·it back in her mouth and finished her dance.

Although Mary wasn't right for a role in the Hammerstein-Harbach-Kern show, Larry Schwab signed her to a 52-week contract, with a part in *Ring in the New*, a musical that he and Oscar were writing, and sent her to New York.

* * *

In late April Oscar came down with a severe case of bronchial pneumonia, with a high fever and constant coughing. The doctors ordered bed rest and then a few weeks in the desert air before resuming work. This was one of the few illnesses of Oscar's adult life.

Although Oscar's health had generally been good, he was troubled by a bad back, to the extent that in his thirties he had been forced to wear braces. Later, after his marriage to Dorothy, he began using a chiropractic masseur whom Dorothy had recommended—Peter Moën, the husband of Dorothy's masseuse. (Peter became a household fixture; besides being Oscar's masseur, he was also chauffeur and general helper.) Oscar established a regimen that he would follow for the rest of his life. Each morning he arose at six, took a swim whenever possible, or a bath, and received an hour-long massage from Peter.

Except in athletics, Oscar approached physical tasks cautiously and reluctantly. He never picked up a tool; he took no part in the physical maintenance of his home. He did not mind being looked after and found it easy to ask servants or family for a physical service. Once, when the children were older, as the family was eating and no servants were around, Oscar said, "I want a glass of water." No one moved. He got up from the table and headed toward the kitchen, whereupon the whole family burst into applause.

When Oscar was allowed out of bed after his bout with bronchial pneumonia, he went to Phoenix, where he could combine his recuperation with working on a future Broadway project with Larry Schwab. Soon after he and Dorothy arrived back at Benedict Canyon, scarlet fever struck Jimmy, Susan and Sarah Titchmarsh, the maid, and they were quarantined.

When the patients recovered and the quarantine was lifted, Oscar left almost immediately for St. Louis, where he would cast and rehearse *Gentlemen Unafraid*. Before his departure he had several long talks with Billy. Oscar's heart-to-heart talks with his children behind closed doors in his study were sometimes lightly referred to by Dorothy as "pulling that Lord-Chesterfield's-letters-to-his-son-business." This time there were serious matters of concern about Billy, who had left high school without completing his final year. In the course of his mother's frequent moves, he had attended many schools and liked few of them. He was now floundering, uncertain of his future direction.

Billy had always been interested in show business; he had typed scripts for Oscar, composed songs and hung around his father's shows or movie studios since he was a young boy. Now Oscar, unlike his own father who had made him promise to stay out of the theater, made arrangements for his son to enter the profession. Dick Berger readily agreed to hire Billy as fourth assistant stage manager and general all-around helper for that summer's stock season in St. Louis. Oscar felt that working on the weekly productions would give him the equivalent of two years of theatrical experience and a good idea of what the theater was all about. Billy was delighted and enthusiastic as he went off to St. Louis.

The one-week run of *Gentlemen Unafraid* in St. Louis made it clear that the production had a background that was interesting to the audience, an exceptionally strong score and a good comedy subplot that held up well, but that it lacked an important element: a good love story.

Max Gordon, who had announced his intention of bringing the show to Broadway, convinced Oscar and Jerry to shelve it for the time being and start on something new. The show never reached New York; Oscar worked on the book from time to time, mainly out of loyalty to Harbach, who was keen on reviving it. Ultimately he abandoned it, but Harbach continued to work on the show almost until the day he died. (A production, under the title of *Hayfoot, Strawfoot*, was given at Syracuse University in 1942, and it has been performed by several colleges since.)

One song, "Your Dream (Is the Same as My Dream)" was interpolated into the film *One Night in the Tropics* (Universal, 1940) which had a Kern-Fields score. Another, "Abe Lincoln Had Just One Country," was endorsed during World War II by Henry Morgenthau, Jr., Secretary of the Treasury, on behalf of the United States and used to promote defense bonds and stamps.

After their work on *Gentlemen Unafraid,* Jerry returned to Hollywood. He said that he loved to write for the stage "when there is a stage to write for" but that he felt the opportunities, the competition and the situation were still with the screen. As a composer, his work was subject to little change by others and so the film-making process had a minimum of frustrations for him. Oscar, on the other hand, was more hopeful about the theater and, with Larry Schwab, went into final preparations for their show *Knights of Song*.

Because Larry was under contract to MGM, it was Oscar who

signed to acquire the property initially. *Knights of Song*, a play that had been tested at the semiprofessional Pasadena Playhouse, was based on the historical fact that Gilbert and Sullivan did not get on well together. Too different in temperament to be genuine friends, working at arm's length, they could get along neither with each other nor without each other. Gilbert was an outspoken man with an explosive temper and a gift for cruel witticisms who continually quarreled with everyone; Sullivan was a sensitive and quiet man who suffered under his overbearing collaborator. Out of their discord came the comic operettas that managed to fuse onstage the temperamental differences which flung them apart offstage.

Interspersed in the plot of *Knights of Song* were several scenes from the operettas. Oscar and Schwab had rewritten Glendon Alvine's book during Oscar's recuperation in Phoenix. "It is not perfect yet, but it is much nearer to a professional legitimate effort than we bought." Now the author was haggling about the changes; Oscar told Reinheimer, "You may have to come out here and defend me against a charge of criminal assault."

Oscar left Hollywood in July to oversee a one-week tryout of *Knights of Song* in St. Louis, while Dorothy and the children drove East and settled once more in the Great Neck house. The show was rough, since it had had only ten days' preparation, but everyone felt that its problems could be easily ironed out before it opened in New York.

Oscar went to London to hire an expert in the D'Oyly Carte staging of Gilbert and Sullivan to act as a technical consultant for the Broadway production. Dorothy was not feeling well during the trip, and when they returned to New York, Harold Hyman told her that she had low blood pressure and also that she would have to lead a more restful life. She reluctantly decided not to reopen her business.

When Oscar moved East, Myra again followed. She took an apartment in New York and enrolled Alice in a private school for her senior year. Alice, who had attended Beverly Hills High School for three years and loved it, was distraught when she heard the news. "I'm not going back. I refuse," she said to her mother. Finally she agreed to return to New York, but only on the condition that she could live with Oscar and Dorothy and attend Great Neck High School. She moved into Kenilworth at the end of the summer. When Billy finished his job in St. Louis, he lived with his mother in Manhattan and worked with his father and his Uncle Reggie, who was production stage manager, on all of Oscar's fall attractions.

Oscar's first Broadway production of the 1938–1939 season was *Knights of Song* at the Fifty-first Street Theatre (now the Mark Hellinger) on October 17. Oscar had done additional rewriting and felt satisfied with the script. Despite the extensive revisions, the show opened "cold" in New York, without the usual out-of-town tryouts or local previews. The critics pointed out the many good things about the production and its appeal for Gilbert and Sullivan fans, but found the play sketchy, heavy-handed and loosely structured. Despite general agreement that the evening's entertainment was pleasant enough, the underpinnings were not strong and the show folded after two weeks.

Oscar hardly had time to feel disappointed as he proceeded with two more productions scheduled to open within weeks of each other in November. The first, *Where Do We Go from Here?*, was a little play about the efforts of some fraternity boys to save their fraternity house. The story of how the play was put together was in itself a minor saga of the cockiness and courage of ambitious youth. A twenty-two-year-old named William Bowers, working in Los Angeles as a ghost writer for a syndicated columnist, devoted his spare moments to writing a play, which he decided to produce at the cost of $708, an amount which he and his friends raised by pawning cameras and borrowing from families and friends. A young scenic designer who was also moonlighting as an actor agreed to design the set for $3.50, providing he received a part. All the cast members were enthusiastic amateurs who hoped for careers in show business. One of them was the nephew of Laurette Taylor, whose son Dwight, an established playwright, was invited to the opening night. Not only busy but suspicious of little-theater offerings, Taylor was reluctant but was finally persuaded to come. Taylor was surprised to find that his brash young cousin was a personable juvenile and that the little play had something appealing about it.

A few nights later Taylor dropped around with playwright Howard Lindsay, who shared his opinion and arranged for him to meet with Oscar, who Lindsay knew was on the lookout for Broadway properties. Oscar was immediately struck with the fresh vitality of the performance and agreed to produce it in New York that fall.

The Broadway production cost $12,000, a meager sum even for

those days. Oscar had no difficulty raising the capital and brought it into the Vanderbilt Theatre on November 15. The critics enjoyed the comedy of the "amiable frolic" and the deft characterizations of its attractive young cast, but found the play lacking in structure and substance. Said Brooks Atkinson: "To make it completely enjoyable, all they need is a play."

The play lasted only fifteen performances, but Bowers and the company were encouraged enough by both the critical and audience reception to try again even after the Broadway engagement ended. Oscar gladly turned over the production to the group of newcomers.* Bowers and five other diehards lived in two rooms on the Upper West Side to keep down expenses while they raised the capital needed for the Equity bond and theater rental. Eventually the play did open again at Orson Welles's Mercury Theatre. Although the story of Bowers' pluck is delightful, the play was another failure for Oscar.

Oscar's third production, *Glorious Morning*, opened on November 27, the night that *Where Do We Go from Here?* closed. When he saw the play by Norman Macowan, starring Jessica Tandy, in London, Oscar had promptly acquired the American rights. It is easy to see the play's appeal for him, aside from its successful West End run. The play was anti-Nazi and antitotalitarian in its theme. Set in a mythical kingdom ruled by a dictator, its Joan of Arc heroine and her followers are eventually sent before a firing squad because of their refusal to recant their belief in religious freedom.

Its theme was, ironically enough, part of the play's downfall on Broadway. Several reviewers pointed out that in those days of 1938, no play could even approach in dramatic quality the ugly reality of daily events in Europe. Hitler was destroying not only people's right to think but their right to live, making the play's impassioned plea for freedom of religion seem feeble and insignificant. In addition, the play appeared tedious and pedestrian, partly because of the script itself and partly because of Oscar's direction. Although one critic praised the staging as intelligent and sympathetic, others found it phlegmatic. The show was a disaster, grossing only $355 at the box office the first week, with only one seat sold in the orchestra on

---

* Those in the *Where Do We Go from Here?* company included Don DeFore, Ralph Holmes and Hugh Martin. The latter, a talented songwriter, along with Ralph Blane, composed for Broadway and Hollywood such songs as "The Trolley Song," "Have Yourself a Merry Little Christmas," "Love" and "Buckle Down Winsocki."

Friday night, though the Mansfield Theatre was partially filled with playgoers holding passes or cut-rate tickets. Oscar called it quits after nine performances.

In his brief career as a producer, Oscar had come up with one play that never arrived in New York and three that closed after twelve, eleven and seven nights, respectively. Obviously, optimism and enthusiasm were not enough. Oscar was discouraged by his poor record. Jerry Kern tried to comfort him with the thought that the years of "*dolce far niente*" in Hollywood had blunted the "old, acute sense of dramatic values for the stage," which a short time back in the theater would undoubtedly resharpen. Frank Mandel's analysis was that Oscar was too nice and gentle to be a producer, a role for which one needed to be a "bastard, to have any success and not get gypped." In both of his last productions, Oscar had let idealism get the better of his sound business judgment, in one instance for a theme that struck a deep response in his political and moral beliefs, in the other for a circumstance that appealed to his romantic love of the theater.

In addition, all four failed because, with all their good attributes, they each lacked a sound underlying structure. His failure to recognize this or to remedy it illuminates one of Oscar's weaknesses as a librettist. Time after time his libretti were strongest when adapted from another source in which the basic structure already existed, weakest when they were originals in which he had to build that structure.

With the resounding failure of his four producing ventures, Oscar plunged into writing again. Jerry wrote, "Your character and guts have been tested before . . . [and] these disappointments are not going to permanently shake your confidence or cause you to temper your artistic honesty or lower your standards." Whatever damage was done to his self-confidence, there was no hint of it in Oscar's actions or correspondence in the months that followed. In the best Hammerstein tradition, he did not dwell on the failures of the past, but looked with optimism to the future and kept busy. He had not decided definitely to give up producing and he pursued several possibilities. He worked on two musical projects with Jerry: *Golden Bells*, based on the Marco Polo novel; and another in collaboration with Alice Duer Miller. Romberg was also pressing to do a show with him in the next season, pointing out that Oscar had tried his luck with everyone but him, and that he had a hunch that this was a good time for them. Jerry also was more than enthusiastic about collaborating and in one of his weekly letters to Oscar on December 13, 1938, he wrote:

> The situation now is past the pleasant, joshing point, and you and I both have got to bang through with something powerful for the stage. We have both been much too long off the boards. While we naturally do not want to roll up on Broadway with just a show, I find the prospect very encouraging. Upon analysis, there was never a thoroughfare more naked of competitive traffic. When you think that only somewhat more than a handful of seasons ago plenty of entertainment was provided by Friml, Romberg, the Gershwins, Berlin, Youmans, Hirsch, us and the Europeans, not to mention the current limited group, the target for a bull's-eye has pretty good visibility.
>
> I am sorry to keep plucking at the same string, but my one and only objective is to dig up a musical play for Broadway for next season, and any by-pass must be sacrificed to that end.
>
> So let's get going, kid. Love to you and Dorothy a/k/a "the incurable decorator" from your little fat friend.

In March, newspapers carried the announcement of a new Kern-Hammerstein show, *Very Warm for May,* an intimate play with music, no chorus, a 28-member cast, and the mood, spirit and size of one of the Princess Theatre shows. Jerry had suggested that they use the character and adventures of Elisabeth Marbury, the Princess Theatre impresario. Born into an old, aristocratic New York family, she had rubbed elbows all her life with the most interesting people of her generation, not only in society but in the literary world and the theater. Oscar loved the idea and thought it lent itself well to one of his favorite themes: "the call of the theater."

Max Gordon was their choice as producer, though he had to remain in Hollywood throughout the preparation and, as it turned out, well into production, with Oscar acting as his New York liaison. George Kaufman wrote Gordon a caustic letter telling him he found it odd for a producer to be producing a show in New York while he remained in Hollywood, and Bernard Baruch warned him that he was doing too many things to do any of them well, but Gordon was optimistic that all would work out well. He wrote that he was pleased with Oscar's concept of keeping the show small, charming, romantic and funny, and added, "Now if you will only fix a capacity audience, there will be nothing left for you to do."

Vincente Minnelli asked to join the show in any capacity. Minnelli had designed sets and costumes and staged musical numbers for several Broadway shows; Gordon signed him as designer of scenery, costumes and lighting and stager of the production numbers, though Oscar was to direct the book and Albertina Rasch and Harry Losee the dances. From the outset the broth seemed to have too many cooks, and in Max Gordon an absentee chef.

Jerry and Max were anxious to open the show on the West Coast, play throughout the country and open in New York in the early spring. Oscar wrote to Jerry: "In other words, we are opening a play in the far west to prime it for the rigors of Lent, followed by a severe attack of Worldfairitis in May. If three experienced showmen ever thought of a screwier idea, I'd like to know what it is . . . Why in the hell are we sneaking in the back door? Why don't we rehearse, open in Philadelphia October 10 and in New York October 24, like a couple of grown men? Or are we mice?" Jerry agreed that his plan was "impracticable, unworkable, and ridiculous" and they convinced Gordon that the show should open in the usual way.

Oscar went to California in July to work with Jerry, staying at Norma Talmadge's ocean-front house in Santa Monica. One evening Oscar was pacing up and down on the beach, trying to get an idea for a song that would fit into the show, when his attention was caught by a pair of lovers. It was a moonlit night and he could see other couples on the sand, but he found this pair especially interesting. Both white-haired, they walked with arms entwined, gazing out over the Pacific with peace and contentment in their eyes. Oscar tried to concentrate on his lyric, but could not stop looking at the two until they rose and walked away, hand in hand. When they had gone, Oscar knew that the tribute he wished to pay these strangers would not fit into the show and that he had no time to waste, but he felt he couldn't proceed with his work until he had written some recognition of the pleasure they had given him. Using a melody Jerry had written in 1927 for *Show Boat* but discarded during the out-of-town tryouts, he wrote the lyric called "Sweetest Sight That I Have Seen," which ended with the following lines:

> I have seen a line of snow-white birds
> Drawn across an evening sky.
> I have seen divine, unspoken words
> Shining in a lover's eye.
> I have seen moonlight on a mountaintop,
> Silver and cool and still.

> I have heard church bells faintly echoing
> Over a distant hill.
> Close enough to beauty I have seen,
> And, in all the whole wide land,
> Here's the sweetest sight that I have seen—
> One old couple walking hand in hand.

The next day he went to Jerry's house, confessed his crime and produced the unusable lyric. Jerry fell in love with it and they worked on the song that day. By evening, the compulsion out of the way, Oscar returned to the work at hand.

One of the songs for *Very Warm for May* became one of their most popular hits: "All the Things You Are." "It was the most surprising hit Jerry and I ever had," Oscar said. "We never thought the public would take it; it had three changes of key in the middle of the refrain, which is a very risky thing to do." One word in the lyric gave Oscar a great deal of trouble. He felt the word "divine" hackneyed and trite because of its overuse in lyrics; he always tried to avoid using it. He didn't like the word when he submitted the song to Jerry and, as he had anticipated, Jerry didn't, either. For days Oscar worked on it, trying to find a substitute in the last lines of the song:

> Someday I'll know that moment divine
> When all the things you are, are mine.

He was trapped. The last line was just what he wished to say and he could not surrender the finish, but it demanded an "ine" rhyme. Oscar never could find a way out and, pleased as he was with the song and its popularity, he was never happy with that word.

Another song in the show—"All in Fun"—indicates that while Oscar was not a "sophisticated" lyricist like Cole Porter or Larry Hart, when a plot situation called for a jaded note, he could write effectively in that vein:

> We are seen around New York
> "El Morocco" and "The Stork"
> And the other stay-up-late cafes,
> I am on the town with you these days
> That's the way it stands.
> Just a fellow and a girl,
> We have had a little whirl,
> And our feet have left the ground a bit.
> We've played around a bit,

That's the way it stands
For we are strictly good-time Charlies
Who like to drink and dance around
And maybe kick romance around
And that's the way it stands.
  All in fun,
  This thing is all in fun,
  When all is said and done
  How far can it go? . . .

They returned to New York to complete casting * and begin rehearsals in September 1939, with the first tryout scheduled for Wilmington on October 20. *Very Warm for May* was a different kind of show for Oscar and Jerry. It was integrated, to be sure, but it was much lighter than anything they had done before. There were no major themes, no heavy characters or glimpses of the deeper struggles of life. It was a gay and light-hearted musical comedy, the kind of youthful romp that was proving popular with the public of the late thirties.†

As the libretto was originally conceived, seventeen-year-old May (Grace McDonald) returns from school to her home in Oyster Bay to find her father (Donald Brian) in heavy debt to gambling gangsters, who plan to use May in their scheme to kidnap one of her rich beaus. May escapes in a motorboat and hides, across the Sound, in a barn on the estate of eccentric Winnie Spofford (Eve Arden) which is being used by her son (Richard Quine), her daughter Liz (Frances Mercer) and Liz's pretentious avant-garde theatrical boyfriend Ogdon [*sic*] Quiller (Hiram "Chubby" Sherman) to produce a surrealistic opus with Quiller's progressive workshop players. The play becomes a satirical spoof of avant-garde theatrics as Quiller postures his way through rehearsals of his bizarre production, the highpoint of which is a narrated ballet entitled "The Strange Case of Adam Standish or Psycho-Analysis Strikes Back," in which Quiller describes his emotional states as dancers representing various parts of the brain act out what is going

---

* Among the youthful cast that subsequently garnered long careers on both stage and screen were Richard Quine, Vera-Ellen, Max Showalter, June Allyson, Avon Long, Billie Worth, Don Loper and Helena Bliss.

† On October 11, NBC scheduled a live telecast of a *Very Warm for May* rehearsal, in what the station said would be the first specific instance of sustained cooperation between the theater and television. Actors Equity, however, stepped in—a television union had not yet been formed—demanding one full week's salary for each performer, thus causing the program to be canceled.

on in his head. A Broadway director, Johnny Graham (Jack Whiting), arrives at the barn in time to save the show—amid love affairs, kidnappings, the arrival of the gangsters and the police, and the reunion of the dotty Mrs. Spofford and her old boyfriend, none other than May's father. The dialogue was fast and witty, the whole infused with a screwball charm that delighted Wilmington audiences, who gave the "triumphant birth" of the show long and loud applause, stopping the show after every number and demanding encores. The *Morning News* critic reported that the audience was "wild with enthusiasm" and predicted that the show, which sparkled with youth, verve and gaiety, would be a big hit; *Variety's* critic reported that it looked like a box-office "click."

The production moved on for a week in Washington where the reaction was the same. In Philadelphia, too, the show provided some of the "loudest laughter and most earsplitting applause heard in years." The play's Boston opening on November 6 prompted critic Elliot Norton to predict that "all points to the fact that the show, a gay and joyous thing now, will be rounded into surefire hit form before its impending Broadway debut."

Between the end of the Boston engagement and the opening night in New York six days later, something happened to *Very Warm for May*. Max Gordon had reappeared on the scene, and he and Minnelli became convinced that the show had to have drastic revisions in order to be "commercially successful." Gordon brought in Hassard Short as consultant. The book was completely rewritten, the gangster plot removed entirely, and along with it an element of fantasy upon which the tone and humor of the play depended. The character of Quiller was so toned down that the satirical element was eliminated and the preposterous, posturing figure became an inexperienced but sympathetic young man. The dialogue was emasculated in the hasty rewrite, losing its wit and verve. The new script showed a tightness that the first version had lacked, but removed the wacky charm of the original without offering any substantially stronger structure. Russell Bennett, the orchestrator of the show, called *Very Warm for May* a "great show that was produced into a failure."

Oscar did not fight for his original conception. It is not difficult to see how he allowed the show to be butchered. Under the stress of pre-Broadway, it is always hard to see a show in perspective A solid phalanx of experienced showmen—the producer and two directors— were convinced that drastic revisions were necessary. In addition, Oscar had been feeling unsure throughout the production. Neither original structuring of plot nor this genre of light, modern musical comedy was his forte. His recent flops and Jerry's long absence from Broadway added to his lack of self-confidence. He wanted a hit badly and was no longer certain that he could write one.

In *Very Warm for May* Oscar had chosen to go for the current "formula." It could never have been an enduring success like *Show Boat* because it did not draw on the deepest part of Oscar's talent. However, though flawed, what he had written was charming and entertaining.

The badly doctored show opened at the Alvin Theatre on November 17, 1939. Oscar and Dorothy had taken a suite at the Weylin Hotel for the opening. The next morning Oscar put on his overcoat over his pajamas and went down to the lobby newsstand to get the papers. When he got back to the room, Dorothy asked, "How are they, Ockie?"

"The worst notices I've ever had in my life!" he said. They dressed and went to an early movie at Radio City Music Hall. The movie didn't provide the diversion that the Hammersteins were looking for, since it was *Babes in Arms*, the Rodgers and Hart hit musical starring Judy Garland and Mickey Rooney, which, unfortunately, was about youngsters making a success in a "summer stock" venture.

"VERY WARM FOR MAY: NOT SO HOT FOR NOVEMBER." The reviews were indeed unfavorable, with only a few exceptions, and the contrast to the out-of-town notices was striking. Richard Watts called the book "excessively tedious and humorless" and the "potentially effective show" disappointing. Atkinson noted, "The book is a singularly haphazard invention that throws the whole show out of focus and makes an appreciation of Mr. Kern's music almost a challenge. . . . There has seldom been a book that fought entertainment as successfully as the story of this musical play." Ironically enough, Oscar, who had so often been ignored as a librettist, now received full credit. Said Richard Lockridge: "Never, I think, have elements so promising been tangled more hopelessly in the barbed wire of a thoroughly exasperating plot. It is not a plot which can be ignored or forgotten. Oscar Hammerstein II, who devised it, has seen to that . . ."

While it is often true that out-of-town success will fail on Broadway, and vice versa, an examination of the two scripts for *Very Warm for May* shows that this failure was due not to the more exacting taste and standards of New York but to a doctoring that could be called malpractice. The New York critics were right in finding the show dull and routine. A very few liked the show. Robert Benchley in *The New Yorker* gave it a rave review that makes one wonder if he didn't see it out of town. John Anderson of the *Journal-American* liked it too, and defended the play in a later column by contending that the drama critics who had come to review musicals were, by training and nature, so prone to pay undue attention to plot that they tended to overlook more important elements in a musical and condemn a show totally if the book was weak.

Oscar took exception to Anderson's piece, writing in a letter which Anderson printed that "the book *does* matter." After a long plea for the importance of the book, he concluded, "I am completely positive of this principle only because I have been kicked in the pants so hard every time I disobeyed it." He always took the responsibility for *Very Warm for May*'s failure and attributed it to the weakness of the play's structure. Borrowing a metaphor from his mentor, Otto, he said, "We had all the logs with which to build the fire but they were never properly piled on top of each other, nor the kindling properly placed. So the thing never took spark."

Max Gordon was as devastated as anyone by the show's reception; "To have been so wrong seemed impossible," he later said. Oscar urged him to close the show but he refused. He finally closed it after fifty-nine performances. Gordon suffered not only the financial setback which followed a long string of failures, but also the pain of self-recrimination as he thought of Baruch's warning, Kaufman's taunt and his own sense of guilt for not having been on the scene from the outset. In his memoirs Gordon recalls that he felt his world "slowly and surely blowing up." Haunted by the memory of a previous nervous breakdown, he entered Leroy Sanitarium. Out of the sanitarium, he went for long walks with Oscar in Central Park. As they walked they discussed the theater and the future. On bad days, when Gordon's old fears and doubts would reappear, Oscar, "quick and sensitive to these moods," Gordon recalls, would reassure him. He talked of future triumphs, assured Gordon that past successes had not been due to luck but to ability and judgment. "You haven't lost them, Max," said Oscar. "You'll come back bigger and better than ever."

Oscar's optimistic encouragement of Max Gordon was in marked contrast to the discouragement that he was feeling about his own future and about his own ability and judgment after the failure of

Very Warm for May There is no evidence to suggest that he was going through an emotional crisis of the sort that Gordon was facing, but he was feeling pessimistic about his own career. It had been a long time since he had had a real hit, and though he was mature and experienced enough to know that no one could expect constant success, his record of failure was now looking ominous. He thought, Things aren't working out. This is just too many failures. He could cope with failure; he was getting to be an old hand at it, in fact. But what of his financial responsibilities and his obligation to be realistic about the future? A letter from Romberg, who had been hounding Oscar for months to do a musical together, shows that Oscar was bitter and had some thoughts of giving up writing entirely.

December 8th, 1939

Dear Oscar:

I received your letter of the 3rd, and . . . your letter made me very sad. Feeling as close to you as I do, I am going to use very plain language, so please forgive me in advance, if I seem to offend you in any way. . . .

Being hounded by critics isn't original with you Oscar. Most writers, and very few exceptions, were hounded by the critics to the point of destruction . . . Nature gives a writer something with which to withstand such blows. One throws it off—and we continue. I beg of you, never expect life to be the way you want it, but come to the realisation that in this rotten world, filled with lousy stinking people, you have to take the other man as he is—and not the way you want him to be.

Of course, the decision as to what you want to do in the future naturally rests with you, and I won't even try to influence you. However, since last summer I have been dreaming of beginning working with you, and waiting patiently for you to get finished with Jerry so that we could get started. . . .

I am not trying to throw bouquets or compliments at you Oscar, but I do have a very soft spot in my heart for you, and somehow or other have the feeling that not only do we understand each other thoroughly, but you have a knack for bringing out my best qualities, and I am vain enough to feel that perhaps I have the same influence on you. After all, our plan and our plot was so very different from what you did with Jerry—so entirely different, but that of course, is all a dream of the past now.

I am getting a little choked up Oscar, and don't intend making this letter too long, and perhaps give you the impression that I am getting "mushy." I know exactly how you feel and honor your decision. I have often felt that way myself, but if you are right, I assure you Oscar, that some of our greatest works by some of our greatest authors and composers would not have been written—if they had allowed themselves to give in and listened too much to criticism. Your statement about the fact that there is never any credit for the man who writes a musical show is an old theory, overexploited in so many versions that it is now wearing a long white beard. Of course you are wrong in your assumption that people will not remember that you write such hits like "Show Boat," "Desert Song," "New Moon" and any of those other shows— but I guess you are in the frame of mind at the present time where no matter what I say will have any effect on you—so I am not even trying to say it.

I'll close now, and just want to tell you that I still love you, and as a parting shot, I'll just tell you one thing more. Out of one hundred outstanding authors, writing dramatic plays, I don't think you'll find three who have the knowledge—the feeling and the sentiment to know how to write a book in which music is supposed to be interwoven with the action. You are one of those few, and that's where the "rub" comes in.

With my love to Dorothy and yourself, in which Lillian joins me,

As ever,

Rommy

As Oscar's career looked more and more dismal, Dorothy's, by contrast, began to flourish anew. When the Hammersteins were vacationing in Florida, Norma Talmadge asked Dorothy to give her house there "your special sparkle" for a large party she had planned. Dorothy was delighted. She had been professionally "retired" for over a year, though she had kept active in the field by doing a little refurbishing for the Harbachs' home in Mamaroneck and a complete redecoration of the Hammerstein's own house which left Oscar sputtering. "Every time I pick up a pad and pencil I find a carpenter or painter underneath it," he complained to Dorothy one day. "I'll have to go into the Stone Room."

"No, I wouldn't do that, Ockie. The men begin in there today."

She had missed her business life and the "decorating disease" was still with her. Shortly after their return from Florida, Dorothy had lunch with Sophie Biow and a friend of hers, Mrs. Herbert Sondheim. Sophie, a very good friend and an enthusiastic booster of her talent, was so persuasive that Mrs. Sondheim (known as Foxy) asked

Dorothy to come back with her to the apartment on Central Park West which she, her husband and her young son Stephen had recently moved into. Foxy entertained frequently and wanted to make her apartment as attractive as possible. She asked Dorothy to take on the job.

After discussing the offer with Oscar, Dorothy agreed to do it, called Louis Bowen, and within a few days had rented a brownstone apartment at 126 East 61st Street. She began to acquire many East Coast clients, and soon her business was thriving in New York as it had in Beverly Hills. It was not a cheerful situation for Oscar. He was happy for her, but couldn't help comparing her success with his own failure. When she was being congratulated for one job or another, he would occasionally make a snide comment, such as "I could have done it cheaper."

During the Florida vacation that led to Dorothy's return to decorating, staying with Arthur in Palm Beach, Oscar saw his cousin Clarence Obendorf, a noted psychiatrist and author, and his sister Beatrice Keyser, the children of Augusta, Oscar I's sister. Beatrice had a fund of stories about Oscar's grandparents she had heard from her own mother, who was a gifted storyteller. Oscar became fascinated once again with his colorful grandfather. He did a good deal of research and several months later sent MGM a 78-page treatment, *Romance with Music,* about the life of Oscar Hammerstein I. He stipulated that he would not sell the property unless he was contracted to write the screenplay. Metro bought the film rights and assigned the project to Arthur Freed, but the movie was never made. Oscar told Freed that in Freed's version, his grandfather had turned out to be a combination of Ronald Colman, Boris Karloff, Edward G. Robinson and Mickey Rooney.

Christmas was not a very happy time that year. Mousie had died two days before and Oscar made all the arrangements for her funeral, keenly feeling the loss of this unique woman who had meant so much to him since his earliest childhood.

It was a help to Oscar's flagging spirits that "All the Things You Are" began to be played with increasing frequency on the radio (Alice reported from her University of Chicago dormitory that sometimes it was as often as three times in half an hour—her friends knocked on her door each time to inform her that it was on), and became the number one song on the Hit Parade for many weeks. The song boosted not only Oscar's ego but his ASCAP income, which now averaged about $25,000 per year.

Whatever the sentiments he had expressed to Rommy in early December, Oscar was negotiating in February to do a show for the World's Fair Corporation, which, despite a financially unprofitable first season, was going to gamble on a second season because of steadily increasing public interest. A 45-minute version of *Show Boat* was originally proposed, but Jerry and Oscar objected to such a presentation. Oscar decided to collaborate with Arthur Schwartz on an original show for the Fair which would consist of a series of events in American history. The show was called *American Jubilee*. One number, "My Bicycle Girl," set in New York at the turn of the century, had twenty-four girls riding bicycles on the stage—the notion that had sparked *Sweet Adeline*, but had proved too difficult to stage in a regular theater. The Hammerstein-Schwartz score was in keeping with the pageant, but none of the songs gained individual popularity.

With *American Jubilee* finished, Oscar began to work on an operetta, *Sunny River*, with Romberg, making sixteen trips to California during the months of preparation. When on June 14, 1940, Paris fell to the Germans, he was so deeply saddened that he found himself unable to work on the show. He walked along the shore in Great Neck, brooding over the news. Try as he might to work, he found that his mind was too crowded with remembrances of the wonderful city he had visited so many times. The first time he saw Paris was when he was a boy, staying at the Grand Hotel with his family while Willie looked over vaudeville acts. He remembered the huge bolsters on beds so high that getting into them was an athletic feat. The next time he saw Paris he was seventeen, promenading the boulevards, sitting at sidewalk cafés, fleeing one in confusion when a pretty girl smiled at him. He pictured the city as it was the last time he was there—the clamor of taxicab horns, the gaiety and beauty and romance of the streets.

Fearing that perhaps all this was never to be again, he thought of those months in 1925 when he had lived in a little apartment near the Arc de Triomphe and began to write a love song to a city he loved which was also a lament.

> A lady known as Paris,
> Romantic and charming,
> Has left her old companions and faded from view.
> Lonely men with lonely eyes are seeking her in vain,
> Her streets are where they were,

But there's no sign of her
She has left the Seine . . .

> The last time I saw Paris
> Her heart was warm and gay.
> I heard the laughter of her heart in ev'ry street cafe.
> The last time I saw Paris,
> Her trees were dressed for Spring
> And lovers walked beneath those trees
> And birds found songs to sing.
> I dodged the same old taxicabs that I had dodged for years
> The chorus of their squeaky horns was music to my ears.
> The last time I saw Paris
> Her heart was warm and gay
> No matter how they change her I'll remember her that way.

I'll think of happy hours,
And people who shared them:
Old women selling flowers in markets at dawn;
Children who applauded Punch and Judy in the park,
And those who danced at night,
And kept their Paris bright
Till the town went dark.*

Oscar had seldom written lyrics for a song without having a situation in a play and a melody to fit them to. A few hours before boarding the Super Chief to California with Dorothy, he called Jerry to read him the words, telling him he really didn't know what he wanted to do with them, but they were something he just had to write. When Dorothy and Oscar stepped off the train in Pasadena, Jerry handed Oscar the music for his lyrics. The full impact of the wonderful surprise hit him only after they arrived at the Kerns' house and Jerry played for him the sprightly and lilting melody he had written to fit the wistful words. Oscar was very happy with the result of the collaboration, and was amused by Jerry's scribbling on the

* "The Last Time I Saw Paris" was bought by Arthur Freed and interpolated into his film musical of *Lady Be Good* (MGM, 1941). Sung in the movie by Ann Sothern, the song went on to win an Academy award that year, giving Oscar his first "Oscar." As pleased as both he and Jerry were, they strongly felt that Harold Arlen and Johnny Mercer deserved the award for "Blues in the Night" and immediately began working toward changing the Academy's bylaws so that only songs specifically written for the screen would be eligible for the industry's highest honor; this has been the rule since 1942.

sheet: "Phone Ira [Gershwin] about George's taxi horns." He had also scribbled the direction "not sadly"—which did not deter a few singers from singing the song dolefully, which annoyed both of them.

Oscar had come to the Coast to attend an ASCAP dinner in honor of Rudolf Friml. He sat on the dais not only as a former collaborator, but as the society's newly elected vice-president and as master of ceremonies of the affair. It was at this dinner that an incident occurred which Oscar often used as ammunition to refute those who called him a kind, thoughtful, well-adjusted, thoroughly good man. He had once backed into a corner a short press agent who was fashioning such garlands for him and, towering over him, said, "Listen, if you want to know what kind of a guy I am, I once stole a radish from a blind man, see?" At this ASCAP dinner, Oscar happened to be seated next to a blind composer who was apparently unaware of the radish on his butter plate. Toward the end of the meal Oscar sneaked the radish off his neighbor's plate and ate it. For the rest of his life he felt bad about it.

In late June he was approached with an offer that foreshadowed an important association. Edna Ferber wired Oscar on June 29 that she had talked to Richard Rodgers about making a musical play from her new serial novel, *Saratoga Trunk*, and "we would be happy if you were willing to do the book." The same day another wire came: LARRY AND I SIT WITH EVERYTHING CROSSED HOPING THAT YOU WILL DO SARATOGA TRUNK WITH US. DICK RODGERS.

By July Rodgers was writing Oscar that Ferber was "acting up," as was Warner Brothers, which owned screen rights to the property, and that the whole project looked like "endless aggravation." Although neither Rodgers nor Hammerstein went ahead with *Saratoga Trunk*, the door to collaboration remained open. Rodgers concluded his letter with the following:

> I can say this, however, I was delighted and warmed by several things in your letter. Even if nothing further comes of this difficult matter it will at least have allowed us to approach each other professionally. Specifically, you feel that I should have a book with "substance" to write to. Will you think seriously about doing such a book?
>
> Let us correspond and when you come east perhaps you and Dorothy will come up here for a week-end.
>
> Love to both of you.
>
> Dick

The months after *Sunny River*'s summer tryout in St. Louis were filled with tribulations. Max Gordon acquired the property, but went through ups and downs in raising the money and booking a theater as the season proceeded and Oscar and Rommy waited for a definite opening date. Finally, again solvent after his successes with *My Sister Eileen* and *Junior Miss*, Gordon set December 4 at the St. James Theatre for the show's premiere An operetta in every sense, a romantic story of separated lovers in the New Orleans of the early 1800's, *Sunny River* opened to scathing critical reviews. John Anderson's "*Sunny River*, stay 'way from my door" summed up the attitude of the reviewers who found the show stuffy, ponderous and hopelessly old-hat. John Mason Brown reported feeling as if a "valentine I had hoped had gone off the market years ago had been delivered in a Bergdorf Goodman box by a messenger who thought he must be carrying a Christmas gift."

The time of the operetta was clearly past, though audience reaction showed that there still existed a portion of the public which appreciated the venerable form and this example of it, which Brooks Atkinson termed "workmanlike." Gordon, hoping that this was a "people's" show, set the box-office price low, and kept the show open despite the devastating reviews. It closed on January 3, 1942, after 36 performances.*

Oscar had a strong feeling that those who said the parade had passed him by were quite right. His letter to Max Gordon just after *Sunny River* closed reveals his mood, which he characterized as "blue."

January 8, 1942

Dear Max:

Thank you for your letters. I feel sure that you did everything that was humanly possible to give the show its chance to find a public, and it didn't. I don't believe there is one—certainly not in New York. Operetta is a dead pigeon and if it ever is revived it won't be by me.

I have no plans and at the moment I don't feel like making any. It looks as if Metro will want me to come out for the final script of "Very Warm For May" in about six weeks. Meanwhile I am trying to write a good song that might do something for the nation's war morale.

* In 1943 *Sunny River,* starring Evelyn Laye and Edith Day, had a lengthy run at London's Piccadilly Theatre.

I am convinced that all the war songs I have heard so far are on the wrong track. But I know that there is a great situation for a great song and I am going to hunt it out—if it takes me a year.

We are in the midst of a terrific cold spell. It's so little above zero that it might as well be below. The snow in the country is beautiful, though, and if you were here I'd dig up a pair of galoshes for you and we'd tear off a few brisk miles.

Sincerely,
Oscar

The letter was sent from Highland Farm, the Bucks County home to which Oscar and his family had moved the year before. They decided on the move not only because of Dorothy's continuing dislike for the Great Neck house and the area itself, with its increasing population, but because of a growing need in Oscar for country life, which had always attracted this city boy. He remembered fondly that vacant lot on Central Park West with a few weeds and spindly trees. He remembered that even in Far Rockaway, where he and Myra had taken a small cottage jammed in among others, he would sit on the porch and enjoy a sense of peace as he looked across at a lone tree silhouetted against the sky in the fading evening light. His friend Walter Redell had kidded Oscar about that tree, which was to him a symbol of Oscar's "naïve idealism." Perhaps it was a symbol to Oscar, too, and he now sought the "peace and systematic living" that the country represented to him.

The Hammersteins had often visited friends in the Bucks County area located in the easternmost section of Pennsylvania. On a rainy autumn day they went to a local real estate agent and looked at many places, but none seemed suitable. After lunch in New Hope, they continued to look at other properties in nearby Doylestown.

As they drove up the long hill at the end of East Street, about a mile and a half outside the small town, to look at a farm, a rainbow suddenly appeared over the early-eighteenth-century main house on the hilltop. Dorothy decided immediately that it was a good-luck omen. Oscar loved the look of the place.

The farm stretched out below a large stone and stucco house that stood on a hill overlooking the property's seventy-two acres of serene, rolling countryside. In addition to the main house which was built in 1740, there was a carriage house and a barn. It was a working farm, which was a particularly appealing notion now that the war had officially begun and food shortages were foreseen.

Dorothy's professional eye saw that a minimum of work would be needed to make the house livable and comfortable for a large family. The master bedroom suite on the second floor contained a room with a fireplace which would be perfect for Oscar's study, and there were plenty of bedrooms for all the children.

The price was $23,000, not as low in 1940 as it now sounds but certainly within their means, particularly since both the Benedict Canyon and Kenilworth houses would be sold. They moved in with children, six dogs, two housekeepers and the Moëns. Peter would continue as Oscar's chiropractic therapist as he and his son Walter managed the farm.

A year later Highland Farm had come to feel like home to the Hammersteins, now "the folks who live on the hill." Their big, disorganized holidays seemed to work perfectly in this sprawling old house in the country where the children gathered for the festivities: Jimmy, Susan, Alice, Henry, Billy and his new wife Maggie. From the time they settled into Highland Farm, "adopted" family members would live with the Hammersteins in times of need or crisis. Among the friends and relatives celebrating Christmas with them in 1941 were Dorothy's sister, Doodie Watanabe, whose part-Japanese husband had been interned at Ellis Island following the outbreak of the war, her daughter Jennifer, and Shawen Lynch, the child of an English friend, who lived there throughout the war and afterwards.

The farm gave Oscar a sense of security that was only partly based on the practical thought that there would always be food for the family from the gardens and the livestock on the farm. Although they still had an apartment in New York where Dorothy spent the weekdays attending to her decorating business, Oscar stayed in Doylestown much of each week. He wanted to be alone there. Every day he took long walks—sometimes he covered three miles, sometimes ten. Or he would sit alone for hours and think. He had much to think about.

He did not panic as he thought of his position and his future. Oscar said about himself, "In a confused world I am confused but I am not thrown into a panic by confusion . . . am not unduly distressed by it. I can take confusion and imperfection in my stride." Nevertheless, he had to take stock of his situation.

Oscar knew Broadway well enough to understand that for all the gossip and pettiness, it was basically a forgiving place. Although his reputation was at a low, there would be collaborators and producers who would take him on. What troubled him now was his own confidence in himself. He had thought himself able and as experienced a professional as there ever was, but something was wrong. In show after show and film after film he had proved to be out of touch with what the public wanted, with what was considered good by current standards. He hadn't been able to write a musical or produce a show that could succeed, on Broadway or in Hollywood, for nearly a decade. He had tried again with the collaborators of his greatest successes, Jerry and Romberg, and it hadn't worked out. True, each of his failures had tested his mettle; he had found out he could take it, could survive.

However, he was forty-six years old and had a big family to provide for. He had his continuing royalties from past successes; he could write the occasional hit song, such as "The Last Time I Saw Paris"; Dorothy was making money. They would not starve, but that was not enough. Although his wounded pride occasionally caused him to react jealously to Dorothy's success, he knew that she, too, needed the satisfaction that she got from her business and her job at home. He had to be able to say to himself the line that he called the most significant in all nursery rhymes: "What a good boy am I." One needed approval from oneself and from one's peers. He had known many people who he felt did not work hard enough to get that approval, and who had then become "paranoics, clinging to the life of their egos, to their own self-approval, and blaming the rest of the world for not endorsing it."

He had had many lucky accidents in his life, and he had made the most of them. Now there seemed to be little luck, and perhaps not as much talent as he had thought, but he was determined not to let that discourage him, lick him, turn him into a bitter, defeated man.

Five

A New Lease on Life

Sitting alone at the farm one day in January 1942, Oscar listened to a recording of Bizet's *Carmen*. He played it over and over as he studied the libretto with an English translation of the original French and the complete piano score. Without saying a word about it to anyone outside his family, he set to work modernizing the opera.

This was not the first time he had thought of such a project. Lunching with MGM musical supervisor Sam Katz one day in 1934, Oscar had suggested that they film an opera to appeal to the movie-going public, adapting the story to the cinematic medium. The night before hearing a concert version of *Carmen* at the Hollywood Bowl, he was struck not only with the beauty of the music and the construction of the work, but with the fact that even without costumes or scenery, sung in a language that most of the listeners didn't understand, the opera had tremendous appeal. A dramatic story, its characters were passionate people who expressed universal emotions. If Bizet's work had such vitality even when presented untheatrically, and in a foreign tongue to boot, what would it be like when presented in a richly dramatic way and in a language accessible to a mass audience?

In a follow-up proposal to Katz, Oscar wrote, "As a popular operatic subject, *Carmen* stands alone. It has a universally interesting story, fine characterizations and as melodic a score as was ever written." Though he found *Carmen* "way out in front," he also saw good possibilities in *Faust, Boheme, Butterfly, Tosca, Pagliacci* and *Louise*. The project was developed to the point that Metro thought of casting possibilities, but never took shape while Oscar was in Hollywood.

His recent screenplay on Oscar I's life, and a memoir he had written afterwards, *A Kind of Grandfather*, had reminded him of the Old Man's passionate ambition to make opera livelier and more accessible to the public by using English translations. Over the years Oscar II himself had developed his own aversion to the kind of opera production in America. Refusing to accept that opera is "over the heads" of most people, he felt that the problem was that a small musical clique had turned it into a pretentious elitist form. He took exception to the way that operas were performed in English with little care given to the words the characters sang. Typical operatic diction turned "romance" into "romonce"; managers allowed a thick foreign accent to mask the words; conductors thought a blast from a horn more important than the words being sung by the characters. Moreover, he objected to the English translations themselves, written by scholarly gentlemen who knew nothing about the science of writing singable lyrics and were neither poets nor showmen; their concern with a literal translation that slavishly followed the text diminished the richness of the characters and the emotional power of the plot.

With this ancient grudge and not much work to do, Oscar attacked the problem of creating an English version of *Carmen* which would present the story to an audience with vitality and theatrical effect.

Bizet's opera was based on a tale by Prosper Mérimée adapted by Henri Meilhac and Ludovic Halévy. When first presented in 1875, it was scornfully rejected, particularly by the press. The vicious attacks on the opera's "odious characters" and "babbling" inharmonious music were thought by some to be a major cause of Bizet's death three months after *Carmen*'s Paris debut. Eventually the opera gained recognition everywhere as the masterpiece it was.

As Oscar studied the La Scala recording until he knew every bar, he realized that he wanted to translate the story into a familiar American setting and time without changing an essential note. He immediately identified black people in the South as an ethnic group that had similarities to the Spanish gypsies and common workers of *Carmen* in that both groups express feelings honestly and directly and belong to a culture steeped in strong music. Bizet's score had an elasticity and "hotness" to it that seemed to Oscar to have an affinity with the sound not only of spirituals and blues, but of the rhythm of the Southern blacks' dialect.

Working with the original score and the libretto, which he called "a model of musical drama architecture," he changed the cigarette factory in Seville to a parachute factory in South Carolina during the World War II years. In Oscar's version Don José becomes Joe, a black Army corporal, while the toreador Escamillo is turned into Husky Miller, a heavyweight prize fighter. Carmen Jones, who works in the factory, steals Joe from Cindy Lou (Micaela), his hometown girl friend. Carmen Jones soon transfers her affections to Husky Miller and follows him to Chicago. Joe comes after her and begs her to return, but she rejects him. Outside the arena on the night of Miller's championship fight, Joe kills Carmen and then himself.

Oscar dropped two arias that did not fit his new two-act libretto, but otherwise did not alter the music in any way. The words, of course, were changed completely. The lyrics were so adeptly fitted to the mood and tempo of the music that they sound completely right. In fact, many people felt that they brought new vitality to the score because they accentuate the wild passion of the music and project the story more powerfully than the original libretto.

The familiar "Habanera" is supposed to be sung in a provocative way by the gypsy girl, but the words in the standard English translation sound stiff:

> Ah! love thou art a wilful wild bird,
> And none may hope thy wings to tame,
> If it please thee to be a rebel,
> Say, who can try and thee reclaim?
> Threat and prayers alike unheeding;
> Oft ardent homage thou'lt refuse,
> Whilst he who doth coldly slight thee
> Thou for thy master oft thou'lt choose.
> Ah, love . . .
> And if I love thee, now beware.

In Oscar's lyrics for the same aria the identical thought is conveyed in a style more in keeping with the earthy character of the girl:

> Love's a baby dat grows up wild
> An' he don' do what you want him to,
> Love ain' nobody's angel child
> An' he won' pay any mind to you . . .
> One man gives me his diamon' stud
> An' I won' give him a cigarette.
> One man treats me like I was mud
> An' all I got dat man c'n get
> Dat's love . . . dat's love!

The "Toreador Song" ingeniously becomes a prize fighter's defiant chant that not only matches the power of the music, but presages the ultimate violent climax more clearly than did the original lyrics:

> Stan' up an' fight until you hear de bell,
> Stan' toe to toe,
> Trade blow fer blow!
> Keep punchin' till you make yer punches tell,
> Show dat crowd watcher know!
> Until you hear dat bell,
> Stan' up an' fight like hell!

Oscar worked without deadlines or pressures, not even certain that the work would ever be produced. He enjoyed this project more than any other he had done. He had written well-crafted lyrics before and occasionally songs that were outstanding, but never had he produced a libretto that was so consistently powerful and artful. Virgil Thomson called the fitting of the words to Bizet's music "ingenious, neat and wholly triumphant." Other music critics called the libretto brilliant, poetic, an extraordinary achievement. The months spent in the country at the lowest ebb of his fortunes marked a turning point for Oscar; in *Carmen Jones* his showmanship became art.

In July 1942, four days after Oscar completed the libretto, he agreed to work on a musical adaptation of Lynn Riggs's *Green Grow the Lilacs* for the Theatre Guild. A few weeks later Max Gordon took an option on *Carmen Jones*; an early fall opening was announced, but the Broadway production was postponed until the following season because Gordon didn't have the necessary capital and Oscar was involved in the Guild project.

There were other minor activities in 1942. Oscar doctored a

show for Irving Caesar in Philadelphia and worked on casting and attempting to raise funds for a revival of *Show Boat*. He talked about ideas for a new show with Jerry, who, very much opposed to letting Irving Caesar handle *Show Boat,* snapped that it sounded like a last stand and he was not *that* desperate. In California in May, Oscar wrote one song for the proposed MGM film of *Very Warm for May* and made some changes in *Music in the Air* for a revival there. In the fall, he was again in Hollywood talking with Metro not only about the script for a movie about his grandfather, but about a forty-week contract that he described as "not heaven but better than hell." He was finally advised by Howard Reinheimer not to sign the $65,000 agreement because taxes and the expense of moving again to California would make it unprofitable to do so.

The Writers' War Board, the American Theatre Wing War Service, the Stage Door Canteen and local Bucks County war efforts occupied some of Oscar's energies. On the day that Germany invaded Russia Beatrice and George S. Kaufman came to Highland Farm for lunch. "What do you make of all this, George?" asked Dorothy.

"I think," Kaufman said, "they're shooting without a script."

The war and its consequences touched the Hammersteins most closely with Billy's enlistment in the Navy and the tragic situation in which their brother-in-law, Jerry Watanabe, was caught.

Married to Dorothy's sister Doodie, Watanabe was the son of a couple unusual in the 1890's: the strong-willed daughter of a British ambassador to Japan and a Japanese director of Mitsui and Company. He was raised in the English manner and educated at Cambridge. A handsome and charming man who was an excellent tennis player and golfer, he was working at Mitsui's New York office when war was declared between the United States and Japan. When the government ordered all citizens of Japan interned, he was arrested and sent to Ellis Island. When the typist working on his transcript broke her leg in a blizzard and the document wasn't filed for months, he was forced to remain at Ellis Island, where he was assigned to maintenance work. Finally released, his Japanese name prevented him from getting a job, so he began to work for Dorothy, handling the financial end of her business.

During her father's internment Jennifer lived in Doylestown. Dorothy and her sister took the little girl to a local school to enroll her and said to the headmaster that they wanted to be sure she would not be hurt by anyone.

"She'll have to pay the price for her antecedents," was his reply. They quickly left. Oscar suggested a Friends school, which he teasingly called "Fiends' Academy" when Jennifer went there. She later went to the George School in Newtown, Pennsylvania, enrolling as Jennifer Blanchard because of the hardships caused by her Japanese name.

Oscar read many books and plays that year in the hope of finding a show to write with Jerry. On a trip to California in May, he told Jerry that he was intrigued with the possibilities of *Green Grow the Lilacs,* which had been produced by the Theatre Guild in 1931. He saw a dramatic vitality under the play's gentle surface and was attracted to the well-defined characters, whose talk was at once earthy and lyrical. Jerry recalled that the show had lasted only a few weeks on Broadway and considered the second act utterly hopeless. His reaction was so negative that Oscar dropped the subject, but remaining strongly attracted, he continued to think about the play's possibilities as a vehicle for a musical.

Back in New York, Oscar received a call from Richard Rodgers, who said that he wanted to talk something over with him. They met for lunch at the Barberry Room, just across the street from Dorothy's decorating studio. Rodgers came right to the point. "The Theatre Guild wants to do a musical based on a play they produced years ago. Terry Helburn feels there are some good elements for a musical and wants me to do the score. I wonder if we could get together. Why don't you read it and see how you like it?"

Oscar almost anticipated the answer as he asked, "What's the play?"

"*Green Grow the Lilacs.*"

"I don't have to read it. I know it and I'm crazy about it. I'd love to do it with you."

With this coincidence began the partnership of Rodgers and Hammerstein. The collaboration itself was not entirely unexpected. It was just a year before, in July 1941, that Rodgers sent Hammerstein the telegram saying that he hoped Oscar would work on *Saratoga Trunk* with Rodgers and Hart. He had again approached Oscar in September. In Philadelphia for the tryout of *Best Foot Forward,* for which he was a silent producer, Dick had called Oscar in nearby Doylestown to ask if he might come to the farm to have a talk. It was then that he told Oscar about the troubles he was having with his long-time partner, Larry Hart. Committed with Hart to do the score of a musical version of Ludwig Bemelman's *Hotel Splendide,* for which Donald Ogden

Stewart was writing the book, Dick was now worried that Larry would not be able to finish the lyrics. He unburdened himself about his fears concerning his partner of over twenty years and asked Oscar to join them on the play. Increasingly convinced that he would need a new collaborator, he turned to Oscar because he respected him and his talent, but he felt despondent and guilty about the situation with Larry.

When Dick finished, Oscar thought for a minute or two and then said, "I think you ought to keep working with Larry just as long as he is able to keep working with you. It would kill him if you walked away while he was still able to function. But if the time ever comes when he cannot function, call me. I'll be there."

The immediate problem was solved when *Hotel Splendide* was canceled shortly thereafter, but Larry Hart's problem remained. Oscar had known Larry since Columbia varsity show days and thought him one of the sweetest men he knew; he was deeply saddened by Larry's condition. A gifted lyricist and a delightful personality, Larry Hart was a lonely, unhappy man whose drinking bouts, which led to disappearances and irresponsibility, had increased throughout the years until they reached alarming proportions. He could no longer be relied on to keep an appointment, to meet a deadline, to be in any condition to work.

Larry Hart had always been a tormented man. Talented and charming as he was, he had always been tortured by his height, a bare five feet, and his homosexuality. The product of a strong, conventional Jewish family, Larry was torn by guilt and dissatisfaction as he lived the double life of a homosexual in a society that neither understood nor accepted homosexuality. The devoted son, the successful writer, the sweet man with loving friends who respected him, was uncontrollably heading toward self-destruction.

Dick Rodgers had always accepted his irresponsible behavior, not only because Larry was so sweet and good-natured that it was difficult to be angry with him, but because he was afraid to upset a working relationship that had proved so successful. When Larry's concentration span became shorter and shorter and he could no longer work alone, Dick gave him the necessary musical themes and whatever drinks were necessary, and sat with him as he worked. He set up a financial scheme to help Larry save money, tried to arrange psychiatric help and took care of all the areas in their professional association except for lyric writing. He indulged Larry as long as he could. When his partner was hospitalized at Doctors Hospital during the writing of *By Jupiter*, Harold Hyman, who was treating Hart, suggested that Rodgers use the piano that Cole Porter, also a patient, had had moved into the interns' quarters and finish the work there. In 1941 Rodgers realized that the situation was critical and that he had to think about the unthinkable: the breakup of Rodgers and Hart, a team that for over twenty years had seemed indivisible.

Despite the similarities in their background, upbringing, education and milieu, Oscar Hammerstein was as different from Larry Hart in personality and technical style as it was possible to be. Larry's words and rhymes were incisive, sophisticated, witty, pyrotechnical; Oscar's were simple in vocabulary, used the phrases of everyday speech, were direct, uncomplicated and sentimental. Oscar had worked with many collaborators; Dick had not, but he felt that despite the contrast, something fresh and worthwhile could emerge from this new combination.

From the beginning of their partnership, Rodgers and Hammerstein reversed the usual process of collaboration. Beginning with their first, "Oh, What a Beautiful Mornin'," Oscar wrote the lyrics first on all but a few Rodgers and Hammerstein songs. This process, as well as the association itself, suited them from the start and profoundly affected the nature and personality of the work of each.

Although early newspaper announcements of the show said that Rodgers, Hart and Hammerstein were working on a musical adaptation of *Green Grow the Lilacs,* in fact Hart had told Rodgers that he didn't want to work on it and had gone to Mexico when the first working conference on the play that would become *Oklahoma!* took place.

Oscar and Dick sat under a large oak tree at the Rodgers' home in Fairfield, Connecticut, and tossing ideas back and forth as they discussed the texture of mood of the play, the songs and their placement, they became familiar not only with every aspect of the play but with each other's way of thinking.

One of the basic traditions of the musical theater had always been that not long after the curtain rose, the audience would be treated to one of musical comedy's most attractive assets: the sight and sound of vital young singers and dancers. Oscar had discarded this convention in the past, but he shared Dick's concern that an ensemble number should not be put off until too late in the play, but that the show, like the play, should start quietly, with one silent character onstage. For days they sought ways of logically introducing a group into the early action of the play. Strawberry festivals, quilting parties, sewing bees were suggested and rejected. After going through long periods of silence staring at each other, unable to think of anything at all, they finally went back to the natural way in which the story seemed to want to be told: to open with a woman, Aunt Eller, seated alone on a stage churning butter while the voice of a cowboy, Curly, is heard offstage. Although the first act would be half over before a chorus appeared, once the decision was made neither of the collaborators was worried by the risk in their course. Oscar explained their attitude as the inner confidence that people feel when they have adopted the direct and honest approach to a problem.

At no point did Oscar and Dick say, "Let's do some great revolutionary things for the American theater." They just tried at every step of the way to do the best they could and to do it honestly. For the first time since *Show Boat,* Oscar was aware of letting the material he was adapting dictate his course. He threw away the traditions he knew when they interfered with that course. Throughout the writing of *Oklahoma!* they remained faithful to the spirit of the original, and though they weren't at all sure that the show would be a success, they felt very good about their work.

As Oscar thought about the opening and searched for a subject for Curly to sing about, he remembered how impressed he had been by Lynn Riggs's stage directions at the start of his play:

> *It is a radiant summer morning several years ago, the kind of morning which, enveloping the shapes of earth—men, cattle in the meadow, blades of the young corn, streams—makes them seem to exist now for the first time, their images giving off a visible golden emanation that is partly true and partly a trick of imagination, focusing to keep alive a loveliness that may pass away.*

He wanted to put the description into the opening song to create the right atmosphere and to introduce Curly, the light-hearted young man who is one of the central characters. He took the cattle and corn and golden haze on the meadow from Riggs and added some observations of his own based on his experience with beautiful mornings at Highland Farm.

Oscar had written "The corn is as high as a cow pony's eye," but when he walked over to a neighbor's corn field he found that the August corn was much higher than that. Even before this discovery he had had reservations about the sound of "cow pony" and so he sacrificed the word that was indigenous to the southwestern territory of the early 1900's—which was the setting of the play—for one that sounded better and was more accurate in terms of measurement.

When he came to the second verse of "Oh, What a Beautiful Mornin'," he remembered sitting on his porch on a summer's day a year before, watching a herd of cows standing on a hillside half a mile away. The day was hot and all was motionless. He did something on that day that he had never done before: he made a poem describing what he saw but did not write it down. Now he remembered it:

> The breeze steps aside
> To let the day pass.
> The cows on the hill
> Are as still as the grass.

The image of the still cows had been crystallized in his memory by the words that he had idly composed, and he used the image now in "All the cattle are standin' like statues."

It took him three weeks to write the song's lyrics, many days of which were spent fussing over whether to insert the "Oh" in the first two lines. Finally he finished the lyric, which is characteristic of the mature Hammerstein style that was so evident in the entire show. Simple and direct, with imagery drawn from the natural setting of the play, the vocabulary and phrases are true to the everyday speech of the character, yet lyrical and expressive:

> There's a bright, golden haze on the meadow,
> There's a bright, golden haze on the meadow.
> The corn is as high as a elephant's eye
> An' it looks like it's climbin' clear up to the sky.
>
>> Oh, what a beautiful mornin',
>> Oh, what a beautiful day.
>> I've got a beautiful feelin'
>> Ev'rythin's goin' my way.
>
> All the cattle are standin' like statues,
> All the cattle are standin' like statues.
> They don't turn their heads as they see me ride by,
> But a little brown mav'rick is winkin' her eye.
>
>> Oh, what a beautiful mornin',
>> Oh, what a beautiful day.
>> I got a beautiful feelin'
>> Ev'rythin's goin' my way.

> All the sounds of the earth are like music—
> All the sounds of the earth are like music.
> The breeze is so busy it don't miss a tree
> And a ol' weepin' willer is laughin' at me!

> Oh, what a beautiful mornin',
> Oh, what a beautiful day.
> I got a beautiful feelin'
> Ev'rythin's goin' my way . . .
> Oh, what a beautiful day!

Oscar took the completed lyric to Dick in Fairfield. "I was a little sick with joy because it was so lovely and so right," recalls Rodgers. "When you're given words like that you get something to say musically. You'd really have to be made of cement not to spark to that." Completed in ten minutes, the music had all the simple, sweet charm of a folk song and a poetic lyricism that was different from Rodgers' previous work. Both Dorothy Hammerstein and Dorothy Rodgers liked the song immensely. (Richard Rodgers' wife being another Dorothy added to the conversational confusion that already existed around the three Dorothy Hammersteins in the family.)*

Stimulated by their feeling that the song was a good one that set the tone they wanted for the play, they tore into work that afternoon and in a short time solved some of the vexatious problems of the play's second act—the killing and the ribald shivaree, which resisted integration with the music and could not possibly be shaped into the healthy gaiety considered appropriate to musical plays. Convinced that much of the flatness commonly found in musical comedy books was due to erroneous ideas of what you can't do in a musical, Oscar proceeded on the principle that if the background is bright and life's joy is present in the story and the characters, then the events of a musical's plot can be as dramatic or tragic as anything found in a play without music, or in life.

He wrote the book quickly, keeping intact the spirit of the original and the characters of Curly, Laurey, Aunt Eller and Jud (whose name was changed from Jeeter). He cut the script to make room for the music, but used many of the lines from the original play. The most radical changes were in the play's second act, where he invented a new finish and compressed events in the original, and in the char-

---

* Uncle Arthur was married to the former Dorothy Dalton; cousin Ted Hammerstein to the former Dorothy Underhill.

acter of Ado Annie, changed from a shy, fat girl to a trim girl who "cain't say no." He wrote a subplot around Ado Annie, adding new characters, such as Will Parker, and building up the Persian peddler, Ali Hakim, in order to vary the musical numbers by having diversity in the characters who sing them.

Lawrence Langner, who ran the Theatre Guild along with Theresa Helburn and Armina Marshall (who was Mrs. Langner), met Oscar for the first time when the first draft of the book was finished in late August. His impression was of a big man with a broad, kindly face who was slow-moving but quick-thinking. He found that unlike many men he had met in the musical field, Oscar had wide interests and had read extensively. Langner felt that his knowledge of philosophy, economics and world affairs was greater than that of almost any other man that he had met in the theater.

The Theatre Guild was in wretched financial condition at the time, their treasury so depleted that they could not produce the show without outside capital. They began to seek backers while work went on.

Early in August, Oscar had begun to think about casting and had written to Charlotte Greenwood to see if she would be free to play a part. Although he didn't specify the part, Charlotte wrote back: "If you're a talking abot thet thar Aunt Eller, 'f it had to be me I'll lose more'n a leg (page 85 *Green Grow the Lilacs*). But oh, Oscar, it's a purty kind a thought." As it turned out, she was not free to do the stage version of *Oklahoma!* *

Later in the month Oscar called Mary Martin, who had by then scored a great hit with "My Heart Belongs to Daddy" and made a name for herself in films. "I'd adore it," Mary said, "but there's a hitch. Vinton Freedley has offered me a show called *Dancing in the Streets* for this winter and I don't see how it can work out." Eventually Mary flipped a quarter to decide between the shows and it came up heads, which meant the Freedley musical.†

The first draft completed, and one song finished, Rodgers and Hammerstein began to work on the rest of the score. Like Gilbert, who also wrote lyrics first, and Sullivan, who fitted the music to them, Oscar and Dick did not actually write together. They worked very

---

* Charlotte Greenwood was available when it came time for *Oklahoma!* to come to the screen.

† *Oklahoma!* and *Dancing in the Streets* had tryouts during the same week as Boston. Oscar sent Mary red roses and said, "I'm going to send you roses for a long time. Had you accepted the role, I would have written a different show."

closely in their office at Max Dreyfus' firm in Rockefeller Center while drawing up the "blueprint," the outline detailing how much of the story would be told in dialogue and how much in song. They discussed characters, mood, plot, and the function and placement of songs. Then they discussed carefully the spots they had chosen for songs. Dick might contribute a lyric idea and Oscar a music idea as they hashed out the play's structure. Their preparation done, they went off to their respective homes to work.

Dick found working with Oscar very different from the system he used with Hart. With Hart, he would provide him with a melody and then virtually lock him up; Hart would write the lyrics quickly and spontaneously, taking almost no more time than it took to scribble the words. Oscar needed no stimulus other than the agreed-upon idea for the song and was, of course, absolutely reliable. Adhering to a disciplined schedule, he worked steadily and painstakingly until he finished.

Oscar would work through the lyrics using a "dummy" melody, usually fragments of other people's tunes in a minor key. It was universally agreed that Oscar's dummy melodies were terrible. He would often leave his study and go into the bedroom, where Dorothy was reading or working, to sing the lyrics he was working on. "Trying it out on the dog," she called it. Suffering through the miserable singing, Dorothy would say, "I think they're lovely words, but I'm dying to hear the happy music."

Both Dick and Oscar felt that their way of collaborating produced songs that were better integrated in terms of character and plot and represented a natural fusion of words and music. The songs sprang directly from the moods and situations of the play. The closer union of words and music was made possible by the collaborators' extensive discussions of the exact kind of song needed and also by Oscar's thorough understanding of music. Oscar was not a musician, but Dick found that he had "a suberb sense of form" and a full understanding of "the architecture" of a song.

Once supplied with a lyric, Dick wrote the music quickly. Oscar once said that the only trouble with Dick was that he worked so fast; he claimed that he was afraid to give him a lyric when they were out with people because Dick would rush off to start composing. Dick said that the reason his composing seemed to be so rapid was that by the time he sat down to write a melody, he and Oscar and talked so much about the play, the story and the characters that ideas would have started germinating, so that the lyrics were but the final stimulus that allowed him to go straight to the piano. He found, too, that the lyrics-first method that gave Oscar greater freedom also gave him a chance to break away more than ever from the generally accepted *aaba* 32-bar song construction because the lyrics suggested new structures to him.

With the book completed, Oscar worked on the show's next song, "The Surrey with the Fringe on Top," which was the second of the two songs in *Oklahoma!* directly inspired by Riggs's words. As Curly tries to tempt Laurey into going to a box social with him he describes the carriage they will ride in: "A bran' new surrey with fringe on the top four inches long—and *yeller!* And two white horses a-rarin' and faunchin' to go! You'd shore ride like a queen. . . . And this yere rig has got four fine side-curtains, case of a rain. And isinglass winders to look out of! And a red and green lamp set on the dashboard, winkin' like a lightnin' bug."

The finished lyric suggested to Dick a "clip-clop rhythm and a melody in which the straight, flat country road could be musically conveyed through a repetition of the straight, flat sound of the D note, followed by a sharp upward flick as fowl scurry to avoid being hit by the moving wheels."

In the last line, "Don't you hurry with the surrey with the fringe on the top," Oscar broke with the convention that dictates an ending that can be sung with the mouth wide open. He realized that the rule was not inviolable, that "fringe," which looks unpromising in print, actually sings well, and that the quiet closed sound of "top" is more appropriate to the naïve and charming lyric than a dramatically vocal finish would be.

In *Oklahoma!*, the songs not only played an important part in telling the story and depicting the characters, but helped to solve the problems presented by the villain, Jud Fry. A collector of dirty pictures who frightened Laurey by walking outside her window every night and a suspected murderer, this character was heavy fare for a musical play. However, he was needed as the bass fiddle that gave body to the orchestration of the story and prevented the play from being so idyllic that it would have been either soporific or nauseating. The question, then, was how to make Jud a plausible figure, not just an unmotivated purveyor of arbitrary evil. The collaborators considered the device of having two other characters discuss him in order to give the audience psychological insights into the character. They decided that this method was not only questionable dramatically, but impossible because there were no suitably educated, articulate characters to do the discussing. They solved the problem with two songs, "Pore Jud" and "Lonely Room."

Both are sung in the dingy smokehouses lined with suggestive pictures where Jud lives. When Curly sarcastically describes his funeral, Jud is so intrigued with the thought that people might discover his good qualities after he is gone that he becomes, for a while, a comic figure. The song also reveals him as a pathetic and lonely figure, and the audience can feel some sympathy for him.

The second song, "Lonely Room," is meant to convey the menace necessary to the story. Jud's song about his solitary life, his hatred of Curly and desire for Laurey, paints a savage picture more rapidly and vividly than dialogue could do. When Lynn Riggs attended a rehearsal of *Oklahoma!* and was asked by Oscar if he approved of the number, he said, "I certainly do. It will scare hell out of the audience." The song made many people so uneasy during rehearsals that they considered cutting it from the show. But during tryouts it became clear that the scene and the play were better with it than without it, and the song remained.

The one song in this show for which the music was written first was "People Will Say We're in Love." Dick wrote the refrain thinking it would be a good duet for the lovers. Both collaborators wanted a love song, but again the play threw up a roadblock. Though the pair is clearly in love from the beginning of the play, the antagonism between them is necessary for the development of the plot. An "I love you" song wouldn't work. After a good deal of worry and talk, they decide to have the lovers obliquely confess their mutual affection while warning each other against any show of tenderness lest other people think they are in love.

Once they had settled on the idea Oscar started to jot down some don'ts: Don't look proud when I rope a steer, bake a cake; don't wax poetical; don't tie my ties for me, don't tell pretty lies for me; don't buy a hat for me, don't turn democrat for me.

When he finished, Oscar was so pleased with the song that had solved so many problems that he called Dick to read him the words:

> Don't throw bouquets at me—
> Don't please my folks too much,
> Don't laugh at my jokes too much—
> People will say we're in love!

> Don't sigh and gaze at me,
> Your sighs are so like mine,
> Your eyes mustn't glow like mine—
> People will say we're in love!
>
> Don't start collecting things—
> Give me my rose and my glove.
> Sweetheart, they're suspecting things—
> People will say we're in love!

While work on the score proceeded,* the Guild began to bring together other production elements. Rouben Mamoulian had been a good-luck charm with his fine direction for the Guild on *Porgy and Bess,* for Rodgers and Hart on *Love Me Tonight* and for Oscar and Jerry on *High, Wide and Handsome.* He came to town in January 1943 and was engaged as director.† Terry Helburn hired two others who had worked for the Guild in the past, Lemuel Ayers for the scenery and Miles White for the costumes.

When Agnes de Mille wrote Lawrence Langner suggesting herself as choreographer for the musical, Terry Helburn persuaded Oscar and Dick to go with her to the opening night of the Ballet Russe de Monte Carlo, in which Agnes was to dance in her own ballet, *Rodeo.* After the performance, they wired Agnes: "We think your work is enchanting. Come talk to us on Monday." Although Agnes de Mille had failed in the musical theater before, she was confident that she had learned and could contribute to this show. Actually, she considered her lack of qualms inexplicable in view of her history. Oscar had followed her career since the night of her first recital, in 1930, when he came backstage, "stood by the side of his handsome wife and gazed with benevolence and kindly enthusiasm." He had told Agnes then that her work showed marked talent, but the problem was how to use it. Twelve years later, this seemed an opportunity to do so. Helburn and Langner

---

* Among the other songs were "Kansas City," "I Cain't Say No," "Many a New Day," "It's a Scandal! It's an Outrage!," "Out of My Dreams," "The Farmer and the Cowman," "All er Nothin'," "Why, Oh Why," "Someone Will Teach You" and "She Likes You."

† Although, in retrospect, Mamoulian seemed the inevitable choice as director for the musical, in fact several others were approached before him. As early as June 1942 Dick Rodgers wrote to Joshua Logan but Logan went into the service that summer. Terry Helburn asked Brentagne Windust and Elia Kazan; the latter replied, "I reread *Green Grow the Lilacs* and I just don't click with it. I'm afraid I'd do a very mediocre job."

thought she might bring something fresh to the production. Dick had certain doubts, and indeed there was risk involved in using this intense and original artist whose roots were in the ballet, not the Broadway stage.

De Mille was so anxious to work on the show that when she ran into Oscar by chance in the Buckingham Pharmacy Coffee Shop on Sixth Avenue, she knocked a plate off the counter in her haste to speak to him and find out if she would get the job.

When she was hired, she went to her first working meeting determined to be very firm. She thought that Oscar seemed understanding but reminded herself that one can never tell. Sitting erect and looking severe, she announced that she must insist that there be no one in the chorus she didn't approve.

"Oh pshaw!" murmured Oscar. With a completely straight face, and in a tone of utmost sincerity, he said he was sorry she was going to take that attitude because there was his regular girlfriend and Lawrence had two, and Dick Rodgers always counted on some. For a moment Agnes took him seriously, and then she "relaxed on that score" for the rest of her life.

Then started the prodigious job of auditioning. Because of the financial plight of the Guild, Terry Helburn felt that established stars could lure backers and audiences; she suggested Groucho Marx for the peddler and, with Mary Martin unavailable, Shirley Temple for Laurey. Oscar and Dick held fast to their determination that the actors and singers must be right for the parts, no matter what their box-office potential was, and they ended up with a cast of competent unknowns.

Joan Roberts, who had played in Oscar's *Sunny River,* won the part of Laurey, and Alfred Drake, known to Dick from *Babes in Arms,* was the perfect Curly. Celeste Holm, who had been in a few dramatic plays, charmed everyone as she sang like a gawky farm girl, throwing in some uninhibited hog-calling, and received the part of Ado Annie. Betty Garde, an established character actress, was cast as Aunt Eller and Joseph Buloff, from the Yiddish theater, as the peddler. Lee Dixon, who had begun his career in Warner Brothers' musicals, was hired for the role of Will Parker, and Howard Da Silva more than qualified for the role of Jud Fry.

Everything looked fine, except that the production was still short of capital and the Theatre Guild was finding it impossible to wheedle money from investors. In the grim war days, not only did investing in a musical seem like fiddling while Rome burned, but the Guild had made money on only two of its last sixteen productions, and its coterie of investors had lost enthusiasm for the Guild's work. In addition, with the exception of Dick Rodgers, no one involved in the show had had any recent Broadway successes, if they had had any at all. The show itself looked unpromising. A cowboy musical with chorus girls in long dresses? A musical based on a folk drama that had been a flop years before? No, thanks.

The show came to be known as Helburn's Folly as the tiny, brisk Terry Helburn doggedly tried to raise money. Once an intellectual snob about musicals, she had come to dream of the production of a new kind of musical, not a musical comedy in the familiar sense, but a musical play of the sort that Oscar had so long believed in. Now she used her fierce energy to make other people share her conviction.

One of the biggest stumbling blocks in raising money was the Guild's inability to offer the lure of potential movie profits, the rights to *Green Grow the Lilacs* having been acquired by MGM from the original purchaser, RKO, years before. Since MGM owned only the dramatic rights, Terry Helburn tried to persuade them to put up $69,000 in return for 50 percent of the show profits, and $75,000 if they wanted film rights. If the show succeeded, they would get back their original investment and more, and if it failed, it would cost them only $69,000, since they wouldn't have to buy the movie rights. MGM turned the deal down cold, contemptuous of "another western."

Oscar called Arthur Freed at Metro to see if he could persuade Louis B. Mayer to at least allow them an option on the motion picture rights so that they could attract other investors. Freed thought he could. At the time, Oscar was negotiating a contract with the studio to act as Freed's associate producer, and Mayer was as anxious as Freed to see that the contract went through. He granted the Theatre Guild and Messrs. Rodgers and Hammerstein an option at $40,000, to be exercised within thirty days of the New York opening. (It took them less than thirty hours!)

Terry next turned to other producers. "Too clean," they said. "It hasn't got a chance." However, through Max Gordon, who made a personal investment, Harry Cohn of Columbia Pictures became interested. Although he could not get the Columbia board of directors to go along with him, Cohn put up $15,000 of his own. The regular Broadway angels were the next step. Their response was "No gags, no girls, no chance." Howard Cullman, one of the most successful backers in the business, dismissed the play with a short *no*. (He later hung over his desk a copy of Miss Helburn's letter, a rueful reminder of the *no* that he estimated cost him over one million dollars in profits.)

Terry Helburn, Oscar and Dick, along with Alfred Drake and Joan Roberts, took to the "penthouse circuit" in their efforts to interest investors. Feeling like wandering minstrels, they would perform in the drawing rooms of rich New Yorkers for small audiences of prospective backers. Dick would play portions of the score while Oscar narrated the story and Joan and Alfred sang the songs, with Oscar joining Alfred for "Pore Jud." The results were discouraging. One evening seventy people sat in a palatial home, listened, nibbled caviar and drank champagne and left with polite thanks and unsullied checkbooks.

Riding in a taxi one night to a fund-raising audition in the apartment of Jules Glaenzer, head of Cartier's and a good friend of the Hammersteins, Terry Helburn said to Oscar, "I wish you and Dick would write a song about the earth."

Startled, Oscar said, "What do you mean, Terry?"

"Oh, I don't know, just a song about the earth—the land."

Oscar thought it was one of the vaguest and silliest ideas he had ever heard. Two days later he found himself writing a lyric he had never intended to write, a lyric describing a "brand-new state" that would provide "barley, carrots and pertaters, pasture fer the cattle." He wrote of the wind sweeping down the plain and how sweet the waving wheat smelled when the wind came right behind the rain. It was a song about a couple expressing happiness that they belonged to the land and that the land they belonged to was grand. It was a song about the earth. Terry's arrow shot in the air became the song "Oklahoma." Oscar felt that this incident showed "producing" at its best. Although a producer is generally thought to be simply a money-raiser, Terry was always poking her nose in everywhere, continually shooting arrows in the air. Agnes said, "Terry is always nipping at my heels." Taking her analogy one step further, Oscar described Terry as a "very small sheepdog always pushing you relentlessly to some pasture that she felt would be good for you."

The money was dribbling in very slowly, in small amounts, throughout the winter. Despite their faith in the show, things looked bleak. Oscar was seriously going ahead with his MGM contract; Dick was expecting a commission in the Air Force to come through any day.

Even when rehearsals began in February, Terry was bringing prospective backers into the theater to watch them, hoping that the enchantment felt by those in the show would bring a response. (At the first rehearsal, a gasp went around the room after "Oh, What a Beautiful Mornin'.") The rehearsal atmosphere was frenzied. Every inch of the Guild Theatre, on West Fifty-second Street, was being used as Russell Bennett worked on the orchestrations and dance arrangements, Rouben and Oscar held book rehearsals on the stage, Dick sat at his keyboard and Agnes drilled her dancers in the downstairs lounge.

De Mille and Mamoulian, both temperamental and used to unquestioned authority, had clashed at the outset of rehearsals. Agnes "blew a fuse" one day when Terry Helburn and her backers interrupted a rehearsal, and she was dragged off screaming by dancer Marc Platt, who held her head under a cold water faucet until she quieted down. Mamoulian went into a rage about the too-bright costumes and the fact that Oscar and Dick had seen the costume and set designs before he did. Despite the sporadic outbursts, everyone worked hard, de Mille driving her dancers relentlessly, Mamoulian sweating at his task as he worked to integrate the drama, song and dance. He wanted to create the atmosphere of a farm with animals and thought of getting cows, horses and chickens but finally settled on pigeons, which made a group flight during the New Haven tryout and never came back.

Oscar and Dick kept their calm and optimism through it all. Dick never lost his temper and frequently met the "It can't be done" of the Guild and of Mamoulian with a "Let's see." Once, on the stage at midnight, he said to the assembled worriers, "Do you know what I think is wrong? Almost nothing. Now, why don't you all quiet down."

In New Haven before the first tryouts, tempers went completely to pieces. Oscar sat through the endless nights "quietly giving off intelligence like a stove," according to Agnes. Terry found him a steady flame, his inner serenity glowing. Says Agnes in her book *Dance to the Piper:*

> He never got angry or hasty or excited, but when people were beating their heads on the orchestra rail, made the one common-sense suggestion that any genius might think of if he was not at the moment consuming himself. Lawrence Langner expounded. Terry Helburn snapped and badgered and barked at our heels, with a housekeeper's insistence on detail. Mamoulian created in spite of the hour and other people's nerves. But Oscar just quietly pointed the way.

As *Away, We Go!* it opened at the Shubert Theatre in New Haven on a blustery night, March 11, 1943, with little publicity. The *Variety* critic reported that its liveliness was "built on an old-fashioned foundation that seemed to ring the bell with first nighters here." However, the New York contingent, the chic opinion-setters whom Oscar referred to as "grave-diggers" or "smarties," rushed off to their train back to the city crying, " 'Bye," and spread the word that the show would never make it: "Too clean"; "They'll have to rewrite the second act; you can't kill people in a musical." Mike Todd left after the first act. Max Gordon wrote to Oscar, "Did I tell you that I thought you ought to try to bring the girls on sooner in Act I?"

In Boston they rewrote and made further production changes during the second week of tryouts, despite the nightmare of illness that descended upon them there. Terry caught a germ which kept her in bed for a week, though she sneaked out to the theater with a trained nurse in attendance and held conferences while she sat in bed with ice packs to lower her temperature. Agnes came down with German measles, which spread to the dancers, who had to cover their spots with grease paint before going on. A good part of the chorus had sore throats and croaked through the numbers. Dorothy was running a raging fever "of undetermined origin," and she lay in bed at Peter Bent Brigham Hospital as Oscar dashed back and forth between theater and hospital.

Two scenes were cut; a love duet in the second act, "Boys and Girls Like You and Me," was felt to slow down the show and was replaced by a reprise of "People Will Say We're in Love," though Oscar generally objected to reprises. The song "Oklahoma" was changed from a duet for Curly and Laurey to a rousing chorale for the whole company. During one of the endless discussions of the show's title, Oscar said, "Why don't we add an exclamation point to Oklahoma and be done with it." He felt it a "good, honest name."

Boston audiences responded enthusiastically and the notices were good. Oscar wrote to Billy, now a quartermaster first class in the Navy, "I think I have something this time." He went on to tell him that the cast had lost the pace of the show while rehearsing the changes, but "we gave them a good drilling and the result was so successful that in one night we suddenly took on the aura of a hit. . . . I now believe that here is the nearest approach to *Show Boat* that the theatre has attained. I don't believe it has as sound a story or that it will be as great a success. But it is comparable in quality. . . . All this is said in the hope that a handful of beer-stupefied critics may not decide that we have tried to write a musical comedy and failed. If they see that this is different and higher in its intent, they should rave. I *know* this is a good show. I cannot believe it will not find a substantial public. There! My neck is out."

Dorothy, who always signed herself "Steppy," wrote to Billy, "Your father deserves a hit badly. There was never such a game sport about his work in the whole world—I won't say that about his ping-pong game, but as far as his work is concerned there has never been a more courageous person." His courage was indeed remarkable. Plagued by failure for years, Oscar had nonetheless found the strength to take risks. He would later joke about a game that he and Dick played in which they explained why *Oklahoma!* had to flop: the chorus girls didn't appear until the curtain had been up for forty minutes; the first act had no plot except a girl deciding which young man to go to a dance with; there were virtually no important new numbers in the second act; and so on and so on. Had the play failed for one reason or another, the elements in it that were hailed as brilliant and revolutionary could easily have been called mistakes.

It must be granted that the confluence of talent and purpose in *Oklahoma!* was extremely serendipitous, with a producer and director who were as interested as Oscar and Dick in presenting a fully integrated musical play, whatever the risks. Dick Rodgers was not only flexible enough to work in a new way, but had a sensitive talent that merged perfectly with Oscar's. It is true, too, that Oscar was once again working in an area best suited to his talents—the adaptation of a work that was simple and honest. Still, it is easy to imagine the word from the Broadway "grave-diggers" if *Oklahoma!* had not succeeded: "That damn fool Hammerstein is out of touch. Here he is writing about farm girls and cowboys with simple-minded lyrics about a beautiful morning and a horse and buggy, when the world has changed. This is wartime, everyone is more sophisticated—no one cares about farms anymore. He's a nice fellow, but the parade has passed him by."

How did Oscar come to lead the parade that had passed him by for so many years, and to do so in a way that brought a resurgence of power and quality to his work? Oscar did not have the highest respect for the judgment of the critics and the smart New York theater crowd, but he had always had faith in the instincts and taste of the nonprofessional audiences that fill theaters, the "common" people, and a belief that they would recognize work of real value. He had told Ben Hecht in February that no matter what the "smarties" said, if an elevator man and a salesgirl at Altman's told him they didn't like a play, he would know there was something wrong with it. For years he had said that popular fads would come and go, and only work that was honest and true would survive. In his forty-seventh year he reached his goal of creating an enduring work; this time he did not try to please current popular taste, as he had in the shallow *Very Warm for May*, or to revive a once-popular form, as he had in *Sunny River*—he simply tried to express his own feelings and thoughts about the things in life that mattered most to him. When he did this, he not only allowed his talent to soar and his work to take on new depth, but almost paradoxically found the success that had eluded him for so long.

Walking on the country road in Doylestown with Dorothy a few hours before *Oklahoma!* was to open in New York on March 31, 1943, he said, "I don't know what to do if they don't like this. I don't know what to do because this is the only kind of show I can write."

Six

Oh, What a Beautiful Mornin'

Oscar sat calmly, holding Dorothy's hand, in the fifth row while Agnes, Dick and the others stood at the back of the St. James Theatre, which was not sold out for the first-night performance of *Oklahoma!* The curtain rose on a country scene, a farm woman seated on a porch churning as a voice from the wings began: *"There's a bright, golden haze on the meadow."* At the end of the song the audience gave an audible sigh, looked at one another, and settled back to love the show.

The last note of "Oklahoma" brought thunderous applause. Crowds of friends and acquaintants pressed around Oscar, Dick, everyone connected with the production, barraging them with the superlatives that the critics would use a few hours later in their notices.

It was a heady time. When Jules Glaezner offered Dick a drink at the cast party he gave after the show, Dick refused: "No, thanks. I don't want to get drunk. I want to feel this!" Trying to decide where to lunch the next day, Dick said, "Shall we sneak off to someplace quiet where we can talk, or shall we go to Sardi's and show off?"

"Hell, let's go to Sardi's and show off," replied Oscar.

As they walked past the theater on their way to lunch, the scene was chaotic, with policemen trying to control the crowds waiting to get to the box office. The difficulties of getting tickets to *Oklahoma!* became legendary. When Oscar's farmer, Peter Moën, asked for tickets for his son and his bride to see the show following their wedding reception, Oscar promised to get them and asked, "When's the wedding?"

"The day you can get the tickets," Moën replied.

Oklahoma! played 2,243 performances on Broadway and then toured for fifty-one weeks, while a national company traveled for ten years, appearing in over two hundred and fifty cities. There were companies on almost every continent (including a USO unit dispatched to every Pacific area to perform for American troops). In London it had the longest run of any play in the 287-year history of the Drury Lane Theatre. In addition, Decca sold over a million albums of the original cast recording, which was the first recording of an entire musical; in 1944 *Oklahoma!* received a special Pulitzer citation.

Oklahoma! was one of the few "real, genuine, 14-carat, true-blue milestones," marking the end of one era and the beginning of a new one, said Alan Jay Lerner twenty years later. Noting that "many a new day of memorable musical theater began the night that *Oklahoma!* opened," Brooks Atkinson says it was the verse of the show's first song that changed the history of the musical theater:

> All the sounds of the earth are like music—
> All the sounds of the earth are like music.
> The breeze is so busy it don't miss a tree
> And a ol' weepin' willer is laughin' at me!

"After a verse like that, sung to a buoyant melody, the banalities of the old musical stage became intolerable."

Show Boat, to which reviewers likened *Oklahoma!,* had been the first milestone for the integrated musical play, breaking with many of the traditions of operetta and vaudeville revue. Musical comedies in the thirties popped up sporadically with a lyric, a book or a character that was weightier or more touching than the usual froth, and dance in other shows took on a new look and a new importance. *Oklahoma!* brought together all the trends that had been growing disparately: each of its component parts was good, but it was the sum of them that made the show so extraordinary. Those showmen who followed often missed the point; believing that the show had succeeded because of one technique or another, they would overdo some element in an effort to outdo *Oklahoma!*, with here an over-serious book, there a dream ballet sequence that became a nightmare. The great musicals that came after the landmark show succeeded be-cause they used the lesson of *Oklahoma!* well: the emphasis was not so much on the freedom from convention as on artistic integrity.

With *Oklahoma!* running smoothly, Oscar turned back to the busi-ness of getting *Carmen Jones* on her feet. After an ASCAP meeting the previous November, he had run into Billy Rose, producer, nightclub entrepreneur and sometime-lyricist.

"What's new, Oscar?" asked Rose.

"Billy," replied Oscar, looking down at his pint-sized colleague, "if you're serious and not just asking a question you don't want an-swered, I'll answer."

As they walked—like Mutt and Jeff—to the cloakroom for their overcoats, Oscar said, "I'm working on a show for the Theatre Guild and I've also written a new musical that Max Gordon has been sitting on for some time. He's been having trouble getting money for it. I think it's the best thing I ever wrote."

"So how come you never sent it over to me?" Rose inquired.

"Frankly, it never occurred to me, Billy. I couldn't imagine it was your sort of show."

Rose pushed aside Oscar's argument: "It's bad enough to take 'no' for an answer when you're looking for a 'yes,' but it's ridiculous to decide a door is bolted before you even try to open it. So send it over tomorrow."

After Oscar went off into the snow, Billy turned to Howard Dietz, who had heard the conversation. "What do you know about *Carmen Jones?*" Billy asked.

"The most turned-down show in town," answered Dietz. "If you were in your right mind, would you sit down and write Bizet's *Carmen* as a modern American musical with an all-black cast?"

The next morning a messenger arrived at the Rose home on Beekman Place with the manuscript together with a note: "Here is my adaptation which I promised to send. It sounds much better with music but I hope you will get some enjoyment out of it just as it is. Kindest regards, Oscar."

Billy instructed his wife, Eleanor Holm, to cancel any appoint-ments. He went up to his room, kicked off his shoes, and proceeded to sing to himself Oscar's lyrics to the Bizet score, which he had learned from his opera-loving mother. It was nearly lunchtime when he turned to the well-thumbed title cover of the manuscript, noted Oscar's phone number down at the farm and called him.

"This is your little friend," he said. "Oscar, you've written the freshest musical anyone ever wrote and I want to produce it."

The smart money thought Rose had lost his mind when the word spread about the Rialto that he was going to produce *Carmen Jones* with an all-black, no-name cast.

While Oscar worked on some rewriting that he wanted to do, Rose's first important step was to engage John Hammond, Jr., an outstanding jazzophile who had been a member of the board of the NAACP since the late thirties. Hammond, a graduate of Yale and the Juilliard School of Music, had formed the first interracial trio for a highly successful tour with Benny Goodman. He also fostered such great artists as Count Basie, Teddy Wilson and Billie Holiday, and for many years he was head of A & R (artist and repertoire) for Columbia Records.

Hammond accepted the task of casting *Carmen Jones* as a labor of love and refused to be paid. The cast called for over a hundred black performers capable of singing an operatic score. Because opera, the ballet and the New York theater had not been open to black performers, there were not many available on Broadway who had trained operatic voices or dancing and acting experience. For six months Hammond toured the country, holding auditions in forty cities, contacting everyone he knew in his search for unknown talent. Luther Saxon, who had been a bellhop, an elevator operator and a chauffeur while he studied music, was working as a checker at the Philadelphia Navy Yard when he landed the role of Joe. Glenn Bryant, cast as Husky Miller, was a six-foot-five-inch New York policeman who was granted a leave of absence for the run of the show. Muriel Smith, who had studied at the Curtis Institute, was working as a film scraper for $15 a week at a photographic laboratory when she auditioned for the role of Carmen Jones. Napoleon Reed was working in the stockyards in Chicago when he was brought to Arthur Hammerstein's attention. Oscar flew to Chicago to hear him and he was signed as the alternate Joe. (The production followed the grand-opera practice of alternating lead singers, eight performances a week being too hard on voices.)

While casting went on, Russell Bennett began to adapt Bizet's score to Oscar's libretto. A composer who had become the most famous musical theater arranger on Broadway, Bennett tried to effect cuts and transpositions while sacrificing as little as possible of the musical substance. He used a good deal of Bizet's orchestration, but had to arrange a score written for a full orchestra of more than ninety instruments for an orchestra of half that number.

Only one of the principals, Muriel Rahn, the alternate Carmen, had been on the legitimate stage before. Charles Friedman, book director, mapped out each actor's every gesture and movement, working intensively with the actors as they learned to wear costumes, get around the stage, to feel at ease in their parts. Elizabeth Westmoreland of the Curtis Institute worked as a voice coach for the principals. Robert Shaw directed the ensemble.

Hassard Short, once an actor in London and New York, had directed over forty shows and was universally respected for his innovative staging. He had long hoped to stage a musical show in primary colors, so when Oscar gave him the *Carmen Jones* script, he said, "Now's my chance." Working with set designer Howard Bay and costume designer Raoul Pène du Bois, he devised a scheme whereby each scene would be bathed in a different color. He used color also as a leitmotif. Carmen Jones was never seen without a splash of red—a rose, a red cape, a magenta flower in her hair or on her shoulder.

The production opened in Philadelphia at the Erlanger Theatre for a three-week run on October 19, 1943, to "the most excited first night audience I have ever seen," Oscar reported in his weekly letter to Billy, stationed in the Pacific. New York visitors, such as Deems Taylor, Donald Ogden Stewart, Max Gordon and Larry Schwab, "raved, tore their hair and frothed at the mouth." Lee Shubert predicted it would be a big hit, but told Oscar it would have been twice as big had he not used Bizet's music! Oscar himself was, of course, very pleased that the show had turned out as he had hoped. He told his son that the show "seems to surprise people, then sort of tickle them (plenty of laughs), then it winds up by sweeping them off their feet and leaving them limp." He added, "I'm not exaggerating—just reporting."

He kept Billy informed of family doings as well. Twelve-year-old Jimmy was planning to go into the chicken business with Peter Moën's stepson, Arny. "As far as I have been able to make out the principle of their enterprise it runs something like this. They are going to take sixty of my chickens, breed them with mine, use my feed, raise them in my chicken house, and then sell them to me to eat."

Dorothy's business, still big, had become such a trial, what with the wartime scarcity of labor and materials, that Oscar persuaded her to ease up a bit, keeping just a skeleton staff to service her clients with repairs and replacements. Despite their desire to be at the farm, the Hammersteins found it necessary to work in the city several days a week. They gave up the cramped quarters of the apartment near her decorating office on East 52nd Street for three-fifths of a brownstone at 157 East 61st Street which had a charming garden with a large tree. Oscar described the small elevator attached to the staircase as a "demi-tasse lift." He used a room on the second floor of the brownstone as his study. Although the success of *Oklahoma!*, added to their other sources, ensured a high income in the years ahead, both Oscar and Dorothy felt they had to rationalize the expense of a relatively large city house. In their letters to Billy they explained that now they would dine in more often, so that the cost of the Barberry, the Stork and "21" could be subtracted from their budget. Susan would leave boarding school to study at a day school in New York while pursuing an acting career, thus the Shipley tuition could be subtracted as well.

During rehearsals of *Carmen Jones* at the Mecca Temple (now the 55th Street City Center), Rose had remarked to Oscar, "I don't think there's a theater in town big enough to hold this show." *Carmen Jones* needed a large stage for its huge cast, and the few large musical theaters were booked solid. Throughout the Philadelphia run, Rose kept on the lookout for a suitable New York house. The show moved up to Boston and the immense Boston Opera House. Although the notices were enthusiastic, the fire and excitement felt in Philadelphia were lost in this "big barn." During the first week it looked certain that they would have to stay there for six weeks, since there was still no easing up of the New York theater situation. By the next week, however, a closing at the huge Broadway Theatre gave them a house and a December 2 opening was announced.

Dorothy wrote to Billy that after she had decided "in a fit of madness" to give a party after the opening, "Your papa has been either feigning worry and lack of confidence in it ever since—or maybe he is really worried." The opening night was in fact a triumph. Drama and music critics alike raved not only about the conception and the libretto, but about the "dream production," the lighting and sets, the costumes that looked as if du Bois had "gone mad, in the best possible taste," the enthusiasm and vitality of the performers, the "miraculous showmanship" of *Carmen Jones*.

Oscar had expected a patronizing attitude from the music critics, despite the fact that *Carmen Jones* was billed as a musical play, not an opera, but most of them were as enthusiastic about the show as the audiences and the drama critics. They thought it had a greater affinity to Bizet's opera than the usual "grand opera" presentations of the work. Virgil Thomson, composer and critic, found the shape of the work intact in a way that was truer to the spirit of the original and more convincingly presented than the current Metropolitan production, despite the latter's orchestral and vocal superiority. Thomson also thought the translation, which "had wit, makes sense and fits the music," superior to anything of its kind in English. A Boston music critic thought that Bizet himself had dreamed of such a *Carmen*, with the story approaching the level of the music, and that though the show needed the Met's orchestra, the result should "give the Metropolitan plenty of pause before it brings back its own quaint conception." Robert Bagar said, "What Messrs. Hammerstein, Bennett, and their associates have done is to reaffirm the greatness of Bizet's *Carmen*. They may have led the way to an operatic resurgence."

The Hammersteins' resident critic, Dorothy, to whom Oscar had given all his rights to the property, wrote Billy that *Carmen Jones* was more exciting than *Oklahoma!* and the lyrics "the best Ockie has done, ever, ever, ever!" This time critics outside the family also gave Oscar full credit for his achievement. "If this reviewer were not given to making a fetish of understatement," said Bagar, "he would call Mr. Hammerstein a genius." George Jean Nathan, pointing out how difficult it was to fashion an intelligent paraphrase of a classical work, said that it was not merely a clever stunt, but a "skillfully maneuvered affair." Hobe Morrison, the *Variety* critic, found that Oscar's lyrical adaptation compared with his best and indicated that he was "at the peak of his career." Oscar Hammerstein, "who must be considered one of the greatest librettists of our day after his superb reworking of *Oklahoma!* and now *Carmen Jones*, has achieved a masterly tour de force," said Howard Barnes.

The notices of both *Oklahoma!* and *Carmen Jones* thus heaped praise not only on a great show but on Oscar himself. The years of seeing his first masterpiece called "Jerome Kern's *Show Boat*," of being held responsible for the wrong things and not receiving credit for the right ones, or of being totally ignored, had left their mark on Oscar. He said, "The librettist is the whipping-boy of musical comedy. When he is whipped only gently he is naively surprised. When he is not whipped at all, he feels as one who has been caressed. When he is actually commended, he loses all control, waltzes down the avenues singing his own lyrics, and wishes he were a dog, with a tail to wag and a long, grateful tongue to lick the hand that pats him." Perhaps drama critics had finally come of age in a more thorough understanding of musicals. Certainly, Oscar's work had come of age.

He wrote Billy about the offers of various jobs now flowing in and commented, "I am suddenly a much cleverer man than the dope who wrote *Sunny River* and *Very Warm for May*." A few weeks later he was asked to buy space in the annual *Variety* anniversary issue, in which theater people traditionally announced their accomplishments of the year while giving holiday greetings to others in the industry. As usual, he did so, but the "ad" that he ran was far from the usual:

Holiday Greetings
from
Oscar Hammerstein, 2?
author of
Sunny River (6 weeks at The St. James)
Very Warm for May (7 weeks at The Alvin)
Three Sisters (7 weeks at The Drury Lane)
Ball at The Savoy (5 weeks at The Drury Lane)
Free For All (3 weeks at The Manhattan)

"I've Done It Before And I Can Do It Again!

The ad was the talk of Broadway. Columnists quoted it and people talked about Oscar's modesty and sweetness. He claimed that he wasn't intending to be modest and sweet at all, and offered two explanations of the ad at various times. One was: "On Broadway, when you're good you're very very good and when you're bad you're terrible. I'm the same guy I used to be, except now I've got hits instead of flops. The ad was just a gentle reminder that times change, and keep changing." The other explanation was less gentle: "What I really was trying to do with that ad was thumb my nose and say: 'Well, you hyenas, so you thought I was all washed up?'"

Bombarded with exciting and lucrative propositions from Hollywood and Broadway, Oscar resolved not to be "diverted into a haphazard and heterogeneous catch-as-catch-can career as I have been in the past fifteen years." The turning point that marked a change in his work marked changes in the man as well.

Oscar's regimen had not varied for years. Awake at seven, he would have a long massage followed by a shower and then breakfast with Dorothy at eight-thirty. He would eat at a small table while she sat in bed with a breakfast tray. Then he would go to his study and work on his current project until eleven-thirty, when he would handle his correspondence and business matters. After lunch at one, he would go back to his study until five, with a half-hour nap in the middle of the afternoon. At the end of his workday, he would pop into a room and ask "What's the score?" if Jimmy was listening to a baseball game, or "Want a game of tennis?" Occasionally he would take Jimmy to a Saturday football game or take part in some other weekend activity, but generally he wrote for five to seven solid hours every day of the week except when a show was in rehearsals and tryouts.

The difference his family noticed since he first began working on *Carmen Jones* was in the concentration that went into his work. When the children's noise occasionally reached his study and distracted him, their father seemed much angrier now. The violence of his temper on these occasions, when he emerged from his study swearing and yelling, surprised them, for he was usually as calm and controlled at home as he was in the theater. The outbursts are a clue to the increase in concentration since 1942 which seems to be responsible for the change in the quality and depth of his writing. The anger was the reaction of someone concentrating so hard that household noises jolted him out of an inner place. It was as if he was meeting the deepest feelings of his characters and himself in those hours in the study—an interaction that made possible the honesty that characterized his best writing.

Outside of his study Oscar changed, too. He became more private than ever, eschewing the New York parties he had come to dislike so much and spending as much time as he could on the farm. He remained devoted to his family and always found time to play games and spend time with the children, but seemed somewhat more withdrawn than he had been in his earlier years. Dorothy often had a feeling that even after he left his study he was abstracted, still involved in some way with the lyric lying on his desk.

Oscar always made time for his work on the Writers' War Board created in the spring of 1942, when the Treasury Department asked Howard Lindsay, then president of the Authors League, to get together a group of writers to help publicize the war bond effort. Oscar was one of the original members of the board, staying with the organization as it expanded its operations to cooperate with several government agencies in liaison with the Office of War Information and even after the war, when it became the Writers' Board for World Government. Rex Stout, who headed the board, was amazed to find that Oscar almost never missed or was even late for any of the board's all-day Wednesday meetings, no matter how busy he became in those years. In 1943 Oscar set up a committee of people in the music industry to look for songs that would help the morale of the country and the war effort. He found that the most constructive efforts came from the younger people in the industry and concluded that the music business was an "old man's comedy of errors." He and Dick wrote three songs, none of them inspired: "The P.T. Boat Song (Steady as You Go)," "We're on Our Way (Infantry Song)," and "Dear Friend." There was a good deal of skepticism about the Music War Committee; Oscar Levant remarked: "You can't win the war with a song."

Oscar Hammerstein answered the doubters with: "You think this is futile, and yet it is a mighty funny thing that shortly after I started to handle the war, Africa fell to the Allies." A few months later he realized that the skeptics were right and he devoted all his war effort to the Writers' War Board, which tackled some major questions of attitudes in the country. Distressed by the racism and anti-Semitism existing in America even while it fought the Nazis, the board not only tried to change attitudes, but pressured the government and other organizations to stop racist practices. Its efforts were instrumental in getting the Army to hire black medical personnel and the Red Cross to stop typing blood by racial group.

Relatives and friends gathered in force again at Highland Farm for Christmas 1943. Oscar loved the holiday and looked forward particularly to Christmas Eve and the traditional trimming of the large tree in the living room. There were sixteen people staying in the compound and eight more who dropped in for the evening. Henry surprised his mother and stepfather by turning up just before dinner on Christmas Eve. Graduated cum laude from Storm King Academy, he was enrolled in a Navy training program at Duke University. At the table set with green cloth and bright red napkins, the Hammersteins drank a toast to the absent family members: Billy and his wife, Maggie, Reggie * and his new wife, Mary.

After the presents were opened the next morning, everyone pitched in to help clean up the debris and prepare for Christmas dinner. All sixteen wrote a message to Billy, which was bound into "a book" by Milton Cohen, a childhood friend of Oscar's, who was invited to spend every Christmas with them. Alice reported on her new job as Oscar's general assistant (replacing Leighton Brill, then overseas with the U.S.O.); she was excited by the chance of learning so much by working with her father.

Oscar wrote of his biggest Christmas surprise. A truck had pulled up bearing a jet-black Aberdeen Angus heifer with a red ribbon around her neck and a card attached—a present from Billy Rose.† Oscar was delighted to have another Angus; he found them "beautiful creatures, straight backed, short-legged, bit barrelled—though barrel is a little unjust. They are more shapely and suggest more muscular power." He planned to breed the four Angus heifers with his neighbor Ray Bitzer's prize bull, keep the offspring and build up the herd, a non-taxable form of increased wealth. The farm provided plenty in times of rationing: two hogs would provide enough ham, pork and lard for a year, chickens and milk were plentiful and the Hammersteins were making their own butter.

Jerry Watanabe, who had spent the Christmas before on Ellis Island, wrote: "There comes a time in every man's life when his world seems shattered—all that he has worked for and hoped for seems but a mirage in the desert of hope. At such a time, lucky is he indeed who has a friend in the real sense of the word. And I, Bill, am one of those lucky ones. That I am here today able to send you these few

---

* Reggie was again associated with Oscar as the production stage manager and supervisor of the *Oklahoma!* National Company after making some independent stabs at producing. He drank more than ever, but was thought by the family to be a "weekend drunk," whose alcoholism never interfered with his ability to work. The family was delighted with his marriage to beautiful ex-Powers model Mary Manners, who had a fourteen-year-old daughter, but had some doubts about its chances for survival. It lasted one year and produced a daughter named Regina.
† The Rose heifer later made local headlines by producing triplets.

lines, with my own wife, daughter, and mother is all due to the Hammersteins—God bless them and theirs."

Lu Hellman, an old Great Neck friend, wrote how remarkable it was that with sixteen people no one got in one another's way. After dinner, family and friends sat around in comfortable firelit rooms reading, writing, listening to music, dozing or playing games. The dominant game this year was chess, introduced to the household the summer before by Stevie Sondheim, he had become such a frequent visitor that he seemed part of the family.

Dorothy's client Foxy Sondheim had moved with her son to a house near Doylestown following her divorce, and had arranged for Steve to meet Jimmy, who was exactly one year and one day younger. Steve was immediately drawn to the Hammersteins and to the atmosphere of their home, so different from his own. He bicycled the twenty minutes to the farm, or was driven by one of his mother's friends, for the day or for visits that often ran to several days. A bright, complex, competitive boy, he immediately took to the games which were an important part of his adopted home. His first day at Highland Farm was spent playing Monopoly; soon he taught Oscar and Jimmy chess, which became a passion for them all.

Oscar loved games. Fiercely competitive, he tuned into the thinking and psychological patterns of an opponent, as good games players do. In the third or fourth chess game that Steve played with Oscar, the twelve-year-old set up a three-move trap, which Oscar started to move into. He put his hand on his piece, moved it forward and then, without taking his hand off the piece, looked up at the boy. As Steve kept a poker face, Oscar took his piece back, thought a few minutes and moved a different piece, avoiding the trap. "How did you know what I was setting up?" asked Stevie.

"I heard your heart beating," replied Oscar.

He entered into games with fervor, wanting to win as much as the boys did. Though most games were played for money, tennis and chess were not. Oscar wanted to win so much that he made blatant gamesmanship ploys. While a chess opponent was thinking, he would drum his fingers on the table or begin to whistle. When the opponent looked up and said, "Would you please stop that?" he would do so, but the damage had been done, the concentration broken. Over the years Oscar consistently beat Steve, Steve consistently beat Jimmy and Jimmy consistently beat Oscar. In anagrams and, later, Scrabble, Oscar and Steve always battled for the lead, while Dorothy, an excellent crossword-puzzle solver, and Jimmy always trailed. When Jimmy was thirteen, he said to his father, "I'm going to beat you in tennis next year."

"No," said Oscar, "not until you're sixteen."

At fourteen, Jimmy had a ranking in the mid-Atlantic states and knew he could play rings around his father, but couldn't win a set against him. At fifteen he finally did it.

"That's a relief," said his father. "That's really a relief."

For Oscar and the children, games provided a medium of knowing and communicating with each other. It was through chess and other games that Jimmy felt he came to know his father's mind. It was not until he was in his twenties that he and his father really began to talk, in a way outside the usual family pattern of "What did you do today?"

The only other medium for discussion in the earlier years was the dinner-table "talks," which were another game. Here, as well as at the chess table, Oscar would find ploys to best whichever of the children he had taken on that night. It usually started when one of them made a generalization of some sort. "Ah, another sweeping statement," Oscar would say, which meant, "Let's go." He would begin tearing the statement to shreds, trapping the victim into contradicting his or her original remark. He would then put the contradictory statement together saying, "I don't understand" with an innocent look on his face. In the process of the verbal battle he might make the child trip over words and then attack the diction or turn to personal teasing. He would never admit that he was wrong or give the youngster the satisfaction of hearing "Well argued." Very often it was Jimmy who was on the spot, though it might be any one of the others.

Steve, who spent more and more time with the Hammersteins as his problems at home worsened, never came under attack—he enjoyed all the advantages of a son without any of the disadvantages. Calling Oscar "the finest man I ever met," Steve has no criticism of the man, major or minor, other than his teasing of his children. He later became an "artistic son" to Oscar, but his relationship with the Hammersteins was deeply personal. "Oscar and Dorothy saved my life on a personal level, and Oscar set my life on a professional level. It's as simple as that. I don't know where I would be today if I hadn't met them, on any level."

The other children did not resent Steve for escaping Oscar's attacks, probably because they could sense the love and concern expressed even in the teasing. In any case, they were able to put the dinner-table needling in perspective even while they went through them, and gradually they learned to toss it back to him.

"It must be awfully dull for people who know all the answers," said Susan one night.

"Yes, it is," Oscar replied.

Henry, who spent most of his vacations on the farm, which he loved and found a "dream world" of order, comfort, good food and fun, began a letter: "Dear Ockie, I miss you also. No longer do I hear a calm and measured voice doling out derogatory remarks to my right at the dinner table . . ."

One night when Jimmy was sixteen and the Rodgers were having dinner at the farm, he finally caught his father in a slip of the tongue. His moment had come. "That's an interesting way of putting it," he said, laughing. Oscar turned red and looked ready to kill him, but said nothing. The game was over—he never made another verbal attack on his youngest son. Perhaps, like the end of his supremacy in tennis, it was a relief.

Dorothy, who tried to cool the competitive spirit of the dinner table but often felt her interference only made matters worse, received her share of teenage humor, too. A woman of sound perceptions and good sense, she had a subtle wit and a healthy sense of the ridiculous, but in the heat of argument made an occasional slip. One night she capped a discussion of religious prejudice with: "Well, I don't care whether a person is a Jew or a Mohammedan or a Buddhist or anything, just as long as he is a good Christian!" The children broke into applause while Oscar smiled at her fondly.

In January Oscar began writing a screenplay for *State Fair*. He and Dick had signed a contract with Twentieth Century-Fox the previous summer to write a musical version of Phil Stong's popular novel. The simple tale of a family's visit to the Iowa State Fair had been filmed once before, in 1933, with Will Rogers, Lew Ayers, Janet Gaynor and Sally Eilers. Now Darryl F. Zanuck, the studio head, wanted to present it as a musical, and when he saw *Oklahoma!* immediately thought of Rodgers and Hammerstein. Oscar liked the idea and promised to have a completed script by February 1, though, as it turned out, the production of *Carmen Jones* made it necessary to extend the date to April 1.

Oscar's scenario caught the spirit of the story, which had no villain and little suspense except for such burning questions as whether prize hog Blue Boy would win the grand championship. He still didn't enjoy writing for the screen as much as he did for the stage, where he could see the whole thing unfold before him. Writing a picture felt like navigating without a compass. "I don't know where the hell I'm going," he declared, and vowed never to write another.

One afternoon, while working with Dick, Oscar brought up a song problem. When the story opens, the young girl, Margy, is unhappy; she is going to a state fair with her family but is not looking forward to it and doesn't know why. A song was needed for her melancholy mood, which sounded to Oscar like spring fever. But he knew, unfortunately, that all state fairs are held in the harvest months of autumn—which knocked out his spring fever song. Rather half-heartedly he threw out the idea of having her say that although it's autumn she has spring fever, so it might as well be spring. Dick jumped up excitedly and said, "That's it!" Within a week Oscar wrote the words for "It Might as Well Be Spring." The lyrics exhibit his skill at its most effective:

> I'm as restless as a willow in a windstorm,
> I'm as jumpy as a puppet on a string.
> I'd say that I had spring fever,
> But I know it isn't spring.
> I am starry-eyed and vaguely discontented,
> Like a nightingale without a song to sing.
> Oh, why should I have spring fever
> When it isn't even spring.
> I keep wishing I were somewhere else,
> Walking down a strange, new street,
> Hearing words that I have never heard
> From a man I've yet to meet.
> I'm as busy as a spider spinning day-dreams,
> I'm as giddy as a baby on a swing.
> I haven't seen a crocus or a rosebud,
> Or a robin on the wing,
> But I feel so gay—(in a melancholy way)—
> That it might as well be spring—
> It might as well be spring!

Oscar and Dick were scheduled to spend five weeks in Hollywood preparing the shooting script, but had to cancel the trip when Oscar was hospitalized in early May. He had an operation for a severe attack of diverticulitis, for which he had undergone surgery the year before. He told Steve Sondheim, who visited him after the operation, that he had had a glimpse of death and that it was a startling and edifying experience. During the weeks of recuperation at the farm, Oscar enjoyed for the first time in his life being "lazy" and having an excuse to sit on the porch and gaze at the fields and dream. Dorothy kept him company, but finding herself unable to be inactive, she kept herself busy nearby painting the outdoor furniture, much of which had come from the set of *East Wind* in 1931.

Twentieth Century-Fox gave *State Fair* a lavish technicolor production with a cast that included Jeanne Crain, Dana Andrews, Dick Haymes, Vivian Blaine, Charles Winninger, Fay Bainter and Donald Meek. Its release in August 1945 was greeted by reviewers as one of the most successful pictures of the year. Archer Winsten said in the *New York Post* that "*State Fair* is to movie musicals what *Oklahoma!* is to stage musicals." Of its six songs, three—"That's for Me," "It's a Grand Night for Singing," and "It Might as Well Be Spring"—became hits, the last receiving an Academy award as the best original song that year.

Pleased with the results of his collaboration with Dick, Oscar was already discussing another stage musical with him. He did not consider it an exclusive partnership, however, for he continued to correspond with Jerry Kern regularly, not only about matters of friendship and the latest on Rommyisms (as when Rommy asked Oscar, "Is it true Lena Horne is an octane?"), but about material for shows they might collaborate on. Independently of each other, each had picked up the old Marco Polo script in the spring of 1944 and become enamored of it all over again. Jerry wrote that he still thought it could well be the "best musical play ever written," and they discussed other possibilities as well.

On Father's Day of that year Jimmy and Alice wrote a new lyric to an aria from *Carmen*. It went in part:

> But every day is father's day for Father
> We know we should repay him but we just can't bother
> Dad we know that you are lovely but
>   outside o' that you're naughty too
> You listen in on conversations that don't
>   belong to you
> You read other people's letters
> You never admit you're wrong—

But you always should remember that it's here
 where you belong—No foolin'
We hope that you like this song.

The lyrics referred to Oscar's habit of listening to Susan's telephone calls or creeping up behind her as she gossiped with a friend on the couch and then repeating the conversation, complete with imitations of the girls, at the dinner table. Susan finally put an end to the telephone snooping by breaking into a stream of profanity whenever she suspected that he was listening on the extension. Her ploy worked; the language was more than Oscar could bear. Oscar seldom used profanity, except when he was yelling for quiet from his study. He chuckled at off-color jokes told by certain old friends like Harold Hyman, but did not talk about sex with his family. He was embarrassed when the children told dirty jokes, with the exception of one joke of Henry's which delighted him. "A man went into a store," said Henry, "and asked the woman there, 'Excuse me, miss, do you keep stationery?' She replied, 'Yes, until the very last minute, and then I go crazy.'"

Though he usually objected to song parodies, Oscar appreciated Jimmy's and Alice's Father's Day effort. When Susan was home from boarding school, he used to sing one of his own to her, to the tune of "All the Things You Are," in what Billy Rose called a voice like a raven: "You are the promised pest of summer / That makes the lovely winter seem short . . ." Susan was amused by the song. She and others in the family were also amused by his old-fashioned expressions: "waist" for "blouse," or "You've got too much lip rouge on!" Studying to be an actress, Susan was sometimes carried away in her efforts to look and act sophisticated. In addition to criticizing her overuse of make-up, Oscar would often remind her that being blasé or pretending to be knowing was really a sign of an unsophisticated person. "The most sophisticated thing you can say is 'I don't know. Tell me about it.'" While he encouraged her acting studies, he was not given to false compliments when it came to the theater, even with his children. After a performance of *Rumpelstiltskin* at Friends Academy in which she played the miller's daughter, Oscar greeted Susan backstage with "The less said about that, the better." When she was sixteen, she announced to him that she was going to try out for Billy Rose's *Seven Lively Arts*. "Doing what?" he asked.

"I'm going to be a show girl," replied Susan.

Stung by his laughter as he regarded her reedlike figure, Susan put on an enormous pair of falsies, an angora beret that she called a "hooker's special," and lots of red-black lipstick and got a part—as one of fourteen show girls.

Though Oscar had an office at 655 Fifth Avenue, he opened another with Dick at 1270 Sixth Avenue, decorated by Dorothy, where they set up a separate business affiliation in addition to their creative one. In partnership with Max Dreyfus at Chappell, they created their own publishing arm, whose first songs were those from *Oklahoma!* In honor of their fathers, both of whom were named William, they named the publishing firm Williamson Music.

Dick's love of producing and Oscar's desire to hedge against the day when his creative abilities might wane led them to become Broadway producers on shows other than those they wrote. Dick found a book of short stories by Kathryn Forbes, *Mama's Bank Account*, which they thought had the makings of a good straight play. Deciding to make this their first joint producing venture, they acquired the rights and engaged John Van Druten, the playwright and novelist, to act as adapter and director.

As for collaborating on a new show, they knew that anything they did would be measured against *Oklahoma!* for years to come. An incident concerning Sam Goldwyn served to remind them of this. After seeing *Oklahoma!* Goldwyn called Dick and asked to meet him to give him some advice.

"*Oklahoma!* is such a wonderful show," Goldwyn said. "You know what you should do next?"

"What?" asked Rodgers.

"Shoot yourself!"

Oscar and Dick were so careful about picking the right property for their next show that when it appeared they initially turned it down.

It happened at a "Gloat Club" lunch. Meeting each Thursday at Sardi's with the Guild's Helburn and Langer, they discussed financial and casting matters and, of course, gloated over *Oklahoma!*'s incredible success.

In November, at one of the weekly lunches, Helburn and Langner conspiratorially looked from left to right to make sure that no one was listening, put their fingers to their lips and whispered, "How would you like to do a musical play based on Ferenc Molnár's *Liliom?*"

Oscar and Dick looked from left to right and whispered back at them in unison, "No."

"Why?" asked Langner.

They took turns listing objections to the play, which had been a great success when first produced by the Guild, in an adaptation by Benjamin F. Glasser with Joseph Schildkraut and Eva Le Gallienne heading the cast, and again in the 1940 revival, featuring Ingrid Bergman and Burgess Meredith. They agreed with the producers that the story was beautiful and the characters interesting, but they felt that the Hungarian setting was impossible. They couldn't conceive of it done in either peasant costume or in drab modern Hungarian dress, and the current volatile political situation made it highly impractical, since they might have to change the play before tryouts.

The following Thursday Terry greeted them with: "Move *Liliom* from Hungary to Louisiana. You boys say you want to write about America; the show is European—Louisiana is an American locale with a European flavor. Liliom can be a Creole."

They promised to think about it. Oscar researched the necessary Creole atmosphere, only to find a disconcerting difficulty: dialect full of "zis" and "zat" and "zose," which would be corny as well as difficult for writing lyrics. However, he had always liked the play and the more he thought about it, the more attracted he was to the bittersweet play that blended realism and fantasy in the tale of a shiftless but charming carnival barker in Budapest. Liliom leaves Julie, the shy but spirited young factory worker who loves him pregnant with his child when he kills himself in order to avoid capture by the police for an attempted robbery. Sent to Heaven, and then tó sixteen years in Purgatory, he is allowed to return to earth for one day to atone for his sins; he tries to give his daughter a star, but when she refuses to take it, slaps her and is led away by his heavenly escort, presumably to Hell.

They all met a few days later to discuss the possibilities further. There were serious problems. One was the locale; another, what Oscar called "the tunnel" of the second act—the gloomy scenes in the Hollander house, followed by Liliom's crime, his death and a bitter, downbeat ending. In addition, the motivation for the crime seemed very difficult to do musically.

Both Oscar and Dick later told a story about the writing of "Soliloquy," the male lead's aria about becoming a father, in which they said that the words about a son named Bill came first and the section about a daughter was added only later at Dick's insistence, since both of the Rodgers children were girls. The story was a charming one, but notes from the December 7 meeting at Oscar's New York home suggest that it was inaccurate: "Mr. Rodgers suggested a fine musical number for the end of the scene where Liliom discovers he is to be a father, in which he sings first with pride of the growth of a boy and then suddenly realizes it might be a girl, and changes completely with that thought." It was this song idea that made the possibility of doing *Liliom* come alive for both of them. Also, the motivation for Liliom's robbery attempt seemed the hardest thing to do musically; they felt sure that once they saw the solution to that problem, they could get the rest of it.

They tentatively told the Guild they would do it, but the locale still bothered them. At the next meeting Dick suddenly suggested transferring the story to a New England setting. The suggestion seemed outlandish for only a moment, and then everything began to fall into place. Immediately Oscar saw that this setting solved the problem of an ensemble that is necessary in a musical, for New England at the turn of the century had girls who worked in the mills and boys who worked as fishermen or on sailing ships. He was attracted to the idea of presenting New Englanders as something other than tight-lipped Puritans, as people who are strong and alive and lusty. The New England speech would be no trouble at all. The inner strength and outer simplicity of Julie seemed to him more characteristic of New Englanders than of people anywhere else, and the strutting carnival barker could fit any surrounding. Once they sorted out the locale and the motivation for the murder, they became enthusiastic about doing the play, even with all the other problems it presented. In fact, the problems made it doubly attractive, for they were aware of the *Oklahoma!* trap: the difficulty of creating a show that was just as good but not imitative of their first joint effort. They would be forced to find imaginative and unusual devices in order to solve the challenges that existed for them in *Liliom*.

Meanwhile the Guild producers had set about getting permission from Ferenc Molnár. He was generally opposed to adaptation of his plays; he had refused Giacomo Puccini's request to use his most successful play as the basis for an opera: "I want it to be remembered as Molnár's *Liliom*, not Puccini's *Liliom*." The Guild decided that the best means of persuasion was to arrange to have Molnár see *Okla-*

homa! In his meeting with Terry and Larry afterwards, Molnár said that if Rodgers and Hammerstein could treat the subject of his play as tastefully and charmingly as they had handled *Green Grow the Lilacs,* he would be pleased to give his consent.

It was summer before substantive work began on even an outline. They were determined from the outset to blend elements of the dramatic stage, opera and dance. Dick decided early on not to have an overture, which usually competed with the noise of people rushing in, banging seats and getting settled. He decided on a musical prelude within the structure of the play, a pantomime establishing the characters and mood, played to a waltz scored for woodwind and brass in imitation of the steady grind of the carousel onstage. They decided to have more music than dialogue; most musicals were 50 percent music, but *Carousel* came closer to 75 percent.

The Rodgerses brought their children with them to the working weekends in Doylestown. Mary, thirteen, and Linda, nine, were lively, articulate children who exhibited musical talents of their own. Mary immediately loved the atmosphere of the Hammersteins' farm and found Oscar warm and friendly, with an air of being quietly amused or bemused by children. At her first meeting with Steve Sondheim, she thought he was the most brilliant, entrancing person she had ever met and they struck up a lasting friendship.

The two Dorothys found themselves in a peculiar position; their husbands' partnership plunged them into a close relationship even before they had a chance to become acquainted with each other's personality. The two women had many similarities in their backgrounds: both were decorators and both were wives of men who had been in the musical theater for years. But they were as different in character as the rooms they created in their work. Dorothy Rodgers' decorating style was as meticulous, measured, thought-out and as correct as she was. Dorothy Hammerstein's reflected her more spontaneous nature and manner, her preference for an easy, colorful tone, rather than correctness of form. Their upbringings and temperaments, too, were very different. For the most part, the relationship went smoothly enough, though there were tensions beneath the surface. Oscar would never discuss any difficulties of the situation. From the beginning of their collaboration, he and Dick worked smoothly together and presented a solid front to the world while maintaining a relationship that was quite impersonal. Bound together in an interdependence closer than that in many families, they were able to preserve an equilibrium that few other collaborators have been able to maintain. The difficulties in such a successful collaboration were enormous. Under the greatest pressure, in public view, they had to share effort, decisions and responsibility, as well as the resulting rewards and recognition. In addition to the bruising exposure of self that any creative process brings, they had to contend with the tensions and jealousies inherent in such a partnership. By nature not alike, perhaps sensing things they did not like about each other, they chose to concentrate on the qualities they did like and leave the others alone. This was a very different kind of relationship for Oscar than his association with Jerry Kern. Jerry and Oscar, someone remarked, were rather like two naughty boys together. Dick and Oscar were like two solid, successful partners whose primary link was professional.

Recognizing their need of each other, they evolved a relationship that would make it possible for them to work well together. The basis of it was formed by the time they worked on *Carousel*. At its core was personal distance, mutual respect, loyalty, discipline and, above all, restraint. At arm's length emotionally, they never confided in each other, never shared conversation about the deeper issues of life, ideals, their feelings for one another. They always presented a common front to others and their loyalty to each other was complete; never did one question the other publicly or utter anything but praise. Those who worked with them found that they came to meetings united and in perfect agreement, made joint decisions quickly and stuck by them. They began to be known as "R & H."

As their basic collaborative relationship was set, the process by which they worked on a show was set as well. Again they used long talking sessions at the home of one or the other to work out the characters, the story, the placement and purpose of the music. After these sessions were over, Oscar and Dick kept in touch on matters of substance but worked side by side even less than they had on *Oklahoma!* Oscar began work on the book that summer, but interrupted his writing in the fall, when John Van Druten's adaptation of *Mama's Bank Account* was ready for their efforts as producers.

Like *Oklahoma!*, the play, now entitled *I Remember Mama*, was a folk drama of heart and spirit with none of the usual ingredients for popular success. Van Druten's script pleased Rodgers and Hammerstein and they assembled an excellent cast, with Mady Christians as Mama and Marlon Brando as Nils, his first Broadway role. Rodgers and Hammerstein found themselves as successful at producing as they were at writing musicals. The play opened to reviews that made much of the impeccable production. It ran for over two years and became something of a modern classic; it was made into a movie and a television series and was used for countless stock and amateur productions.

In the fall the Hammersteins closed their house in Doylestown and planned to spend most of their winter in the city because Oscar would be busy with two shows and his Writers' War Board work, and because in September Jimmy left for his first year at George School, a boarding school.

With *I Remember Mama* successfully launched, Oscar turned again to the adaptation of *Liliom*. He still felt somewhat uneasy as he proceeded because he was admittedly afraid of Molnár's disapproval —he was aware that no matter how faithful he was to the story and the characters, some dialogue values would have to be sacrificed to make room for the music.

He felt, too, the pressure of *Oklahoma!*'s success. In November he wrote, "We're all fools. No matter what we do, everyone is bound to say 'This is not another *Oklahoma!*' It isn't trying to be, but that will make no difference. As a matter of fact, every musical play that everyone else writes meets the same irrelevant comment, so that every time a new musical opens, *Oklahoma!* gets another string of good notices."

With the scene changed to Maine in 1873, Liliom became Billy Bigelow, but remained the handsome amusement-park barker who means well but is a rough-and-ready bully, as incapable of making money as he is of showing love. In Oscar's version, Julie is not the barker's mistress but his wife, though her character, too, retains the original's unique qualities and odd values, expressed in the song "You're a Queer One, Julie Jordan." Oscar changed the words of the dialogue more than he had in *Green Grow the Lilacs,* to give the speech a more authentic ring. Molnár's "I suppose I'm to ask your permission before I touch another girl!" became "Can't put my arm around a girl without I ask you permission! That how it is?" Other lines were dropped or changed entirely, but the feelings, the interactions and the characters in the opening scene remained the same. The inspiration for the song "If I Loved You" came directly from Molnár's dialogue in the first scene.

LILIOM: But you wouldn't marry a rough guy like me—that is,—eh—
　if you loved me—
JULIE: Yes, I would—if I loved you, Mister Liliom.

The song makes explicit the theme of Molnár's play: the inability of
the couple to express to each other the deep love that each feels.

When Irving Berlin said, "The difference between Oscar and the
rest of us lyric writers is that he is a poet," he illustrated his point
with these words:

> You can't hear a sound—not the turn of a leaf,
> Nor the fall of a wave, hittin' the sand.
> The tide's creepin' up on the beach like a thief,
> Afraid to be caught, stealin' the land. . . .

In his first script, Oscar used dialogue to get across the inability
of Billy and Julie to articulate their feelings and wrote a very different
version of the song:

BILLY: Ah . . . How do you know what you'd do if you loved me?
　Or how you'd feel . . . or anythin'?
JULIE: I dunno how I know.
BILLY: Ah
JULIE: Sometimes you know things that y' can't say so good why
　ya know 'em but you do.

> If I loved you
> I would tremble ev'ry time you'd say my name,
> But I'd long to hear you say it just the same.
> I dunno jest how I know, but I ken see
> How everythin' would be
> If I loved you . . .
> If I loved you
> I'd be too a-skeered t'say what's in my heart
> I'd be too a-skeered to even make a start
> And my golden chance to speak would come and go
> And you would never know
> How I loved you—
> If I loved you.

In the next version the dialogue was dropped and the song sim-
plified and clarified, pared to the essence of the meaning that it
carries:

> If I loved you
> Time and again I would try to say

> All I'd want you to know
> If I loved you
> Words wouldn't come in an easy way—
> 'Round in circles I'd go!
> Longin' to tell you, but afraid and shy,
> I'd let my golden chances pass me by
> Soon you'd leave me
> Off you would go in the mist of day
> Never, never to know
> How I loved you—
> If I loved you.

Oscar ended the scene as Molnár did, with acacia blossoms falling around the awkward lovers.

As he progressed on the libretto, the ending continued to trouble him. He lightened the tone of the "tunnel" that had worried him by moving the action out of the dreary Hollander house to a spa on the ocean, preparations for a clambake and the event itself. The very end of the Molnár play is bleak and pessimistic. Liliom defiantly tells Heaven's policemen that he does not regret his actions and is led away, as frustrated and unable to communicate as ever. It was not a desire for a "happy" ending that made Oscar shy away from Molnár's, but what he called an inability to conceive of an unregenerate soul, of a dead end to existence.

In *Carousel*, Oscar followed the original plot through Billy's death by his own hand when he is caught in an attempted robbery, and Julie's articulation of her love and understanding as she cradles his body.

> "Sleep, Billy—sleep. Sleep peaceful, like a good boy. You weren't a good boy—you were bad and quick tempered and unhappy. But sleep peaceful now. I knew why you hit me. I always knew everythin' you were thinkin' . . . One thing I never told you—skeered you'd laugh at me. I'll tell you now—[*Even now she has to make an effort to overcome her shyness in saying it*] I love you. I love you. [*In a whisper*] I love—you."

It was in the development of the character of Billy's daughter that he radically changed the ending. In *Liliom* the daughter is simply a figure who appears briefly and reacts to her father's slap. Oscar and Dick from the beginning had planned a sequence using dance and music to show the fifteen years of Billy's daughter's life. Now the second act went on from there to develop more fully the father-child relationship. Although Billy hits his daughter, as Liliom did, he is also able to help the unhappy child—whose problems are so like his own—face life more positively. "You'll Never Walk Alone" is used in the final scene to emphasize the hope and love that Billy is able to give his daughter on the one day he is allowed to spend on earth. Lawrence Langner remarked that this "uncanny collaboration" of composer and librettist made the musical play considerably deeper than the original play by exploring the new dimension presented by the child and her problems. Oscar claimed it was only to indulge himself that he made the change in the play, but the results were artistically satisfying, removing the gloomy tragedy of *Liliom's* ending without altering the bittersweet tone of the story.

The lyrics of "You'll Never Walk Alone" embody the essence of Oscar's optimistic and hopeful philosophy in a melody that matches the words in solid simplicity. Once again Oscar and a collaborator were able to write a song that had a comfortable air of familiarity about it. "Ol' Man River" seemed from the beginning to be an old spiritual; "You'll Never Walk Alone" sounded like an oft-sung hymn— it has already become such an established favorite at weddings, funerals and graduations that many people forget it was written for a Broadway show in the 1940's. Irving Berlin believes this the greatest song Oscar ever wrote because when he heard it at a funeral he realized that it had as much impact on him as the Twenty-third Psalm.

Oscar said he was sometimes "poisoned" by the research he did in his desire for accuracy. When he and Dick decided they needed "This Was a Real Nice Clambake" as an ensemble song, he realized that he had no idea what a clambake was like, so he began to research the matter. Learning that a clambake began with chowder, he read several books by historians, cooks and experts on dialect before he wrote:

> First come codfish chowder
> Cooked in iron kettles
> Onions floatin' on the top
> Curlin' up in petals!

Unfortunately, after he finished the verse he read another book and discovered that the authentic clambake chowder is codhead, not codfish, chowder. Should he use the new word, "codhead," which he was so proud of discovering, or retain "codfish," which would make more sense to more people even if it was wrong? Suppressing his researcher's pride, he kept "codfish" and went on. When he got to lobsters, he wrote:

> We slit 'em down the back
> And peppered 'em good
> And doused 'em in melted butter . . .

A friend, Ted Ely, who had a home near Gloucester, Massachusetts, said, "Oc, how could you? Don't you know you slit lobsters up the front?" Oscar was grieved at this news, since his line was better for singing. He sent out his chief researcher, Alice, who called on the chef of the King of the Sea restaurant and found out that he slit them "down the back—always." Oscar concluded that people probably all slit lobsters the same way, but some call the back the front and vice versa.

In writing "June Is Bustin' Out All Over" he thought he knew enough about things in June to proceed without research. One verse ran:

> June is bustin' out all over
> The sheep aren't sleepin' any more!
> All the rams that chase the ewe sheep
> Are determined there'll be new sheep
> And the ewe sheep aren't even keepin' score!

It was after the lyric was finished that Peter Moën pointed out to him that sheep do not mate in June; they mate in winter and bear their young in the spring. Oscar hated his lyrics to be inaccurate, but he let the stanza remain, explaining to purists, "What you say about sheep may all be very true for most years, sir, but not in 1873. 1873 is my year and that year, curiously enough, the sheep mated in the spring."

Just after the mail brought the lyrics to "June Is Bustin' Out All Over" to the Rodgerses' house, Dorothy Rodgers left on a short errand. When she returned, less than a half-hour later, Dick had completed the music to the song. Oscar was a much slower worker; the lyrics to Billy's "Soliloquy" took him over two weeks. It is probably the most important song in *Carousel* because it explains Billy's sudden change of heart about committing the crime that leads to the climax of the drama. After he realizes the baby might be a girl, he sings:

"I got to get ready before she comes!
I got to make certain that she
Won't be dragged up in slums
With a lot o' bums—
Like me!
She's got to be sheltered and fed, and dressed
In the best that money can buy!
I never know how to get money,
But I'll try—
By God! I'll try!
I'll go out and make it
Or steal it or take it
Or die!"

The problem presented earlier by Jud, the bad character who had to be shown in all his complexity in order to generate some sympathy for him, was even more pressing in creating the character of Billy Bigelow. A ne'er-do-well who beats his wife, gets involved in a crime and commits suicide, he can hardly be viewed as a sympathetic character. And yet the long "Soliloquy" he sings in his blustering way reveals a gentler Billy—one who yearns and who wants to do the right thing but isn't sure how. The lyrics give a clue to his background and the grudges he bears that make him a "bad fellow," and create strong sympathy for him as a very human being.

My boy, Bill—
He'll be tall
And as tough
As a tree,
Will Bill!
Like a tree he'll grow
With his head held high
And his feet planted firm on the ground,
And you won't see no—
body dare to try
To boss him or toss him around!
No pot-bellied, baggy-eyed bully'll boss him around . . .

After considering that his son might do anything, as long as he does what he likes, might be a boat pilot or a cowboy or a carousel barker or heavyweight champ or President of the United States ("That'd be all right, too—"), he sings:

"Wait a minute! Could it be—?
What the hell! What if he
Is a girl! [*Rises in anguish.*]
Bill!
Oh, Bill! [*He sits on bait box and holds his head in his
        hands . . . speaks over music in a moaning voice.*]
What would I do with her? What could I do for her?
A bum—with no money!
   You can have fun with a son,
   But you got to be a FATHER
   To a girl!"

When they first discussed "Soliloquy," Dick improvised on the piano to give Oscar an idea of the kind of music he envisioned—the tone, color and emotion. Oscar wrote the lyrics with this feel of the music in his head, then gave six typewritten pages to Dick, who set the eight-minute melody in just two hours. The final composition shows integration of words and music so complete that it seems as if one man had written both.

"What's the Use of Wonderin' " was often used by Oscar to illustrate his theory about phonetics, which, after rhyming, is the most important device used by a lyricist. He believed that proper phonetics not only made a song good, but determined its popularity. He never agreed with people who called him a "poet," partly because he knew that the lyricist had a job different from the poet's. While the poet must find the exact word and put it in the right place, in a sense he is freer than the lyric writer, who must not only find the right word but must be sure that it is a word that is clear when sung and not too difficult to sing on a given note. In vocal climaxes and on high notes, singers are comfortable only with vowels that have an open sound. A word like "sweet," for instance, would be a bad choice for a high note because the *e* sound closes the larynx and the singer cannot let go with his full voice; in addition, the *t* ending is a hard consonant which would make it impossible to sustain the note.

In "What's the Use of Wonderin'," Oscar broke the rule of ending a climactic word with an open sound. The last two lines are: "You're his girl and he's your feller—/And all the rest is talk." "Talk" finished the song quietly and abruptly. The song worked well in the play, but was never sung much on the radio or on records, and Oscar was convinced that the problem of phonetics was responsible for its lack of popularity.

Although the Hammersteins had planned to spend most of the winter in their home on 61st Street, in December Dorothy became ill and they went to Doylestown for several months while she recuperated. Her high fever was at first diagnosed by Harold Hyman as tuberculosis, but when all tests were negative, it was attributed to extreme nervous exhaustion. Dorothy had been working hard, and Oscar felt that what she needed was relaxation. He was happy to retreat to the country with her to finish his work on *Carousel*, due to go into rehearsals at the beginning of February.

Rodgers and Hammerstein had signed a contract for *Carousel* with the Guild whereby they would also act as producers, though the billing would remain "The Theatre Guild Presents." Oscar and Dick would jointly receive a straight 7½ percent of the weekly gross (the usual percentage in those days was 2 percent for both composer and lyricist, and 1 percent for the bookwriter) plus 40 percent of the Guild's share of profits, after repayment to investors, of which there was no shortage this time. This phenomenally good contract had been the Guild's own proposition when they first began their talks.

They assembled virtually the same staff that had done so well with *Oklahoma!*: Rouben Mamoulian as director, Agnes de Mille as choreographer, Miles White as costume designer. Only Jo Mielziner was new to the group, replacing Lem Ayres as scenic and lighting designer. Mielziner, probably the most talented designer of his day, had over a hundred shows to his credit, among them *Pygmalion*, *Street Scene*, *Of Thee I Sing* and *Knickerbocker Holiday*, as well as several shows for the Guild and for Rodgers and Hart. Oscar and Dick took it for granted that Russell Bennett would handle the orchestration. They were deaf to his protestations that a radio contract he had signed would make it impossible for him to do the show. "In your spare time you can do this," Dick would say as he handed him the music. Bennett did arrange the prologue and "Mister Snow," but eventually the responsibility was transferred to orchestrator Don Walker and dance arranger Trude Rittman. John Fearnley was production stage manager. Remembering the nervous tension during the preparation of *Oklahoma!*, Dick and Oscar warned Mamoulian at the outset that he had to maintain a good relationship with Agnes. The two worked much more closely in this production, and the prologue was in fact a joint effort.

Molnár first saw *Carousel* at the "run-through," a rehearsal with no stops for corrections, just two weeks into production. When Oscar saw Molnár in the theater, he was nervous about having the author see his adaptation, particularly the drastically revised ending, and was angry at Langner for inviting him: "We're not ready for Molnár. Why not let him come next week when we can give him a better show?" Oscar apologized to Molnár for the rough performance he was about to witness. The playwright smiled and nodded. "That is the theater. That is the part of the theater I like. Good rough rehearsals." Somewhat reassured, Oscar sat down to watch the show. Throughout the performance, he kept seeing it through Molnár's eyes, hearing it through his ears. What would he think of this? What would he say to that?

At the end of the performance Oscar didn't move. He would allow the playwright to leave the theater if he wanted to, without the embarrassment of talking to Oscar. Soon Molnár was at his side, his eyes wet with tears as he told Oscar how much he liked the show. "What you have done is so beautiful!" He understood perfectly the reasons for the changes that had been made; he liked the music. "And you know what I like best? The ending."

Throughout auditions, rehearsals and tryouts, Oscar and Dick watched every detail. One of them was always there and usually both. They had the final say on everything, from props to costumes to vocal inflections. They were as demanding of others as they were of themselves. Rehearsals and tryouts were always hard but seldom unpleasant. Oscar was affectionate and patient. Assistant stage managers, stars, young people, hard-bitten Broadway pros all found him approachable, easy to talk to and sympathetic. He listened well and responded simply and directly to what he heard. People found that he could strip away nonessentials and see to the heart of a problem. The most temperamental behavior was handled by him with patience and good humor.

In fact, it was humor that Dick and Oscar used to take the edge off their driving perfectionism. Agnes de Mille had become good friends with both and loved to work with them. They would press unmercifully until something was right, but they were never rough in manner. Dick hid his high-voltage tension under a constant stream of quips and jokes. Oscar played small jokes or improvised *sotto voce* parodies and puns, always delivered with a straight face as if he were expecting no reaction at all. Once he and de Mille argued for a long time about a dance cut which she bitterly opposed. When they could come to no agreement on the matter, he ordered the cut and said to her, "And don't come out of that rehearsal hall until it's done." He sent a tray of twenty containers of coffee into the room after her.

Opening night in New Haven on March 22, 1945, was a disappointment. The first act went well; the second didn't. After the performance, the staff sat down to a two-hour conference that showed the R & H professionalism at its best. The plan that came out of the meeting drastically altered most of the troubled act, cutting five scenes, half a ballet, two complete songs and several verses in others. The move meant heavy work and personal sacrifice, for the roles of several actors were eliminated, one of them an elderly actress whose part represented the first big chance of her career. John Fearnley remarked afterwards, "Now I see why these people have hits. I never witnessed anything so brisk and brave in my life." One of the major changes was to make God less austere, a lighter and more benign figure, because the original conception was felt to be too shocking or gloomy for the general audience.

With an enormous amount of rewriting to do, he was up before dawn each morning working through the revisions, one of which had been suggested by Molnár. Rodgers and Hammerstein worked constantly through the two days at the Shubert in New Haven and well into the three-week engagement in Boston where the reviews and audience reaction were better but still reflected something wrong with the show.

The dress rehearsal in New York went badly and everyone was apprehensive. As Oscar and Dick walked out of the Majestic Theatre on 44th Street, their discouragement deepened when they saw the marquee of the St. James Theatre directly across the street: *Oklahoma!* The mood was temporary, for the opening-night performance on April 19, 1945, was triumphant, the audience laughing, crying and applauding throughout the show and for a long time afterwards. When Bambi Linn appeared again after her show-stopping ballet sequence performance, the audience greeted her with such a roar that she had to step forward and bow. Mary Rodgers and Steve Sondheim caught sight of each other across several rows of seats, both with tears streaming down their faces.

Although such critics as Louis Kronenberger, Robert Garland, George Jean Nathan and Lewis Nichols were eloquent in their praise, other reviewers proved Oscar right in his prediction that people would say, "This is not another *Oklahoma!*" Some of them seemed to be so busy ticking off items of comparison of the two that they forgot to be moved by *Carousel*. Kronenberger, who pointed out that the shows were so different that comparisons were unprofitable, ended his review with a comparison, a favorable one. He said that this musical play held him as *Oklahoma!* had not, and that he believed it might seem a greater milestone in the years ahead.

The show ran for over two years, followed by a two-year road tour and a run of over a year at the Drury Lane in London. In 1956 Twentieth Century-Fox made a successful Cinemascope 55 film that starred Gordon MacRae and Shirley Jones. It was presented by the New York City Light Opera Company in 1958, with Jan Clayton recreating her original role. *Carousel* was not the incredible financial success that its predecessor was, but for Oscar it was probably an even bigger artistic success. Many theater historians refer to it as his most important work. Certainly, the play shows him as a master of technique and of poetic expression.

Oscar's fiftieth birthday on July 12, 1945, was celebrated at a luncheon given by the Guild at the Waldorf-Astoria Hotel. There was much to celebrate. Four years before, it had seemed that he was finished professionally. Now columnist James Gray suggested that he deserved the title "The Man Who Owns Broadway." *Variety* issued the following report: *Carousel*, in its thirteenth week, gross leader selling out, receipts $43,000 the previous week; *I Remember Mama*, in its tenth month, fortieth week, would maintain capacity into next season, receipts $21,000; *Oklahoma!*, one hundred and twentieth week, gross has reached $4,120,000 (not including road show), $31,000 plus; *Carmen Jones* brought in $35,096 at San Francisco's Curran Theatre, biggest week locally since *Lady in the Dark*; *Oklahoma!*, in eleventh week in Philadelphia, grossed $37,200 the previous week; *Rose-Marie*, in second week at Los Angeles' Philharmonic Auditorium, grossed $45,900; a revival of *Show Boat* planned for the Ziegfeld Theatre was being held up by the author's insistence on high production standards; *State Fair* appeared likely to be one of the coming season's big movies.

The menus for the Guild's luncheon, made up to look like *Oklahoma!* souvenir programs, announced:

LUNCHEON
given for
Oscar Hammerstein II

with the grateful appreciation of
Theresa Helburn and Lawrence Langner
for his foresight in arranging to have his
Fiftieth Birthday
on the occasion of the 1000th performance of *Oklahoma!*

Forty friends and relatives ate lobster and paid tribute to Oscar. Max Gordon, who produced several of the flops, got a laugh when he said, "I let Oscar go just in time." Gordon spoke seriously of the time, five years before, when he was through, "broken in spirit and later in body," and how on his worst night Oscar had bucked him up and provided a turning point: "Everything begins with character—and Oscar has a monopoly." The luncheon ended with laughter as Dick Rodgers complained that when he was associated with his late partner, Larry Hart, people used to say that the little fellow (Hart) was nice, while the big one (Rodgers) was a "son-of-a-bitch." "Now," said Dick, "it's changed. The big fellow (Hammerstein) is considered the nice guy, and the little one is the son-of-a-bitch!"

Although the war seemed to be almost over, Writers' War Board work continued. Oscar was in charge of writing "The Myth That Threatens America" and presenting it to influential leaders of the communications industry—writers, radio producers, advertising people. The message was an important one: even writers with no racist bias can inadvertently give support to prejudice and do more harm than hatemongers when they use the devices of stereotype as a lazy way of getting laughs and making quick characterization.

Oscar also found time to write a piece about Jerry Kern for *Vogue* magazine's February 1945 issue, a brief sketch about Jerry's humor. Eva Kern wrote him an appreciative letter and said of "our pixie," "I feel you love him almost as much as I do."

Oscar saw the pixie in California that August. He and Jerry wrote "All Through the Day" for *Centennial Summer* and worked on revisions of *Show Boat* for the revival they were planning at the Ziegfeld Theatre.

Time had brought a new perspective. Eighteen years before, when Ziegfeld had pleaded for further cuts to bring the curtain down before overtime wages began at eleven-thirty, Oscar couldn't find a word he didn't think necessary. Now he discovered an entire scene and three songs that he felt they could do without, and shortened the play by twenty minutes. They wrote a new song, "Nobody Else But

Me," to replace an imitation specialty that Norma Terris had done in the original.

Oscar used the revival to try to persuade Jerry to write a show with Dorothy Fields which he and Dick would produce on Broadway. Jerry was interested but resistant. Referring to *Very Warm for May,* he said, "I'm not going to go through *that* again." Oscar told him that the revival would help him get the feel of the theater after all his movie years.

"I'm too old," said Jerry.

"That's no excuse," Oscar retorted. "If you said you'd written enough, I'd be convinced. This would be your one hundred and seventh score, and I figure you're good for another forty-eight." He reminded his friend of the telegram he had sent to Jimmy on the day of his birth, promising to do a show with him in 1947. Finally Jerry agreed to do it.

In Hollywood Oscar also conferred with Twentieth Century-Fox, signing a contract with a guarantee of $150,000 against 15 percent of profits over $4 million for a screenplay about his grandfather's life, which he would write in the East and co-produce with Otto Preminger. He agreed to the project not only because it would be a tonic for Arthur, who had just undergone a major operation to remove a tumor, but because the subject still interested him. He wrote to his cousin, noted psychiatrist Clarence Obendorf, to ask his view about the Old Man's subconscious drives. Obendorf answered that Oscar I had probably been one of those people who shatter when they meet success because it burdens them with a sense of guilt; they may pick themselves up and succeed again, but inevitably they again turn success into failure, continuing the pattern throughout their lives.

Oscar also discussed with MGM the $275,000 it was putting up for the *Show Boat* revival. (Arthur Freed wanted to make a new film version and hoped to stimulate public interest by the Broadway revival.) He also discussed his role in Freed's *Till the Clouds Roll By,* a biographical film about Jerry. He agreed to being portrayed in the film, but only with script approval of the scenes involving him. He made a few changes, one of them in a line that had him saying, "I came across a book that I think is going to make one of the great shows of all time!" No librettist over the age of fourteen, he felt, would say such a thing.

In November Jerry arrived in New York. He and Oscar had talked almost daily for weeks about the preparations for *Show Boat*. They were determined to do a first-class production.

Jerry and Eva had settled into the St. Regis Hotel on the day of their arrival, November 2, 1945, and spent the weekend at Highland Farm. Jerry was bright and chipper, enthusiastic about the revival and the new show he had agreed to write. Back in the city on Monday morning, Oscar called the Kerns' hotel room just as breakfast was being brought in. "Have it at your leisure, Jerry," said Oscar. "There's no need to rush to the theater. I'll see you there at two for the chorus audition."

Dorothy Fields called to arrange to have lunch with Eva. "All right," Jerry said. "You know better than to call at this hour. Eva's asleep, but I'll leave her a message on the bathroom mirror where she's sure to see it." He took a bar of soap and scribbled on the mirror, "Meet the bitch at Pavillion at 1 o'clock! See you later and don't eat too much!" He left the hotel on 55th and Fifth Avenue at eleven-thirty and walked toward Park Avenue, heading for Arthur Ackerman's on 57th Street to buy his daughter Betty the breakfront she had reserved there. When he was about to round the corner of Park and 57th Street, he collapsed.

At one-thirty, Leighton Brill called Oscar at a Dramatists Guild luncheon to tell him that ASCAP had phoned the office to report that a man carrying an ASCAP card in his pocket with the name Jerome Kern on it had collapsed on 57th Street and Park Avenue. They phoned every hospital in town, but found Jerry in none of them. At the scene of the collapse it was discovered that Jerry had been taken to the city hospital on Welfare Island, under the Queensboro Bridge.

Oscar rushed to the hospital and found Jerry unconscious in the neurological ward. He was lying on a cot cut off by curtains from the crowded ward of the city hospital. The indigent patients, derelicts, alcoholics and addicts had heard who the new patient was and, in deference to Jerome Kern, maintained absolute silence as the doctors attended to him. A nurse came over to Oscar and said, "I will stay on duty for twenty-four, forty-eight, seventy-two hours for Jerome Kern. I will do anything for him because he has given me so much with his music. He will be well taken care of, Mr. Hammerstein."

Harold Hyman arrived and pronounced Jerry's condition very serious—a cerebral hemorrhage; he said that even if Jerry recovered, he couldn't say in what condition his brain or body might be. Oscar couldn't sleep for the few remaining hours of the night. He realized what a grip Jerry had on his affections, greater even than he had known.

On Wednesday Jerry was moved to Doctors Hospital, where Oscar and Dorothy took a room near Eva and Betty and remained for three days. On Sunday, November 11, Oscar was alone with Jerry when, at ten minutes after one, his labored breathing stopped. Although he had steeled himself to expect the inevitable, he didn't want to believe that Jerry was dead. Oscar lifted the oxygen tent, and whispered in his ear, "I've told ev'ry little star," but there was no response. Oscar broke down. When he again gained control of himself, he left the room to tell Eva and the others that it was over.

When Eva asked him to speak at the services, Oscar agreed to try. He almost made it through his brief speech, but by his own description "went to pieces" at the end and could not finish the last sentence.

The day before *Show Boat* returned to the stage Oscar told a *New York Times* reporter: "For both Jerry and me this new production was a labor of love. The only mitigation of my pleasure is the fact that he isn't here to share it." Jerry would have been as pleased as Oscar was with the praise bestowed on the show again; it was still the "greatest of all musical comedies."

Seven

R&H and
Their First Original

It was just after *Show Boat* was revived that Steve Sondheim spent a memorable afternoon with Oscar, an afternoon in which he learned "everything I know, basically, about the theater and songs." Although Steve had taken piano lessons and had always liked to fool around on the piano (he had been known to wake up the Hammerstein family with "Flight of the Bumble Bee"), as a child he wasn't particularly interested in the musical theater. He thinks that Oscar must have smelled something, though, because he began to interest the boy in the theater, and by the time Steve was fifteen he knew that was what he wanted to do.

Steve was a "compulsive nut" who wanted to learn how to act, produce, direct, "wanted to be Noël Coward at fourteen," says Jimmy Hammerstein. To have a competitive, successful father, and then "to find that the guy who's become my foster brother is also a genius," was difficult for young Hammerstein, but he enjoyed Steve's company and learned to accept the close relationship between his father and Steve. Oscar later helped Jimmy to learn about the theater, but in his adolescent years Jimmy showed little interest in it. Steve, on the other hand, was deeply involved: "He wanted everything and he wanted it soon and he had the talent and the drive to do it."

In 1946 Steve and three classmates at George School wrote a musical about campus life called *By George*. Steve thought it was terrific and wanted Oscar to read it. He sent it to him with a note saying, "Please don't treat it as if you knew me. Treat it as if it were just a script that crossed your desk." Delusions of grandeur danced in his head that night; R & H would produce it, he would be the youngest composer on Broadway; *By George* would make theater history.

The next day they met and Oscar reiterated Steve's stipulation: "You asked me to treat this as if I'd never heard of the author."

"Yes," Steve said.

"In that case, it's the worst thing I've ever read."

As Steve's lower lip trembled, Oscar went on, "I didn't say it doesn't show talent. But it's just terrible. If you want to know why it's terrible, I'll tell you."

"Yes," said Steve, "tell me."

So Oscar started with the very first line, the very first stage direction, and pointed out how untheatrical it was and then proceeded to go through every scene, every song, every line of dialogue. He treated the libretto as if it were a mature work, not the school show that it was, with thinly disguised teachers and campus setting, and he was dead serious about everything in it. The big, shaggy man and the boy sat for hours in the study and pored over the script.

There were basic rules of lyric writing and show construction that Oscar considered essential knowledge. He told Steve that later he might break the rules, as Oscar had done so often, but to be a professional he must know them. Steve remembered every one of them and has in turn passed them on to younger writers because he finds them "unarguably true."

Oscar stressed the opening of a show: the first lyric the audience hears, the first song, is what makes or breaks a show. "If you start with the right opening, you can ride for forty-five minutes on the telephone book. On the other hand, if you start off with a wrong one, it's an uphill fight all the way." And in constructing a song, "Everything should develop, every word should count, nothing should be reiterated or repeated unless you're doing it for effect."

Oscar said, "Don't imitate other people's emotions. Speak your own." When Steve wrote of wind and willows and robins and larks, in imitation of Oscar, his mentor said, "You know, you don't believe in any of this stuff. Write what you feel. Don't write what *I* feel. I really believe all this stuff. *You* don't." Because he knew Steve so well and because he wanted so much to make an impact on him, Oscar automatically knew how to appeal to him; he added, "If you write what you believe, you'll be ninety percent ahead of all other songwriters." The boy was so competitive that the minute Oscar put it on that basis, the very next lyric he wrote was personal.

The major principle in songwriting, he said, was that "the thought counts more than the rhyme." Rhyme, he believed, is the easiest thing in the world; it is expressing a thought with clarity that is so difficult and so important. (Sondheim today feels that very few songwriters have been consistent about this "unarguably true principle.")

Steve remembers being "snotty" when he was fifteen. When Oscar said, "This doesn't say anything," Steve shot back a challenge: "Well, what does "Oh, What a Beautiful Mornin'" say?" To which Oscar said firmly, "Oh, it says a lot."

Steve, then in high school, thought that "to say something" meant a message you can reduce to one sentence and hand back on a test. What he learned from Oscar was that "saying something" in a lyric doesn't always mean that you are expressing a profound philosophical truth, but that you are simply saying something true about human beings.

When he finished with the last line of the script, Oscar told Steve that in the next few years, he should put himself through four stages. First, he should take a play he really liked and thought was good and make a musical out of it in order to learn something about play structure from having to closely examine a work he admired. Second, he should take a play that he didn't think was so good but try to improve it and make a musical out of it. Third, he should take a nontheatrical work, such as a short story or a novel, and make that into a musical. And last, he should write an original, making up a story himself and telling it in a musical. "By the time you get through that, you'll know something of what we've been talking about this afternoon."

This is exactly what Steve did. He went through the four tasks while he was at Williams College, and found that by the time he was twenty-three, he was a professional—"It's as simple as that." Very few songwriters are professionals at that age, but when he finished his four musicals, Steve says, "I really knew what I was doing."

Since the meeting with Oscar a decade would pass before Steve's brilliance as a lyricist and composer/lyricist would be seen on Broadway, first in *West Side Story* and *Gypsy,* and then in such musicals as *A Funny Thing Happened on the Way to the Forum, Anyone Can Whistle, Company, Follies, A Little Night Music* and *Pacific Overtures.* (Though Steve was Oscar's most special pupil there were also other young people that he taught.)

Oscar and Dick established early in their partnership the pattern of writing a musical every other year and producing shows written by others in the intervening years. As R & H, Oscar was willing to produce, not only because Dick wanted to, but because as partners they complemented each other so well. He couldn't understand why Dick liked dealing with administrative and financial matters, but it was fine with him because it allowed him to deal primarily with other aspects of the job that he liked best.

In 1946 the team produced a musical based on the life of Annie Oakley. The idea for the show began the summer before with Dorothy Fields, who had left Hollywood a year after Oscar did, to write exclusively for Broadway, often in collaboration with her brother, Herbert.

One night she left the Stage Door Canteen, where she worked with Oscar and Dorothy, to eat a late-night supper at "21." In the middle of someone's story about a sharpshooter, she had a flash of inspiration: "Sharpshooter. Ethel Merman as Annie Oakley." The next day she and Herb went to see Mike Todd, with whom they had a commitment for a show with Merman. Dorothy feverishly told him of their idea and the great show they could do.

"A show about a dame who knows from nothing but guns? I wouldn't touch it," replied Todd, the man who had walked out during the first act of *Oklahoma!* in New Haven.

"Are we out of our commitment, Mike?" she asked, "because we want to do the show."

"You got it—yes. I don't want any part of it!"

Dorothy left Todd's office to attend a Writers' War Board committee meeting which Oscar was chairing. Afterwards she went over

A study of Jerry and Eva Kern made by George Gershwin.

At the Benedict Canyon Drive home with six-year-old Jimmy and the "boat" he had just built.

At work in the Kerns' Whittier Drive residence in Beverly Hills.

During their first year at Highland Farm.

An aerial view of Highland Farm, Doylestown, Pennsylvania.

The main house.

The family at Highland Farm (1942). (Back row, left to right): Jerry Watanabe, Dorothy, Oscar, Billy, Doodie, Henry, Susan, Alice, Reggie. Front row: Jimmy, Madame Watanabe and Jennifer.

R & H: Oscar and Dick Rodgers at the start of Oklahoma! *and their twenty-seven-year collaboration.*

Mexican painter Covarrubias interpreted the final scene from Carmen Jones.

To Dorothy and Ockie
In deep appreciation
and love,
Steve
12/25/45

Fifteen-year-old Stephen Sondheim.

TWENTY CENTS   OCTOBER 20, 1947

TIME

THE WEEKLY NEWSMAGAZINE

Boris Chaliapin

OSCAR HAMMERSTEIN II
In musicomedy, a New Look.
(Theater)

$6.50 A YEAR   (REG. U. S. PAT. OFF.)   VOL. L NO. 16

October 20, 1947.

After a radio broadcast on which Frank Sinatra sang "The Last Time I Saw Paris."

With daughter Alice in the study at East 61st Street.

In his study at Highland Farm Oscar preferred to work standing up.

Working on Carousel.

Three Hammersteins: Oscar, Arthur and Reggie.

A favorite pastime at Highland Farm.

Mary Martin as a teenager at summer camp. Oscar put this picture by his mirror where he shaved every morning after writing under it: "This proves there is hope for everyone."

At the opening-night party of South Pacific. *Photo by Slim Aarons.*

The creators of South Pacific: *Josh Logan, Dick Rodgers, Oscar, Mary Martin and James Michener.*

Next to standing, this was Oscar's favorite way of working.

On location for Oklahoma! *with director Fred Zinnemann.*

At a Flower Drum Song *rehearsal.*

In Negril, Jamaica, while scouting locations for the film version of South Pacific.

Oscar's last gift to Dorothy given to her on Valentine's Day the year he died. He wrote: "In New York I could go to Schling's/For sentimental, floral things,/But on a Pennsylvania farm/One must rely on home-made charm./An enterprise like this from me,/Certainly you've never reckoned—/But there it is, with all my love,/Oscar Valentine, the second. February 14, 1960"

Mrs. Oscar Hammerstein II in the 1970's.

"Bless my homeland forever."

OSCAR HAMMERSTEIN, II

Tribute

Mayor Robert F. Wagner asks that tomorrow night, (Thursday, Sept. 1st), at 9 P.M., all lights on Broadway between 42nd and 53rd Streets; and the side streets between 6th and 8th Avenues, be extinguished as a token of our city's respect for the late Oscar Hammerstein, II.

The blackout will be signalled at 8:57 P.M. by a flare over Father Duffy Square. This will be followed by the sounding of Taps.

BLACKOUT AREA

Broadway and 7th Avenue from 42nd to 53rd Streets. Also side streets from 42nd to 53rd, between 6th and 8th Avenues.

Lights on after second flare signal.

PLEASE CO-OPERATE

The night the lights went out over Broadway. London's West End had already done the same ten days earlier.

to talk to him. "Ockie, what do you think of Ethel Merman as Annie Oakley?"

He thought the idea was terrific and Dick agreed. Perhaps the alacrity with which he accepted Dorothy's idea was caused by a childhood memory: *Buffalo Bill's Wild West Show*, in Sheepshead Bay, which had enthralled him as a boy.

This show with the Fields team was the one that Jerry had finally agreed to do. With his death, the show was without a composer. At a meeting to discuss who could possibly take his place, Irving Berlin was mentioned. "Just go on," someone said, "because he'd never do it unless he were the head of the show and had his own ideas."

"Wait a minute," Oscar interjected. "I don't think you should eliminate him until you've asked him."

Oscar was sixteen years old when he first met Irving Berlin, introduced to him by his father backstage at the Victoria, where Berlin was appearing as "the composer of the recent hit 'Alexander's Ragtime Band.' " He and Oscar's father were good friends, often shooting craps together after the show at the Hermitage Hotel, across the street from the theater on 42nd Street. Berlin knew Oscar's grandfather, too, from the time when his *Yip Yip Yaphank* played at the Old Man's Lexington Opera House, which Irving had chosen to present his 1918 Army musical. "Oscar is the only 'great' in my business who truly came from a theatrical family—no, rather a theatrical dynasty," says Berlin. "There were the Barrymores and the Drews, but they were all actors. But here were three generations of Hammersteins —each in his own way a 'great,' a 'genius.' " About Oscar himself he says, "I ask you—would you believe that one and the same person wrote 'When I'm Calling You-ooo' and 'I'm as Restless as a Willow in a Windstorm'? This is a great talent. He's never really been given the credit that he deserves. There's only one lyric writer that came close to being a poet and that's Oscar Hammerstein."

Irving Berlin was "more or less impressed and awed" by the idea of R & H producing a show of his, but he resisted doing *Annie* for many reasons. He was tired, and he didn't feel that he wanted to step into Jerry Kern's shoes.

"Why don't you read Dorothy and Herb's script, Irving?" said Oscar.

Berlin read it. "This is up your alley. Why don't you and Dick do it?" he asked Oscar.

"It's not up our alley," said Oscar. Berlin felt what he really meant was that it was a run-of-the-mill musical, a star vehicle, which in a sense it was.

Berlin was not sure that after a long career as an independent songwriter he could compose this type of score. He had written his last Broadway show, *Louisiana Purchase,* in 1939. He thought of more objections.

"That hillbilly stuff, Oscar—it's not for me. I don't know the first thing about this kind of lyric."

"That's ridiculous," Oscar countered. "All you have to do is drop the g's."

Berlin went home and reread the script. Then he sat down and, almost without effort, wrote "Doin' What Comes Natur'lly" and "They Say It's Wonderful."

A few days later he met with Oscar and Dick at their office. Still cautious, Irving said, "Give me another week."

"Why another week?" said Dick bluntly. "Do you want to do it or don't you want to do it?"

"I want to do it," said Berlin, and sheepishly pulled out his two songs.

They concluded the business part of the arrangement in five minutes. Since in his previous ventures Berlin had always been part of the production, Oscar said they didn't know what to offer him.

"How about five percent of the gross," suggested the composer.

"That's fine."

"What about billing?" asked Dick.

"We'll all be billed in the same type," was his generous reply.

After he started working on the score, Berlin realized that many of his song ideas and titles were coming out of the book. The Fieldses were getting 4 percent while he was getting 5 percent, and he felt that he should cut his percentage to 4½ percent.

"You know you don't have to do it," Oscar told him.

"But the songs are coming out of the script. The idea . . ."

"Where do you think the songs from *Oklahoma!* came from?" was Oscar's reply.

Berlin wrote the songs quickly, usually trying them out on Herb and Dorothy Fields before handing them in to R & H. Once, though, when he had to write a song for a scene change, he called Oscar.

"I've got an idea for a song called 'There's No Business Like Show Business.'"

"That's great! Write it."

And Berlin wrote it.

The only criticism he got on the score from anybody was from Oscar. His first version of "They Say It's Wonderful" was:

> They say that falling in love is wonderful
> Wonderful so they say
> To bill and coo like a dove is wonderful . . .

When he saw the lyrics, Oscar grinned and said, "Are you sure you like that, Irving?" Berlin knew that what he really meant was "It's corny as hell." The next morning he called him and said, " 'And with a moon up above.' Is that better?"

"Much better," said Oscar.

Oscar was as restrained in his praise as he was in his criticism, but when he praised something everyone knew he meant it.

Josh Logan, who had worked before with Dick Rodgers, was just getting out of the Army when R & H asked him to direct *Annie Get Your Gun*. As they began rehearsals Josh's staging of "The Girl That I Marry" impressed Oscar with its honesty simplicity. He became Josh's champion and they began to be friends. Josh found the large "seemingly benign" man so warm that "it was hard to see the glints of steel in his eyes. He had a way of judging songs, scenes and people that seemed completely sympathetic, yet contained. And he was able to make me laugh whenever he wanted to; there was an incipient smile, almost a wicked one, at the corner of his mouth. I discovered he enjoyed preparing very personal practical jokes and I'm afraid they were designed to make people squirm a bit—but he was so delighted when they were a success that he was forgiven immediately."

Two days before rehearsals started, at a conference with the entire production staff at Oscar's house, Josh whispered to him that he was worried about the score, that there weren't enough duets. As Oscar finished whispering back that he agreed but didn't want to panic Irving just before the opening, Berlin bounded across the room and said to Oscar, "Do you need another song?"

Before Oscar could reply, Berlin was announcing, "Just a minute, everybody. There's been a request for another song. I want to take over this meeting and have a full discussion as to what it should be . . ."

"I didn't . . ." said Oscar.

"You did, too. I heard you. You want another song. Now, where could it be and what could it be about?"

Berlin knew that it couldn't be a love song because Annie and Frank don't come together until the end. As they discussed putting it in just before the shooting match, someone said, "How about some sort of contest song?"

"Contest song?" said Berlin. He started across the room to the door. "That's right. All right. That's all. Go ahead. Good-bye, everybody."

The meeting broke up soon afterwards, and Josh went back to the hotel suite where he was living, six blocks away from Oscar's house. As he walked in the door the phone was ringing.

"Hello?"

"Josh? This is Irving. How's this?" He began to sing, "Anything you can do I can do better/I can do anything better than you . . ." and went through the entire song.

"That's perfect," Josh shouted. "When in hell did you write that?"

"In a taxicab. I had to, didn't I? We go into rehearsal Monday."

The Fieldses' book was a rousing story of the romance between hillbilly sharpshooter Annie Oakley, a role tailor-made for the boisterous, gutsy, electric Ethel Merman, and Frank Butler, a crack rifle shot, played by Ray Middleton. Like Oscar, Dorothy Fields had a career spanning four decades, encompassing both Broadway and Hollywood, as both lyricist and librettist. *Annie* proved that her talent had continued to grow and that she was able to keep step with the changing world.

Annie provided the only time in the history of the theater that two of America's greatest songwriters acted as the producers of a musical comedy for which another "great" * in American popular music wrote the score. This unusual association went smoothly, R & H never encroaching on Berlin's domain, and he never venturing into theirs. The score, with nineteen new songs, was a miracle, with over half a dozen hit numbers—pure Berlin gold—including "You Can't Get a Man with a Gun," "My Defenses Are Down," "Doin' What Comes Natur'lly," "The Girl That I Marry," "They Say It's Wonderful," "Anything You Can Do" and "There's No Business Like Show

---

* Two years after *Annie* opened, Oscar and Dick, honoring Berlin's sixtieth birthday and his fortieth anniversary as a songwriter, established the Irving Berlin Scholarship in Composition (a full four-year course) at the Juilliard School of Music.

Business," which became the unofficial anthem of the American theater.

Opening on May 16, 1946, the production had 1,147 performances, making it second to *Oklahoma!* as the longest running musical in New York theater history, a record not broken until *South Pacific* surpassed it in 1952. The London edition, presented by Prince Littler, was as great a success, running 1,304 performances, and in France, Germany and the Scandinavian countries it ran for more than a year. Arthur Freed made an equally successful MGM film version in 1950, with Betty Hutton and Howard Keel. When someone remarked to Berlin that *Annie* was old-fashioned, his answer was, "Yeah, an old-fashioned smash!"

Annie's arrival on Broadway set for Oscar an all-time record that is still unsurpassed. Ed Sullivan christened him "Mr. Hit"; *Variety* referred to his feat as "Broadway's One-Man Show Biz Dynasty." For running on Broadway in 1946 were five shows that he wrote: the marathon *Oklahoma!* at the St. James, *Carousel* at the Majestic, *The Desert Song* at the City Center with *Carmen Jones* to follow, *Show Boat* anchored at the Ziegfeld, and two that he co-produced: *Annie* and *I Remember Mama. Variety*, trying to compute Oscar's annual gross earnings, taking into account his "pix," recordings, ASCAP (double-A rating) royalties and "legit" earnings, concluded it would stagger a crew of certified public accountants and tax experts and would put him "in the top coin class in America, in and out of show biz."

The Hammersteins were at sea on the S.S. *Mariposa* on *Annie's* opening night. When the Broadway premiere was postponed, Oscar decided to go ahead with their plans for an important trip to Australia. He had been there only once, sixteen years before, and now Dorothy felt an urgent need to see her mother, who was seventy-nine years old.

On the ship on May 14, Oscar and Dorothy celebrated their seventeenth wedding anniversary. They had found their love growing deeper, their respect for each other stronger as the years passed. There were problems, of course. The children were "yours, mine or ours," depending on how matters stood. There was Oscar's jealousy of Dorothy and of her work. There was just plain jealousy. According to her daughter Susan, Dorothy "contemplated calling a lawyer" if Oscar danced with another woman twice. In Boston, Dorothy went to the Colonial Theatre during a rehearsal one day and from the back of the house saw Oscar on the stage next to a show girl who had her arm around his back. When lunch was called and Oscar started to walk up an aisle of the darkened theater, the girl called, "Ockie, would you pick up a sandwich for me too?" Oscar saw Dorothy flee and followed her to the Boston Common, where they talked, both in tears as Oscar assured her it was nothing, it meant nothing. In the theatrical world, in which extramarital affairs are the rule, only once were there rumors about Oscar and another woman. Given the realities of human nature and the gossiping endemic to the theatrical world, where malicious envy thrives, particularly of someone as successful, good and even awesome as Oscar, it is remarkable that there was only one such rumor.

Oscar's "sweeping things under the carpet," the part of him that staunchly refused to look at unpleasantness and badness, always bothered Dorothy. He would forget things he did not wish to remember. "Remember how we worried about Susan's operation?" Dorothy asked. Oscar did not remember an operation. When small things went wrong at home, Oscar looked the other way. Dorothy accepted this part of him, but with mixed feelings. A pessimist is somebody who has lived all his life with an optimist, she thought ruefully. However, she was willing to deal with unpleasantness and she made Oscar's life at home as smooth and trouble-free as possible. She saw to it that everything was comfortable and to his liking, took care of the annoying details, provided the haven of "orderly and systematic living" that Oscar had always craved and needed.

There was a part of Oscar that he would not share with anyone, not even Dorothy, and she felt it more as their years together went on. She, too, held something back. Friends and children saw that she was quieter when Oscar was with her. She let him have the floor, deferred to him, didn't want to bore him.

Still, their closeness and commitment to each other were evident. They kept the vow they had made before their marriage that they would always be together. Dorothy left her business, her home, her children to go with Oscar to tryouts, meetings, wherever he had to go. The only time she left him was when her dear friend Sophie Biow was dying and Dorothy went to Paris to be with her. Otherwise, they were together almost every night of his life. It was obvious that for Oscar and Dorothy the relationship between them came first.

The heart of such a relationship lies hidden from the world; the evidence is superficial. After all the years together, they still held hands when they rode in a car together. In the house Oscar would often sneak up behind Dorothy and kiss her. And he would leave notes for her, full of the language of intimacy. He would write a note in lipstick on the bathtub, leave on a coffee table a series of little notes to be pieced together "by Woodsilheim McCarthy" (one of Oscar's nicknames for her). Inside a jar of cold cream was stuck a small pink note in an envelope to "Mrs. W. B." which said "Happy Easter to the Woodle Beaut from the Bady."

Alice wrote Dorothy a letter just before the trip to Australia in which she expressed her feelings about their relationship. In California working as a story analyst for RKO, she had become very close to Susan, who was there as a starlet, under a long-term contract to Twentieth Century-Fox. In her letter Alice tried to explain why Susan was angry at her parents at the moment:

> I sat here while Henry fumed about your not being able to come West a few days before Dad so you could see him in Los Angeles, before you went to Australia. He resented the fact that Dad meant more to you than he did. He said he would not go to San Francisco to see you, but he did, because he does love you. Now I hear Susan resent the same thing, because it looks to her as if you are not interested enough to meet her boy until he is able to go East and meet you. But I know that Susan loves you and idolizes you, both of you, and you and she are probably both under the same false illusion that each is disinterested in the other. I also believe that you and Dad mean more to each other than your children mean to you, but I do not resent it. I used to, but I believe I have gotten over that constant yearning for attention, if only quite recently. Perhaps it is because I am older, or perhaps I have gained more understanding. I think your attitude toward each other is admirable, and I'm all for it. I think it is much more difficult to maintain a deep love for, and an avid interest in, one's husband and wife thru the years than it is to feel this way for one's children, because love for your own child is a natural love, while love for your partner must always be built up and renewed. But when your children feel the lack, it must mean that you haven't got it across to them that they rate pretty high.
>
> But I often think of you both as standing on top of a mountain, together, surveying the land and people below with bemused expressions, and it is hard to reach up to you.
>
> Please don't feel that I am being disloyal or disrespectful. I'm not writing as a step-daughter, or a daughter, but more as an onlooker, an amateur observer, and Susan's friend. I don't have the

feeling anymore that my father isn't concerned about me. I am sure of his love, and though I'm not as close to him as I would like to be, there is a warmth that will always be there, and I know that he is interested. But a few years ago I wasn't sure, less than a few years ago,—as Susan isn't sure now of your interest.

On board ship Oscar began the book for an original musical that he and Dick had decided to do next, the story of a man's struggle to make his way in the world without compromising his principles. He mailed about a fifth of the script and several lyrics to Dick when the ship docked in Brisbane.

They saw Dorothy's mother for the first time in twelve years. At seventy-nine she was still active and was even tempted to make the trip back to America with them, but finally decided not to. (She died later that year.) They saw friends and visited Dorothy's birthplace in Tasmania.

When they returned home, Oscar gave his immediate attention to the next show that he and Dick were scheduled to produce. Earlier that year Anita Loos had sent them her new play, *Happy Birthday*, a delightful and sentimental comedy that was something of a combination of *The Iceman Cometh* and *Cinderella*. R & H immediately acquired the property and signed Helen Hayes for the lead. While Oscar was away, Rouben Mamoulian withdrew as director and Josh Logan took over. Though it was not a musical, *Happy Birthday* required one song for Helen Hayes to sing and Dick and Oscar wrote "I Haven't Got a Worry in the World." The show was a success and ran for over a year and a half.

In early 1947 Oscar was asked to be president of the Authors League. He remained in office for two terms, four years. One meeting of the League was called to discuss an actors' strike. The members talked heatedly about how the strike would affect their royalties, whether or not to go along with the producers although it was evident that this would be hard on the actors. After an hour and a half they decided to bring to a vote the most effective action they could take: throwing in their weight with the producers. Oscar had said nothing throughout the meeting. Just before the vote he stood and said, "It's immoral." He sat down again and the room was silent. Everyone knew he was right; the proposal was not passed.

Shortly after *Happy Birthday* opened, Josh suggested that Oscar and Dick join him in producing a farce by Norman Krasna—*John Loves Mary*—which he planned to direct. They read it and liked it, but Oscar felt he had to say, "Good God, don't you think people are going to look down their noses at three big guys like us doing a little tiny play like this? Won't they make fun of us?"

The only problem they had with *John Loves Mary* was with the ending. Oscar, Dick, Josh and playwright Norman Krasna went at it hot and heavy after every performance during the out-of-town break-in. Suddenly Josh knew what should happen. "The father and mother see the boy out and go to bed, and the boy comes back in the room, kisses the girl and takes her off into the bedroom." Oscar rose with a purple face and said, "Anyone who would make a suggestion like *that* is a *cad!*" When the meeting broke, Krasna said to Logan, "Everybody used to tell me that Oscar was cool as a cucumber. Well, he's the most belligerent cucumber I ever met."

They fixed the end of *John Loves Mary* by simply bringing down the curtain, cutting the scene. The play, which opened in New York in February 1947, didn't get distinguished notices, but audiences liked the "tiny" show so much that they kept it running for 421 performances.

During a working weekend that summer at the Rodgerses' home in Connecticut, Dick, Oscar and both Dorothys went to have lunch at the nearby home of Armina and Lawrence Langner. Other guests included Terry Helburn, Ina Claire, Mary Martin and Richard Halliday. After lunch the hosts asked everybody to get up and do something entertaining. Ina Claire did a brilliant job of mimicking famous people; Mary, who came next, had to think of something spectacular to top her; she let go with "You Can't Get a Man with a Gun." This was not the kind of song she usually sang, but she did it so well that Oscar and Dick were "laid out cold," and soon after signed Mary for the starring role in the national company of *Annie*. As many times as Oscar's and Mary's lives had crossed before, this was the first time they worked together.

The early months of 1947 were occupied by preparations for the original musical *Allegro*, which turned out to be the first unsuccessful show written by Rodgers and Hammerstein. Not unacquainted with failures, Oscar generally dismissed them quickly, but this one he continued to regard with "pride and affection." It "churned" inside him years after the original Broadway production; just before he died he was rewriting the musical for television.

Oscar's original intention was to write a universal story of the life of a man from birth to death. He wanted to deal with the assaults on the individual integrity, forces that make him adopt false values, the "conspiracy of the world" that keeps him from his true path of satisfaction and fulfillment. He meant it to be not strictly autobiographical, though in some ways it was, but personal in that it contained his own experiences and feelings.

The collaborators realized that what they were writing was a modern allegory and agreed that the play called for an unorthodox presentation. Oscar envisioned a play like *Our Town* which would be so simply staged that it would lend itself to college productions after its first run. They decided that dance, movement, would be a prime factor in the telling of the story. There would be songs, orchestral interludes and dialogue, but a good part of the story would be told through a "Greek chorus."

The theme could be applied to a man in any profession, but they chose a doctor, Joe Taylor. The play begins with his birth and shows various stages of his life by means of the chorus, rear-screen projections, short scenes, dances and songs. Joe marries his hometown sweetheart, Jenny, who craves wealth and power and succeeds in making him take the position offered him in a big city hospital. There he achieves success; he becomes so busy running the hospital, as well as attending board meetings and cocktail parties for trustees, that he has no time to be a good doctor and treats his patients cynically and dishonestly.

Joe's friend Charlie, so disgusted by the rat race that he has taken to drink, and Emily, the sensible nurse who loves Joe, sing "Allegro," the play's title song, to him as chorus and dancers join in. The ironic, satirical lyrics are more "clever" than those usually identified with Oscar, but the message they carry is pure Hammerstein. Since the word "sentimental" was so often used pejoratively to describe Oscar, it is interesting to note the meaning he gave the term "sentimental folk" in this song, with its connotation of people who live an authentic life, as opposed to those who pursue superficial ways:

> Our world is for the forceful,
> And not for sentimental folk,
> But brilliant and resourceful
> And paranoiac gentle folk . . .
> "Allegro" a musician
> Would so describe the speed of it,
> The clash and competition
> Of counterpoint—

> . . . we know no other way
> Of living out a day.
> Our music must be galloping and gay!
> We muffle all the undertones
> The minor blood-and-thunder tones
> The overtones are all we care to play!
> . . . Allegro!

When he looks at his life and at what his wife has become, a "chic" woman having an affair with a member of the board of trustees, Joe says, "There's nothing real about any of it—nothing real about the whole damn place. What the hell am I doing here! What the hell am I doing!" Joe drops his head as the chorus and his mother remind him of his boyhood ideals and values. When Joe lifts his head and speaks to Emily, he says, "I went kind of haywire, I guess." The chorus sings:

> A man's brain is sometimes cleared
> By the sudden light of one word.
> In the flash of a split second
> He sees a signpost, pointing down a new road,
> And he may take a new turning
> That will affect the rest of his life.

Joe turns down an offer to become chief physician at the big hospital. With Charlie and Emily he returns to his hometown and the real practice of medicine.

Oscar and Dick wanted to experiment in the staging of *Allegro*. Unfortunately, somewhere along the way, their simple allegory acquired a heavy-handed production that rested uneasily on the play's weak structure. Jo Mielziner's set was an intricate series of platforms, treadmills, pendulum stages, curtains and loudspeakers, in front of a huge screen on which images were flashed. The cast was enormous—forty-one principals and almost a hundred more people, speaking in chorus, dancing, singing, moving about the complex set. Both the musical score and the production introduced a lushness that worked against the simplicity of the story.

R & H asked Agnes de Mille to direct. She read the first scenes in bed recovering from giving birth to her son, and found them so beautiful that she cried. When the next batch of material came to her, she called Oscar.

"Oscar, you're writing several plays at once. You're all over the map."

"Well, I'm deep into Act Two. When I'm finished, we'll get together."

Oscar had spent almost a year to write the first act, taking infinite pains. He didn't have time to work the same way on the second act. Rushing to a deadline, he finished one week before rehearsals began.

Four days before they went into production, de Mille asked him, "Oscar, what is this play about?"

"It's about a man not being allowed to do his own work because of worldly pressures."

"That's not the play you've written. You haven't written your second act."

Oscar's comment was, "But we're already committed to the theater in New York."

Rehearsals were a nightmare. Oscar had offered Steve Sondheim, who was seventeen, a summer job as "go-fer," fetching coffee, typing scripts. "Now you'll learn something about the other side of the theater," he said, "about the *geshrei* we go through." Steve indeed saw the *geshrei*, with Dick redoing songs and scenes, Oscar rewriting from five in the morning, de Mille, who had never before directed an entire show, trying to cope with the unwieldy production and an enormous cast. Finally she said, "I can't do the new dances and the new songs and the new book," and Oscar stepped in to direct the book during rehearsals while he was rewriting during the rest of the day and night.

Ironically enough, Oscar himself proved that *Allegro*'s theme was a valid one because, like the play's protagonist, he was pressed by worldly considerations into doing less than his best work. Oscar had envisioned a simple setting but had agreed to a sophisticated, elaborate one; he had wanted to write about "birth to death" but he had been dissuaded from ending the play with death because people said it would be "depressing." He knew that the second act was unfinished, but was pressed by practical, financial considerations to go ahead with it. In fact, he had run out of time to write because he spent so much of that year as producer of other people's plays and as president and board member of worthy organizations. Oscar had come a long way in his struggle not to squander his time and usefulness on the wrong things so that he could devote enough of himself to his real work, but the struggle remained.

When *Allegro* began its pre-Broadway tryouts, accident followed accident. At the New Haven Shubert Theatre premiere, in September 1947, the first-act scenery collapsed; Lisa Kirk fell into the orchestra pit as she was singing "The Gentleman Is a Dope" (ironically just after the line "A clumsy Joe who wouldn't know a rhumba from a waltz"); smoke from trash burning at the Taft Hotel next door panicked some of the audience and sent them rushing to the exits. The following week in Boston, obstreperous conventioneers full of spirits, holiday and otherwise, disrupted the play until Oscar yelled out "Shut up!" and the disturbance subsided.

The 40-week Broadway run and the 31-week tour that followed would have ensured financial success for most musicals, but despite a $75,000 advance sale, the huge production overhead put the show into the Theatre Guild's red column. *Allegro* received the coveted Donaldson Award in three categories (book, lyrics, musical score), and many good, even rapturous reviews, but at heart it was an artistic failure, as well as a financial one.

The critical reaction to the play was sharply divided. In Boston, Elinor Hughes said it was "a sentimental chronicle, lacking in cohesion and humor," while Elliot Norton found it "the most remarkable musical play I have ever seen." A few weeks later, in New York, Louis Kronenberger called it "a grave disappointment . . . an out-and-out failure"; Ward Morehouse, "a distinguished and tumultuous musical play . . . excitingly unconventional." John Chapman said R & H had "gone philosophical; sententious even." Robert Coleman said they had reached "perfection." Brooks Atkinson said that in their step forward —a musical play without any of the conventions of form—they had created a first act "of great beauty and purity, as if *Our Town* could be written to music."

With the play's long run and many favorable critical reactions, Oscar could have rationalized that it was a success. But he remained troubled, partly because among those who thought the play failed were many whose opinions he respected, partly because both critics and audiences had so misinterpreted what he was saying that he knew it was he who had failed to get the meaning across. If an audience runs away with the play, like a horse who runs away with his rider, he said, it meant that the playwright's grip was not strong enough. In this case many theatergoers and critics thought Oscar was saying that small-town people were honest and good and that big-city people were neurotic, materialistic and venal. He could and did point out that the worst character in the play was a small-town girl, but he knew it was his fault that his message was not clear.

Rodgers later said he thought the show was "too preachy, which was the one fault that Oscar had, if any." He thought it was the moralizing that led people to go overboard in seeing things that weren't there. The "Greek chorus" that Oscar used in the play to comment on the action and the characters not only lent a verbose, rather pretentious note to the play, but by giving the characters little to do except respond, prevented them from coming to life strongly enough to engage the audience. When he was revising the play for television thirteen years later, Oscar toyed with the idea of keeping the chorus concept only as unseen voices of the characters themselves, not "a lot of people [who] march up and down the stage aimlessly."

For all its flaws, *Allegro* represented serious attempts at experimentation in the form of the musical and was more iconoclastic than either *Oklahoma!* or *Carousel*. Characters diminished in importance as other elements carried the plot. On an abstract set, the living and the dead, a Greek chorus, dancers, and photographic images moved in a unified pattern. Few of the songs were designed to be hits; there were no stars; important songs were given to minor characters and only one to the principal actor. The intention was to draw the audience into the show as each action onstage was seen subjectively. Hiring a choreographer as director was not a capricious decision; the authors wanted a consistency of visual pattern, a frame of movement and rhythm, a continuity of design. Brooks Atkinson said that it was as if R & H "were trying to create a musical play from the inside out, as if music and ballet were a single form of expression . . . all contributing equally to the whole impression." To some extent the reason that the play was not successful was that it was so innovative, there were many places where it could fail. Still, it may prove in retrospect to have been a milestone, albeit a rather weak one.

In any event, R & H never again attempted such a major experiment. Perhaps it was not in the nature of their partnership to do so. The limit imposed upon any collaboration is the common ground on which two men's talents and personalities can work together. Although many flaws in *Allegro* were due to weaknesses in Oscar's book and mistakes in judgment on the production, for which he correctly took responsibility, it was he who was more responsible for the successful innovations.

Though R & H presented a unified façade to the world, and Oscar seemed the more conservative and stolid of the two, he was in fact that more experimental. Agnes de Mille says that Oscar, with his cracker-barrel, folksy reputation, was "actually prone to considerable daring in his search for new forms. [He] attempted startling and lovely experiments." She talks of a quality of "dry toughness" that Oscar "frequently had to yield before audience hesitation or surprise. This occurred in one-third of the scenes in *Allegro*." Dick, she says, "is more conventional, classic . . . not so interested in experimenting as in reaching the audience emotionally and he prefers direct and proven methods for doing this."

Oscar was a practical man of the theater, a craftsman who in four hours could convey to Steve Sondheim the basic principles of the musical theater. Yet there was another part of Oscar. His son Jimmy remembers the time Reggie was discussing one of his projects with Oscar and kept referring to rules, such as "The hero comes in too early," and Oscar exploded in anger toward the brother he usually treated with such gentleness. "There's just one thing I hate and that's rules. The theater should have no rules."

Oscar's loyalty to Dick was so complete that he almost never distinguished between their efforts, even in talking with family and close friends. However, once in a while, he let something slip, as he did while recording a tape interview for the Columbia University Oral History Program. Referring to the chorus in *Allegro*, he said, "I intended Dick to write music for it, but we wound up reciting the chorus instead; we also wound up with a great deal of scenery . . . without this device, it was much better, I thought." He caught the slip and continued, "I'm not blaming anyone, because we all accepted it, we all collaborated . . . but it was a mistake."

One of the basic failures in *Allegro* was that the styles of the two men simply did not match in this show. The rather austere simplicity that Oscar strove for was not matched by the music.* "It is not possible to avoid the tender subject of Mr. Rodgers' music any longer," said Cecil Smith in writing about *Allegro* for *Theatre Arts*. "It seems that the minute he leaves the métier of conventional musical comedy, in which he excels, and ventures into a more exacting area of theatre music, he passes outside the limits of his technique and his ideas alike. . . . The instrumental passages accompanying dramatic scenes are really terrible; they lean on repetitions of catch-lines and empty build-ups orchestrated by Russell Bennett exactly as he has orches-

---

* Jerry Kern's music in such songs as "Sweetest Sights That I Have Seen" and "Lonely Feet" has the spare purity and harmonic simplicity that better suited the kind of lyrics that Oscar wrote for *Allegro*.

trated countless other Broadway shows by rule of thumb. . . . The score as a whole is not very good Broadway—though its pretentions are likely to impress a good many Broadway sophisticates—nor does it satisfy the minimal requirements of the lyric theatre."

A superb musician, Dick might well have been able to go in directions of another kind that were not possible for Oscar and therefore in their collaboration. It is clear, however, that Oscar could have gone further in the direction of changing the form of the musical, but not as R & H. He was neither articulate about his visionary impulse nor particularly driven by it in his later years. If he had been younger, more frustrated, less content with life, perhaps he would have been as instrumental in creating the next form of the musical as he had been in formulating the present one. If he had been willing to forgo the satisfactions of his collaboration with Dick, he might have worked with a composer better suited to the move toward a less commercial musical. The careful dreamer himself would have deplored such speculation. The fact is, R & H were never again innovative. They spent the rest of their years together refining the dramatic musical play until they took their particular brand of it as far as it could go.

Eight

Some Enchanted Evening

"Rodgers and Hammerstein would be perfect for this property," said Josh Logan to Leland Hayward.

"Of course, but don't you mention it to them. They'll want the whole goddam thing. They'd gobble us up for breakfast!"

The property was a collection of stories called *Tales of the South Pacific*, for which Logan and Hayward had made an informal producers' agreement to acquire theatrical rights from its little-known author, James Michener. Since no contract had been signed, Leland ordered the voluble Josh not to blab about it.

When Logan saw Rodgers at a cocktail party a few days later, he knew "how Eve felt when she saw the apple," and couldn't resist saying, "Don't tell anyone I've told you this, but I own a story you and Oscar might make a musical of. It's called 'Fo' Dolla' and it's from *Tales of the South Pacific*."

His sense that R & H were absolutely right for this show dimmed Josh's remorse at breaking his word to Leland as he watched Dick jot on the small note pad he always carried: "Fo' Dolla—T of the SP."

Before the rights were acquired, Logan blabbed again—this time to Oscar, who had recently returned from a two-month tour of Scandinavia and was in Philadelphia with Dorothy on January 31, 1948, to see *Mister Roberts,* which he wrote and directed. Oscar mentioned to Logan that he and Dick couldn't find anything for their next show.

"Hasn't Dick told you my idea?"

"No. What is it?"

Logan told him of their conversation about "T of the SP" and suggested that he read it. Oscar bought a copy the next day, and when he finished it he immediately called Dick.

"Dick, I think *Tales of the South Pacific* would be great for our next."

"I was crazy about it, too," said Rodgers, "but some son-of-a-bitch I met at a cocktail party owns it. I can't remember who it was, but we haven't got a chance."

"Was that 'son-of-a-bitch' Josh?" asked Oscar.

"Logan! That's the son-of-a-bitch!"

They called Logan and Hayward. Dick and Oscar said they wanted to write the show but would do so only under the condition that they co-produce with Logan and Hayward and retain 51 percent of the property. Hayward was not happy about the majority interest factor, but knowing that R & H would do a show only if they had final say, he and his partner agreed. The next step was to locate the author of the book. It took Oscar several days of New York phone calls to track down James Michener at his home, which was in Doylestown, only a ten-minute walk from Highland Farm.

When they met Michener, they found that the quiet man in conservative tweeds and rimless round eyeglasses had never written before. He had sailed as an able-bodied seaman in the British Merchant Navy after his graduation from Swarthmore College, studied painting at the British Museum, worked as a teacher, and spent years as a textbook editor at Macmillan. Assigned by the Navy in World War II to a roving job that took him back and forth among several islands in the Pacific, Michener found himself with plenty of time to observe his fellow men—and women—and to study the way that people of two cultures reacted to each other in the unfamiliar environment and situations created by the war. He began to write a series of realistic stories, some amusing, some romantic, loosely tied together by the narrator and by a large-scale military operation called "Alligator." He sent his completed manuscript to Macmillan under an assumed name so that he would not seem to be trading on his former position there.

Not only Macmillan but the public liked the work of this natural storyteller.

At that first meeting Michener sensed that both Oscar and Dick were still smarting from the reception accorded *Allegro* and noted to himself, "Those fellows are so mad they could make a great musical out of three pages from the Bronx telephone directory." Their attitude seemed to be that there would be no pitfalls on their next venture. Michener was confident they would create an important work from his stories, even though their lawyer, Howard Reinheimer, made a habit of criticizing the author's property in order to extract a better deal for his clients: "You yourself admit it isn't a novel." The fifty-page contract that he finally signed gave him a nominal advance and only 1 percent of the gross. Michener had nothing more to do with the production and only saw it for the first time at the final run-through in New York. He did, however, buy two shares in the venture, and while he was short of cash when the time came to put up the money, R & H lent him the capital, which he paid back painlessly by deductions from his weekly royalties.

Tales of the South Pacific, with no single protagonist and dozens of characters who appear and frequently reappear in nineteen loosely linked sketches, presented tough structural problems for adaptation. One problem it did not present was that eternal question of the musical—who will make up the ensemble—for nurses and Seabees abounded in the tales. Another immediate R & H decision was not to use a ballet, since the atmosphere of the *Tales* was so realistic that it would not lend itself to fantasy. They liked, as Josh had, the story called "Fo' Dolla," which describes the love of Lieutenant Joseph Cable for Liat, the daughter of a disreputable, betel-chewing old Tonkinese woman known as Bloody Mary, and the young man's difficulty in overcoming the prejudices created by his Main Line, Philadelphia, background, despite his love for the beautiful Oriental girl. Concerned that this love story might seem just a variation of *Madame Butterfly*, Oscar spent several months carefully studying the other stories, marking characters and incidents with the thought of combining several of the tales.

He kept coming back to "Our Heroine," a story that had appealed to him from the beginning. A story about the romance between Ensign Nellie Forbush, a young nurse from Otolousa, Arkansas, a small town near Little Rock, and a middle-aged French planter named Emile de Becque, "Our Heroine" again dealt with racial prejudice, as the Southern girl found herself unable to accept either de Becque's former liaison with a dark-skinned woman or the children of that union. Oscar and Dick realized that using the two love stories would be a serious departure from the accepted musical-play form. Usually, if the main love story was serious, it was felt that the secondary one should be lighthearted and amusing. They decided to go with the two serious love stories, and to provide comic relief with a character from a third story, a tattooed wheeler-dealer named Luther Billis. To fuse the two plots they decided to use details from still other stories that described preparations for the large Japanese attack.

By late May, after they had agreed on the basis for the musical, they received a call from Edwin Lester, the Los Angeles Civic Light Opera Association's producer. He had signed Ezio Pinza, the distinguished Metropolitan basso, to a $25,000 contract for the lead in *Mr. Ambassador,* but now decided to cancel the production and inquired if R & H could use Pinza, thereby relieving him of his financial obligation. They began to flirt with the notion of engaging the opera singer for the role of the French planter and making him the leading character, subordinating the story of the young lovers. A middle-aged hero would be another serious departure, for the musical theater had traditionally glorified youth. But they liked the idea, and a few weeks later they lunched with Pinza and signed him for the role of Emile de Becque.

Their next thought was to get Mary Martin to play Nellie Forbush. Years before, at the opening night of *One Touch of Venus,* when Mary appeared in the final scene in a simple gingham dress, Oscar had turned to Dorothy and said, "This is the real Mary—a corn-fed girl from Texas—and that's the kind of part she should play." He had tried to get Mary for *Oklahoma!* but a toss of a coin sent her to another musical. Now he tried again. Mary was starring in *Annie Get Your Gun* in San Francisco when he and Dick called about their new show.

"What on earth do you want, two basses?" asked Mary. She was terrified at the thought of playing with a leading man who had a beautiful operatic voice. Dick promised that she would never have to sing "in competition" with Pinza. Mary told him that as soon as she returned home she would talk to them further.

Back in the East, still not convinced that she should play Nellie, Mary went to Dick's house, near hers in Connecticut, to hear some of the songs that had been written. Dick played while Oscar sang—first "Twin Soliloquies," then "Some Enchanted Evening"—most of which

Oscar had written during a weekend visit to Billy and Eleanor Rose's home in Mt. Kisco. They told Mary that although the show was far from finished, they wanted her and asked her to think it over for a few days and let them know. Unable to get the glorious "Some Enchanted Evening" out of her head she called Dick's house at 3 A.M. to say, "Do I have to wait three days? Can't I say *yes* right now?"

Other parts, too, had been virtually cast even before the book was written. Juanita Hall seemed a natural for Bloody Mary. Betta St. John, who had been a chorus member and Bambi Linn's understudy and then her replacement as Louise in *Carousel,* was in Oscar's mind for the part of Liat from the very beginning.

As usual, Oscar found writing the book a laborious process. He had always found this part of his job much more painful than lyric-writing; later he would say that he never particularly wanted to write the books of his shows, but wrote them because he could never find anyone else who was good enough. This adaptation proved particularly difficult and Oscar was finding it slow going during the summer. When Logan called to see if he could help, Oscar said he was having trouble with military talk and behavior. "I hate the military so much that I'm ignorant of it." Josh was something of an expert in such matters, with military school, the service and *Mr. Roberts,* also an adaptation of several stories, behind him. He and Oscar arranged for the Logans to spend the weekend at the farm.

Josh got out the Dictaphone he had brought along and he and Oscar began to take various parts and speak their lines into the machine. One line followed another as they threw themselves into their acting.

> Oscar (Bloody Mary): Hallo, G. I. . . . Grass skirt? Very saxy! Fo' dollar? . . . Saxy grass skirt . . . Fo' dollar . . . Send home Chicago . . . You like? . . . You buy?—
> Josh: [stage notes] Her eyes pan left to right as if her customer is walking away. She rises. Her crafty smile fades to a quick scowl as he apparently passes without buying. She calls after him.
> Oscar (Mary): Where you go? Come back! Buy! Chipskate' Crummy G.I.! Sad-sack—Droopy drawers!
> Josh (Adams): Tell him good, Mary!
> Oscar (Mary): What is 'good'?
> Josh (Adams): Tell him he is a stingy bastard!
> Oscar (Mary): Stingy bastard!—That good?
> Josh (Adams): That's great, Mary. You're learning fast.

Oscar (Mary): Stingy bastard! I learn fast. Pretty soon I talk English as good as any crummy Marine. Stingy bastard!

They were both so stimulated by each other that they worked late
into the night. Josh stayed on for another week and they worked intensely. The whole household became involved in the task: Shirley
Potash, a friend of Susan's from California who had been living with
the Hammersteins for months and had begun to work as Oscar's
secretary, transcribed the Dictabelts, and Dorothy and Nedda Logan
collated the pages.

Oscar's shows had always been free of sexual allusions. When he
and Josh reached the point where Lieutenant Cable and Liat make
love, Oscar's puritanical spirit rose. In the Michener story Cable
slowly pulled off Liat's clothing until she was lying nude on the mat.
Oscar's first draft of the scene suggested the sexual act simply by
having a blackout as the fully dressed lovers sat on the mat. Josh
argued that after the blackout they must give some indication that
clothes would be removed, perhaps by having Cable take off his shirt
during the blackout.

Oscar was silent. "You're emphatic, aren't you?" he said finally.

"Well, yes. Would you rather not do it?"

"No, no. It's a good idea," Oscar said. "It's just that I had to get
my breath, that's all."

The lyrics were completed one after another, usually in the order
in which they occurred in the play. One night Mary went to the
Logans' New York apartment, where Oscar and Dick had said they
would give her a "present." The gift was a song that had sprung as
much from Mary's personality as from the character's: "A Wonderful
Guy." The picture of Mary as "a corn-fed girl" in a gingham dress in
Venus came into Oscar's mind again as he wrote, "I'm as corny as
Kansas in August." He used Kansas instead of her native Texas because
the two k sounds gave a nice alliteration to the line. Oscar was fond
of this song. The only emotion he wanted to express in it was the sentimental, exuberant sailing spirit of this girl in love. He usually used
rhymes sparingly, but he felt that this simple song could be decorated
with more ingenious rhyming, and he provided embroidery with in-
terior rhymes and alliteration.

I expect every one,
Of my crowd to make fun,
Of my proud protestations of faith in romance.

And they'll say I'm naive,
As a babe to believe,
Ev'ry fable I hear from a person in pants!

Fearlessly I'll face them and argue their doubts away
Loudly I'll sing about flowers in spring;
Flatly I'll stand on my little flat feet and say
Love is a grand and a beautiful thing.

I'm not ashamed to reveal
The world famous feeling I feel.
I'm as corny as Kansas in August,
I'm as normal as blueberry pie,
No more a smart
Little girl with no heart,
I have found me a wonderful guy.

I am in a conventional dither,
With a conventional star in my eye,
And you will note
There's a lump in my throat
When I speak of that wonderful guy.

I'm as trite and as gay
As a daisy in May,
A cliche coming true!
I'm bromidic and bright
As a moon-happy night
Pouring light on the dew!

I'm as corny as Kansas in August
High as a flag on the fourth of July,
If you'll excuse an expression I use,
I'm in love
I'm in love
I'm in love
I'm in love
I'm in love
I'm in love with a wonderful guy.

"This is your song, Mary," they said, and Dick played while Oscar "said-sang" the words. Mary loved it. She sat down on the piano bench to sing it herself, throwing herself into it, waving her arms, getting more excited with every "I'm in love," until on "with a wonderful guy," she fell off the bench onto the floor.

"Never sing it any other way," said Dick. Mary went on and on singing it until the Logans' River House neighbors began to call with complaints about all that noise coming from their apartment. Logan answered the complaints with "You'll be sorry. Someday it's going to cost you a lot to hear all this."

During the course of the year that it took to write the musical, which was eventually titled *South Pacific*, the Hammersteins moved from their 61st Street apartment to 10 East 63rd Street. Going toward Central Park one Sunday for a walk, as they passed a town house near Fifth Avenue Dorothy said, "That's a lovely house. We could get that."

"Really?" replied Oscar.

"Would you like to see it? There are servants who can show it to us."

"So that's why you wanted to walk this way!" said Oscar.

As they went through the six-story red-brick building, Oscar could sense her good feelings about the gracious house, with its sweeping staircase and ample rooms, and he liked it, too. When they moved in a few months later, the huge eight-paneled Chinese screen that Oscar had bought for Dorothy in Paris the previous year had to be disassembled and moved in by pieces to its place behind the couch in the living room. Oscar had a study on the third floor and an office on the first floor as well, where his secretary worked and kept his files and correspondence.

Susan was now living with her parents again; she had so hated her Hollywood "starlet" years that she had lost her desire to be an actress. She was seeing quite a lot of Henry Fonda, who was starring in *Mister Roberts* in New York.

Billy, who was twenty-seven and married, had worked as an assistant stage manager on the revival of *Show Boat* when he was discharged from the Navy. He was happy to get the job but disappointed at his low salary, $75 a week. Oscar explained that with Reggie as stage manager he couldn't pay Billy more because it looked bad enough to have "all those Hammersteins on the payroll." A few months later Billy discovered that his father had in fact been paying him $125 a week, but had asked the general manager to put $50 each week into a savings account. Billy took this as an expression not only of Oscar's protective impulses but of a lack of confidence in him. His next job was as production stage manager for *Mister Roberts*.

Jimmy was in college at the University of North Carolina. After pestering his father to send him a draft of *South Pacific*, he had neglected to mail it back. Oscar wrote telling him to deposit it in an envelope "even as you safely deposit girls in their dormitories. . . . if there is no post office in Chapel Hill, send it by Pony Express, and if there are no ponies, take the cover off the script, roll it up, put it in a bottle, have it hitch-hiked to the seaboard and thrown in the Atlantic. . . . The only other thing I can suggest is that you do nothing at all about it, but this has probably already occurred to you."

During the year, pre-production on *South Pacific* proceeded smoothly. No longer did the producers have to scramble for money as Terry Helburn had done for *Oklahoma!* Backers were so anxious to invest in R & H shows that the four producers were able to finance this show not by the usual limited partnership agreement but by forming a corporation which restricts the number of investors to ten. The sum of $225,000 was raised, but because the show actually cost $180,000, they were able to set a precedent by paying the shareholders $25,000 the day of the New York premiere.

By January 1949, just a year after Josh had mentioned "Fo' Dolla," both cast and production staff were assembled. Josh was to direct the book and musical numbers, Russell Bennett and Trude Rittman were attending to the orchestrations, Jo Mielziner created the scenery and lighting, and Motley the costumes. (It was actually Liz Montgomery who did the designs for *South Pacific*, since the rest of "Motley," Sophia and Margaret Harris, were busy in London at the time.) In addition to Ezio Pinza, Mary Martin, Juanita Hall and Betta St. John, the cast, which had been carefully chosen in seemingly endless auditions, included Myron McCormick as Luther Billis, and William Tabbert as Lieutenant Joseph Cable.

Collaboration is vitally important in the theater—not just the collaboration between author and composer, but the convergence and coordination of every talent in a play, from lighting to set designing to direction to acting to writing. Oscar warned young people that to get along in the theater you must enjoy working side by side with other people. He said that a certain novelist who had left the theater to return to writing for the printed page because she couldn't stand so many people advising her and butting in on her work was right to leave. "The theater is a welding. . . . You must be willing not only to give your best to [the others] but to accept their best and give them the opportunity of adding their efforts to yours."

Even more than most shows, *South Pacific* represented a mingling of the ideas and talents of everyone involved in the show. One song, "Bali Ha'i," provides a good example of the process. Michener had described Bali Ha'i, the small jewel of an island, so vividly that from the beginning Oscar and Dick knew that they wanted a song about it. Before he actually wrote the music, Dick envisioned not only the languorous, mystical Oriental quality called for by the story, but the range and pitch that would suit Juanita Hall's voice. Oscar wrote several verses, taking almost a week to do so, and handed Dick a typewritten sheet of the words when he went to Josh Logan's apartment for lunch one day. Because he had the sound clearly in mind, Dick wrote the music in record time, even for him. By his own account, "I spent a minute or so studying the words, turned the paper over and scribbled some notes, then went into the next room where there was a piano, and played the song. The whole thing couldn't have taken more than five minutes."

Jo Mielziner, who was working on the designs, was so excited when he heard the song that he went back to his studio and started to draw the island. Dissatisfied with his sketch, feeling that it did not have enough mystery to it, he dipped his brush in water and blurred the top of the island so that it looked as if it were surrounded by mist. When Oscar saw Jo's drawing, he thought of an additional verse for the song:

> Someday you'll see me,
> Floating in the sunshine,
> My head sticking out
> From a low-flying cloud.

Thus the song was a collaboration involving not only author, composer and lyricist but set designer as well.

Another song was "collaborated" on by a singer. One day while Mary was taking a shower a "crazy idea" came to her and she ran out of the bathroom, dripping water on the floor, to share it with her husband Richard, working at his desk. "Wouldn't it be a great scene for a movie or play if sometime I washed my hair right onstage and then came out all dripping?"

"Don't you dare tell that to anyone," he said. "Not a soul. If you do, they'll go for it, and then you'll have to do it onstage eight times a week." The first person who called after that conversation was Josh, and Mary heard Richard say to him, "Josh, Mary has a great idea . . ."

"Don't you dare tell Dick and Oscar," said Logan. "You know what will happen."

Of course, they told Dick and Oscar, who happened to be struggling with a song that would convey Nellie's reluctance to marry de Becque and her decision to break off her romance with him. The scene in which she washed her hair onstage while singing "I'm Gonna Wash That Man Right Outa My Hair" became one of the most talked-about things in the show. Mary cut her hair short so that it would dry quickly. She held a bar of soap in her down-stage hand and a palmful of liquid shampoo in the other because it produced bubbles faster. Everything she did or said about the song became fodder for newspaper articles—such as the glamorous turbans she began to wear offstage as a change from the little-boy look that the cropped hair gave her. Others speculated about the effect on her scalp and the number of times (1,886!) she had washed it onstage. Mary became such a hair expert, not only cutting her own frequently but using the time between rehearsals and evening performances to give haircuts to the cast and crew, that Oscar, Dick and the production staff bought her a red-and-white barber pole and put a fake barber's license on her dressing-room door.

Mary was also responsible for one of the hit costumes of the play. One day she showed Oscar a picture that someone had just sent her of herself as a gawky, grinning child in summer camp wearing a pair of men's shorts with wide stripes, a long shirt, a sailor hat and a man's necktie. Oscar put the picture by his mirror where he shaved every morning after writing under it: "This proves there is hope for everyone." When Logan saw the picture he said, "You've come a long way, honey, but you're still a baggy-pants comedian at heart," and thought up the baggy sailor suit with cap and long tie that she would wear for "Honey Bun" in the show-within-a-show of the second act.

The feeling was still widespread in 1948 that social problems had no place in the musical theater. Oscar did not set about writing a play with a "message," but a strong theme critical of racial prejudice existed in the work he was adapting, and he did not shy away from it. "You've Got to Be Carefully Taught" is sung by Cable when he realizes that the differences in race and background make it impossible for him to marry Liat. It is a shocking discovery, and as he reflects upon the injustice of racial prejudice he exclaims bitterly, "It's not born in you! It happens *after* you're born." Then follows an eloquent plea for tolerance as he sings. Oscar's original lyrics were:

You've got to be taught to hate and fear.
You've got to be taught from year to year,
It's got to be drummed in your dear little ear—
You've got to be carefully taught!

You've got to be taught to be afraid
Of people whose eyes are oddly made
And people whose skin is a different shade—
You've got to be carefully taught.

You've got to be taught before it's too late,
Before you are six or seven or eight,
To hate all the people your relatives hate—
You've got to be carefully taught!

Love is quite different.
It grows by itself.

It will grow like a weed
On a mountain of stones;
You don't have to feed
Or put fat on its bones;
It can live on a smile
Or a note of a song;
It may starve for a while,
But it stumbles along,
Stumbles along with its banner unfurled,
The joy and the beauty, the hope of the world.

Dick objected to the last section of the song and they removed it, but once he agreed to the rest he was as staunch as Oscar in withstanding pressure not to use the song which came from many quarters. After a tryout performance, a group of "experienced theatrical people" urged Michener to tell Oscar and Dick that their show would be a greater success if they eliminated this controversial song.*

* In 1953, after a road company performance of South Pacific in Atlanta, some Georgia legislators issued a vehement protest against the song, and introduced legislation to outlaw entertainment works having "an underlying philosophy inspired by Moscow." State Representative David C. Jones, who still believes in 1976 that his original charge is true, said that the song urging "justification of interracial marriage" was "to us . . . very offensive. Intermarriage produces halfbreeds, and halfbreeds are not conducive to the higher type of society. . . . In the South we have pure bloodlines and we intend to keep it that way." Oscar replied to reporters that he didn't think the legislators were representing the people of Georgia very well and he was surprised by the idea that "anything kind and humane must necessarily originate in Moscow."

Michener reported with pleasure: "The authors replied stubbornly that this number represented why they had wanted to do this play, and that even if it meant the failure of the production, it was going to stay in."

Oscar did not think that the alternative to the hate that we are carefully taught was necessarily love. When an interviewer asked him about his supposed "love" for people, he replied, "I don't idealize people. I am conscious of their imperfections. In fact, I haven't got a high opinion of human beings. When they make mistakes, I am not surprised. It is the perfectionist who gets indignant when people let him down. If a man is disillusioned about people, it is his fault. He had no business having illusions. I love people but not the way Saroyan says he loves the human race. I don't think everyone is beautiful or wonderful, the way he says. I know damned well they are not." The alternative to hate, he said, was not blind love but understanding. When the same interviewer asked him if understanding wasn't a road to love, he said, "Not necessarily. I understand a lot of people I don't like at all."

For all his realism, Oscar was not a cynic. He saw clearly weaknesses, imperfections and problems; he saw just as clearly strengths, good motives and hopeful solutions. He preferred to emphasize the latter, in his life and his work. The song he wrote for Nellie to sing, "A Cockeyed Optimist," though put into the words of a character less sophisticated and articulate than he, expresses his own optimism:

> When the sky is a bright canary yellow
> I forget ev'ry cloud I've ever seen—
> So they call me a cockeyed optimist,
> Immature and incurably green!
>
> I have heard people rant and rave and bellow
> That we're done and we might as well be dead—
> But I'm only a cockeyed optimist
> And I can't get it into my head.
>   I hear the human race
>   Is falling on its face
>   And hasn't very far to go,
>   But ev'ry whip-poor-will
>   Is selling me a bill
>   And telling me it just ain't so!
> I could say life is just a bowl of jello
> And appear more intelligent and smart,

> But I'm stuck
> (Like a dope!)
> With a thing called hope,
> And I can't get it out of my heart! . . . Not this heart.

A week before rehearsals Josh Logan and Oscar were sitting in the Logans' living room reading over the script and discussing the alternate endings. In their first ending Cable dies on the mission, but they had switched to one in which he is saved, thinking it would be too hard to kill him. They agreed now that the one in which he dies was a much better solution and decided to use it in the final script.

As Oscar sat reading the last pages of the libretto, Josh finally worked up the courage to speak to him about a matter that had been bothering him for months: credit for the book. Although Oscar had worked out the essential structure and several scenes before Josh appeared in Doylestown, the script itself was a collaborative effort. Josh had recently gone through an unpleasant episode with Thomas Heggen, the author of *Mister Roberts*, who had only reluctantly agreed to giving Josh credit and one-third of the royalties for the play adaptation, on which Josh had worked so hard with him. Now a somewhat similar situation had arisen, for he and Oscar had never discussed the matter of credit. For months his wife, Nedda, had been saying, "Well, are you going to get credit? Are you going to share in the royalties?"

"Oh, I couldn't ask Oscar," Josh would reply, evading the issue.

"Why can't you? You've got to!"

Josh still was loath to confront Oscar but he kept thinking: Suppose it wins the Pulitzer Prize? I'll absolutely cut my throat. This is my one chance ever to win that prize. His embarrassment was finally overcome by this insistent thought, plus Nedda's prodding and the urging of his doctor, who had told him if he didn't confront Oscar, he'd be a wreck. "They'll have to take you away to another hospital," he said, referring to the emotional breakdown that Josh had suffered nine years earlier. Summoning all his courage, as Oscar sat reading the script, Josh blurted out, "Oscar, I'd like to have credit on this."

After a pause Oscar said, "I should have suggested it myself. Of course!"

"That's wonderful," Josh said in relief. "I just couldn't bear the thought that this might win a prize and that all during rehearsals I would have to say 'Mr. Hammerstein wants it this way,' not 'We want it this way.' I just would feel . . ."

"I understand completely," Oscar said.

After a meeting the following day with Howard, Dick and Morrie Jacobs, R & H's general manager, Oscar telephoned Josh to say that he was coming back to talk further. He asked Shirley, his secretary, to accompany him. As they waited for a cab she said, "Boss, I gave Nedda all the scripts." A week or two before, Nedda Logan had told the young secretary that she was collecting all of her husband's scripts to give to some college or theater collection and had asked for the scripts of *South Pacific*, which Shirley had obligingly given her. Worried that she hadn't told him at the time, she asked, "Did I do something wrong?"

"No," Oscar replied. He never said a critical word to her about acting without consulting him.

When they arrived at the Logans' apartment, Oscar and Josh left the two women and went into another room for their meeting. "I was a little premature about the agreement," Oscar began. "I've talked it over with Dick and Howard and here's the deal." He outlined the plan whereby Josh would share the book credit but in a typeface smaller than that for the music and lyrics.

"I'm sorry about that," said Josh, who was already receiving large-size billing as director, "but if that's the way it is—fine. As long as the credit can be there."

Oscar continued: "You will not receive any share of the book royalties nor be a part of the copyright. R & H controls the copyright ownership on everything Dick and I write, and we can't share it with anybody else."

"Well, I didn't ask for money," countered Josh, "but what about taking a portion of my director's percentage and transferring it to co-authorship?"

"I don't know whether that's possible or not," Oscar answered. (He later informed Josh it was not.)

"Tell me one final thing, Oscar. Why did you agree yesterday to an equal division down the line and then hit me so hard with this today?"

Oscar's explanation, according to Josh, was that since the public was expecting him to write it alone (actually, newspapers had for months been referring to the joint effort on the book), he had been penalized by sharing credit with Josh, and now Josh, too, was being penalized.

It was Josh's feeling that Oscar was "speaking lines that he had been instructed to say—whether by Dick or Howard." He was articulating a committee decision rather than his own. Oscar's expression showed him "how hard he must have fought to secure for me as much as he did, and how equally hard it was for him to look me in the eye as he said what he had to say."

Josh left that day for Bill Brown's Health Farm, where he so often went to rest before rehearsals. While he was there, Reinheimer's associate brought Josh's lawyer a contract to sign. He specified that if it was not signed within two hours Logan needn't come to rehearsals. Josh's lawyer signed it and decided not to tell his client about the stipulation until after the play was done.

At first Josh felt grateful that he had been given co-author credit. It is clear that after Oscar had decided on the basic framework of the story and worked out "a few scenes," Logan did co-author the book. He thanked Oscar several times for "the co-author thing" and, in a letter to John Mason Brown, said that his work had come in the second draft. He preferred to blame Howard Reinheimer, as he did in a letter to the Hammersteins, for the fact that he was not to receive author's royalties.

So Logan was stunned when his lawyer told him that it was R & H that had said he was not to come to rehearsals if the contract wasn't executed immediately. "I didn't believe it," says Josh. "I still felt Dick and Oscar were my friends. They were incapable of such gangster threats. It must have been someone else's idea to bully me like that. I forced myself to believe in them."

Josh's feelings remained ambivalent toward both Dick and Oscar. His relationship with Dick altered rather drastically at about this time. Dick had helped Josh early in his career and had insisted on his directing *Higher and Higher* after his well-publicized nervous breakdown. In addition, they had been not only friends but pals, having relaxed evenings together on the road and in New York. Now he felt that Dick had changed, that the fun seemed to have gone out of him as he closeted himself in the office and wrapped himself in business affairs. As to Oscar, Josh respected him as a professional and as a human being. He continued to respect him and to care for him, but he never felt quite the same way about him again.

In the world of the theater the attitudes toward R & H and toward Oscar personally were somewhat paradoxical: R & H would gobble you up for breakfast, R & H always got everything it wanted, looked out for its own interests, R & H was tough and powerful;

Oscar Hammerstein was a good, kind man, a poet ("You just wanted to hug him," many said), a man respected and honored for his personal qualities as well as his talent. Yet Oscar was a full part of that entity known as R & H which gobbled you up for breakfast.

How did the Oscar Hammerstein worshipers reconcile these views? "Oh, Oscar never went to the office. He hated it. He didn't really understand the business side." Or, "Dick Rodgers was a bastard," "Howard Reinheimer was a cold son-of-a-bitch," "You can't trust Morrie Jacobs." Those who probe a little deeper say that Oscar was so delighted to have found a collaboration that worked so well that he didn't want to rock the boat. Eleven years of failure had been quite enough for him; he liked success better and he and Dick were successful together. He put up with personal as well as professional decisions he didn't like in order to be able to live with his partner. If there were a drawing room and a compartment on a train, Dick would take the larger accommodations. Dick liked to sit one row ahead of Oscar at auditions; Dick took 75 percent of the space below a picture of the two for his signature, leaving his partner the rest. Oscar would neither complain nor allow Dorothy to complain about petty matters. It was a successful collaboration and he meant to keep it that way.

Perhaps Oscar's role in the business decisions was another manifestation of his sweeping things under the carpet. Many of his admirers prefer to think that he simply didn't care much about the business side and blandly went along with decisions made by Dick and Howard and Morrie because he didn't want unpleasant confrontations. The decisions were usually fair and easy enough to go along with, though in some cases, such as Logan's, they were not. It is certainly true that Oscar did not enjoy going to the office or attending to small business details. However, it is inaccurate to suggest that R & H decisions did not reflect Oscar's participation as well as Dick's.

Oscar was not unconcerned with money or with artistic power—he enjoyed them both. He knew a great deal about the practical, business side of the theater, though he preferred not to spend his time working on such details. Dorothy says that Oscar made it clear to her that he felt he was better than Dick at handling many aspects of business. Although he did not have a law degree, his legal training made him proficient at reading and understanding contracts, and he had a very logical, mathematical mind. Above all, no one who knew Oscar Hammerstein thought of him as a weak man. "He could have mowed Dick down if he had wanted to," says Logan. If Oscar agreed to R & H decisions it was because he wanted to do so. There was in him, for all his tender qualities and sympathetic understanding, a selfishness that allowed him to look after his own best interests; he knew what he wanted and usually managed to achieve it. Those who knew and loved him most recognized the quality and accepted it. "Anyone in the world who is a creator is selfish," says Mary Martin. It was, in fact, one aspect of the strength that kept him going through eleven years of failure, and gave integrity to his work and his life. Oscar knew what he believed was right for him and he did what was necessary in order to stick to it. "A careful dreamer," Dick called him. Logan put it another way: "He was a dreamer with his feet on the ground and a whole erector set inside of him." Within the poet, with his kindness and humor and caring, there was steel. The nature of R & H reflected the character of the two men who formed the entity. "They were both tough as nails," says Logan.

The co-author dispute did not affect *South Pacific* rehearsals, which were exciting and fun from the very beginning. One of Josh Logan's special attributes as a director is his strong personal commitment, a sense of involvement that cast members find infectious. He threw himself into the show and he encouraged them not only to do their best but to give special contributions.

One of the first scenes to be blocked was "There Is Nothin' Like a Dame." Josh began pacing up and down the stage, the men following him, to suggest the caged-animal quality of frustrated men trapped by the war on an island with no women. He motioned one man to pace one way, another the other way. The result was a scene filled with movement.

A major departure from convention was to treat the chorus less as an ensemble and more as a collection of individuals who had differentiated characters and spoke separate lines of dialogue. Most of them were listed in the playbill. When the Seabees sang of their lonely, frustrated state in "There Is Nothin' Like a Dame," the lines were divided among them, with only the refrain sung in chorus. The lyrics for this song and "Honey Bun" were somewhat earthier than was usual for the puritanical Oscar. Although personally he was the least flirtatious or bawdy of men, he wrote in "Honey Bun":

> My doll is as dainty as a sparrow,
> Her figure is something to applaud.
> When she's narrow, she's narrow as an arrow
> And she's broad, where a broad, should be broad.

Her lips are pips!
I call her hips!
"Twirly—and whirly."

When Oscar first sang the lyrics to Mary, he had a half-embarrassed but pleased look on his face. The song was originally supposed to be sung only by McCormick as Billis, but as the "amateur show" put on by the nurses and sailors in the second act developed, Mary in her oversized sailor suit joined McCormick in his grass skirt, mop wig and brassiere made from two large coconuts.

Dances were not choreographed, they simply developed. Most of the dancing came in the second act. The show-within-a-show staged by the military men and women—ancient device though it was—became one of the high points of *South Pacific* because of its spontaneous quality. The act opened with a soft-shoe hitch-kick and scissors suggested by Oscar, who remembered that in his days as a stage manager such dances were so simple that he could put them on himself. Another routine was actually worked out by Mary, who had once taught tap-dancing back in her hometown of Weatherford, Texas. When Logan discovered that one of the actors could stand on his hands, the feat was "choreographed" into the scene.

When Logan and Myron McCormick were students at Princeton, McCormick had displayed his remarkable stomach gyrations to get them free beer at parties. He was dying to try it onstage and Josh loved the idea. McCormick had a large ship "tattooed" on his abdomen and it rocked back and forth with each roll of his stomach as he wiggled in his grass skirt and coconut bosom. Mary's sailor outfit for the same number, "Honey Bun," kept getting more and more outlandish as rehearsals went on. The sleeves were made longer, the pants baggier and finally elastic was added to make them bounce more. The routine never failed to bring down the house. Josh discovered that one girl could do a barrel roll and another acrobatics and that one of the actors, Archie Savage, had been a member of the Katherine Dunham company; he used them all. To stage one of the last songs, "Happy Talk," Logan took Juanita Hall, Betta St. John and Bill Tabbert to the lobby of the theater where there was a piano, and while Hall sang he sat on the floor with the others and worked out with them the little finger gestures that so charmingly pantomimed the words of the song.

Trying to figure out a fresh way to move immediately from song to story without encores or a break, Oscar, Dick, Josh and Jo Mielziner decided upon the "lap dissolve" method, used for the first time by Mielziner in *Allegro*. There was never a darkened stage; each scene started just before the preceding scene finished. Scene changes were made while the cast was onstage or in front of the scrim. The musical score contributed its part to this continuity; the orchestrations providing transitions as well as "background" music that suited the action indicated the emotional content of the scene or even helped to tell the story. The use of leit-motifs in musical plays—an innovation by Jerry Kern in *Show Boat*—was here brought to full development by Russell Bennett and Trude Rittman.

One day during Mary's "A Wonderful Guy" number, Josh was trying to figure out how to get her from one side of the stage to the other.

"I can do cartwheels across the stage," Mary suggested.

"And sing at the same time?"

"Why not? I used to do them all the way home from school in Weatherford."

Between every "I'm in love" Mary did a cartwheel until she reached the other side of the stage. She rehearsed it until it was perfect.

Just before the company left for New Haven, Josh decided to replace the dim rehearsal work lamps at the Majestic with more powerful theatrical lights onstage so that he could judge the performance from out front. When Mary started her cartwheels, everything went fine until, upside down, she was temporarily blinded by one of the bright spotlights. She didn't know where the floor was, but the momentum was such that she went over again, flipped into the air and landed briefly on conductor Salvatore Dell'Isola's head before crashing into Trude Rittman as she sat at the piano and then onto the floor of the pit. Sitting out front, Oscar heard a loud *thump, thump, thump* and then silence, broken by Trude's voice saying, "Oh God, my neck is broken." He rushed to see if Trude and Mary were seriously hurt. They weren't. When the show opened, Mary didn't do cartwheels—she just skipped to the other side of the stage.

South Pacific offered Mary her first chance to show audiences the essence of Mary Martin as well as the character she was playing; this was to be expected, since Oscar had written the character with Mary in mind. She charmed audiences with her clowning and acting, as well as her singing and dancing. Oscar felt her performance was a "convergence" of all her talents and dreams and energies, her good instincts and technical skill. One night later in the run Oscar and

Dorothy came to see Mary backstage after a performance they had seen. Mary was "having a ball" and greeted Oscar with "Now, tell me—isn't it better?"

He was very serious. "No, it isn't."

"What do you mean it's not better?"

"It isn't," said Oscar. "You're pushing too much. You're having too much fun. You're not Nellie."

"Oh, Oscar." Mary was embarrassed but knew that she *had* been having too much fun—playing Mary Martin. She also knew that Oscar couldn't tell an untruth.

"I'll come back in a couple of nights and see if you've gotten it back," he said.

She worked hard. Two nights later he came backstage and said, "It's back now."

There were several song changes during rehearsals. Late in the second act, Pinza sang "Now Is the Time" before he and Cable embarked on a dangerous military mission. The lyric began, "Now!/Now is the time,/The time to act." They liked the song, but felt that the very act of singing before setting out was a procrastination that belied the words. Pinza had only one other major song, so a replacement was needed.

"Perhaps he could lament losing Nellie before going on the mission," Oscar suggested.

"His decision to go on the mission could come out of the song," Josh threw in.

"Let me have a working title," said Dick.

"This Nearly Was Mine," Oscar promptly suggested. Dick wrote a slow waltz and Oscar wrote lyrics to it to create one of the most moving songs in the show.

The other *South Pacific* song for which the music was written before the words was also put into the show during rehearsals. Oscar was unhappy with his efforts on a song for Cable to sing after he had made love to Liat, feeling his first effort too light and unsuitable for the character. During rehearsals he remembered an unusual melody that Dick had written for *Allegro*. Tentatively entitled "My Wife," it was a tune Oscar loved, but he had never worked out the appropriate words for it. He now wrote lyrics for it in just two days, showed it to Dick the morning he finished and put it into the rehearsal that afternoon. Both of them thought the song, "Younger Than Springtime," one of the best in the score.

The new Rodgers and Hammerstein show with two big stars was so eagerly awaited that there were people standing in line outside the Shubert Theatre in New Haven for three weeks prior to its world premiere on the evening of March 7. The entire one-week engagement was sold out. The show was too long, partly because of the applause for every number, and needed tightening, but the audience was enthusiastic. Mike Todd said after the show, "Don't take it to New York." Silence. "It's too good for them. It's too goddam good for New York!"

The show needed work and they began to cut, tighten, revise. British actor and playwright Emlyn Williams, who was a friend of Josh Logan's, was in New Haven for the first performance. Knowing that someone who is not too close to a play can often see possible cuts more clearly, Oscar asked him to take a look at the script. Working with a blue pencil, Williams was able to pare ten minutes from the show by making small, judicious cuts in the dialogue. Oscar, Dick and Josh chipped in to buy him a small pair of gold scissors and a gold-plated blue pencil inscribed "To Emlyn the Ripper."

Shows invariably need work out of town because of the nature of the medium. Rehearsing in an empty theater, the company is missing an important ingredient that all the experience in the world cannot provide. It is only when the performers respond to the roar of laughter and applause that the show comes fully alive, only when they play to a silence relieved only by coughing that they know something is wrong.

Everyone in the company thought "A Wonderful Guy," sung by Mary to her fellow nurses, one of the best numbers in the show. They were puzzled to find that audiences were not applauding after the song. No one could figure out why. One day Josh said to Oscar, "Too bad it isn't a soliloquy."

Oscar's face was expressionless as he rethought the scene. "Of course. Good idea. I'll do it immediately." Before the evening performance he changed the *you*'s to *they*'s and they restaged the scene, having the other nurses exit to leave Mary sitting on a box singing the song, punctuated by a small exuberant dance and some business with a hat. Now the scene worked. That night and ever after, Mary received a huge ovation for the number.

An actor who had been turned down for a small role in the show turned up as a waiter at Kaysey's, the theater hangout in New Haven. He introduced himself to Dick and Hayward when they were eating there one night and told them he had taken the job to be close to his girl, who played one of the nurses in the show. Dick and Leland came back to the hotel enthralled with the romance of it all and suggested to Oscar and Josh that they hire him for the play. Oscar listened to their story and said, "You know what's going to happen, don't you? He's going to fall for another girl in the show and she's going to marry a waiter from Kaysey's!"

From New Haven they went on to Boston, where the opening night was triumphant. Elliot Norton wrote that his only frustration was, "It is impossible in a small space to do more than hint at all the wonders of *South Pacific*," and Elinor Hughes began her review by noting that "Everyone knows it's dangerous to expect too much from any show, even a Rodgers and Hammerstein musical, but whatever anyone expected from *South Pacific*, which tore the lid off the Shubert Theatre last night, it fell short of what actually took place . . ." She concluded by proclaiming that *South Pacific* was in truth "South Terrific, and then some!"

South Pacific's advance sale on Broadway set an all-time record: $400,000 at pre-opening and $700,000 after the premiere. Because of pre-production word of mouth and out-of-town advance building, there was an unprecedented demand for opening-night tickets (the Majestic Theatre's capacity was 1,696). *Variety* reported that the premiere audience (April 7, 1949) was virtually a who's who of show business and the arts. It was a particularly responsive first-night audience that repeatedly stopped the show with applause and cheers and gave a prolonged standing ovation at the final curtain calls.

Oscar and Dick were so confident about the opening this time that they broke their own precedent and rented the St. Regis Roof for a party after the show. They even ordered two hundred copies of *The New York Times* to hand out to the guests. Brooks Atkinson didn't disappoint them—he loved the show, as did all the other critics. All noted that more than any previous musical, it was strong enough to stand on its own feet dramatically, even without the incredible score, and that it would make it difficult for dramatically implausible musical plays to be accepted in the future. What made *South Pacific* so special was not any particular innovation but the craft that went into every aspect of it. It seemed to many the ultimate musical drama, which would "stand as a model for a long time to come."

When asked to name the most profound change in the musical theater in recent years, Cole Porter replied, "Rodgers and Hammerstein." This was generous indeed, since Porter's own *Kiss Me Kate* was overwhelmingly defeated by *South Pacific* for the New York Drama Critics' Award of 1948–49. *South Pacific* set more records and won more prizes than any other musical. It won Donaldson awards in nine categories and Tonys in eight. Eleven of its thirteen songs, all of which had been written to be integral to the play, became familiar standards. ("Dites-Moi" and "Twin Soliloquies" are the two exceptions.) The prize that pleased Oscar and Dick most was the Pulitzer Prize, not a "special award" as *Oklahoma!*'s had been, but the real thing—the Pulitzer Prize for Drama.

Tickets became so hard to get that "house seats," the tickets reserved each night for important members of the production staff and the stars of a show, began to be sold by theater and ticket broker personnel at premiums of as much as two hundred dollars. The attorney general's office threatened to close the show but found it difficult to find out who was responsible for the practice, which came to be known as "ice," and still continues for hit shows.

The show ran for five years in New York, its 1,925 performances second only to *Oklahoma!* The original cast album sold over a million copies. R & H produced a movie of *South Pacific*, directed by Josh Logan, in 1957. There were innumerable road companies, foreign companies and revivals, which continue in the 1970's.

Oscar and Dorothy attended the last Broadway performance of *South Pacific* on January 16, 1954. At the end of the show the curtain did not fall. The only original cast member still in the show, Myron McCormick, with tears in his eyes led the cast and audience in singing "Auld Lang Syne." Then the cast slowly left the stage and the audience reluctantly moved out of the theater as the curtain remained unlowered.

Nine

One Hit, One Miss

"My days have been pretty well filled as orator, politician, lawyer and diplomat," wrote Oscar to Larry Schwab in the summer of 1949. He was not only president of the Authors League and vice-president of ASCAP, but a board member of several councils as well. Aside from the time he devoted to organizations related to his profession, his involvement was always with those that reflected ideals and values important to him. *Oscar Hammerstein II* on an organization's letterhead meant that the group was helping to promote understanding between people of different races and nationalities and that more than a "name" was being contributed.

The cause that was most important to him was the World Federalism movement, in which he began to be active in earnest when the Writers' War Board became the Writers' Board for World Government in 1949. Through the years he became one of the leading spokesmen for the movement. Norman Cousins described him as "one of the first starry-eyed and divinely discontented" people to bring the concept and its importance to the country's attention. Aware that the problems in the way of achieving world law were so enormous that attempting to bring it about might seem like dreaming, he said it was people who thought that the old ways would work in the nuclear age who were dreaming, that the task that seemed impractical was in fact practical because there was nothing else to be done. The organization's first major effort was a presentation called *The Myth That Threatens the World*, which Oscar arranged and directed, using material written by Abe Burrows, Russel Crouse, Carl Van Doren and others, and with a cast that included Marian Anderson, Robert E. Sherwood and Henry Fonda. An audience of powerful figures in the communications field settled in their seats at New York's Coronet Theatre (now the Eugene O'Neill) and listened for a few minutes to what seemed to be the usual dreary evening of speeches. When the microphone went dead, they began to make rude remarks as master of ceremonies Clifton Fadiman searched frantically for an electrician. The electrician appeared and began to chat with Fadiman as he tinkered with the mike. Slowly the audience caught on to the gag—the electrician was Eddie Albert. The show that followed was fast-paced and entertaining, so successful that although intended for only one performance, it was subsequently repeated in principal cities throughout the United States and Great Britain.

In the same year, 1949, Oscar and Dorothy became deeply involved in another organization that would engage their time and energy for years. Their Bucks County neighbor, novelist Pearl S. Buck, had just begun Welcome House when James Michener asked Oscar to help in any way that he could. He expressed his interest and willingness to help and soon became its president. Welcome House began in an almost accidental way. Pearl Buck received a letter from a state adoption agency asking her to help them in a difficult matter: they were unable to place for adoption a child whose parents, a brilliant young Indian and the young American daughter of a missionary, were unable to marry because of strong parental opposition. Although she and her husband, Richard Walsh, were too old to adopt the little boy, she told the agency to send him to her and she would care for him until they could find adoptive parents. By coincidence, the same week she was given a newborn half-Chinese baby to care for. One adoption agency after another refused to take the children, claiming they were unadoptable and nothing could be done. Her "stubborn pioneer blood" aroused, the novelist obtained a charter from the State of Pennsylvania, and soon had nine children of mixed racial background living with her and later at a home that was set up as

Welcome House. As the work went on, Welcome House found it necessary to try to combat racial prejudice and old misconceptions about "hybrids."

One of the first babies to be adopted through Welcome House became the Hammersteins' first grandchild. When Alice and her second husband, Phil Mathias, whom she had met while picketing MGM studios, expressed interest in adopting a child, Dorothy suggested that they consider Welcome House. The Mathiases were living in New York, where Phil was a stage manager, and their adoption took a long time because it was a test case for parents and children who were "matched" only by love and not by ethnic background. A few years later they provided a brother for their daughter, Melinda, when they adopted their son, Peter, also through Welcome House. Phil wrote with Oscar a show called *With the Happy Children*, to promote good will for and understanding about the organization among their Bucks County neighbors.

Jimmy was still at the University of North Carolina, where he did some studying (his father made dry references to the fact that he was collecting C's) between acting, tennis playing and playwriting. He had written tunes as a small boy, but in his middle childhood gave it up when he felt he was no longer any more talented than anyone else. Now he had returned to writing and in the summer collaborated on a musical show called *Meow*. When he asked his father to take a look at the script, he found that he was a sympathetic but forthright editor. "He knew exactly where the bullshit was before he'd read what the point of the story was."

It was at this time, when Jimmy was nineteen, that he and his father became "fast friends." Their communication was no longer limited to games. Now, as they sat in the kitchen sharing a beer, Oscar would talk to Jimmy about the theater and about his own life. Although Oscar expressed his opinions forcefully, he left decisions up to Jimmy, who was then dissatisfied with college, dropping behind in his grades and wondering whether he was learning anything or just filling in time. That summer Jimmy received what seemed to him a biweekly "check-up-on-the-son" call from his father. At the end of the conversation Oscar said casually, "Oh, by the way, Billy's assistant has gone from Leland's office; they just fired him. Is there any graduate from the senior class you know that wants a job? It doesn't start at much."

Jimmy started to suggest names and Oscar told him to call his brother. The boy hung up and went out to the porch to sun himself, one of his major occupations that summer. Suddenly he realized, in a long double-take, that his father had laid a trap for him. He went back to the phone and dialed home.

"Dad? I just thought of a terrific assistant for Bill."

"Who?"

"Me. I'll be up in a couple of weeks."

And so he left college for good and began his career in the theater. Oscar never pushed his children to complete college; Alice and Henry were the only two who received degrees. He sensed that Jimmy was doing very little at school and was not involved, but he didn't ask Jimmy if he wanted to drop out.

Oscar was responsible the same summer for getting Steve Sondheim his first job in the business. One night just after his graduation from Williams, Steve went with Dorothy and Oscar to dinner at Pat and Donald Klopfer's country house in nearby Clinton, New Jersey. The Klopfers and the Hammersteins had been close friends for many years. Oscar first met Pat at Myra's house when she was thirteen and he twenty, but both his father and his uncle Arthur were good friends of her uncles, the Selwyn brothers, who owned and operated Broadway theaters, and another uncle who had been Willie's stage manager. (One of Oscar's favorite shows, which he had seen when he was eight years old, had been *The Fisher Maiden,* partially written by Pat's father, Vincent Bryan.) During the war, he and Pat Klopfer had worked together on the Writers' War Board.

Dorothy and Donald Klopfer called each other "cousin" because his widowed mother had married Henry Jacobson's uncle. When she was still in *Charlot's Revue of 1924,* Dorothy had met Klopfer and Bennett Cerf. "Just because I'm in the chorus, I'm not going to sink into anonymity," she said, inviting them to tea. The two young men had just begun a publishing venture after buying Modern Library from Horace Liveright's publishing company. When they decided to branch out, in the fall of 1927, they commissioned Rockwell Kent, already assigned to illustrate some of their books, to design a logo for them. They planned to publish luxury editions of books chosen at random. "We're going to call it Random House," they told Kent, who promptly sketched the familiar gated house.

Now they sat in the Klopfers' comfortable living room after dinner with another longtime friend, George Oppenheimer. He told Oscar that he had signed a contract to write the *Topper* series for television but needed a writer to help him once he went to Hollywood.

"I don't know where to turn, Oc. I've gone to the Writers Guild. Where next?"

"Here," said Oscar, pointing to Steve. "I think your problems are over."

Oppenheimer asked Steve to bring him whatever he had written. Steve returned early the next morning with samples of his writing. George thought he had enormous talent and immediately hired him.

There were several family marriages in 1950. Both Billy and Reggie remarried, and Susan married Henry Fonda in the 63rd Street house on December 28. No one, including Oscar and Dorothy, knew about the romance until the couple had made plans to marry. Fonda, starring in *Mister Roberts*, had had an enormously successful year professionally but a very difficult one personally. His wife, Frances Seymour Brokaw, a New York socialite whom he had married in 1936 after his brief marriage to Margaret Sullavan, had been confined to a mental institution and had committed suicide the previous spring. Susan and Hank Fonda lived in a townhouse on East 74th Street with his children, thirteen-year-old Jane and ten-year-old Peter. The year had not been easy for them, but they adjusted quickly to their stepmother, Jane and Susan establishing a close relationship that has continued.

The same day that Susan and Hank were married, Dorothy and Oscar attended another wedding, that of John Steinbeck and Elaine Scott. That ceremony was held just around the corner from their house at Steinbeck's publisher's home on East 64th Street. They had first met Elaine, a handsome, bright, astute woman, who worked for the Theatre Guild, when she was an assistant stage manager on *Oklahoma!* Because she was from Texas, Oscar would ask her to pronounce certain words as he wrote the lyrics for "I Cain't Say No," and they became fast friends. When the Guild decided to assign her to another show temporarily, Elaine Scott heard Oscar's voice from the back of the theater proclaiming, "We'll only trade her for a good right-fielder and a shortstop." She became friendly with both the Hammersteins and the Rodgerses and introduced them to Steinbeck when she met him a few years later. She found Oscar one of the kindest men she had ever met and realized that everyone on Broadway felt the same way. One night, Ludwig Bemelmans, who loved to say outrageous things to her to "get her dander up," said he didn't like Oscar. Elaine had never heard anyone say such a thing. "I almost killed him." She became so impassioned that Bemelmans stopped her with "Calm down, Elaine. It was only one of my ploys to rile you up."

Between shows, Oscar and Dorothy spent as much time as possible at Highland Farm and took several trips. The first was to Florida, where they visited the Schwabs, fished, swam and took a short trip to Bimini. Schwab introduced Oscar to a new project of his, the first "music tent," which was initiated by ex-actor St. John Terrell. This new method of bringing Broadway musicals to the public outside of metropolitan areas immediately appealed to Oscar. "This is going to take the country by storm," he told Larry. "It will be an important force someday and I'm going to help as much as I can." He not only invested in both the Florida venture and its subsequent counterpart in Lambertville, New Jersey, but more important, opened his catalogue of shows to Terrell at reasonable terms, often making revisions to accommodate this new theater-in-the-round.

In a suite at the Berkeley Hotel in London, on the morning of Dorothy's birthday, June 7, 1950, she awoke to find that Oscar had left her a letter addressed to "Mrs. Oscar Hammerstein 2nd (Very Personal)." She opened it to find that, in the Hammerstein tradition, he had eloquently expressed his emotions in writing:

My dearest Dorothy, my darling wife, my only love:
  I have bought no surprise present for your birthday. I hope we can go out together and find one for you today. The only surprise I can give you is this letter. Its purpose is not only to surprise but to use this chance to tell you how deeply I love you and how much I thank you for being the sweet and wonderful wife you are. It is a long time since I have written to you. We have been together so much in these very happy years, there has been no need to write. And there has been no need to document my feelings for you—not for me, anyway. Those earlier letters were filled with extravagant protestations and, God knows they were honest and sincere. But a young man starting his love is telling himself about it as much as he is telling the one he loves. I don't have to tell myself how much I love you because you have become so much a part of my life. You and I live together in my heart and my mind, and it will always be so. You are not so much aware of this as I

because, after all, it is *my* heart and *my* mind. And so I am telling you what goes on in those places—you, you go on, ever and ever. Please know this and remember this always. It can never be any different. I love you, I love you, I love you, for what you are to me as well as for what I see you are to other people. Here is a man, nearly fifty-five, who knows what he is saying, who has been married to you for twenty-one years and has felt this love growing all this time. Perhaps this solid edifice is less attractive to you than the impulsively built flying towers of my early desire for you but to me it is more attractive, infinitely more important, more gratifying, more secure.

If this letter seems alarmingly literal, unplayful and even pompous don't be deceived by style. My eyes are wet with tears as I write this unflowery and unpoetic statement. I am saying exactly what I mean and expressing exactly what I feel.

Don't ever forget any of it—

Your Ockie

After their return from London, Oscar completed the manuscript for a book of his lyrics for Simon and Schuster. In addition to choosing the lyrics for publication, he wrote a 48-page foreword. He decided to refer to some of his "worst early efforts," believing that a writer's early imperfections were important to guide and encourage young people. In addition, he discussed the principles and practical aspects of lyric-writing, with reference to particular songs. He expressed his "blind infatuation" with Broadway and ended with: "I'm in love with a wonderful theater." The book was well received by book reviewers.

Oscar's love for the theater was the theme of a speech he gave when he accepted an honorary doctorate of law at Drury College. The standards of the theater were fundamental, he said, because they were determined by the public. People who achieved success in it had usually done so by being punished with failure for cheapness and insincerity and careless work. The theater, with its severe penalties for failure and extravagant rewards for success, he called a world where "only stern and rugged dreamers survive. One needs the heart of a poet and the hide of a rhinoceros. . . . In the theater, toughness is of equal importance with talent, and neither is any good without the other."

R & H produced a trio of straight shows in 1950. The first was *The Happy Time,* an adaptation by Samuel Taylor of Robert Fontaine's biography, a warm story of a boy's emergence into manhood in an eccentric French-Canadian family in the twenties. They signed the talented Bobby Lewis to direct, and spent months looking for a youngster to play the lead; finally they signed Johnny Stewart, but worried that the thirteen-year-old would quickly outgrow the part. *The Happy Time* was dubbed *I Remember Papa* by some and was a hit. It ran for a year and a half on Broadway before becoming a Columbia film in 1952 and then back to the stage as a musical in 1968.

The two other plays that R & H produced that season were not successful. *The Heart of the Matter,* written by Graham Greene and Basil Dean, had a disastrous first-night tryout in Boston. The novel's powerful story of a man's conflict with God was so static and uncohesive in the stage adaptation that it seemed a routine and not very original tale of adultery. The decision was made to close the production at the end of the engagement in Boston. Oscar was sorry to lose the first-rate cast, several of whom had been brought over from England and one of whom, Norah Howard, was the Hammersteins' longtime friend, but he and Dick knew that the play would not have stood a chance on Broadway.

At the outset *Burning Bright,* the third production, seemed to have everything going for it. When John Steinbeck mentioned that he was writing a play, R & H asked to read it and immediately decided to present it. They engaged the distinguished director Guthrie McClintic, designer Jo Mielziner and a capable cast: Kent Smith, Barbara Bel Geddes, Brooks Martin and Howard Da Silva. Cautioned not to hire Da Silva, who was returning from Hollywood after being blacklisted and labeled a Communist, Oscar said, "I don't care what he's called. He's perfect for the play and he has the part." The out-of-town critics saw much merit in the play, but New York audiences didn't and it ran only two weeks. The script read well, but it never worked on the stage.

This was the last show other than their own that Oscar and Dick produced in this country, though their London office continued to present non-R & H shows.* Both decided that producing was too time-consuming and not financially rewarding enough, even with hits, to justify the time and effort involved.

---

* Their London productions included *The Pajama Game, Damn Yankees, Teahouse of the August Moon, The Desperate Hours, The Seven-Year Itch* and *A Shot in the Dark.*

One day in late January 1950 Fanny Holtzman, the shrewd theatrical attorney, was walking up Madison Avenue on her way to client
Gertrude Lawrence's house to talk about the right vehicle and writer
for a musical that Miss Lawrence could do. Crossing 62nd Street, she
met Dorothy, who said, "Ockie's not coming home for lunch. I'm on
my way to Sammy's Deli for a sandwich."

Ockie, thought Fanny. But of course! Who would be better to
write a musical for Gertie?

She grabbed Dorothy's arm. "Listen, why don't the boys do a
show for Gertie. If I send a book over, will you see that Ockie reads
it?"

Dorothy nodded and continued on her way. Later that afternoon a
messenger delivered the book. As she so often did, Dorothy read it
before giving it to Oscar. He respected her judgment, not only reading whatever she suggested but usually asking her opinion on properties he had read first. She was not impressed with the story of a
Jewish actress married to a German general.

"I don't think it's good for Gertie," she said to Fanny over the telephone. "Especially the end, where she winds up working in the War-
saw ghetto."

"Well, I'll think of something else. But I definitely think the boys
should do a show for Gertie."

Oscar, sitting in the other room with Dick, was amused to over-
hear Dorothy's next remark. "I don't know why they should. She'll
want it all."

"That's just what we would have said!" he said to Dick.

The following day Fanny sent another book, *Anna and the King
of Siam*. Dorothy read the book, liked it very much and told Oscar
that he should read it. He did and readily agreed that it had rich
possibilities. The book, written by Margaret Landon in 1943, was
based on the account by a British widow, Anna H. Leonowens, of the
years she spent in Siam in the 1860's as tutor to King Mongkut's children. Not for many years had Oscar or Dick written a "star vehicle,"
and their star had not done a musical since *Lady in the Dark*, ten
years before. Her singing voice was neither strong nor polished, but
they admired her acting and what Oscar called the "magic light" that
made her such a compelling figure on the stage, and thought her
perfect for the strong character of Anna. A few days after they
agreed to do the show, Dorothy and Dick Rodgers, Gertrude Law-

rence and Fanny Holtzman had lunch at the Hammersteins', followed by a story conference that lasted for several hours. When the meeting was over, the project was under way.

Once again the problem presented by the material was also its attraction for Oscar and Dick. Because the two principals did not identify their deep feelings for each other as romantic ones, there could be no "love story" except in the most oblique way. More than any of their previous musicals, this would be a play about ideas and human behavior, since the plot was not one of action and suspense but, rather, an unfolding of the relationship between the King and Anna. Inherent in the relationship was the fading of racial and ethnic differences that occurs when people of alien cultures begin to know and understand one another. This was, of course, as attractive a theme to Oscar and Dick as was another important idea in the story: the dignity and rights of each individual and the extent to which they are threatened by slavery and tyranny.

Always anxious not to repeat themselves, they were happy to have a story so different from their previous works, but they had some jitters about the project. They were surprised to find themselves being congratulated on it from the time the show was first announced. The more normal reaction to their projects in the past had been, as it was for *Tales of the South Pacific*, "How in the world do you expect to pull that off and why are you trying to?" Now all their friends seemed more confident than they that *The King and I* would be marvelously successful, mainly because of Miss Lawrence and the Siamese background, so rich in set and costume possibilities. R & H immediately asked Jo Mielziner to begin work on the set designs in concert with Irene Sharaff.

Probably the foremost costume designer in the theater, Irene Sharaff's credits read like a list of both Broadway's and Hollywood's finest: *The Great Waltz, Idiot's Delight* and *Lady in the Dark* on the stage; *Meet Me in St. Louis, Yolanda and the Thief* and *Ziegfeld Follies* on film. She was working on *An American in Paris* when R & H signed her, but she immediately began to do some sketching and research for *The King and I*. For several months she felt as if she were living in two countries—France in the daytime and Siam in the evenings. One of her first steps was to contact Jim Thompson, an American who had become so involved in a project with refugee silk weavers that he had virtually revolutionized the industry and created a booming export trade for Thailand. He started to send Irene not only fabric samples but pictures of Siamese dress in the mid-1800's.

Oscar and Dick knew that their greatest task was to maintain the story's realism. This was always a problem in a musical, since the very act of bursting into song is itself unreal. They did not wish to present a starkly realistic "documentary" work on the Orient in the mid-nineteenth century, Oscar said, but wanted to "capture this remote reality and still give our production the lift and glow that all musicals must have."

One of the biggest problems for both men was creating an Oriental flavor within a context that American audiences would accept. Dick realized that a too-accurate reproduction of nineteenth-century Siamese sounds would give small pleasure to the Occidental ear and might send audiences howling out of the theater. He purposely avoided this particular bit of realism by deciding against research into Oriental music, though he made an occasional pass at the five-tone scale for the sake of color. His aim was to express the atmosphere musically in his own terms and in a manner comprehensible to American ears. Illustrating their basic approach, Dick said that if Grant Wood had spent a few weeks painting in Bangkok, whatever work he did there would look very much like Thailand to us, but would also look like Grant Wood.

Oscar had a similar problem in dealing with speech. When he was in London for *Carousel*, he had heard someone from the Thai embassy speaking his native tongue. The sound was so odd that Oscar decided to use little runs on musical instruments to represent what was being said in Siamese onstage. He had another, more important problem: he had to capture the exotic quality of the Oriental characters without turning them into oddities or stereotypes.

For the speech of the King, Oscar developed an emphatic, abrupt style that matched the personality of the character; the syntax was elliptical and, like that of Oriental languages, free of articles. The non-idiomatic, formal diction captured the quality of English learned from a British tutor. While planning a banquet for visiting dignitaries, the King says:

> "Ha! We shall give them theatrical performance. We shall show them who is barbarian! Line up! Line up! Line up! Lady Thiang! On Saturday next, at nine o'clock post meridian, we shall give fine

dinner. . . . You are to make tablecloth of finest white silk for very long table. Also instruct court musicians to learn music of Europe for dancing, etcetera. What? What? What? Am I to be annoyed by children at this moment?"

The word "etcetera," repeated throughout the play, effectively showed that the King, for all his blustering insistence that he knew best, really was anxious to learn. He asks Anna at the beginning of the play what the word means when she uses it for the first time, and then incorporates it into his vocabulary.

The King soliloquizes in the song "A Puzzlement," in which he describes his confusion in trying to reconcile tradition with the modern world:

> When I was a boy
> World was better spot
> What was so was so,
> What was not was not.
> Now I am a man;
> World have change a lot:
> Some things *nearly* so,
> Others *nearly* not.
> There are times I almost think
> I am not sure of what I absolutely know.
> Very often find confusion
> In conclusion I concluded long ago.
> In my head are many facts
> That, as a student, I have studied to procure,
> In my head are many facts . . .
> Of which I wish I was more certain I was sure!
> Is a puzzlement!

The complex character of the King emerged in all its dimensions: he was arrogant and autocratic, but vulnerable and even lovable. The development of character was particularly important in *The King and I* because the dramatic conflict in the play is based on the inability of the major characters to understand each other. The strong, proud woman, who believes firmly in human dignity and individual rights, and the equally strong, proud man, whose life is based on the ancient kingly authority that gives him absolute power over others, gradually come to respect and care for each other as they come to appreciate the essential humanity of the other.

"Something Wonderful," a song that became a hit out of the context of the show, is important to the play not only because it is an astute analysis of the King by Lady Thiang, the "head wife," who loves him deeply, but because it motivates Anna's change in attitude toward him:

What more can I say to you?
This is a man who thinks with his heart,
His heart is not always wise.
This is a man who stumbles and falls,
But this is a man who tries.
This is a man you'll forgive and forgive,
And help and protect, as long as you live . . .

He will not always say
What you would have him say,
But now and then he'll say
                    Something wonderful.

The thoughtless things he'll do
Will hurt and worry you,
Then all at once he'll do
                    Something wonderful.

He has a thousand dreams
That won't come true,
You know that he believes in them
And that's enough for you.
You'll always go along,
Defend him when he's wrong
And tell him, when he's strong
                    He is wonderful.

He'll always need your love,
And so he'll get your love—
A man who needs your love
                    Can be wonderful.

Oscar succeeded so well in creating a dynamic, full-bodied character for the Oriental potentate that the King, played by Yul Brynner, came close to stealing the show from one of the most charismatic actresses in the theater.

Since Dick was laid up with a recurrence of his back trouble, Oscar finished most of the dialogue before many songs were completed. Dictaphone tapes show that, as usual, Oscar wrote not only the dialogue but full stage directions as well. Further departures from convention emerged as the libretto took shape. Not only was the show to begin and end without music, but one of the leads, the King, was to die onstage. When he had finished Act I, Oscar wrote to Josh Logan, "I believe I have caught the quality that made the book so strangely appealing. I don't know. By its very nature, the story will not permit the pace and lustiness of a play like *South Pacific* and I am sharpening a very long knife for the first one who tells me that it hasn't the qualities of *South Pacific*. It is a very strange play and must be accepted on its own terms, or not at all."

Oscar had asked Logan to collaborate with him on the book and to direct, but when he turned both offers down, Oscar approached John Van Druten, who agreed to stage the book. Van Druten had never before directed either a musical or a play that he hadn't written.

In November Leland Hayward wrote to them from Paris that he had discussed *The King and I* libretto with choreographer Jerry Robbins on the ship to Europe and that he was "nutty about it. He thought the entire script was wonderful and was absolutely off his head about The Uncle Tom's Cabin ballet." R & H had originally asked Robbins to stage only the ballet, since no other major dancing was planned. Jerry said that he would like to stage all the musical numbers and Leland suggested that they have him do so. After seeing Indonesian dancing with its "quiet, non-balletic tone," he felt that the Uncle Tom's Cabin ballet should be not a huge production number, but "like a polished jewel, delicately performed and intimately done." He threw out an idea about fake paper snow through which the dancers would move. He suggested also that all the movement in the show be of a particular style, including the entrances of the children and the servants and the general deportment of the court, thus giving a certain unity of movement to the entire show.

Meanwhile, back in New York, Irene Sharaff was examining the pictures that Jim Thompson had dug out of the Royal Archives in Bangkok. One that she showed to Oscar, of a delicate Siamese woman dressed in a Victorian bodice, native panung, embroidered Western stockings, high-heeled slippers and a wide silk ribbon with a jeweled border across her bosom, inspired "Western People Funny" in Act II, sung by Lady Thiang, whose costume resembled that of the woman in the picture.

Sharaff ordered silk woven in Thailand in the colors she was planning, and she sketched the costumes worn in Siam in the mid-

1800's. Oscar, Dick and Van Druten were surprised by the unusual dress but gave her permission to go ahead.

One of the first actors auditioned * was Yul Brynner, who sat cross-legged on the stage, scowling, strumming chords and singing a fierce ballad in a strange tongue. Brynner, born on Sakhalin island (north of Japan) in 1920 of a Romany gypsy mother who had renounced her clan and a Mongolian father whose family predated Genghis Khan—a heritage that led Noël Coward to comment, "To have a background like that is like living with a woman who always wears red"—had worked as a folk singer and an acrobat in Europe before studying acting with Michael Chekhov in New York. He had played in only one Broadway show, *Lute Song,* in 1950 with Mary Martin, and was directing and acting as a singing host with his then wife Virginia Gilmore on a CBS TV variety series. Although he had auditioned for the part, he was making a great deal of money on TV and wouldn't take the calls from R & H's casting director, John Fearnley. Finally Brynner's agent, William Liebling, along with Mary Martin and Brynner's wife, convinced him that such a part on the legitimate stage was too important to turn down. When he read the script, he found the character of the King irresistible. Mary had told Oscar, "No one can play this part but Yul Brynner. Kidnap him if you have to, but get him!" They had been impressed with his authority, style and savage quality, and were happy to sign him for the role.

At his first meeting with Sharaff, Brynner said, "What shall I do about my hair?" He was bald except for a few strands on the top of his head and a fringe around the back.

"Shave it," she said impetuously.

A look of horror crossed Brynner's face. "No! I can't do that. I have a dip on the top of my head and I'd look dreadful!"

She continued to urge him to shave his head, telling him he could always wear a wig if he hated it, but he continued to resist. Finally, during the New Haven tryout, Brynner shaved off every hair and covered his head with the same dark make-up that he

* When they could not get their first choice for the King, Alfred Drake, R & H resorted to auditions. (Drake loved the play and was sure it would be a success, but decided not to take the role, partly because he felt the King did not have enough to sing, but primarily because he had just been offered his first chance to direct a new Broadway play. Drake did, however, assume the role later, when Brynner went on vacation for eleven weeks.)

used on his body. The effect was sensational and the shaven head became Brynner's trademark.

Of all the songs in the show, "Hello, Young Lovers" took Oscar the longest to write. Since there could be few love songs because the King and Anna are never in love in the usual sense, Oscar first chose "Tom" as a title, to express Anna's love for her dead husband. He struggled for over a month with the lyrics for "Tom," and then for a second version called "Home" and for a third, "I Have Been in Love."

He had written in his preface to *Lyrics* the year before that the term "inspiration" was annoying to a professional writer, implying as it did that ideas and words were gifts from heaven. In fact, he said, writing is very hard work and no professional sat around waiting to be inspired. Like him, they went to work every day. "Some days the work comes easier than other days, but you keep going because the chances of getting good ideas are more likely while you are trying to get them than when you are doing nothing at all."

He described writing a lyric as a long wrestling match in which the lyric gets to be an enemy. "I have to get its death grip off me and get a death grip on it." He finally got a "half nelson" on "Hello, Young Lovers" after five weeks of struggling, and wrote most of the song in a "final burst of perspiration" in forty-eight hours. The lyrics flow easily as if they had indeed come to him by inspiration:

> When I think of Tom
> I think about a night
> When the earth smelled of summer
> And the sky was streaked with white,
> And the soft mist of England
> Was sleeping on a hill—
> I remember this,
> And I always will . . .
> There are new lovers now on the same silent hill,
> Looking on the same blue sea,
> And I know Tom and I are a part of them all,
> And they're all a part of Tom and me.
>
>> Hello, young lovers, whoever you are,
>> I hope your troubles are few.
>> All my good wishes go with you tonight,
>> I've been in love like you.
>> Be brave, young lovers, and follow your star,
>> Be brave and faithful and true,

Cling very close to each other tonight—
I've been in love like you.
I know how it feels to have wings on your heels,
And to fly down a street in a trance.
You fly down a street on the chance that you'll meet,
And you meet—not really by chance.
Don't cry, young lovers, whatever you do,
Don't cry because I'm alone;
All of my memories are happy tonight,
I've had a love of my own,
I've had a love of my own, like yours—
I've had a love of my own.

One day Oscar showed the lyrics to Josh Logan and asked him what he thought of them. "Certainly I've never read anything better. But why do you seem so upset? You should be happy. Isn't Dick crazy about them?"

"I don't know," Oscar replied. Uncharacteristically, he told Logan in some detail what had happened when he finished the lyrics. He sent them by special messenger to Dick, instructing the man to wait for an answer. The afternoon went by with no reply and no phone call from Dick. In fact, he didn't hear from Dick for four days about the lyric that he had liked so much. On the fourth day Dick called: "Oscar, Howard wants to know whether they could have an R & H night in Kansas City next March. Would that be all right?" Oscar responded briefly. They went on to discuss other business matters. Just before Dick hung up, he said, "Oh, I got that lyric. It works fine."

This was one of the very few times that Oscar expressed any criticism or frustration with his partner. Logan found the usually cool and controlled Oscar agitated and upset. He tried to soothe his friend, reminding him how Dick always understated things, relating instances where Dick had done the same sort of thing to him. Oscar began to pour out his feelings and then abruptly stopped and held out his hand to shake hands. "Okay. That's it. You've helped me. Thanks."

The King and I rehearsal and pre-Broadway tryout period, which began in January 1951, was even more hectic and difficult than usual. The fifteen children in the cast were adorable but trying. If they weren't flushing their hats down the toilets, they were into some other mischief or were sick. Colds and flus swept through the youngest cast members and affected the adults as well. Gertie Lawrence had a 103-degree temperature when the show reached New Haven.

Len Mence, a cast member who had been in Hammerstein shows for over thirty years, remembers that the children were mad about Oscar. When he came backstage, they would all crowd around him, plucking at his sleeves and clamoring for attention from him. He would talk to them, chuck them under the chin and say, "I'm watching it. You're doing very nicely."

R & H frequently hired directors, such as Van Druten, who were unfamiliar with musicals. Van Druten was having trouble with the elaborate production, even though, as one production staff member said, "Oscar's book directed itself." Although Oscar was a talented director who had often staged shows earlier in his career, he chose not to do so now, though he frequently became involved with the directing. Never one to say "I'll take over," he was enormously tactful when, on occasion, he worked with Van Druten; his approach was, "Wouldn't it be better if . . . ," and he never made his role obvious to the rest of the company.

Jerry Robbins was asked to take charge of all the musical sequences, though virtually none were "numbers" in the traditional sense. The routine where the children were introduced was a charming one that showed the King's paternal pride and affection amid all the trappings of the royal court. While Robbins was explaining the elaborate patterns, he noticed that the smallest one didn't seem to be paying attention. He turned to the boy and said, "Eh, what count do you do this on?" The child replied, "What's the matter, don't you know?" and went through the routine perfectly.

The conception of the movement for "The Small House of Uncle Thomas" ballet that Jerry had hit upon in Hayward's Paris hotel suite became one of the most unusual and memorable scenes in the play. In masks and jeweled headdresses, the actors danced with delicate, geometric movements as Doretta Morrow, as Tuptim, recited her version of Harriet Beecher Stowe's tale.

Eliza flew from Simon Legree's bloodhounds to a river represented by a rippling silk scarf that stiffened as Buddha produced a miracle and froze the river. Hopping on one foot, she "skated" between actors carrying poles with silk banners, printed with large, ornate snowflakes, to a score composed by Trude Rittman with wood blocks, cymbals and other percussive instruments to match the stylized movements of the performers. The funny, charming "play within a play" pointed up the central issue in the larger play: slavery.

Gertrude Lawrence gave a touching and sympathetic interpretation of Anna from the beginning, but had constant trouble with her singing voice. Never strong, it had worn badly through the years and now she was not only plagued with bouts of laryngitis and ill-health, but with a score that was set in a key too high for her.

The hooped skirts that Gertie wore made her seven costume changes difficult, but she, Sharaff and the dressers finally established a procedure whereby the dresses were laid on the floor backstage at her exit point with two wardrobe women standing by to help her disrobe, get zipped into the new dress, touch up her hair and makeup and reappear on stage, immaculate and in command, in less than a minute!

In the scene where Anna keeps her promise to the King that even though she will not prostrate herself before him as his subjects do, she will follow court etiquette and keep her head from being higher than his, she must sit, kneel and finally lie on the floor as he constantly changes position while dictating to her a letter to President Lincoln. Gertie's hoop kept popping up over her head as she went through the actions required by the script and Sharaff constantly worked on new ways to weight it. However, in another scene, "Shall We Dance," which was added in Boston, the imaginative star used the hoop to advantage. She discovered that by holding one of the thin bamboo hoops that made up the underpinning of her pale-pink satin ball gown, she could swing the whole skirt into a graceful arc as she danced the polka with the King, until, as Sharaff said, "the gown became another element with her and Yul in the dance."

The King and I was not only the most expensive (it cost $360,000) but by far the most opulent and spectacular R & H show, with six carloads of costumes and sets. The brilliantly colored, shimmering satins and silks of the costumes, worn with intricate Oriental jewelry, were matched by Mielziner's elaborate sets representing the luxurious Siamese palace.

The musical was well received during its four-week break-in out of town, but forty-five minutes had to be cut from the running time. A good deal of dialogue went, and several songs were dropped but three were added. One addition was the popular "Getting to Know You." The tune had originally been written for *South Pacific* with the title "Suddenly Lucky," but was never used. When everyone agreed that *The King and I* needed more light touches, particularly since there were no "comic" characters at all, Gertrude Lawrence suggested that she sing a song with the children in the first act. Using the "Suddenly Lucky" tune, Oscar wrote lyrics that lightly expressed the play's serious theme:

It's a very ancient saying
But a true and honest thought
That if you become a teacher,
By your pupils you'll be taught.
As a teacher I've been learning,
(You'll forgive me if I boast)
And I've now become an expert,
On the subject I like most.
Getting to know you.

Oscar dryly commented that, as far as he knew, it was not an ancient saying at all. He did feel, though, that the idea itself was old and certainly it was one that he believed in strongly. Robbins created a delightful piece of staging for the number, in which the topknots that Irene had discovered in her research about nineteenth-century Siamese hair styles became an important prop, and the song became a show-stopper.

Even with the extra work of cutting and revising the show, there were light moments during the weeks in Boston. After a grueling day of rehearsals and performances, Oscar always joined the large group that would go out dancing after the show. Although he normally headed for bed early, away from home Oscar loved to dance and enjoyed sitting around with members of the company. One of its lowliest members, assistant stage manager Ruth Mitchell,* felt she was as welcome as the biggest star. She was amazed to find that everyone in the R & H organization treated her as a person, not a function. She would often take walks along the Charles River with Oscar, talking about the theater, herself, "anything and everything." She found him always approachable, comfortable and willing to listen. While she thought he was perhaps a "bit of a chauvinist" with his family, she saw that he treated women as human beings. In fact, she thinks it was almost certainly he who was responsible for giving her the title of stage manager, still rare for women in the fifties.

Because of the extensive out-of-town versions, Oscar and Dick

* Now a successful producer, in association with Hal Prince she has been responsible for such shows as Company, Follies, A Little Night Music and Pacific Overtures.

were somewhat nervous before the New York opening on March 29 at the St. James. They needn't have worried. The audience was "enthralled" with the beautiful show, said Hobe Morrison, *Variety's* critic. Except for a few comparisons to *South Pacific,* which had by now replaced *Oklahoma!* as the standard to which every musical was compared, the critics said everything R & H might have wished. They appreciated the show's subtlety, depth of character, impeccable taste and the skill with which score and play were blended. "This time Messrs. Rogers and Hammerstein are not breaking any fresh trails," said Brooks Atkinson. "But they are accomplished artists of song and words in the theater; and *The King and I* is a beautiful and lovable musical play."

During the first year's run of *The King and I,* Gertrude Lawrence was plagued by poor health. Her voice weakened; she became thinner and thinner and was replaced with increasing frequency by her understudy, Connie Carpenter. Her lawyers, Fanny and David Holtzman, who served also as agents and friends, assured everyone that Gertie was fine, that her illness was just temporary. R & H could see her condition, but didn't know how to deal with it. A letter written by Oscar and Dick on May 20, 1952, telling her frankly that her singing had deteriorated "to an alarming extent" is marked *Not mailed.* They wrote: "Eight times a week you are losing the respect of 1500 people. This is a serious thing to be happening to one of the great women of our theatre, and it would be dishonest and unfriendly of us to stand by any longer without making you aware of the tarnish you are putting on your past triumphs and your future prospects. . . . We are sorry that you were unable to see us either Monday or Tuesday. . . . We have expressed our feelings to Fanny and David Holtzman, but they apparently are not in agreement with us—or perhaps they misunderstand us." On occasion she was even booed by audiences, but she was determined to carry on with the show.

A few weeks later, on September 7, 1952, after entering New York Hospital for treatment of "hepatitis," Gertrude Lawrence died of cancer. She was buried in the ball gown that she wore in *The King and I.* Oscar delivered a eulogy for Gertie at the funeral service at the Fifth Avenue Presbyterian Church. He spoke movingly of the "magic light" that had made Gertie a star.

The King and I more than made up its high production costs, with a 1,246-performance Broadway run, a year-and-a-half tour and

926 performances in London.* It had been Gertrude Lawrence's great wish to play Anna in the West End, but since this was now impossible, Valerie Hobson assumed the role. In 1956 Twentieth Century-Fox made a very successful film version with Deborah Kerr (her voice dubbed by Marni Nixon) and Yul Brynner. The movie added six Academy Awards to its three Tonys and five Donaldson awards.

That year Oscar earned close to a million dollars. He made a chart of his ASCAP earnings as compared to those of Ira Gershwin and Larry Hart, the other big earners among lyricists. His yearly income from ASCAP in 1951 was $340,028 to Ira's $204,816 and Larry's estate's $191,910. In addition to this weekly $6,500, two road companies of *South Pacific* were bringing him $9,000 per week. *The King and I* was selling out, *Oklahoma!* and *Carousel* were still touring, and profits were rolling in from stock and amateur rights on shows that he wrote before and after his collaboration with Rodgers. It all added up to a personal income of over $17,500 every week.

Oscar sometimes grumbled about the enormous taxes he paid as one of the country's highest-paid men, but pay them he did. The Hammersteins were sitting on the lawn at Highland Farm one afternoon that summer, with Elaine and John Steinbeck and Eleanor and Billy Rose, when Billy said, "Let me tell you about this wonderful new lawyer I've got. Now, he's not going to do anything illegal, mind you, but he's got a lot of new tax dodges. Let me tell you—"

"We don't want to hear about it," said Oscar and John, almost in one voice.

While Steinbeck nodded in agreement, Oscar said, "That's not the way I operate, Billy. I live in a land that I approve of, and I take off what I can legitimately, but the rest I want to pay."

Jimmy Hammerstein remembers the time during *The King and I* period when Oscar said angrily, "Don't ever do anything out of pity. It is the lowest motivation to help somebody out of pity. I've just learned. I'm fifty-six years old and I've just learned. Pity is a base thing." The outburst had a long story behind it.

Years before, in 1924, Oscar had collaborated on two plays with a Columbia classmate, Milton Gropper. Both were flops; one, *Gypsy Jim*, occasioned the remark from Alexander Woollcott: "Oscar Ham-

---

* The profits have not ceased; a twenty-fifth anniversary revival opened in April 1977, with Yul Brynner re-creating the role of the King (a part for which the fifty-seven-year-old actor is now more suited in terms of age).

merstein 2d and Milton Gropper/Wrote a comedy that came in awful cropper." Gropper had written one hit in the 1924–25 season, but the years since had brought him no success; he continued to write, but was barely able to eke out a living. From time to time, Oscar "employed" his old classmate to make digests of new novels and stories or do research. Shirley Potash, Oscar's secretary, would receive Gropper's weekly envelope in the office in the Hammersteins' home, give him the $75 that Oscar had told her to do, and stick the envelope, unopened, among the others on a high shelf. On occasion Gropper would drop in at the theater or the office to offer "advice." Dorothy's reaction was, "What a heck of a nerve he's got," but she was used to the old friends that Oscar treated with such patience.

Several months after the Broadway opening Gropper said that he should have a share of the show's profits for his contributions of "parts of the hit musical, including the conception and writing of 'The Small House of Uncle Thomas.'" Although the claim was absurd to everyone who knew Gropper, Howard Reinheimer paid him $1,500 plus $10,750 in weekly installments, for which he signed a waiver. (With the money he had previously been paid, it added up to $16,200.) Some months later Gropper filed a suit against Oscar for $233,800. (On the allegation that "his rights" were worth $250,000, he was suing for the difference.)

Oscar asked Gropper to come see him in his study on 63rd Street. He was trying to reason with him when Gropper suddenly looked at the Dictaphone and yelled, "You've got that machine on, don't you?"

This was the moment that made Oscar see red. For years he had helped Gropper because he felt sorry for him, disguising the charity by giving him useless assignments, and Gropper was now accusing him of wanting to trick him.

"Get out or I'll throw you down the stairs," he said to Gropper.

Oscar called Howard Reinheimer and told him to fight Gropper's suit. His lawyer convinced him that it was not worth the time he would have to spend in court and persuaded him to agree to an out-of-court settlement of $50,000 to get the matter disposed of quickly. The story ended when Milton Gropper died two years later and not only left the $50,000 to Oscar but willed his mother's jewelry to Dorothy.

It was in 1953 that Steve Sondheim finished an original musical play, the fourth step in the plan that Oscar had outlined for him so many years before. He sent the script to Oscar from Hollywood, where he was still working with George Oppenheimer on the *Topper* series.

Oscar sent back the script with extensive notations and a long letter that illustrates the honest, tough but constructive criticism that his colleagues so often sought.

Dear Stevie:

When I read your script I carried on an experiment. I made notes on the pages as they occurred to me. They are very true and quick reactions. I didn't want to have to think back and remember how it affected me, and I thought it might be valuable to you as an author to get these reactions, however much you might disagree with them, and however much some of them might irritate you.

I believe there is irritation in them for you because they are born of irritation in me—some of them. My basic irritation lies in my deep faith in you and in your future. This faith is endorsed and substantiated by so much of the good writing that has been put into this play. What I resent is the story itself and the characters. They are getting far better treatment than they deserve, and so whatever irritation I have against the play is felt on behalf of the author, not on my own behalf. . . .

[Oscar refers to the real-life incident that served as a basis for the play.] You were in the middle of this crisis, and you were whirled around in it, and it seemed very big to you. But the trouble is it is not really big. It is quite an ordinary phenomenon, this kind of discovery on the part of a young girl. It is not earth shaking, and it wouldn't even shake Sardi's—nor a table at Sardi's.

I know that the smallest kind of story can be made to be earth-shaking if the characters are examined closely enough, and if the choice of incident is ingenious enough, and if the narrative of the incident is told with enough depth and human observation. But this is not the case here. This play is a hybrid, made of a true story wedded with fiction. The fiction does not strengthen the truth, and the truth would not be worth telling if it were not fictionized.

Granting the uncertainties in the theatre, I feel quite certain that you will not succeed in getting an audience's interest, and certainly not in sustaining this interest throughout an evening for this group of characters.

The writing is in spots very very good indeed, and I have marked some of it as good, not to balance the "bad markings," but in the interest of truth and fairness. Please read my comments and forgive them if they seem cruel. Surely they are not meant to be.

I don't feel cruel or hypocritical about this play. In a curious way it enhances my confidence in you. It proves to me that you can and will some day write a very brilliant play which will be a thing very much your own, and I hope you will follow it up with many more.

What does all this add up to? My advice to you is not to produce this play, not to let anyone else produce it, but to call it what it certainly is, a very important stepping stone in your libretto writing and composing education. When you get time, start and finish another musical play, but spend a lot of time making up your mind as to its fundamental quality of human interest. (How I hate that phrase! Why do I use it?) What I mean is, I want you to say: "Can I interest an audience in this to the extent that I am interested in it?" I invite you to try it out on me before you start to write, and let me attack it—if I think it should be attacked. I do not ask you to let me be the be all and end all of your playwriting decisions. I volunteer merely to be a wall off which you may bounce an idea. (I don't like that expression very much either.)

Oscar had planned to produce a show using Jerry Kern's unpublished music, with new lyrics and a book devised by Herb and Dorothy Fields. When the project fell through, he decided to revive *Music in the Air*, directing it himself as he had originally, with Reggie as producer and Billy Rose as the sole backer. Before the end-of-summer tryout in Olney, Maryland, Oscar modified the script, moving the locale from Bavaria to Switzerland, cutting some dialogue and interpolating "All the Things You Are" into the score.

The production provided Jimmy's first opportunity to work with his father. He had spent a year in Leland Hayward's office, but had not been given the assistant stage manager's position that was promised him, and when his uncle Reggie asked him if he would like to be second assistant stage manager on the show, Jimmy was delighted with the chance to be something other than an "extra."

Now a successful director in his own right, Jimmy says his father was "an amazing director," with great self-control and a clear and logical approach, who said simply and directly what he was looking for. Jimmy remembers a nightmare technical run-through in Olney— the kind of disaster that doesn't happen often in the professional theater—when Oscar sat patiently in the front row for four hours and spoke only when it was helpful to do so, with no recriminations or angry outbursts. Jimmy saw his father in a new light. He felt that his father was more natural, more relaxed in a theater than he was even at home. He seemed to be completely at ease once he stepped inside a theater. Jimmy attributes this Hammerstein trait that he shares with his father, his grandfather and his great-grandfather to personal shyness that vanishes when he walks into a theater. Because he understands the theater's framework of rules, conventions and expectations so thoroughly, he experiences a self-confidence in his workplace that he never feels anywhere else.

As Jimmy worked with his father and uncle, he saw again how much they enjoyed being together. They shared a similar sense of humor, but otherwise were so different that they exemplified different kinds of theater people. Reggie, like Uncle Arthur, cousin Teddy Hammerstein and other theatrical "old-timers," spoke a rough language, drank, smoked, pursued women and played favorites shamelessly. On the first day Jimmy worked for him, Reggie said, "Who's going to get my chocolate milk shake?"

"I'm the second assistant, so I guess it's up to me," replied Jimmy.

"You're my nephew," said Reggie. "Somebody else is going to go."

Although Reggie was the younger brother, had grown up in the same household and followed Oscar to Columbia, he behaved like a member of the older group. Oscar's manner, on the other hand, was of the new breed of theatrical people. He was more "gentlemanly," cursed and drank little, never smoked in his life and was unflirtatious. "You could tell he wasn't looking," says a woman who worked with him.

The Broadway judges found that though the score was still one of the best, *Music in the Air*'s book did not hold up after nineteen years, and the revival, which opened at the Ziegfeld in October 1951, lasted only two months. Brooks Atkinson said, "Mr. Hammerstein was writing tender, effortless lyrics in those days, with a little star-dust shaken over them. But the plot has a lot of hackneyed playwriting in it. He writes with much greater simplicity now."

Rodgers and Hammerstein shows were never complete flops because of advance sales and a public that thought their worst efforts were worth seeing. The next two shows they did were their weakest, though both ran over a year and had the usual first-class physical production.

Me and Juliet was, as George Jean Nathan said, "a show without a show with all the necessary externals for a good show but missing the internals." The trouble began at conception. Not only was the play an original, never Oscar's forte, but he lacked enthusiasm for the idea behind it. This seems an instance when Oscar's and Dick's smooth indifference to each other hurt rather than helped them. Upset by some *King and I* reviews critical of his music, Dick was anxious to try a show he had always wanted to do, one that took place in a theater and showed the musical theater from backstage. The score would allow him a brassier sound and some dance tunes he had been dying to get out of his system. Oscar didn't like the idea because he thought it was trivial, and he didn't "believe in it." However, he agreed to do the show because he had had his turn with *Allegro* and he thought it necessary to compromise "in order to keep the partnership together." Within the framework of backstage life in the musical theater he decided to write about something that did interest him: what it means to be a physically big man. Oscar had always been aware of his own size, and he created a plot about the conflict between a large man and a small one.

Their first step was to talk to Jo Mielziner about the set. Mielziner told them it would be possible to play a scene partly onstage and partly off, to set scenes on the light bridge and at other points around the theater, but that it would be complicated and expensive. As Mielziner and his several assistants began to design the twelve sets, Oscar and Dick began the libretto and score.

The script was sent to George Abbott in early autumn. He had never worked with Oscar, though he had long admired and liked him, having served with him on several committees. Abbott's long experience as a director of musicals made him a perfect choice for this musical about musicals, but he didn't much like the script. Oscar told him to cut whatever he wanted: "Treat it as ruthlessly as if it were your own." Abbott thought that perhaps when the "onstage play," barely described in the script, was fully choreographed, it would give it the excitement he felt was lacking, though he was disappointed when Bob Alton, a choreographer he thought "old-fashioned," was signed. Nonetheless, the director didn't want to turn down the chance to work with R & H, and went ahead despite his qualms.

Me and Juliet was booked into the Majestic Theatre, scheduled to open in May 1953, and Irene Sharaff began working on the three hundred costumes as Mielziner and thirty carpenters and painters worked on the elaborate sets. Auditions were held while Isabel Bigley, Bill Hayes, Joan McCracken and Ray Walston were signed to lead the huge cast.

Oscar was revising the libretto extensively and still working on lyrics when the musical went into rehearsals in March. Although he always felt very nervous at certain points in the progress of the play —when he began to write, when he first heard the actors reading his lines and just before an opening—his nervousness was seldom apparent to others. George Abbott found that both Oscar and Dick exuded self-confidence. Both seemed to be absolutely sure and almost "unassailable"—understandably so, for they were at the very peak of their success, with ten years of legendary hits behind them, and with awards and tributes continually showered upon them one after another.

Now R & H had a show that seemed shaky. It was obvious to Abbott that the score was less than their best, and the play-within-a-play, so nebulously sketched in the script, never took much shape, the dances doing little to clarify it; Abbott found Oscar to be "almost Sphinxlike" about it.

Whatever Oscar's public face, Jimmy Hammerstein, who joined the company in Boston as an assistant stage manager, found his private face very different. Staying in Oscar's suite at the Ritz, he discovered his father's "classic writer's ego." One night, Jimmy told him that *Me and Juliet* wasn't very good and wasn't working well. Oscar exploded, and they had a "slam-bang" fight that sent Jimmy from the room in tears.

Although they worked hard and made many revisions, *Me and Juliet* remained flawed. The strongest element in the production was Mielziner's set, a masterpiece of aesthetic and technical design that allowed the musical to shift between the onstage and backstage stories. "Keep It Gay" illustrated the ingenious collaboration between librettist, choreographer and set designer which allowed three scenes to be shown during one musical number.

It was in fact the audience's talk about the sets as they left the theater that confirmed Dick and Oscar's doubts about the play itself. They had become very adept at judging playgoers' reactions, and circulated through the lobby at intermission and after the show to hear what people were talking about. If they were discussing golf scores and restaurants, Oscar knew it meant they wanted to get away from it. If they left a theater noisily, it usually meant that they were stimulated by the play. Often Oscar sat in an upstairs stage box so that he could watch people in the balcony and the orchestra. The thing he looked for was a certain expression on their faces, what he called a "glow," a steady smile that stayed there when they were enjoying a show. He didn't trust coughing, applause or laughter as accurate gauges of their feelings. Coughs could simply mean a high number of colds or flu that month. Applause could be a response to effort or a particular actor, or some sure applause-getting dramatic effect, such as the right kind of cymbal crash or timpani roll. An audience could laugh throughout a show and go out hating it. Conversely, they could sit in silence and later tell all their friends to go see it. Facial expressions, relaxed bodies, intermission topics of conversation and the buzz of excitement as the audience left were much more accurate clues to their involvement. Oscar said that although he could tell what an audience felt, sometimes he didn't want to admit it to himself if the news was bad.

Unmemorable as the *Me and Juliet* score is (only two songs became popular, "No Other Love" and "Keep It Gay"), "The Big Black Giant" is interesting in terms of Oscar's attitudes toward an audience, which he characterized as "that big black giant who looks and listens with thousands of eyes and ears" whom "every night you fight." The years had dimmed neither his respect nor his fear of the audience. He viewed the function of an artist as communicating in such a way that a substantial number of people would understand; he said he could "see no sense in expressing something to a handful of people or to oneself."

Broadway audiences liked *Me and Juliet* well enough to keep it running for a year and thereby earn back more than its production costs. (The $350,000 capital had been put up entirely by RCA for a 50 percent interest and rights to the cast album.) However, the newspaper reports made it clear that this was no R & H smash, nor even an admirable failure like *Allegro*. In fact, the New York reviews read like the usual out-of-town notices. The score was called mediocre by some and adequate but without distinction by others, though it was pointed out that R & H at less than their best were still better than most composers and lyricists at their best. The sets, acting and costumes were universally praised and the mechanical aspects termed "pure magic." The trouble with the musical seemed to reside in the problems of the show-within-a-show. The intended contrast between onstage and backstage life was never achieved because the onstage show was so tepid and confusing. Having no cohesive point of view, the show started as an interesting, off-beat musical, then shifted to satire and ended as dance numbers whose sole purpose seemed to be to keep up a fast pace.

When Oscar's passport expired in July 1953, he was required to file an affidavit stating that he was not and never had been a member of the Communist Party. After he duly signed and filed the affidavit, he was issued a limited passport, good for only six months, with the explanation that some information received by the Passport Division of the Department of State reflected on his loyalty to the United States. He was told that in order to be issued a regular passport, he would have to file a statement of his political beliefs. His first reaction was one of outrage: "To hell with them."

Some of his children and his friends felt that it was demeaning for him to justify himself in order to receive the passport that was rightfully his. However, persuaded that getting only a limited passport could lead to practical complications with all the R & H business in London (four companies were then playing in England), he decided to write a statement, and labored over a 29-page document to submit to the Passport Division.

He answered charges point by point, from his association with the Hollywood Anti-Nazi League to his $2 yearly contribution to the Abraham Lincoln Brigade (the contribution was stopped when Reinheimer noticed it was on the Attorney General's list). He gave examples from his songs that praised the ideals which "the Communists call *bourgeois*," and listed honors and awards he had received; "If I am a security risk, I have been fooling a great many people—including myself." He said he had a healthy fear of international Communism, "but not a hysterical fear," and thought that we must be vigilant, but only within the framework of our own principles of thought and speech. Explaining at length his support of Paul Robeson's right to speak, no matter what his views, he said, "I must tell you that if this episode were to take place today, my thinking and acting would be the same. Disagreeing with what is said gives no one the right to suspend freedoms guaranteed by the Constitution. You do not protect rights by abrogating them." He made it clear, too, that he was opposed to "blacklisting" on the basis of personal politics rather than on the content of an artist's work.

It is not out of character that Oscar reacted as he did; he was, after all, a careful dreamer. By philosophy a liberal, by nature, as he himself said, he was "not a non-conformist." But it is also not out of character that he hired accused actors and publicly supported his old friend Hy Kraft, who was blacklisted in the fifties. When Kraft came back to New York after his interrogation by the House Un-American Activities Committee, whose questions he repeatedly declined to answer by citing the Fifth Amendment, there were two messages waiting for him. One was not a message but a command by Oscar and Dorothy Hammerstein to appear for dinner. After a movie that evening Oscar insisted that they go to Sardi's. Kraft was apprehensive about a visit to that gathering place of the theatrical world. The papers would have carried the news of his performance before the committee, and in those days, said Kraft, no one wanted to be seen with an unfriendly witness—particularly at Sardi's. Although Kraft admitted that no committee or columnist could damage Oscar's standing in the theater, nevertheless "the gesture of hosting a Fifth Amendment friend was a defiant commitment that raised plenty of eyebrows." The gesture meant a great deal to Kraft, who said later, "The man was my friend. I liked the world a lot better when he lived in it."

Ten

RH Negative

Since 1943, when *Oklahoma!* first electrified Broadway, film producers and studios had been trying to acquire the motion picture rights to it. Oscar and Dick were not anxious to sell. They wanted to keep the musical running as long as possible, and knew that as time went on it would not become less valuable. In 1951 R & H acquired sole rights by buying out the interests of the Theatre Guild and its original investors for $851,000, but continued to turn down even the most staggering Hollywood bids.

It was the demonstration of a new cinematic process that changed their minds in 1953. Arthur Hornblow, Jr., now an officer of Magna Theatre Corporation, sponsors of the development of the Todd-AO process, urged Oscar and Dick to attend a demonstration in their experimental laboratory in Buffalo, New York. Inspired by Mike Todd and developed by the research staff of the American Optical Company, Todd-AO was a single-camera process projected on a huge, curved screen that combined a 128-degree scope with remarkable clarity and depth of field, utilizing six-track orthosonic sound. Oscar and Dick were bowled over by the demonstration. Oscar had the impression that instead of looking through a window at the scene, he became part of it with a sense of sharing an experience with the characters in the film. The new invention, with its single strip of 70 mm. positive film, was much cleaner than the three-camera Cinerama process and, through advances in close-up lenses, not only produced a sweeping picture but effectively photographed intimate scenes to enhance character portrayal. They were convinced that with Todd-AO, new values could be added to the story without diminishing the already established ones.

Although both were excited at the prospect of filming *Oklahoma!* in Todd-AO, Dick was so disgusted with a crude shouting match between Todd and Magna president George Skouras that he came out of the preliminary meeting saying he wanted nothing further to do with them. A few days later Oscar and Reinheimer called Magna to say that R & H would be delighted to become associated with them in the production. "Had I made an issue of this, I'm sure it would have caused a serious rift between Oscar and me," says Dick in his autiobiography, *Musical Stages.* The terms of the agreement were very good, artistically and financially; Dick said nothing and went along with the contract. In fact, both he and Oscar purchased shares of Magna stock.

They wanted to trust no one else with their baby, their first joint Broadway hit and now the first film of one of their shows, and they set up Rodgers and Hammerstein Pictures, Inc., to produce it. Although they would have full control over every aspect, they nonetheless appointed Hornblow producer. He immediately asked screenwriters Sonya Levien and William Ludwig to prepare a scenario, following the original closely. The three spent a week at Highland Farm making various changes and additions with Oscar.

They signed Fred Zinnemann as director. For the Austrian-born director, whose work included such dramatic films as *The Search, Member of the Wedding* and *High Noon,* the directing of a musical was a new experience. Their choice of Zinnemann reflected their desire not to make yet another "Hollywood version" of a Broadway show.

The first tasks, nearly a year before *Oklahoma!* went into production, were to choose a location and to begin the arduous job of casting. Although movie musicals rarely went on location because of prohibitive costs, R & H were determined to bring the story to life by photographing most of the film in an authentic setting. They had hoped to use Oklahoma, but it proved to be too commercially developed to provide a suitably vast, empty site without some anachronism that would be visible in the wide landscape shots the Todd-AO "bug-eye" lens would pick up. Inspections of neighboring Kansas yielded the same results. Iowa had plenty of corn, but not enough open spaces. Finally, one day Hornblow saw *Arizona Highways Magazine*'s cover picture of an unidentified rich, fertile valley that looked perfect. It turned out to be the San Rafael Valley thirty-six miles northeast of Nogales, near the Mexican border. The second site was to be at the railway station at Elgin, fifty miles north. Oliver Smith, the outstanding Broadway and motion picture designer, began to build a full-scale model of the farm that would be erected between two giant cottonwoods on the 1,100-acre Arizona location, with a two story house, a barn, windmill, smokehouse and hurricane cellar.

In early September 1953, a lengthy correspondence about corn began. When Hornblow estimated the cost at $250 per acre, Pennsylvania farmer Hammerstein said that seemed a bit high to him. (In fact the estimate was much lower than the final cost.) The explanation from Hollywood, in a memo entitled "Budget Estimate of Corn," was that the site for the corn was an hour and a half's drive from Nogales, at an altitude of 5,000 feet with no natural water supply, on virgin grazing land that had never been cultivated. Each of the 2,100 stalks, planted far enough apart so that Curly could ride through them singing "Oh What a Beautiful Mornin'," had to be individually watered and cultivated to force growth that would be "unquestionably as high as an elephant's eye."

The corn was planted in January 1954 so that it would reach its fullest height in late July and early August. When it looked as if it wasn't growing as fast as they had anticipated, Oscar said he might have to change the lyric to "The corn is as low as an elephant's toe." But the rains came, and the sun shone, and the corn grew; at shooting time, it was sixteen feet high. "It looks as high as the eye of an elephant who is standing on another elephant," Oscar remarked when he first saw the field. Some of the corn was transplanted into movable boxes the camera could pass through in the opening shots of the film. Oscar figured by that time each ear had cost $8.95!

Meanwhile screen tests were being made to find actors for the principal roles. At first they looked for dramatic actors without regard to their singing voices, which could be dubbed. Oscar saw Richard Burton in London, but Burton was tied up with other commitments and couldn't be considered for Jud. Zinnemann wrote Oscar in England on September 30 that so far the New York actors who looked most promising were Eli Wallach and Rod Steiger for Jud, Joanne Woodward for Laurey, James Dean and Paul Newman for Curly. Newman, referred to as "the boy from *Picnic*," had been suggested by Oscar and Dick.

"Paul Newman is a handsome boy but quite stiff, to my disappointment," Zinnemann reported. "He lacks experience and would need a great deal of work. Still, in the long run he may be the right boy for us. He certainly has a most winning personality although I wish he had a little more cockiness and bravado."

Rod Steiger made a strong impression on Hornblow: "He has a real grasp of the character. He manages to make Jud an understandable human being. I believe that he sets a standard of performance which will not be easy to improve upon." Steiger played the role in the film.

James Dean was tested as Curly: "Dean seems to me to be an extraordinarily brilliant talent," wrote Zinnemann. "I am not sure that he has the necessary romantic quality. Just the same I shot his scenes with great detail because I felt that with an actor of his calibre a standard of performance would be set up which would later on become very helpful as a reference and comparison."

"This is a remarkably good young actor," commented Hornblow. "His instincts and talent are very solid and his scene with Jud had us all excited. His timing and his personal force are remarkable, but to me there is a lack of romantic appeal. Freddie likes him immensely, and Barbara thought that he had more sex appeal than Newman, but I think that we should explore him further with a romantic test and perhaps one in which he dubs back to one of Curly's songs. We'll watch him in the meantime, and will hold the test that we have for your return." Zinnemann later said, accurately, that it would have been a very different movie with James Dean in the lead.

After all the testing of dramatic actors, they finally cast the picture with actors who could sing, and none of the voices was dubbed. Charlotte Greenwood, who had starred in Oscar's London musical *Three Sisters*, had been unable to play Aunt Eller on Broadway, but was signed for that role in the film. Gordon MacRae was cast as Curly and Shirley Jones as Laurey.

Shirley Jones's career as an actress was a highly unusual success story. She arrived in New York with $200 in savings from Smithtown,

Pennsylvania, in 1952, when she was nineteen years old, with the intention of enrolling in a city college. She was introduced to agent Gus Schirmer, who persuaded her to attend an open R & H audition for *South Pacific* at the Majestic Theatre. After waiting in a line that seemed endless, she finally sang for John Fearnley, who said, "Miss Jones, what have you done?"

"Nothing, really," she replied. "I was in a Pittsburgh Civic Light Opera production, and I've done some little theater and things like that."

"Could you wait for a few minutes? Mr. Rodgers is across the street rehearsing the City Center Orchestra and I'd like him to hear you personally."

Soon Dick appeared and she sang for him.

"Miss Jones," he said, "I'm going to call Oscar Hammerstein at home. I want him to come hear you."

When her accompanist said he had to catch a plane, Dick said that she could sing with his orchestra across the street.

Shirley was feeling very nervous, very young and green, as she waited for Osar. When he arrived, she remembers, "That was the first moment I really felt relaxed and more self-assured. Something about the man made me feel that way, some strange kind of way of making you feel comfortable."

He said reassuringly, "Don't be nervous. Everything's all right." When they went across to the St. James, where the huge orchestra was waiting, Oscar muttered, "Boy, I couldn't get up on that stage and sing with this orchestra."

Handing her a score, he said, "Forget not knowing the words. Just stand up and read it, just sing along like you're in your own living room and just forget the orchestra's there."

She sang five or six songs from *Oklahoma!* as they listened. Dick, Shirley noticed, was the spokesman at the audition. R & H hired her that day. And so, ten days after arriving in New York, Shirley Jones had a job as a replacement in *South Pacific* at what seemed a princely salary.

She played for several months in *South Pacific* and was amazed to find that the producers hadn't disappeared from the scene. At least once a week both would visit the show, Dick usually more often. Oscar always knocked on the door of the chorus dressing room to say "How are you?" He knew everyone's first name, what they were like, what they were doing. He would ask, "Is everything all right? Are you enjoying the show?"

When *South Pacific* closed, Miss Jones's agent set up an audition for her to try out for the road company of *The King and I*. R & H said they didn't want her to go out of town, that they wanted her available, and offered her the role of Juliet, a small but featured part in *Me and Juliet*, then playing on Broadway.

A few weeks later she found out what had been in the back of their minds at the first audition—the role of Laurey in the film version of *Oklahoma!* Again she auditioned for Oscar and Dick, this time in their offices, where Oscar particularly wanted to hear her sing "A Cockeyed Optimist," even though she didn't know the words. The audition was successful, but Zinnemann and Hornblow were apprehensive about using a novice in such a big role in such a big picture. They continued to test more experienced actresses. A month later Shirley Jones flew to California to make a screen test opposite Gordon MacRae. Within a year of coming to New York, she was awarded the lead role in a multimillion-dollar motion picture. She was also the only performer ever put under an exclusive contract to R & H.

Two months before the start of production, Dorothy and Oscar celebrated their silver wedding anniversary by giving a dinner-dance for a hundred and twenty friends in the roof garden of the Pierre Hotel. Oscar gave a speech about their marriage and about good unions in general, the fitting of the holes in one partner's head to the bumps in the other's. They had, he said, adjusted their faults and their virtues, their weaknesses and strengths, to each other.

When the Hammersteins arrived in Arizona, Oscar was astounded by the set that had been built. He said that no one driving up to the farm would doubt that it had been lived in for many years. In contrast to the papier-mâché used to build the outdoor set for *High, Wide and Handsome* in 1937, this one had been constructed entirely of weathered, rough-sawn wood, for which every lumberyard within a radius of five hundred miles had been scoured. In the case of the smokehouse, which needed a tumbled-down look, the company had bought a deserted mining shack, torn it down and used the old timbers.

The expensive corn was ready and the cattle were standing like statues. The peach orchard that had been planted near the house was not bearing enough fruit, so every morning the crew hung two thousand fuzzy wax peaches on the trees and every evening harvested the crop. In one of the biggest location jaunts in Hollywood history, seventy trucks and trailers transported the props and equipment to Nogales and three hundred and twenty-five people stayed on location for over seven weeks. The exposed film was flown each day to laboratories in New Jersey, shipped back to Hollywood for editing, and then to Nogales for screening. Two cameras had to be used to film each scene; since only a limited number of theaters would be projecting 70 mm. Todd-AO, the movie was photographed in standard 35 mm. CinemaScope as well.

Back in Hollywood, two sound stages were leased at MGM (the same studio that had signed away its original rights to *Green Grow the Lilacs!*). Stage 2 housed the first Todd-AO projector and a half-million dollars' worth of recording equipment was installed. Stage 15, the world's largest sound stage, contained one of the largest sets ever built: the interiors of the houses and bunkhouse with porch, stables, corral, cattle trough, windmill and fence.

The first sequence shot by Zinnemann and top cinematographer Robert Surtees was the vast, elaborate scene that showed carriages, people, horses, driving away over the plains to the box-supper. Sitting at dinner that first evening with Dorothy, Oscar turned to his director and said, "Sorry, Fred, but the money has run out." Zinnemann still has the picture that was snapped at the very moment that Oscar, full of smiling benevolence, delivered the line.

During the preparations and the production, Zinnemann had come to know the Hammersteins well; with his family, he spent Christmas at Highland Farm. Although R & H maintained complete control of the picture, he had no difficulty in working with them. He had responded immediately to Oscar's warmth, which he characterized as a love of people. "I never remember him saying anything ugly or nasty about anybody or anything," says Zinnemann. "I felt very strongly about him and he was one of the very important people in my life."

Agnes de Mille was signed to create the dances for the film, an assignment she found formidable because ballet had always been confined to restricted areas, and now Todd-AO opened up the possibilities and the complications. She had not worked with Dick and Oscar since *Allegro*, but their paths had crossed often, and she was one of the many who turned to Oscar at moments of need. She remembers the time she went to see him when her Ballet Theatre was desperately in need of funds. It was one of the few times that she had approached someone for money and she hadn't warned him why she had asked to come. She entered the study on 63rd Street and sat nervously in an antique chair, facing him across the polished mahogany desk. Oscar smiled at her and waited. Agnes moistened her lips and shifted in the chair.

"It's just this—" Agnes blurted.

"All right. Yes," he said.

"Yes, what?"

"Yes, a thousand dollars. Never mind the pitch. Do you want Scotch or bourbon?"

During production, de Mille's relationship with Dick was strained. He didn't approve of her dances, which had been opened up for the new medium, and he vetoed a couple of her dancers after Zinnemann had approved them, curtly dismissing them with "Not on this set." She retaliated with sharp comments and her own demands. It was Shirley Jones's observation that both Zinnemann and Oscar tended to walk away from such troubles and that Dick would attempt to solve whatever problems came up. She felt that Oscar always had the "underline" in everything, but that he was happy to have Dick act as spokesman and that it seemed one of the reasons they were such a good team.

De Mille, Zinnemann, Surtees and the dancers worked in concert to devise dances that suited the wider scope of the film. "Everything's Up to Date in Kansas City" was performed at the Elgin station, which now had kerosene lanterns, old-fashioned grillwork and gingerbread trim to look like a turn-of-the-century Oklahoma station.

The "Out of My Dreams" ballet was danced by Bambi Linn, James Mitchell and Rod Steiger and a chorus of thirty-two, in front of a 40-by-50-foot backdrop on eight stage sets over an area of 54,000 square feet. The sequence, which was the last to be photographed, took seventeen days to film, with five hundred pounds of dry ice used each day to create the eerie smoke effect.

Oklahoma! started production on July 14, and a hundred and seven days later, on December 6, 1954, it was completed. It was, at the time, the most expensive motion picture ever made, its final cost totaling nearly seven million dollars. For the next seven months, the film was prepared for release and it opened on October 11, 1955, at the Rivoli Theatre in New York to excellent reviews and public response.

During the year that Oscar worked on the film he was also searching for the basis of the next R & H Broadway show. One was suggested by Josh Logan. A St. Louis lawyer who had come to New York to be a producer showed him the films of a trilogy of plays about the Marseilles waterfront by Marcel Pagnol to which he had acquired the stage rights. The lawyer, David Merrick, thought the stories would be good for a musical. Logan agreed, but he said, "It's too big a subject for anybody except Oscar and Dick."

"You'll never get them," said Merrick. "Besides, they'll want to produce it themselves and I won't let them take it away from me now —it's my career at stake."

When Logan arranged a private screening, Oscar turned to him at the end and said, "It's the greatest. What an opportunity for a lyricist."

A meeting was arranged between Merrick and R & H. They told him that if they wrote the show they would have to produce it, too. Merrick told them that he would be amenable to associate-producer billing, but that under no circumstances would he take his name off the show entirely. Oscar was enthusiastic about the project and said that as long as Merrick didn't interfere with decision making, he would go along with the arrangement. However, when Dick refused to do the show if Merrick's name was on it, Oscar accepted his partner's word on the matter. Merrick arranged for Harold Rome to write the score, and S. N. Behrman the book, for what would become *Fanny*. The coda to the story, says Logan, is that every time he saw Oscar after that Oscar always said, "Why the hell did we give up *Fanny*? What on earth were we trying to prove? My God, that's a great story and look at some of the junk we've done!"

Another project that R & H turned down was one they had considered before—*Saratoga Trunk*. Edna Ferber and Moss Hart were writing the book and wanted them to do the score and produce it. Oscar and Dick refused, but told them, "It would have been a lot of fun for the four of us to work together on a play, so let's do it sometime on some other play." They decided against it because another project had come up that looked like a more radical departure from the kind of characters they had dealt with in the past, the change of pace that they always looked for to stimulate them in a new work.

Producers Cy Feuer and Ernest Martin had approached their friend John Steinbeck about doing a musical based on the sequel to *Cannery Row* which he was writing. They said to him, "What would you think if Oscar and Dick did it?"

"What do you say but hurray! Hallelujah!"

Steinbeck was writing the novel *Big Bear Cafe* (later entitled *Sweet Thursday*) when Oscar left for England to produce *The King and I*, so the novelist sent sections of his first draft as he finished them to Oscar in London. Oscar wrote to Dick that the novel was very interesting, particularly the characters. Dick answered that he was concerned about one point: "Whether we can get away with a factual house of prostitution and make one of the leading characters a working prostitute is something else again." He said he was not inclined to be against it but thought they must be careful about it.

R & H might have done well to be more careful about this problem before they got involved in *Sweet Thursday*, which became the musical *Pipe Dream*. It was widely believed by their critics and their friends that the reason *Pipe Dream* was a disappointing show was that the material was not suited to R & H. It was not that the Steinbeck novel was heavy; on the contrary, the story was "so gaily inconsequential that it might serve as the working script for a musical comedy on the order, say, of *Pal Joey*," said Carlos Baker in the *New York Times*. Steinbeck tended to idealize the riffraff of the small northern California coast town. His prostitutes have hearts of gold; the madam is a former social worker who teaches the girls how to set a table properly in the hope that they will marry substantial citizens; the flophouse residents are philosophical charmers who are entirely contented with their lives. For all the idealization of their lives, however, the whores are whores, the bums are for the most part on the wrong side of the law, and Steinbeck presents these facts of life with a certain clear-eyed toughness that later eluded R & H.

The novel's principal character is Doc, the Cannery Row marine biologist who had always been content, working just enough to earn money for beer, whiskey and peanut butter, but returns from the war restless and discontented. Fauna, the neighborhood madam, and Doc's flophouse friends, correctly diagnosing his condition as loneliness, scheme to get him together with Suzy, a drifting hooker who has landed at the local bordello, the Bear Cafe. Their matchmaking backfires when Suzy senses Doc's reluctance to become involved with her, and realizes that she is ashamed of herself. She moves into an abandoned boiler to build her independence and self-esteem, and is eventually successfully wooed by Doc.

The novel was written almost as a play, with extensive dialogue in short chapters that are almost scenes. Its possibilities as a musical play were immediately apparent, and R & H were attracted to the unconventional, raffish characters and the colorful setting. They decided to write and produce it. The property was turned over to R & H from Feuer and Martin, who became silent partners in the venture and received 20 percent of the producers' share of the profits. Steinbeck was delighted with Oscar's first draft, which made liberal use of the original dialogue. In fact, in no other work that he adapted for the stage had he used so much of the actual dialogue of the original source.

In one of Feuer and Martin's first letters to R & H in September 1953 they had said, "Doc would, of course, be played by Hank Fonda." An old friend of the novelist, Fonda had been taking singing lessons for a year in preparation for the part, which was a natural for him. However, when auditioned, he was turned down for the part. Steinbeck later wrote Fonda, "You will remember . . . that when I was writing *Sweet Thursday* I had you always in mind as the prototype of Doc. And I think that one of my sharp bitternesses is that due to circumstances personality-wise and otherwise beyond our control you did not play it when it finally came up. I think it might have been a different story if you had." The part went to a singer named William Johnson, and the role of Suzy to Judy Tyler. (Both were killed in separate automobile collisions the year after *Pipe Dream* closed.)

Reggie saw Met star Helen Traubel on a television show and called Oscar to suggest that she would be a good Fauna. Oscar had seen Traubel in her first New York nightclub engagement at the Copacabana and afterwards had gone backstage to wag a finger at her and say, "You realize, young lady, you are headed straight for Broadway, don't you?" After Dick had seen her at a subsequent performance in Las Vegas, Oscar visited her again and said, "We've got just the role for you."

"What is that?"

"It's the wholesome madam of a house," he announced.

R & H signed Harold Clurman as director. Again they chose a man who had never directed a Broadway musical. Clurman had an illustrious reputation as founder of the Group Theatre and director of such shows as *Member of the Wedding*, *Bus Stop* and *Tiger at the Gates*. Again, too, they found that a competent director of straight dramatic plays could have trouble with a musical. As had happened so frequently before, Oscar moved over from the sidelines to help out.

The production period for *Pipe Dream* in the fall of 1955 was a particularly harrowing time. During the summer, Dick had begun to feel a pain in his left jaw which by September was diagnosed as cancer. On the day that rehearsals began he entered the hospital to undergo extensive surgery to remove the malignancy. The operation was successful, and although Dick had not fully regained his vitality, he insisted on attending the out-of-town tryouts. He began to be plagued by periods of depression; in his autobiography, he speculates that returning to work so soon after his operation might have "triggered the situation. . . . One of the most disturbing manifestations was that I began to drink," he says. During this period, more of the duties of the partnership fell on Oscar, though he tactfully tried to support Dick and smooth the way for him. After Dick had stayed in the background for several weeks, one day during a rehearsal when Oscar was up front talking to the company, he turned to his partner and asked casually, "Want to take over now?" He moved to a back seat, making it almost mandatory for Dick to step in.

In October Oscar received word that Uncle Arthur was dead at eighty-three. He had remained an active, volatile man to the very end. Never overtly bitter about the bankruptcy that forced him out of the business years before, he puttered with his inventions and even achieved a modicum of success in his old theatrical world with his collaboration on the song "Because of You" that was number one on the Hit Parade in 1951–52. Recently he had been confined to his Florida home, where he devoted all his time to the biography of his father that was finally being written by Vincent Sheean.

His personality had not changed a whit in old age. On his last visit to New York the previous summer, he stayed at East 63rd Street. One day he was lying in the darkened guest room after receiving female hormone injections for the trouble he was having with his eyes when Billy came to see him. "Willie, come over here, I can't see you," beckoned his great-uncle. "God-damn it, they've been putting these God-damned female hormones in me and sailors are chasing me down the street!"

Pipe Dream rehearsals were not going well. A magnificent opera singer, Traubel herself admits that she never claimed to be much of an actress and that the emphasis on words rather than music in the musical theater, as opposed to opera, "changed my actions, my expressions, my very attitude—and even the particular singing of a note." Unlike Pinza, she was having difficulty adapting to the new medium;

it was evident to everyone, including Traubel, that she was not right for the part and that even her voice was not projecting well in this specialized song style. Elaine Steinbeck says that it was clear by New Haven that they should have gotten rid of Traubel. Worried about Dick, and even in the best of times loath to confront unpleasantness, Oscar did not fire her; he "miked" her and tried such changes as adding two children to a scene in an effort to improve matters.

The greatest problems, however, were not in the cast but in the heart of the play. On September 22 John Steinbeck had written Oscar: "I am delighted with *Pipe Dream*—with book and score and direction and cast. It is a thing of joy, and will be for a long time to come." But as rehearsals and the accompanying revisions of the script proceeded, Steinbeck became less and less delighted. The play was being "cleaned up," according to Traubel, "to the point of innocuousness . . . as scene after scene became emasculated."

The novelist typed long memos of suggestions, couched in apologies about his lack of theatrical experience and knowledge. His memos make it apparent that the basic differences in conception and approach which were beginning to emerge were serious ones. Oscar had from the beginning changed the cause of Doc's inner discontent by attributing it to his first meeting with Suzy. Steinbeck objected to this, as well as to the general lack of clarity about Doc's character, but his greatest objection was to the cuts that R & H made as rehearsals proceeded.

The steady revisions and cuts had fudged the whole issue of Suzy's being a prostitute. At the beginning of the play when she was supposed to be a tough, dirty "road kid," Suzy was dressed in a neat blue dress and looked well-groomed as she sang "Everybody's Got a Home But Me." Steinbeck commented that she didn't look like a whore but "like an off-duty visiting nurse." The way the libretto now read, she had no police record for vagrancy and could possibly have been just rooming at the "happiest house on the block," as one lyric states, which "is friendly and foolish and gay." At the top of a page of dialogue changes Steinbeck noted:

> One of the most serious criticisms is the uncertainty of Suzy's position in the Bear Flag. It's either a whore house, or it isn't. Suzy either took a job there, or she didn't. The play doesn't give satisfaction here and it leaves an audience wondering. My position is that she took the job all right but she wasn't any good at it. In the book, Fauna explains that Suzy's no good as a hustler because

she's got a streak of lady in her. I wish we could keep this thought because it explains a lot in a short time.

In his next memo, the author correctly pinpointed the scene that contains the essence of the play's problem as the one where Doc goes to Suzy in her boiler and is rejected by her. The scene didn't come off, he said; it contained no tension, no drama, because the conflict between Doc and Suzy had been reduced to "two immature people who are piqued at each other." Evading the issue of Suzy being a prostitute had taken the heart out of Doc's rejection of her, her motivation for change, and the hurt that caused her rejection of him:

> I think if you will finally bring the theme of this play into the open, but wide open, you will have solved its great weakness and have raised it to a high level. You will have also overcome the most universal and consistent criticism we have had, that the show side-steps, hesitates, mish-mashes and never faces its theme. Please consider this and let us talk about it. If this is not done, I can neither believe nor take *Pipe Dream* seriously. The shock of the killing on stage in *Oklahoma!* was what gave it its final backbone and that made it last.

In Boston, during the second leg of its out-of-town engagement, Steinbeck continued to write long letters to Oscar. Writing as an old friend as well as an associate, he pointed out that the show was particularly disappointing because of Rodgers and Hammerstein's tradition of flouting convention.

> Dear Oscar:
> I come now to what I consider the most important matter of all. I feel it very strongly and the only two thoughtful reviews we got, Norton and the Xtian Sci. Mon. both made a point of it and I get it from all sides on all levels. Norton used the word *conventional* to describe his uneasiness. I have heard others describe the same thing, sweetness, loss of toughness, lack of definition, whatever people say when they feel they are being let down. And believe me, Oscar, this is the way audiences feel. What emerges now is an old-fashioned love story. And that is not good enough to people who have looked forward to this show based on you and me and Dick. You and Dick invented this form and carried it to its high point with South Pacific. When Oklahoma! came out it violated every conventional rule of Musical Comedy. You were out on a limb. They loved it and were for you. South Pacific made a great jump ahead. And even more you were ordered to go ahead.

But, Oscar, time has moved. The form has moved. People love Oklahoma! as a classic, but if you brought it in as a new show now, people would find it old-fashioned and conventional because S.P. and King and I carried it farther. You're stuck with it. You can't stand still. You could bring in this show right now and have an E-flat hit that would run maybe eighteen months but you would have disappointed your audiences. That's the price you have to pay for being Rodgers and Hammerstein . . .

The only thing this story has besides some curious characters is the almost tragic situation that a man of high mind and background and culture takes to his breast an ignorant, ill-tempered little hooker who isn't even very good at that. He has to take her, knowing that a great part of it is going to be misery . . . [but knowing] that the worse hell is the penalty of separation.

Now that is not a conventional situation or a conventional story . . . To avoid this fact that Suzy is a hooker is to throw out the only story there is in this particular thing . . .

Yours in good faith,
John

Why, indeed, had the men who had broken so many traditions, who had for so long sought to bring greater depth and realism to the musical, pulled up short this time? John Steinbeck said, "It's a beautiful show. It needs only guts." R & H had never before lacked guts; they had, in fact, broken barrier after barrier in the musical theater because of their courage in tackling unconventional subjects in unconventional ways. Their primary concern had always been to keep the integrity of the original work intact, but in *Pipe Dream* they did not do so; they diminished the very qualities that had originally attracted them to *Sweet Thursday*. The difference between this work and those in which Oscar was willing to defy convention was the novel's explicitly sexual subject matter. A word often used to describe Oscar's attitude toward sex was "conventional," though many went further and described it as "prudish" or "Victorian."

After seeing *Pipe Dream*, Billy Rose said, "You know why Oscar shouldn't have written that? The guy has never been in a whorehouse in his life." That this was undoubtedly true is verified by Oscar's reaction to his son Billy's announcement, years earlier, that some friends had taken him to a house of prostitution. " 'What was it like?' Dad said. He was so eager. I'll never forget the expression on his face. He hadn't ever been near one, and never would be," Billy says. Although Dick was personally not as strait-laced as Oscar, he seemed to share his partner's view of the handling of sex in an R & H show. "We do family shows," he said to Steinbeck.

South Pacific, Carousel and *Carmen Jones* have stories that rest on the power of sexual attraction. As long as the sexuality was implicit, Oscar could treat it with the same understanding that he brought to other aspects of human behavior. In fact, he said to Josh Logan shortly before he died, "You know something I've decided —that's that there's only one thing important enough to write a story about, and that's sex. I've discovered that it's under almost every good story, and unless it's there you shouldn't write the story. It's not worth it." His problem was dealing openly with sexual material; because of this reticence *Pipe Dream* was not what it might have been.

Steinbeck held no grudge, however; he told Oscar that despite his disagreements on the libretto, he accepted the fact that R & H were ultimately responsible for the show and had every right to make the final decision, as he himself would have done if the positions were reversed.

Pipe Dream opened at the Shubert in New York on November 30, 1955, with the largest advance sale of any R & H show: $1.2 million. The reviewers were divided, with some praising the show's enchantment and others finding it "RH negative." Helen Traubel's performance led someone to inquire, "What's all the Traubel about it?" In general, the criticism of the musical centered on the very issue that Steinbeck had raised. Hobe Morrison noted that it was done with the usual R & H "unerring taste—possibly too much," and John Chapman ventured that "perhaps Hammerstein and Rodgers are too gentlemanly to be dealing with Steinbeck's sleazy and raffish denizens." *Pipe Dream* had the shortest run of any R & H play (246 performances) and incurred the greatest financial loss.

About this time, Steve Sondheim came to Oscar with a problem. On his return from Hollywood he had been signed by designer-producer Lemuel Ayers to write the score for an original musical, *Saturday Night*. Although he completed the work, Ayers' death brought an end to the project. Now Arthur Laurents was at work with Jerry Robbins on the book for a musical, *West Side Story*, for which Leonard Bernstein was writing the score. Bernstein was dissatisfied with his own lyrics and Steve was asked to write them. Steve complained to Oscar that he didn't want to accept the job because he wanted to compose.

"I think you ought to do this," Oscar said.

"Why?" Steve asked.

"Because to work with men of the professional caliber of Bernstein and Laurents and Robbins is invaluable experience," Oscar explained. "And, I think also it'll be a foot in the theater for you. You can always do music on your next show." Steve got the tacit message from Oscar that while he would do everything he could to help Steve personally he should not be counted on to open more doors for him than he already had. Steve knew that this was the same attitude he had toward his own children and did not want to impose on him.

He brought Oscar the first seven songs for the show about a year later and remembers that when he finished playing and singing "Maria," Dorothy came across the room with tears in her eyes and kissed him. Dorothy remembers thinking as she listened to it, "The boy's grown up." Steve had a mixed reaction; he was moved that she was moved, but he himself didn't much like the lyric stylistically. He knew, though, that it was a very "Hammerstein" lyric in that it had the one quality Oscar valued above all others: absolute honesty about a character and what he is saying. Steve says that he still tries to keep this quality in his lyrics, even when he is being un-Hammerstein in style.

When Oscar couldn't attend a rehearsal of the entire show, a special run-through was staged for him prior to the Philadelphia break-in. He was thrilled with it, but had a couple of major criticisms, the principal one being that "Tonight" was not a sufficiently soaring song for the balcony scene. "It's a nice song, but it doesn't seem to me to take off enough," Oscar said. His instinct was unerring, says Steve, because the truth was that the song had not been written for that scene but was used there as a last resort. Even though Steve and the others knew he was right about it, they were never able to fix it.

Steve again went to Oscar when he was offered the lyric-writing assignment for *Gypsy*, which would star Ethel Merman. This time he had absolutely refused, but Oscar again advised him to change his mind. He said that he knew how frustrated Steve must feel, but that he had never had any experience writing for a star and it could be very valuable. "It goes into rehearsal in six months," Oscar added, "so the most it would be is six months out of your life."

Glad that he had followed his advice the last time, he did so once more and took the job. Arthur Laurents and Steve asked Oscar to come to see the show in Philadelphia, where they were trying to solve second-act problems. Dying to hear Oscar's opinion because they thought it would be an important key to the solution of their problems, they were in great suspense as he watched the show. Afterwards, he said, "I think you have two serious problems."

"Arthur and I looked at each other," says Steve, "and thought 'Thank God! Now we don't have to think anymore and stay up all night.'"

"First," said Oscar, "the doorknob to the kitchen keeps falling off all during the first act."

"Is this the time to make a joke?" Steve retorted.

"No—that's a serious problem," Oscar replied. "It interrupts the concentration."

"But, come on," said Steve.

"Well, I think you've got to give Ethel a hand at the end of 'Rose's Turn,'" Oscar continued.

Steve had argued against giving her an applause-getting high note because the character was a woman having a breakdown. "It seems dishonest to me," Steve said.

"Yes, it's dishonest," Oscar explained, "and it's the kind of dishonesty that you have to take into account in the theater, particularly the musical theater. Don't forget: there's an audience out there and they want to applaud. The result of your doing it honestly is that they don't listen to the last two minutes of the show, because they feel so frustrated and cheated. And if you want them to listen to those last two pages of dialogue, then you've got to give them their release at the end of that song. It's dishonest psychologically, but there's another kind of honesty, and that has to do with theater honesty."

Steve says that he still hates the last note they gave the song, but "he was dead *right*, because the minute we put on the high note for her and gave her applause, there was dead silence instead of the restlessness there had always been." Oscar gave similar advice to Jule Styne, *Gypsy*'s composer, when he and producer Herman Levin asked his counsel on *Gentlemen Prefer Blondes*. After Carol Channing sang "Diamonds Are a Girl's Best Friend," the show went right into another dialogue scene and the audience was frustrated in its desire to applaud the song. In that case Oscar advised a momentary blackout after the number.

The R & H effort that followed *Pipe Dream* presented none of *Pipe Dream*'s problems in displaying the tawdry aspects of life; it was an adaptation of *Cinderella*. For years Oscar had wanted to write a children's opera and in 1948 he had talked to Josh Logan and Mary Martin about doing a musical *Peter Pan* with Ezio Pinza as Captain Hook. In 1956, Hubbell Robinson of the Columbia Broadcasting System asked R & H to write a musical version of *Cinderella* for Julie Andrews, who had just taken Broadway by storm via *My Fair Lady*.

Oscar had no objection at all to working in television. He liked the medium, claiming that he even enjoyed watching the commercials. As much as he loved the theater, he had no elitist feelings about television. Both movies and television, he thought, were valid dramatic arenas with many of the same goals as the theater. One of his major objections to the thesis that the theater was "dying" was that more actors, writers, directors and technical people were being employed in movies and TV than ever before. Dick had written *Victory at Sea* for television, but Oscar had never written for the medium before, though he had appeared on programs such as a two-part *Ed Sullivan Show* tribute to him, an Edward R. Murrow *Person to Person* with Dorothy, a thirty-minute interview with Mike Wallace, and even Groucho Marx's *You Bet Your Life!* As in his early Hollywood days and in the filming of *Oklahoma!*, he was interested to learn the techniques and processes of a new medium. He found that TV had all the advantages of the movies, with the dissolve taking care of such problems as inventing exits and entrances, to say nothing of turning pumpkins into coaches. Other major differences, Oscar found, were the intimacy required by the small picture and more precise timing than was necessary on the stage.

The ninety-minute show would be seen only once, but it was estimated that the number of people who would see *Cinderella* would be twice that of those who saw even the longest-running Broadway show. The arrangement was for R & H to sell the show to CBS as a package: that is, they would supervise as well as write the show and would retain all rights to the property, with the network having an option for one re-broadcast. CBS decided to use a live color technique for the production.

Seven months before it was televised, Oscar wrote a story outline indicating the basic ideas and the placement of musical numbers. They decided to make no serious departures from the story as it was first told by Charles Perrault in the seventeenth century. "The traditional *Cinderella* has done very well," Oscar explained. "Why should we trick her up? We decided at once Cinderella would not become a shopgirl from Macy's who is spotted by the proprietor's son and wafted to El Morocco. There will be absolutely no updating, no naturalistic or Freudian explanations. We wanted to do a musical version of the story that everyone remembers from childhood."

They did, however, humanize the characters and bring wit to the show. The stepmother (Ilka Chase) and stepsisters (Kaye Ballard and Alice Ghostley) are more human, slightly stupid and comic rather than wicked. The King and Queen (Howard Lindsay and Dorothy Stickney) are rather appealing, worried, somewhat bumbling parents. Oscar didn't much like magic as an explanation or motivation, so he de-emphasized the fairy aspect of the godmother (Edie Adams) and presented her as a matter-of-fact young woman with a sense of humor who incidentally had magical powers. In her first scene with Cinderella she even tries to talk the girl out of her wild idea of going to the ball. In the song "Impossible," she dismisses miracles, with "Such fol-de-rol and fiddledy dee of course is impossible!" Finally won over by Cinderella's innocent faith and hope, she admits that "Impossible things are happening every day."

The score, with such songs as "My Own Little Corner," "Ten Minutes Ago" and "A Lovely Night," showed Oscar and Dick in a lighthearted mood that matched the story. Looking for a love song for the show, Oscar had the feeling once again that he had looked at love from every conceivable side of the subject and had said all he had to say about it. "But when I am pushed into a corner, suddenly, sometimes, if I am lucky, I get a new thought about people in love that I haven't had before and wonder why I hadn't gotten it long ago." In this case, the thought was, Do I love you because you're beautiful? Or are you beautiful because I love you?

On March 6 the working script and the entire score were completed and rehearsals began. Executive Producer Dick Lewine employed a new technique that had never before been used in television production in order to give the show two full weeks of sharpening, rewriting, restaging and polishing. Two weeks before the air date *Cinderella* had a full-scale presentation that was like a New Haven tryout. Recorded on black-and-white Kinescope, the show was viewed by R & H, Lewine and director Ralph Nelson who made comments and noted changes in lines and routines, as well as in lighting, set design and background music. At that time the creative staff of a television program usually did not see the full-scale production until a dress rehearsal just before the airing—too late to make extensive changes. The method used on *Cinderella* added $20,000 to the $375,000 budget, but resulted in quality far superior to most television productions of the time. "It was a class show," in the words of the *Variety* critic.

There had been talk among Broadwayites for years about erecting a statue of George M. Cohan, and in 1957 Oscar accepted the role of chairman of the committee raising funds for the memorial. Although he had not personally known the songwriter-playwright-showman well, he admired the songs that said in plain, unequivocal words exactly what Cohan wanted them to say and had such an enormous impact on the country. Songs like "Over There," "It's a Grand Old Flag," "I'm A Yankee Doodle Dandy" and "Give My Regards to Broadway" took on symbolic significance for millions of Americans. Oscar couldn't remember seeing statues of American actors, playwrights or songwriters and thought it was high time that the contributions of theatrical people received the kind of recognition so long accorded to those of political and military figures. It turned out to be less simple than he had thought. The committee needed only $100,000, but it took an interminable length of time to raise the sum. Oscar discovered that many people had not liked Cohan as a man, and that grudges and petty grievances were still being nursed. Actors Equity sent only a token contribution, and referred to Cohan's pro-management position in the actors' strike of 1919 that had shut down Broadway. Oscar returned their check with the following letter:

> 10 East 63 St.
> New York City
>
> February 3, 1958
>
> Mr. Angus Duncan
> Actors' Equity Association
> 226 West 47 Street
> New York City
>
> Dear Mr. Duncan:
>   Max Gordon has sent me your check from the Actors' Equity Association to the George M. Cohan Memorial Committee. I have also read your letter to him.
>   Although the last paragraph of your letter states: "And so the Council concluded that indeed the bitterness of the past should be forgotten and concluded—" it seems to me that a donation in an amount "equal to the cost of a life membership in the Actors'

Equity Association" carries with it an ironical suggestion that a few stray grains of bitterness remain.

I remember the old situation very well indeed, and I do not dispute your right to continue a resentment so deep. I must, however, refuse to cooperate with you in pinpricking George's ghost. I am therefore returning the check, thanking you for your sincere but unsuccessful effort to forget.

> Very truly yours,
> Oscar Hammerstein II

The money was finally raised and Oscar presided over the dedication ceremony on September 11, 1959. Ten thousand people jammed into the appropriate site, Duffy Square at Broadway and 46th Street, to witness the unveiling of the statue; at the end of the ceremony, they sang "Give My Regards to Broadway."

A 1957 effort that ended less successfully than the Cohan memorial drive was a book that Oscar planned to write with Pearl Buck and James Michener. The three neighbors were talking one afternoon about some recent incidents involving racial discrimination in housing and decided to write a book together, a "short, unhysterical, profound and unequivocal statement concerning America and the race problem."

Each wrote several chapters about the causes and effects of prejudice. The titles of some of the chapters—Oscar's "Dear Believer in White Supremacy," Buck's "The Effect of Prejudice upon the Individual" and Michener's "Prejudice Is Wrong"—give some idea of the rather polemical, heavy-handed tone. In March 1958 Buck wrote to Oscar that the publishers and agents had decided not to go ahead with it, the general feeling being that the various chapters did not add up to a real book.

Two R & H films had been made since *Oklahoma!*, but Oscar and Dick had had virtually nothing to do with their production. Twentieth Century-Fox had acquired the rights to *Carousel* through its prior claim on *Liliom* and to *The King and I* through its previous filming of Margaret Landon's novel. Oscar and Dick thought the studio had done well by both properties, and when they decided in 1957 to film *South Pacific* they went with Fox (and the $1.2 million that it offered). The film would again be made in association with Magna Theatre Corporation, using Todd-AO, but they asked Buddy Adler, Fox's production chief, to serve as producer. Oscar asked Josh Logan to direct, commenting: "I don't know who else could do it." Although Josh was first offered a straight salary, he held out for a percentage of the potential gross and R & H agreed. (The movie was not being made by R & H Pictures, but through South Pacific Enterprises, Inc., which Oscar and Dick had set up.) Logan doesn't know whether he got back all the money that he lost by not having co-author royalties on the Broadway play, but, he says, "I sure got back some of it, and I'll be able to live on what I got [on the film] for the rest of my life."

Oscar was involved in every aspect of the production, beginning in March 1957 with a preliminary tour of several Pacific islands to scout locations for the film. The location site was of vital importance because Oscar and Dick wanted to adhere as closely as possible to the original presentation, yet give audiences something new in terms of setting; all but a few scenes called for exterior photography in authentic, tropical surroundings. Oscar, Logan, Adler and cinematographer Leon Shamroy finally decided to use Kauai, an island at the northern end of the Hawaiian chain, which had first been used in 1950 for MGM's *Pagan Love Song*. Even though the tidal wave that had struck just before their visit would necessitate some rebuilding of bridges and roads, the island contained so many scenic splendors—from spectacular beaches to some of the lushest foliage and flowers in the world —that it was worth the time and expense. The island matched Michener's description of the jewel-like Bali H'ai.

The casting of the picture was haphazard and filled with mistakes. Ezio Pinza was dead and Rossano Brazzi had already been signed, but his singing voice necessitated dubbing. Mary Martin was primarily a stage actress and was older than Brazzi in any case, so they looked elsewhere for Nellie. Logan was eager to have Elizabeth Taylor, who was "a young thing and had a freckled face and was adorable." She wanted the part and sang for him and Dick, but was so nervous that her voice came out a croak. R & H, he claims, was unwilling to dub her voice. Although Doris Day was Brazzi's age, instead of being fifteen years younger as required by the story, she was so perfect in type that they were seriously considering her. One night when Logan was at a party at Rosalind Russell's, where Dean Martin, Frank Sinatra and others were gathered around the piano harmonizing, Josh asked Doris to sing. "I never sing," she replied. Piqued, he decided to find someone else. Mitzi Gaynor came to him looking for a small part, but assuming it was the role of Nellie she was after, he tested her for it and hired her. She and France Nuyen, who played Liat, were the only leads whose vocals were not dubbed. John Kerr, who played Cable, couldn't sing, and though Juanita Hall could sing extremely well, Dick was worried about how she would record on film and insisted on having her songs dubbed by Muriel Smith. Whatever the reasons, the cast was not what one would regard as top-drawer R & H, to say the least, and the decision to have off-screen, poorly matched voice doubles detracted from the quality of the movie.

Principal photography began at Lihue, Kauai, on August 12. Oscar and Dorothy spent several weeks there. The unit was the largest ever to be sent by a studio to an overseas location. Four cargo ships were leased to transport equipment and properties to the island.

Although the movie was extremely successful financially, it did not have the usual high-quality look that was the hallmark of most R & H productions. In addition to the weak cast and the questionable practice of dubbing most of the voices, the film had a screenplay by Paul Osborn that did not do justice to the property, and mediocre choreography by LeRoy Prinz. Logan's direction was not of the caliber of his work in *Picnic* and *Sayonara*. The most outstandingly bad feature of the film, the reason Logan calls it "the shame of my life," was the color. In an effort to give a different hue to each musical sequence, the kind of effect that Hassard Short had created for *Carmen Jones* on Broadway, special filters were used. It is difficult to understand how Oscar, Logan, the usually excellent cinematographer Leon Shamroy and others, seeing daily rushes, could have allowed the entire film to be shot through the filters that gave an obvious, unrealistic, forced color to so many scenes. However, with all its defects, the movie was a smash hit. Critics were divided between love and hate, but moviegoers loved it to the tune of an $18 million gross.

In the Fox commissary one day during production on *South Pacific*, Oscar saw Joe Fields. He had known Fields since 1902, when both were actors in the P.S. 9 Christmas play. Since then, Fields had spent many years as a successful writer-producer, with such hits as *My Sister Eileen, Junior Miss* and *The Desk Set*. When he mentioned that he was negotiating for the rights to a novel called *The Flower Drum Song*, Oscar was intrigued by the title and asked to read it. He liked the story of Chinese immigrants in San Francisco adjusting to a new culture, which he described as "sort of a Chinese *Life with Father*." Dick and he decided to make it their next show, writing and producing it in association with Joe Fields.

The Hammerstein-Fields book took great liberties with C. Y. Lee's novel. Wang Chi Yang, the patriarch, was eased into the background to make room for two love stories, only one of which was in the original. Following a familiar pattern, one was a tender love story about Wang's old-fashioned son and a demure mail-order bride; the other a comic one about two brash, modern young Chinese-Americans.

Old and new cultures were contrasted in the songs; "I Enjoy Being a Girl" is in the brassy American pop idiom, while "You Are Beautiful" purports to be an old Chinese poem. Once again R & H were faced with the need to capture an Oriental flavor without actually duplicating the sounds of Eastern music. "I Am Going to Like It Here," sung by the mail-order bride when she has just fallen in love, has a slightly singsong melody that is matched by an unusual kind of repetition in the lyrics. The second and fourth lines of each stanza are used as the first and third lines of the following stanzas, except in the final one.

I am going to like it here.
There is something about the place,
An encouraging atmosphere
Like a smile on a friendly face

There is something about the place,
So caressing and warm it is—
Like a smile on a friendly face,
Like a port in a storm it is!

So caressing and warm it is,
All the people are so sincere,
Like a port in a storm it is
I am going to like it here!

All the people are so sincere,
There's especially one I like.
I am going to like it here.
It's the father's first son I like!

There's especially one I like
There is something about his face.
It's the father's first son I like
He's the reason I love the place.

There is something about his face,
I would follow him anywhere . . .
If he goes to another place . . .
I am going to like it there!

As he grew older, Oscar began to keep folders containing his work on lyrics from the first scribblings to the finished, typed version. "A Hundred Million Miracles" began with:

> The dark blue curtain
>   That hangs over night
> Is pinned by the stars to the sky.

Oscar reworked this verse, scribbled other images and rhymes and included the dialogue that leads into the song. Midway through the folder, a sheet shows the outline for the entire song. His completed lyric was much longer than the version used onstage. The omitted "Miracle of Illusion," as well as the rest of the song, expressed his own deep belief that "truth" depends on how one views the world:

> The miracle of . . . Illusion.
> The swans are making
> A snow white chain,
> Crossing the blue of the sky,
> But the snow white chain
> Is as black as rain
> When across the snow white moon they fly.
> How can we be certain
> How well we can know
> That which is true or untrue
> When a swan in flight
> Can be black or white,
> Depending on the point of view
>   A hundred million miracles
>   Are happening ev'ry day
> Before you disagree with me
> Be sure you're sure of what you see!
>   A hundred million miracles
>   Are happening ev'ry day!

Oscar thought that he was judged "sentimental" by some because he chose the brighter point of view rather than the currently fashionable "wasteland" viewpoint. In his opinion, there was no more validity to the belief that life was one great snake pit than to the idea that it was all one huge sunlit meadow, and the wide prevalence of the former viewpoint disturbed him. He was "enraged" when a despairing character in Tennessee Williams' *Sweet Bird of Youth* stepped to the footlights and asked the audience to identify with him because there was some of him in all of us. "There was nothing of me in that character. And it is both ridiculous and phony to make such an appeal to an audience. The accepted and fallacious assumption, in some circles, that this viewpoint is more true to life than decent hopes is nonsense."

Casting the show proved difficult. The production staff discovered early on that there was a scarcity of Oriental theatrical professionals. An advertisement in a New York Chinese newspaper brought only one response. When the cast was finally assembled, few of its members were experienced stage actors and even fewer were Chinese. Japanese film actress Miyoshi Umeki played the mail-order bride, Japanese-American nightclub singer Pat Suzuki the brash Linda Low, and Japanese-American Jack Suzuki (who changed his name to Soo) the part of a nightclub M.C. A Hawaiian, Ed Kenney, was signed for one male lead, and non-Oriental Larry Storch, a nightclub comic, for another. Juanita Hall was the only seasoned stage actress in the cast; veteran movie actor Keye Luke was signed to play the patriarch.

Just after auditions began, both Oscar and Dick were hospitalized for several weeks. Dick's emotional problem—the depression that manifested itself in increasing moodiness, withdrawal and drinking—finally reached such serious proportions that in June he sought treatment at the Payne Whitney Clinic at New York Hospital, where he stayed for twelve weeks. On July 15 Oscar entered Doctors Hospital for an operation to remove his gall bladder. During the month-long stay, he also had a prostatectomy.

On the morning of August 9, while Oscar was still in the hospital recovering from his two operations, Reggie was discovered dead of a heart attack by friends who were part of Reggie's "separate world," people who did not know much about his family or his work. Eventually Dick Rodgers was notified and he telephoned Dorothy at the hospital, where she was writing thank-you notes for the many flowers that Oscar had received. "Is Oscar asleep?" he asked.

"No."

"Then don't say anything more, but go out and pick up the phone in the hall. I've got something to tell you."

When Dorothy returned to the room Oscar, looking straight at her, said, "That was about Reggie."

"Yes," she said. "He's very, very ill."

"He's dead, isn't he?"

"Yes, Ockie."

Oscar turned away for a few moments, and then said, "Would you mind leaving the room for a while?"

About three-quarters of an hour later a nurse told Dorothy, "Mr. Hammerstein wants you to come back."

He was calm when she walked in, his tears over. He had handled the death of his only brother as he had handled that of his mother so many years before—privately. As close to Reggie as he had been to anyone in the world, he had protected and supported him for most of the sixty-one years of his life.

Billy joined Jimmy at the apartment and they attended to all the details of the death and cremation. They waited until Oscar was fully recovered to present him with the problem of what to do with the ashes. Finally Dorothy provided a solution that Oscar liked. She put Reggie's ashes under one of the white rose bushes that lined the much traveled path between the terrace of the house and the swimming pool. "Don't tell me which one," instructed Oscar. "And don't tell the children—they'll be horrified." In fact they were not. Billy found it touching to walk up the path and know that Reggie was under one of those roses.

When *Flower Drum Song* rehearsals began in September, Oscar was recuperating at home. Jimmy came to tell him that he'd better get down to the theater as soon as he safely could because he could see that the show was in trouble. Gene Kelly, who had never before directed a Broadway musical, seemed confused and unconfident. At ten one night, he candidly confessed to the cast that "things were a hodge-podge" the last few days and that he knew it was difficult. With a small smile at the cast sagging in chairs, he said, "Think of the fun we're having." Joe and Jimmy were doing most of the blocking; Carol Haney, the work with the dancers. When Oscar returned to the theater, he was writing script changes at the back of the house, changing lyrics onstage, and attending to some technical details. Jimmy remembers that Oscar stayed cool, usually grinning like a Cheshire cat, but that he was worried about the play. One morning he said to Jimmy, "I had a dream last night that I knew where to fix the entire show and I really thought I had it. I woke up this morning and realized that I had it except for one minor detail. The scene that I was going to cut is a lousy one, but it occurred to me over breakfast that it's the scene where the boy meets the girl."

The Boston reviews made it evident that fixing was needed. The plot dragged, the production was faulty, and the "extraordinary" performances of Miyoshi Umeki and Pat Suzuki were offset by a few poor ones, some so bad as to be "jarringly off-key." The script was rewritten to make the parts played by Umeki and Suzuki larger and to diminish those of the weak performers. Larry Storch was a good nightclub comedian, but he had gotten off on the wrong track in his role and Gene Kelly seemed unable to get him back on the right one. They had been thinking of firing Storch, and he himself was suffering, but almost a week went by without discussion of a possible replacement. Tough as R & H were in many ways, they always tried to avoid firing actors, preferring rewrites to correct difficulties, but finally they replaced Storch with Larry Blyden.

Flower Drum Song opened at the St. James on December 1, 1958, with over a million dollars' advance. First-nighters greeted the show affectionately and reviewers were positive. Brooks Atkinson reported, "Since [R & H] are the masters of the medium, it is customary to discuss them in more legendary language. But this is an occasion when their good feeling for the human race, their warmth and their professionalism are the factors that make something pleasant out of something that does not have the distinction of their great works."

Somewhere between Boston and New York, R & H had pulled off the hundred million miracles, of cutting and polishing, that turned a weak, dragging show into a hit that earned a profit of close to a half-million dollars with its 75-week run, a national tour and even a motion picture version.

About a month after the Broadway opening night, Oscar remarked to Jimmy, "I've had some unlucky flops in my life. I've had some plays that deserved to run better than they did. And then I've had some well deserved hits. But this is the first lucky hit I've ever had."

Eleven

The Shadows Fall

Oscar told Dorothy, his children and friends that he was seriously thinking of taking time off from writing and producing shows to work independently on lyrics and other writing. He had already promised to write the lyrics for *The Sound of Music* when *Flower Drum Song* was finished, but his family had the impression that he was deriving less and less pleasure from his work on such shows and from his collaboration with Dick.

In the last year of his life, Oscar said to Steve Sondheim one day, "What do you think of Dick?" Steve wondered why Oscar had asked. "Because I don't know him at all. We've worked together all these years and I don't really know him." He thought that because Steve was such a good friend of Mary Rodgers', he might have a viewpoint that would offer some kind of insight. "Dick's life is the office or the box office or the theater," Oscar said. "I just don't understand."

Fifteen years after Oscar's death Dick said, "I was very fond of him—very fond of him—and I never did find out whether he liked me or not. To this day I don't know." Both felt it was the other who was hidden, unknowable. Oscar thought that Dick's life was curiously impersonal and Dick thought that Oscar was "not very communicative." They never confided in each other, seldom talked of personal matters. One of the incidents that Dick recalls with hurt is that he found out about a trip to Jamaica that Oscar and Dorothy were making in two weeks only by overhearing a conversation in the office. Even though the Hammersteins later invited the Rodgerses to visit them in Jamaica, Dick was bothered that Oscar had not told him before he told others. There were no major disagreements between them, but there was also no conduit for expressing minor irritations. "I let it brush over, but it bothered me," said Dick of the Jamaica incident. "It was all very placid. For the most part, the shows were successful, so we didn't fight about them." Oscar, too, brushed over the petty things that annoyed him and only mentioned them to Dorothy in the very last years of the R & H partnership.

For eighteen years they kept the lid on a potential powder keg of resentment, jealousy and conflict by maintaining emotional arm's length. However, a few months before he died, Oscar said to Steve, "If anything happened to me, Dick would feel very lost and I'd like you to consider doing a show with him." When Dick approached him to be his collaborator after Oscar's death, Steve suspected that Oscar had "put the bug in his ear" and felt sure that he had cared a great deal about Dick's future.

After the *Flower Drum Song* opening, R & H began to write the score they had promised for *The Sound of Music*. Three years earlier, director Vincent Donahue was shown a German film based on the true story of the Trapp family. Paramount was considering remaking the film with Audrey Hepburn, but Donahue had his eye on it as a perfect property for Mary Martin. Mary and Dick Halliday agreed, and when Paramount dropped its option, they began to secure the rights from the German producers and permission from the Trapp family. Since the baroness and her children were scattered around the globe, it took Halliday and his partner, Leland Hayward, many months and many miles of air travel to complete the process.

Russel "Buck" Crouse, an old Hammerstein friend and neighbor, and his partner, Howard Lindsay, with whom he had written *Life with Father*, *State of the Union* and *Call Me Madam*, were signed to write the book. The producers planned to use the authentic Trapp family music—religious and folk songs—but asked Oscar and Dick to supply a few new songs.

"Compete with Mozart and Brahms? Not on your life," was their reply. They told the producers that they thought mixing old and new songs would be a mistake. Asked to write a complete new score, they said they couldn't do it until *Flower Drum Song* was finished. Halliday and Hayward said they would wait, and agreed to co-produce with R & H.

In early March 1959 Oscar and Dick laid out the placement of the songs and dummy titles, using a 60-page treatment that Lindsay and Crouse had prepared two years before. It was now R & H's turn to wait, for the other team had turned to a Broadway play in the interim.

Oscar decided to spend a month at the Jamaica home that he and Dorothy had bought in the beautiful community of Round Hill, near Montego Bay, which they had discovered while scouting suitable locations for *South Pacific*. Although he usually found it difficult to work in the tropics, Oscar wrote the lyrics for the title song, "The Sound of Music," and began those for "Climb Every Mountain" while he was in Jamaica.

Relieved not to have to write the book, Oscar told Jimmy that he would have given up book writing years before if he had been able to find people good enough to do it, as Lindsay and Crouse were. Lyric writing was different for him; he told a television interviewer that he still felt that he was learning the craft. He also said it was the only thing he was "temperamental" about.

The painstaking effort he put into writing lyrics is revealed in the complete files that he kept of his worksheets for *The Sound of Music*'s score, the numbered and dated pages showing how each song developed. The title song began with a description of Mary Martin sitting in a tree "looking out dreamily." Then the lines: "The hillside is sweet/Today the air is sweet with summer music/And my heart wants to sing/Every song it hears . . ." "Summer music" became "sound of summer" and finally "sound of music." In this song, the multitude of variations is in the same meter that he began with; in others, he arrived at the meter much later in the process.

Oscar's final, typed version of *The Sound of Music* was not the one sung onstage. The number of changes made in lyrics to accommodate the music varied from song to song; some remained exactly the same.

In this one, words, lines and entire verses were different. (Ironically, a line frequently used by detractors of his work, "Like a lark that is learning to pray," was not in the original lyric.) The last refrain of the song was considerably changed; Oscar's first version is on the left:

The hills give me strength	I go to the hills
When my heart is lonely,	When my heart is lonely,
And lost in the fog	I know I will hear
Of a thousand fears.	What I've heard before.
The hills fill my heart	My heart will be blessed
With the sound of music	With the sound of music
And my heart wants to sing . . .	And I'll sing once more.
Every song it hears.	

According to the song layout, the third was to be a sad song, followed by a happy song, to be sung by Maria and the Abbess. The happy song turned out to be "My Favorite Things." Although it was never used, Oscar also worked on the sad song:

> The shadows fall
> on the cold blue snow
> The naked birch
> In the wind
> is weaving, weaving . . .
> Brief are the summers that swiftly go
> But winters are long
> for grieving, grieving

In May, Lindsay and Crouse began the book. In the past, when Oscar wrote the entire libretto, he often found his lyric-writing self "stealing" a scene from his book-writing self because he knew that frequently a point could be expressed much more clearly and economically in a lyric than in dialogue. His new collaborators proved amenable to such pilferage. Sometimes Oscar was offered the gift outright. Lindsay and Crouse were having difficulty with the scene where Maria and the Captain finally get together; they found the dialogue labored and were glad to have the lyrics for "An Ordinary Couple" to pull the scene together.

A song that Oscar did "steal" was "How Do You Solve a Problem Like Maria?" Lindsay and Crouse had written a scene where the Sisters were discussing Maria, but agreed with him that her contradictory character and her life at the convent could be described effectively and economically in a song. He began it on May 20 and spent days writing lists of adjectives, such as "unpredictable, inconsiderate, generous, careless" and so on. Not until May 25 did he write a full line: "What are we going to do about Maria?" He went back to more lists of words: "Paradoxical, confounding, inconsistent, erratic, skittish, ambiguous, capricious, nebulous . . ." Oscar was fond of saying that he didn't have a big vocabulary, and that it was just as well because if he knew a lot of unusual words he'd want to show off. "I'd want to use them and confound my friends." He said that he was more at home with characters who didn't have a big vocabulary and that he was "frightened at the thought of the number of words that I am not familiar with." He claimed that he tried to improve his vocabulary but didn't seem to make much headway. It is true that he never used particularly abstruse words, even in speeches or letters, but his protestations were at least in some measure part of the "homespun" image that he liked to project. This is not to say that he did not enjoy the simple things of life; in fact, his love for simplicity was a very real part of his nature. He admitted that the writer he most admired was Winston Churchill, who, he said, achieved clarity not through "unusual or fancy words" but by "the right shading of a word for what he wants to say." The care with which Oscar chose and substituted words reveals his own sensitivity to them.

On May 29 he began to list nouns—"She is . . . a child, a lamb, a vixen, an angel, a girl," etc.—with scattered longer sentences. The next day he wrote lists of rhymes in the margin, and the song's form began to evolve. Two days later Oscar hit upon his final version of the key line: "How do you solve a problem like Maria?" He went back to lists of words, with "gamin, hoodlum, bother, calamity, disaster, imp, pest, shrew, brat . . . ," but on the same day the basic pattern of the song's refrain was set:

> How do you solve a problem like Maria?
> How do you catch a cloud and pin it down?
> So many different words describe Maria—
> > She's a shrew
> > > She's a child
> > > > She's a clown . . .

Oscar repeated the form over and over, on June 2 and 3, trying different words and phrases. The familiar words of the final version emerged in the line "Maria is a flibbertigibbet, a will-o-the-wisp, a clown." On June 5 he wrote the question that ends the lyric. "How do you hold a moonbeam in your hand?"

On June 6, seventeen days after he began work on the lyric, he finished it. The only changes made when the music was written were a repetition of the first verse later in the song and revision of four lines.

Oscar has never been regarded as a clever or witty lyricist, and compared with Larry Hart and others he was not. Still, while it is neither sophisticated nor witty, "Do-Re-Mi" is a clever song, using the simple phonics of the scale to create a charming music lesson for Maria and the Trapp children.

"My Favorite Things" is clever in a different way. Although the things make up a simple list, they evoke the flavor of a time and place as well as the homey warmth and security of remembered childhood. Here is the familiar Hammerstein message that joy and comfort can be derived from small, ordinary things:

> Raindrops on roses and whiskers on kittens,
> Bright copper kettles and warm woolen mittens,
> Brown paper packages tied up with strings—
> These are a few of my favorite things.
>
> Cream colored ponies and crisp apple strudels,
> Doorbells and sleigh bells and schnitzel with noodles,
> Wild geese that fly with the moon on their wings—
> These are a few of my favorite things.
>
> Girls in white dresses with blue satin sashes,
> Snowflakes that stay on my nose and eyelashes,
> Silver-white winters that melt into springs—
> These are a few of my favorite things.
>
> When the dog bites,
> When the bee stings,
> When I'm feeling sad,
> I simply remember my favorite things
> And then I don't feel so bad!

In New York some weeks later Dorothy Stickney Lindsay and Anna Crouse invited the Rodgerses and the Hammersteins to celebrate the twenty-fifth anniversary of their husbands' first show together, *Anything Goes*. After dinner, Oscar got up and proposed a toast to Anna Crouse. As the others sat puzzled, he raised his glass and said, "To Anna, because she has the strength of character to be the only woman here not named Dorothy."

In the summer, the production took shape; Oliver Smith designed sets; Mainbocher and Lucinda Ballard, the costumes. Director Vincent Donahue worked with R & H's casting director, Edward Blum. As Mary prepared for her role she consulted the real Maria von Trapp, who owned and operated a music school and ski resort in Stowe, Vermont. The baroness recalls that she met so many unfamiliar people that she has no clear mental image of most of those connected with the show—with the exception of Oscar. She barely knew him, but the impression he made on her was a deep one. She writes, "I can only tell you what is in my heart and not in my head. I am Catholic and I would say that he was a living saint. That means that a person is as close to perfection as one can get and still be alive. It just emanated from him and I'm sure he didn't know it himself."

Another of Mary's advisers was Sister Gregory, the head of the Drama Department at Rosary College in River Forest, Illinois, with whom she had struck up a correspondence and then a lasting friendship. Mary and Dick Halliday asked her for technical advice and insights into convent life, and though she never officially joined the production staff, her letters and memos had a strong influence on the show. Oscar's files contain copies of many of her letters to Mary and to him. In one, written the year before production, describing the process by which young women chose a religious life, she said that their decisions, like Maria's, simply pinpointed the search for a purpose in life that every human being must make. Everyone, she said, must find answers to the question: "What does God want me to do with my life? How does He wish me to spend my love?"

As he began the song tentatively titled "Face Life," Oscar wrote these two questions on one of his pages. On another, he scribbled, "You can't hide here. Don't think that these walls shut out problems . . . You have to face life wherever you are. You have to look for life, for the life you were meant to lead. Until you find it you are not living." He also wrote notes under "Face Life" about climbing a hill, getting to the top, "which doesn't bring you much closer to the moon, but closer to the next hill, which you must also climb." Under these notes he wrote, "Don't let it be too obviously a 'philosophical number.' "

Although the idea of climbing a hill had been in his mind from the beginning, in planning the song that would become "Climb Ev'ry

Mountain," his first work sheets, entitled "Face Life," show the following, which was probably meant to be the verse:

> A song is no song
> Till you sing it
> A bell is no bell
> Till you ring it
> And love in your heart
> Isn't put there to stay
> Love isn't love
> Till you give it away.

As the song developed and was set to music in August the verse was abandoned. This decision, as well as Dick's music, helped to give a hymnlike simplicity to the two spare stanzas, made up of simple, short phrases and resonant vowel sounds.

After receiving a manuscript copy of the song, Sister Gregory wrote to Mary and Dick Halliday: "It drove me to the Chapel (Relax, chums, I'm sure it will not affect your audiences in the same way). It made me acutely aware of how tremendously fortunate are those who find a dream that will absorb all their love and, finding it, embrace it to the end . . ." After saying how much she liked the music, she went on, "However, it was the lyrics that sent me to the Chapel. Mr. Hammerstein's lyrics seem perfectly yet effortlessly to express what we ordinary souls feel but cannot communicate."

Rehearsals began the last week in August. On September 16 Oscar went for his annual checkup by his doctor, Ben Kean, who had taken over Harold Hyman's practice upon his retirement. As they sat late in the afternoon in his office Kean told Oscar that he was fine and asked if there was anything else he wanted to discuss.

"No," Oscar said as he got up and went toward the door. Then, just before he closed it, he stuck his head in for a moment. "Oh, yes. You know I've been awakening in the middle of the night hungry. I take a glass of milk and then it's fine."

After Oscar left, Kean suddenly said to himself, That's not much of a complaint but it's the only one he ever made. What the hell, for a hundred dollars we should be sure.

He ran out on Park Avenue and caught up with Oscar near the corner. He told him to come back the next day for a test to determine if he had an ulcer. Oscar walked home and entered the house muttering, "God damn it, I have an ulcer. That son-of-a-bitch has done it to me."

The X-rays and tests showed that it was not an ulcer but cancer of the stomach. Kean immediately scheduled surgery and told Oscar to report to New York Hospital on the nineteenth.

When Mary Martin walked up to the stage door of the Lunt-Fontanne on the eighteenth, Oscar was standing there. "Do you have a few minutes?" he asked.

"Always, darling," she replied.

"Well, I wrote a little couplet and I really don't know where it's going to go in the show because I haven't thought past this, but I'd like you to have it." He put a small piece of paper in her hand, saying, "Don't look at it now. Look at it later."

Mary watched him walk slowly down West 46th Street and thought how massive he looked, what a mountain of a man he was. She went into her dressing room and a few minutes later Dick came in. He told her that Oscar had cancer, but that they didn't know how bad it was. He pointed to himself as a living example that one could have cancer and survive. "Don't let this upset you. We are going to work as long as we can."

He left, and Mary opened the little piece of paper that she still had in her hand. It said: "A bell is no bell till you ring it/A song is no song till you sing it/And love in your heart wasn't put there to stay/Love isn't love till you give it away." Mary eventually sang the lines as the verse for her reprise of "Sixteen Going on Seventeen." The lines meant so much to her that she felt they were a legacy from Oscar, who seemed to her the "epitome of love for his fellow man and to live by love—and he did it." When she did *Hello, Dolly!* years later, Mary sang the couplet at the end of each performance, learning it in several languages, including Japanese.

While Dr. Frank Glenn, chief surgeon at New York Hospital and head of Cornell University's Medical College, operated on Oscar, the five children and Dorothy sat in the waiting room. Dorothy was wearing a bright red coat, as if to make any dark news impossible. Late in the day, Harold Hyman and Dr. Glenn came into the waiting room and, each taking an arm, walked her to the end of the corridor. There, as she stood under the bright lights the children saw her erect body suddenly slump.

The carcinoma was Grade IV; they had removed three-quarters of his stomach, but Oscar would be dead in six months to a year. They all sat numbly, Susan and Alice clutching each other's hands as they heard the doctor's report. Later they discussed it and voted not to tell

Oscar. They also agreed to meet with a cancer expert to find out more about chemotherapy, then in its early stages of development. After seeing the expert, it was decided that the treatment would be fruitless.

It was Ben Kean's opinion that Oscar knew perfectly well that he would die soon, though the understanding between them was a tacit one. Several days after the operation he asked Dorothy, "Why haven't they told me what they did?"

"They just cut it all out," she replied, feeling keenly how unlike their usual relationship it was for her to lie to him.

On another occasion, as Dorothy sat in the room with him, Oscar began talking about his life, how he wouldn't have changed one thing in it, about their life together. She felt it was the most beautiful night she had had since the day she met Oscar—more beautiful even than falling in love with him. When she left the hospital that night, wanting to tell somebody, she stopped in at a friend's, unaware that the children, waiting for her at home, were worried about her.

Oscar remained in the hospital until October 4 and at home for another ten days; he recovered rapidly from the operation itself. He read the reviews from the New Haven tryouts, all of them predicting a smash hit, some saying that R & H had surpassed themselves, but did not see the production until its Boston opening on the fourteenth. It was the first show that he had written in which he didn't see the rough spots and technical mishaps as it took shape. He had missed the baby's childhood, and its emergence full-grown came as a shock to him. He cried as he watched the performance from an aisle seat next to Dorothy. When the final curtain came down, he went backstage to talk to the company onstage. Now it was Dorothy's turn to cry. She stood in tears behind some scenery as she watched him read his notes to the cast, make comments to each, watched him go back to work on the show that was the forty-fourth he had written and that she knew would be his last.

The production was going so well that not many changes were necessary in Boston. Among the few were script changes to emphasize the family's grief over leaving their native land to live in exile.

Oscar worked on a new song from the fifteenth of October through the twenty-first, beginning with a description of edelweiss, the lovely blossoming plant that grows in the Alps. He made no lists of words and rhymes for it, but started to jot down phrases about the sentiments he wanted to express. At the bottom of a page he wrote the name of the flower twice, which seemed to suggest the song's pattern to him. The earliest version of "Edelweiss" contains two lines that poignantly reflect what must have been much on his mind: "Look for your lover and hold him tight/While your health you're keeping."

These were the last lyrics that Oscar ever wrote, his 1,589th. Discarding most of the images and phrases that had occurred to him, he finally chose simply to describe the flower as it appeared to the singer. The feeling of patriotism that he wanted to express came through the words and the music so powerfully, and the song had such an authentic air, that from the time it was first introduced, many people assumed that it was really the Austrian national song, just as they had assumed that "Ol' Man River," from *Show Boat,* was an old work song and " 'Twas Not So Long Ago," from *Sweet Adeline,* a German folk song.

Opening in New York on November 16, with a record-breaking advance, *The Sound of Music* was virtually certain to recoup its $400,000 investment within thirty weeks. However, critical reaction to an R & H show was never as certain as public reaction, and this was no exception. Whitney Bolton noted in his review in the *Morning Telegraph,* "With better than two million dollars sacked up in the till, it couldn't matter less what a critic might think." No matter what the financial picture was, it always mattered to Oscar what the critics thought. Even those who had harsh words for the "hackneyed sentimentality and syrupy sweetness" of the book praised the score. It was said that R & H were in "top form," and that the score represented the "full ripening of these two extraordinary talents." By 1959, critics were sensitive to the work of a lyricist: Oscar received not only due credit but some of the highest praise that he had ever received from the members of the press. Walter Kerr called the lyrics those of a skilled craftsman; Richard Watts described them as "particularly rich in freshness and imagination . . . modest and unhackneyed." Hobe Morrison wrote, "As always, Hammerstein's lyrics have the deceptive simplicity, the seeming effortlessness and naturalness of painstaking artistry. The lyricist seems increasingly to be writing about ordinary things, with an eloquence that lends universality and throat-catching impact."

In December Oscar and Dorothy left for a month's vacation in Jamaica, where they were joined by the children for Christmas. Ben Kean had reported no change and Oscar was feeling well. As usual, he worked during the day in their cottage. He prepared a new treatment of *State Fair* for a remake of that film. A much larger project,

however, was a thorough revision of *Allegro* for a television presentation. Elliot Norton had become a good friend, despite Oscar's mixed
feelings about drama critics, and he wrote that he was glad to hear
about the *Allegro* plans. "Perhaps at this time it will be more ac-
ceptable. I have often thought about the play, and came to the con-
clusion long since that perhaps your thinking was ahead of its time."

Oscar was writing friends that he was completely fit and recovered from his operation, but one day at Round Hill, while floating in
the water as he loved to do, Oscar said to his stepson, Henry, "I've
decided to cut you into my will." He did not have to, since the understanding and agreement in Dorothy's divorce from Henry Jacobson
had been that Henry would be taken care of by his father and Susan
by Oscar. Henry, now thirty and a successful advertising executive,
said, "Fine," and the conversation was dropped.

Back in New York, Oscar went over his will but did not discuss the
subject with anyone. He planned appearances at benefits, gave a dinner for New Jersey's Governor Robert Meyner, corresponded with
friends and associates and prepared for a trip to England. He and
Dorothy left with the Rodgerses on March 7 for a five-week trip to
England, where Oscar and Dick would supervise the West End
production of *Flower Drum Song*. Dorothy often met friends in the
lobby of Claridge's, where they were staying, so that Oscar could rest
in their suite, which he did with increasing frequency.

X-rays taken by Ben Kean soon after they returned showed no
change, but he gave Oscar B-12 and iron shots to help combat the
tiredness. There were small signs that he did not feel as well as he
looked. The first weekend back at Highland Farm he tried to play
tennis with Jimmy. Oscar no longer tried to beat his son, who was by
this time of almost professional caliber in the game. Knowing his father was dying, Jimmy felt inhibited in his playing. He tried to hit
the ball with less power than usual, and then he thought, No, we
have to play. We've always communicated that way. He hit one or two
devastating shots to show him that he could. At the end of one set
of singles, Oscar said, "Gosh, I've never been so tired in my life. I
think I'm too old for tennis." He never played again. By the next
week they were all playing croquet.

In letters to friends, Oscar reported that he felt fine and that he
rather liked being in a position where he was not planning a show. He
told Walter Knapp in April, "I like getting up in the morning with no
anxiety whatever and no songs to write," and said he was kept pretty

busy anyway with the old things and with all the committees he was on.

In May they drove to Williamsburg, Virginia, with the Hymans, but soon after, Dorothy noticed that Oscar no longer had his pro- verbially hearty appetite. They stopped meeting at Dinty Moore's on Thursdays for the tripe and onions special that he had always loved. Never much of a drinker, he stopped having even his occasional glass of wine with dinner.

As his physical deterioration became more visible, the reality of the information that they had accepted months before as an abstrac- tion became more and more painful for the family. And, of course, the deception was difficult. They had all agreed that not telling Oscar the surgeon's prognosis was the right thing to do, but now Jimmy found himself disturbed, affronted by the games they were playing with a man of his father's stature. Although the conventional wisdom of the time was against him, he realized that it didn't make sense to respect the way a man ran his life and then not allow him to run his own death.

During the spring and early summer Oscar seemed content to go along with his daily life as if everything was fine. Finally in June he brought it out in the open when he told Dorothy that he had spoken to the doctor and knew that he hadn't long to live.

On July 7 Ben Kean informed him that X-rays showed a recur- rence of the carcinoma and suggested a course of chemotherapy to retard the advancement of the cancer. The following day Oscar came back to his office and said, "Ben, I've considered very carefully your recommendation. In this showdown I must really decide whether to die possibly a little later in the hospital, or on Dorothy's pillow." He told Ben that he had chosen the latter, and added, "I'm really lucky and never knew how much until now."

Later that same week Oscar sat in his study at the farm and jotted notes for an autobiography. These were the last words he would write:

> Today is July 12, 1960: my birthday. I am sixty-five. This is the accepted age of retirement. I do not want to retire, am in no mood to retire.
>
> This is considered a good time to come to a stop. Perhaps it is, but not for me . . .
>
> I make no room to die with my boots on. Some day I may leave the theatre. But I couldn't walk out suddenly. I would have to linger a while and take a few last looks. I would have to blow a

few fond kisses as I edged towards the stage door. I would have to look around and sigh, and remember a few things, a few people —No, many things, many people.

Is this a book about myself? What does a man know about himself? He has opinions. This is a book rather about the world and my life and all as I see it, as I have seen it during the first 65 years. It is a book not about what I know. It is a book about what I think. If what I think reveals to the reader myself—then it is indirectly a book about myself. But many readers will draw different conclusions from what I've done and from what I think about what I've done and about what other people have done . . .

Life as seen through the eyes of any man is life seen through eyes that are only sometimes clear. All eyes are blurred—no cloud darkened . . .

Oscar wrote about his earlier attempts to send autobiographical letters to his son, Billy, and how he could not seem to get out of his childhood. He said that he was going to write backwards this time. He wanted to tell what is seen by the eyes of a grown man. He wrote an outline for the book, starting from the present. On one page he scribbled in pencil: "I am not by nature a non-conformist. Big talk, yes— But in my behavior have always stayed pretty well in line—(not a rebellious boy)."

He wrote no more on this project, but told Dorothy and the rest of the family, "I hope none of my children ever try to write my biography because they'll get it all wrong." He quoted one of his favorite poets, Robert Burns, to whom he had been compared by some writers: "Oh wad some power the giftie gie us/To see oursels as others see us!"

While he did not wish to have the way his children saw him recorded as his biography, his relationship with them, so contradictory and conflicted in earlier years, was positive and peaceful in later years. After being named Father of the Year in 1959, he wrote some comments in a tone of wry acceptance. Noting that the award may be a "big surprise" to his children, he said that one never really knew if he was a good father and that he didn't know any more about the subject than could fill one page. The most direct method for becoming a good father, he thought, was to try to be a good man. Children never listened much to advice, but they watched their fathers live and used them as a gauge to measure the values of life. While advising against advice-giving, he recommended being there to give help should children want it. A wise father, he concluded, didn't ask for too much reward for bringing up children, just a hope that "they like you and are perhaps a little bit proud of you. If they are not, don't blame them. It's probably your fault."

For all the harsh teasing and competitiveness that characterized his treatment of them in their early years, Oscar's children were very proud of him. In the ordeal of facing his death and saying good-bye to him, they realized how much they loved him, if they had not fully realized it before. They have reason to be his severest critics, having experienced unkindness and anger that the outside world never saw. Yet, in an age when it is fashionable to hate one's parents, none of the Hammerstein children gives any indication of doing so.

On his birthday the family and such honorary family members as Steve gathered at the farm for a celebration. Oscar gave them presents —photographs of him by Philippe Halsman which were piled on the piano in the living room. Steve chose one and then, on impulse, asked Oscar to sign it for him. Oscar looked at him oddly because it seemed like asking one's father to sign something. Dinner was announced and everyone left to file into the dining room. Oscar sat thinking for a few minutes and then, with a mischievous grin, scribbled something in the corner and went in to join the others. Steve looked at the in- scription, "For Steve, my friend and teacher. Ockie." His memory is that he was so on the verge of cracking, of giving way to the tears that welled up, that he didn't make it through dinner that night.

Oscar continued to commute between Doylestown and New York, attending committee meetings, taking care of business decisions. In his last letter to Josh Logan on July 28 he talked about his work on *State Fair* and responded to his friend's suggestion that they do another show together with, "I agree with you that it would be won- derful for us all to get together on something."

But he began to make his farewells. One by one he asked each of the children to sit and talk with him while he still had his full capacities and wasn't in pain. Jimmy was by now twenty-nine, had co-produced *Blue Denim* the year before and was turning to full-time directing. When his son burst into tears, Oscar yelled, "God damn it! I'm the one who's dying, not you." Although Jimmy sensed that it was difficult for his father to talk of it, he could see, too, that he had no foolish romantic notions of fighting death. As they talked Oscar said, "I've had a very happy childhood. I've had a good time as a young man. And I've had a terrific middle age. The only thing that

I'm disappointed in is that I was looking forward to having a really good old age, too."

Susan never realized until then not only how much he meant in her life but how immortal he had always seemed to her. She couldn't believed that he was so ill, and was disturbed by his resignation. When he called her in for their talk, he said, "I know I'm going to die. I don't want to die but I know I'm going to. But I've been a very lucky man. I've had the work that I wanted to do. I've been married to the woman that I love and I've had a good life. I've had everything. I'd like it to last longer, but since it isn't I'm not dissatisfied." Susan remembers that he said it with great humor, not in a stiff-upper-lip way but so openly and positively that she couldn't cry just then. He told her, "Don't let your mother do anything impulsive."

Oscar talked with Dorothy about her future, helped her plan her life. He told her he thought that she should sell the farm and take frequent trips to Australia. "When I've gone, don't go to pieces," he told her, "because it would be like having everything in the world and crying for more. To whine and cry would be pure greediness." When told by Ben Kean that in his twenty-five years of medicine, he had never seen anyone handle so difficult a situation as well as she, Dorothy said, "It was not difficult really to behave well. Oscar and I had a wonderful thirty-one years together with very few sour notes and so there are no regrets for what might have been. He left us all with emotional strength and balance."

Oscar asked Dick to meet him at the Oak Room of the Plaza for lunch. He told him matter-of-factly that he knew he would die soon, that he had decided against treatments that would leave him in discomfort but could not cure him. He discussed Dick's future and suggested that he find a younger man to work with. "We discussed many things that day, two somber, middle-aged men sitting in a crowded restaurant talking unemotionally of the imminent death of one and the need for the other to keep going," Dick recalls. A man seated a few tables away came over to ask them to sign his menu. The stranger told them that he couldn't imagine why they looked so sad—they were so successful they couldn't have a worry in the world.

Oscar asked Steve to have lunch with him at the Lotus Club one day, Hy Kraft at the Brussels on another. Kraft remembered that the conversation was casual, but when Oscar got out of the car at 63rd Street, they kissed and said good-bye.

Soon Oscar went to the farm to stay. Always a man with little tolerance for illness, furious when he had a simple cold, in his terminal condition he never complained, demanded or whined. But he did say to his family that he didn't want to disintegrate before their eyes into a horrible vegetable—"I want to go out with dignity."

Writing of his mother's death, Oscar said his attitude toward death had been crystallized then. "I resisted as an enemy the grief that comes after death rather than giving way to it. I get stubborn about it and say this is not going to lick me, because it didn't then." He was still stubbornly determined that death should not rob him of his reason, his dignity, his control over his own life. One day, sitting on the porch with Harold Hyman, he said, "You know, I've had a good life and I want you to promise me a good death."

In August Oscar became so thin that his hands on the sheet covers reminded Susan of the gray, elongated hands in a painting by El Greco. He sipped essence of sarsaparilla and ate almost nothing. He now spent his time in bed. Bounding up the stairs one day, Henry said, "How's it going, Oc?"

"I guess it's going the way it's supposed to," he replied.

Each day he asked Dorothy what time Harold was expected. His old friend, though retired, was still attending Oscar unofficially and would come every day. When he arrived, Oscar would ask Dorothy to leave the room.

He was heavily sedated against the increasing pain when his children gathered at the farm on the weekend of August 20. After watching a football game on television, he said to Jimmy, "There's a game that people are playing now as to who would you rather be than yourself if you had your life to live over. I'm actually dying so I should play the game better than anybody. Yet I can't figure out whether I'd rather be Albert Einstein or Babe Ruth." He explained, "Einstein's mind and feeling for people, his sense of music, makes me feel he's the most sensitive and best man of this country. But as soon as I think of that—just the feel and hearing the ball hit the bat and see it go over the fence— So I don't know."

On Monday night, August 22, Dorothy stayed with Oscar until just before midnight. When Harold Hyman told her to leave the room, she went into the study to join Susan and Billy.

In the bedroom Oscar was murmuring the names of baseball players: "Ruth, Gehrig, Rizzuto . . ."

Harold Hyman came in ten minutes later and told them Oscar was dead. They stared at each other. Then Dorothy and Susan went to the guest room on the third floor. Dorothy turned out the light and lay very quietly so as not to disturb her daughter. In a few minutes Susan got up and went downstairs.

A little while later Dorothy saw the room swept by headlights coming up the long drive. She walked to the window, from which she saw a long car pull up in front of the door and men go into the house. She pulled down the shade. In the dark room she felt Oscar put his arms around her in the way he had so often done in order to comfort her and say, "Everything is all right."

Selected Bibliography

Abbott, George, *Mister Abbott*, Random House.

Aldrich, Richard Stoddard, *Gertrude Lawrence as Mrs. A.*, Greystone.

Arnold, Elliott, *Deep In My Heart* (biography of Sigmund Romberg), Regnery.

Atkinson, Brooks, *Broadway*, Macmillan.

Berkman, Ted, *The Lady and the Law* (biography of Fanny Holtzmann), Little, Brown.

Blumenthal, George, *My Sixty Years in Show Business* (autobiography of general manager to Oscar I and Willie Hammerstein), Osberg.

de Mille, Agnes, *And Promenade Home*, Little, Brown.

———, *Dance to the Piper*, Little, Brown.

Ferber, Edna, *A Peculiar Treasure*, Doubleday.

Gilbert, Douglas, *American Vaudeville, Its Life and Times*.

Gordon, Max, *Max Gordon Presents*, Geis.

Green, Abel, and Joe Laurie, *Show Biz, from Vaude to Video*, Holt.

Green, Stanley, *The Rogers and Hammerstein Story*, Holt.

Hammerstein, Oscar II, *Lyrics*, Simon & Schuster.

———, *Jerome Kern Song Book*, Simon & Schuster.

————, *Rogers and Hart Song Book,* Simon & Schuster.

————, *Sigmund Romberg* (liner notes for records), RCA.

Harriman, Margaret Case, *Take Them Up Tenderly,* Knopf.

Kraft, Hy, *On My Way to the Theatre,* Macmillan.

Langner, Lawrence, *The Magic Curtain,* Dutton.

Logan, Joshua, *Josh,* Delacorte.

Marks, Edward A., *They All Sang,* Viking.

Martin, Mary, *My Heart Belongs To,* Morrow.

Maxwell, Gilbert, *Helen Morgan, Her Life and Legend,* Hawthorn.

Oppenheimer, George, *The View from the Sixties,* McKay.

Rodgers, Richard, *Musical Stages,* Random House.

Rogers, Will, *The Autobiography of Will Rogers,* Hougton Mifflin.

Sharaff, Irene, *Broadway and Hollywood,* Van Nostrand Reinhold.

Sheean, Vincent, *Oscar Hammerstein I: The Life and Exploits of an Impresario,* introduction by Oscar Hammerstein II, Simon & Schuster.

Smith, Cecil, *Musical Comedy in America,* Theatre Arts Books.

Stewart, Donald Ogden, *By a Stroke of Luck,* Paddington Press.

Stoddard, Dayton, *Lord Broadway, Variety's Sime,* Funk.

Taylor, Deems, *Some Enchanted Evenings* (biography of Rodgers and Hammerstein), Harper.

Van Vechten, Carl, *In the Garret,* Knopf.

Wilder, Alec, *American Popular Song,* Oxford.

Books and Plays Adapted to the Musical Stage and Screen
by Oscar Hammerstein II

Baum, Vicki, untitled work (*The Night Is Young*).

Boykin, Edward, untitled work (*Gentlemen Unafraid*).

Byrne, Donn, *Messer Marco Polo,* Appleton-Century (*Golden Bells*).

Castle, Irene, *My Memories of Vernon Castle,* Little, Brown (*The Story of Irene and Vernon Castle*).

Ferber, Edna, *Show Boat,* Doubleday.

Hopkins, Arthur, and George M. Waters, *Burlesque,* Samuel French, Inc. (*Swing High, Swing Low*).

Landon, Margaret, *Anna and the King of Siam,* Macmillan (*The King and I*).

Lee, C. Y. *The Flower Drum Song,* Farrar, Straus & Cudahy.

Mérimée, Prosper, *Carmen, Opéra-Comique* (Carmen Jones).

Michener, James, *Tales of the South Pacific,* Macmillan.

Misson, Robert, *An Autobiography,* T.N.P. (*New Moon*).

Molnár, Ferenc, adaptation by Benjamin Glazer, *Liliom,* Samuel French, Ltd. (*Carousel*).

Riggs, Lynn, *Green Grow the Lilacs,* Samuel French (*Oklahoma!*).

Steinbeck, John, *Sweet Thursday,* Viking (*Pipe Dream*).

Stong, Phil, *State Fair,* Grosset & Dunlap.

Index

Abbott, George, 309–10
"Abe Lincoln Had Just One Country," 157
Abraham Lincoln Brigade, 312
Abraham, Paul, 124
"A Cockeyed Optimist," 271–72, 319
Actors Equity Association, 42–43, 334–35
Adams, Edie, 333
Adams, Maude, 13
Adler, Buddy, 335–36
A Funny Thing Happened on the Way to the Forum, 242
"A Hundred Million Miracles," 339
A Kind Of Grandfather, 180
Akron Club, 31
Albert, Eddie, 284
Alcott, Chauncey, 13
"Alexander's Ragtime Band," 243

A Little Night Music, 242, 302n
"Allegheny Al," 148
Allegro, 93, 251–56, 261, 278–79, 309, 311 320
Allegro (TV version), 251, 256, 354
"Allegro," 252–53
"All 'r Nothing," 194n
"All in Fun," 164–65
All Quiet on the Western Front, 107
"All the Things You Are," 164, 171, 218, 307
"All Through the Day," 235
Allyson, June, 165n
"A Lovely Night," 333
Alter, Louis, 108–11
Alton, Robert, 309
Alvine, Glendon, 158
Always You, 45–46, 50
Americana, 85

American Jubilee, 172

American Optical Company, 314

American Theatre Wing War Service, 183

An American in Paris, 147, 292

Anderson, Marion, 284

Anderson, Maxwell, 94

Anderson, John, 138, 168, 175

Anderson Tapes, The, 65n

André Charlot's Revue of 1924, 77, 286

Andrews, Dana, 217

Andrews, Julie, 332

Anna and the King of Siam (see also *King and I, The*), 291

Annie Get Your Gun, 245–47, 251, 262

"Annie McGinnis Pavlova," 30

"An Ordinary Couple," 346

Anyone Can Whistle, 242

Anything Goes, 348

"Anything You Can Do," 246

"A Puzzlement," 294

Arden, Eve, 165

Arlen, Harold, 173n

Arliss, George, 18

Arms, Louise, 77

A Romance of Althone, 13

ASCAP (American Society of Composers, Authors and Publishers), 56, 68, 128, 172, 174, 204, 237, 247, 283, 304

A Shot in the Dark (London), 290n

Astaire, Fred, 62n, 147, 152

Atkinson, Brooks, 44, 88, 93, 101, 112, 160, 167, 175, 203, 256, 281, 303, 308, 342

"At the Casino," 60

Authors League, 211, 250, 283

Away, We Go! (see also *Oklahoma!*), 199

"A Wonderful Guy," 264–65, 278

Axelrod, Betty, 40, 98

Axelrod, Herman, 26, 28–31, 40, 98

Ayers, Lemuel, 194, 231, 329

Ayers, Lew, 215

Babes in Arms, 167, 195

Bagar, Robert, 208

Bainter, Fay, 217

"Bali Ha'i," 268

Ballard, Kaye, 333

Ballard, Lucinda, 349

Ball at the Savoy, 124, 209

Ballet Russe de Monte Carlo, 194

Ballyhoo, 108–11, 114

Barnes, Howard, 149, 208

Barrymore, Maurice, 13

Barthelmess, Richard, 54

Baruch, Bernard, 162, 168

Bay, Howard, 206

Bayes, Nora, 49–50

"Because of You," 325

Becky Sharp, 13

Beery, Wallace, 137

Behrman, S.N., 322

Belasco, David, 38, 47, 53

Bel Geddes, Barbara, 290

Bemelmans, Ludwig, 184, 288

Benchley, Robert, 128, 130, 168

Bennett, Robert Russell, 99, 166, 198, 205–6, 208, 231, 257, 267, 278

Berger, Richard, 155, 157

Bergman, Ingrid, 220

Berkeley, Busby, 147

Berlin, Irving, 21, 114, 162, 225, 227, 243–47

Berman, Pandro S., 143, 152

Bernstein, Leonard, 329–30

Best Foot Forward, 184

Bickford, Charles, 146

Big Bear Cafe, 323

"Big Black Giant, The," 311

Bigley, Isabel, 310

"Big Spender," 145

"Bill," 80n
Biow, Sophie, 170, 248
Bitzer, Ray, 212
Bizet, Georges, 179–82, 204–8
Blaine, Vivian, 217
Blanchard, Florence ("Dubby"), 105
Blanchard, Henry James, 76, 105, 115
Blanchard, Marion, 76, 105, 139, 250
Blane, Ralph, 160n
Bledsoe, Jules, 85
Bliss, Helena, 165n
Blossom Time, 67
Blue, Ben, 146
Blue Denim, 357
"Blues in the Night," 173n
Blum, Edward, 349
Blumenstiel & Blumenstiel, 31
Blyden, Larry, 342
Boles, John, 122, 140
Bolton, Guy, 47, 49, 54, 60
Bolton, Whitney, 353
Bonci, Alexander, 20
Bow, Clara, 68
Bowen, Louis, 144, 154, 171
Bowers, William, 159–60
"Boys and Girls Like You and Me," 199
Brando, Marlon, 223
Brazzi, Rossano, 336
Brian, Donald, 165
Brice, Fanny, 21, 48, 109
Brill, Leighton ("Goofy"), 90–92, 96, 98, 100, 108–9, 127, 212, 237
Brokaw, Frances Seymour, 287
Broun, Heywood, 45
Brown, John Mason, 138, 175, 274
Bryan, Vincent, 286
Bryant, Glenn, 205
Brynner, Yul, 297, 301, 304, 304n
Buchanan, Jack, 77

Buck, Pearl S., 115, 284, 335
Buloff, Joseph, 195
Burlesque, 141
Burning Bright, 290
Burns, Robert, 356
Burrows, Abe, 284
Burton, Richard, 316
Bus Stop, 324
Butterworth, A.C., 129–30
Butterworth, Charles, 100, 128–30
By George, 240
By Jupiter, 186
Byrne, Donne, 125–26, 145

Caesar, Irving, 68, 183
Caldwell, Anne, 145
Call Me Madam, 344
Calvé, Emma, 20
Camille, 108
Campbell, Alan, 130, 142
"Can It," 31
Cannery Row, 322
"Can't Help Lovin' Dat Man," 80n, 81, 83
Carmen, 179–81, 204, 207–8, 217
Carmen Jones, 181–82, 204–10, 234, 247, 329, 337
Carminati, Tullio, 122
Carousel, 4, 66, 126n, 222–34, 247, 256, 263, 293, 304, 329, 335
Carpenter, Constance 303
Carrillo, Leo, 53
Caruso, Enrico, 20
Casino, Theatre, 37, 69
Cassall, Gould, 149
Castle, Irene, 152
Castle, Vernon, 152
Castles in the Air, 152
Cavalleria Rusticana, 6
CBS-TV, 297, 332, 334
Centennial Summer, 235
"Ceremony of the Sacred Bath, The," 48

Cerf, Bennett, 25, 286
Champagne and Orchids, 137
Channing, Carol, 331
Chapman, John, 255, 329
Chappell & Co., 124, 219
Charrell, Erik, 145
Chase, Ilka, 333
Chekhov, Michael, 297
Children of Dreams, 106, 107n
Chocolate Soldier, The, 124
Christians, Mady, 223
Churchill, Winston, 347
Ciannelli, Eduardo, 55
Cimarron, 139
Cinderella, 250, 332–34
Cinders, 55
Cinerama, 315
Citizen Kane, 28n
Claire, Ina, 251
Clark, Edward, 35
Clayton, Jan., 234
"Climb Ev'ry Mountain," 345, 349–50
Clurman, Harold, 324
Cochran, Chrales O., 124
Cohan, George M., 38, 63, 334–35
Cohen, Milton, 24, 212
Cohen, Harry, 196
Coleman, Cy, 145
Coleman, Robert, 255
Collier, Constance, 137
Colman, Ronald, 171
Columbia Pictures, 149–51, 196, 290
Columbia Records, 205
Columbia University Players, 27–31, 40, 185
Columbus Theatre, 7
"Come On and Pet Me," 52n
Communist Party, 312
Company, 242, 302n
Compson, Betty, 76
"Concerto in F," 64
Connelly, Marc, 70, 114, 128–30

Coolidge, President Calvin, 103–4
Count Basie, 205
Count of Luxembourg, The, 140
Cousins, Norman, 283
Coward, Noël, 239, 297
Crain, Jeanne, 217
Criss-Cross, 71
Crosland, Alan, 103–4, 106
Crouse, Anna, 238
Crouse, Russel, 114, 284, 344–46
"Cuddle Up a Little Closer," 46
Cullman, Howard, 196
"Cupid Knows the Way," 87–88

Daffy Dill, 49–50
Dale, Alan, 83
Dalton, John H., 113
Damn Yankees (London), 290n
Damrosch, Walter, 6
Dance of Life, 141
Dance to the Piper, 198
Dancing in the Streets, 190
Da Silva, Howard, 195, 290
"Dat's Love," 182
Day, Doris, 336
Day, Edith, 51, 58, 90, 175n
Dean, Basil, 290
Dean, James, 317
"Dear Believer in White Supremacy," 335
"Dear Friend," 211
Decca Records, 203
DeFore, Don, 160n
Dell'Isola, Salvatore, 278
De Mille, Agnes, 194–95, 197–98, 202, 231–32, 253–54, 256, 320–21
Desert Song, The, 66–70, 247
Desert Song, The (London), 69, 73–75, 126n, 170
"Desert Song, The," 69
Desk Set, The, 337
Desperate Hours, The (London), 290n

Devil, The, 18

"Diamonds Are a Girl's Best Friend," 331

Dietz, Howard, 25, 204

Dillingham, Charles, 61–63, 114

"Dites-Moi," 282

Dixon, Lee, 195

Dockstader, Lew, 22

"Doin' What Comes Natur'lly," 244, 246

Dolan, Robert Emmett, 126*n*

Dolly Sisters, 21

Donahue, Jack, 62–63

Donahue, Vincent, 344, 349

Donen, Stanley, 147*n*

Donlevy, Brian, 95

Donnelly, Dorothy, 90, 145

"Don't Ever Leave Me," 99

"Door of My Dreams, The," 56

"Do-Re-Mi," 348

Douglas, Melvyn, 150

"D' Ye Love Me?," 64

Drake, Alfred, 195, 197, 297*n*

Dressler, Marie, 11, 61

Dreyfus, Louis, 124, 126–27, 150, 154

Dreyfus, Max, 46, 50, 52, 61, 132, 191, 219

Drury College, 289

Drury Lane Theatre, London, 59, 69, 124–27, 203, 234

du Bois, Raoul Pène, 206

Duckham, Sir Arthur, 77

Duncan, Angus, 334

Duncan, William Carey, 52

Dunne, Irene, 139, 146, 148

Duvuvier, Julien, 151–52

East Wind, 116, 138, 217

Eddy, Nelson, 137, 140

"Edelweiss," 102, 353

Edens, Roger, 147*n*

Edwards, Cliff, 62

"*Effect of Prejudice Upon the Individual, The,*" 335

Eilers, Sally, 215

Einstein, Albert, 359

Eldridge, Florence, 142

Elektra, 20

Ely, Ted, 228

Emperor Jones, The, 48

Erlanger, Abraham, 38

Erskine, John, 25

Evans, Maurice, 125

"Everybody's Got a Home But Me," 326

"Everyday Is Father's Day for Father," 217

"Every Little Movement Has a Meaning All Its Own," 46

"Face Life," 349–50

Fadiman, Clifton, 4, 284

Fanny, 322

"Farmer and the Cowman, The," 194*n*

Faust, 180

Fearnley, John, 231, 233, 297, 318

Fears, Peggy, 117

"Feasting Song," 69

Ferber, Edna, 70–71, 78, 80–83, 89, 174, 322

Feuer, Cy, 322, 324

Fields, Dorothy, 92*n*, 144–45, 149, 157, 236–37, 242–44, 246, 307

Fields, Frances, 145

Fields, Herbert, 52, 145, 242–44, 246, 307

Fields, Joseph, 145, 337, 341

Fields, Lew, 47, 145, 152

Fields, Rose, 145

Fields, W.C., 48, 108, 112*n*

Finn, Florence, 32, 106

Finn, Frank, 32

Finn, Willy, 32–33, 106

Firefly, The, 33, 46, 114

Fisher Maiden, The, 17, 286
Fiske, Minnie Madden, 13
Fitzgerald, Scott and Zelda, 54
Fleming, Victor, 152
Floradora, 13
Flower Drum Song, The, 337–43, 354
Fluffy Ruffles, 126n
"Fo' Dolla," 259, 261, 267
"Folks Who Live on the Hill, The," 148–49
Follies, 242, 302n
Fonda, Henry, 266, 284, 287, 324
Fonda, Jane, 287
Fonda, Peter, 287
Fontaine, Robert, 289
Forbes, Kathryn, 219
Frawley, Paul, 62
Frawley, William, 146
Freed, Arthur, 147, 147n, 171, 173n, 196, 236, 247
Freedley, Vinton, 190
Free for All, 117, 209
Friedman, Charles, 206
"Friendly Little Farm," 133
Friml, Rudolf, 33, 36, 42, 44, 46, 52, 54–55, 64, 66, 87–108, 162, 174
Furs and Frills, 35

Gabriel, Gilbert, 112, 116
Gang's All Here, The, 114
Garde, Betty, 195
Gardella, Tess, 85
Garden, Mary, 20
Garland, Judy, 167
Garland, Robert, 233
Gaynor, Janet, 215
Gaynor, Mitzi, 336
Gehrig, Lou, 359
Gensler, Lewis, 50, 114, 153
"Gentleman Is a Dope, The," 255

Gentlemen Prefer Blondes, 331
Gentlemen Unafraid, 154, 156–57
George and Margaret, 150
George M. Cohan Memorial Committee, 334
George School, 184, 224, 240
Gershwin, George, 44, 46, 52, 64, 81, 86, 89, 102, 126, 138, 151, 162, 174
Gershwin, Ira, 52, 64, 102, 138, 162, 174, 304
Gest, Morris, 38
"Getting to Know You," 301–2
Ghostley, Alice, 333
Gigi, 147
Gilbert, W.S., 44, 148n, 158–59, 190
Gilmore, Virginia, 297
"Girl That I Marry, The," 245, 247
"Give My Regards to Broadway," 334–35
Give Us This Night, 140
Glaenzer, Jules, 197, 202
Glasser, Benjamin F., 220
Glenn, Dr. Frank, 351
Glorious Morning, 160
Golden Bells (see also *Messer Marco Polo*), 126, 161
Golden Dawn, 83, 107
Goldwyn, Samuel, 219
Good Boy, 91, 100
Good Earth, The, 115
Goodman, Philip, 94
Gordon, Max, 126n, 150, 157, 162–63, 166, 168–69, 175, 182, 196, 199, 204, 206, 235, 334
Grady, Hugh, 113
Grant, Cary, 83
Gray, Alexander, 103
Gray, James, 234
Great Waltz, The, 151, 292
Green, Abel, 149

Greene, Graham, 290

Green Grow The Lilacs (see also *Oklahoma!*), 182, 184, 186, 190, 196, 224, 320

Greenwood, Charlotte, 128, 190, 317

Gregory, Paul, 106, 140

Gropper, Milton, 52–53, 304–5

Group Theatre, 324

Gypsy, 242, 330–31

Gypsy Jim, 52–53, 305

Hale, Alan, 146

Halévy, Ludovic, 180

Hall, Juanita, 263, 267–68, 277, 337, 340

Halliday, Richard, 251, 268, 344–45, 349–50

Hal Roach Studios, 135

Halsman, Philippe, 357

Hamilton Echo, 14

Hamilton Institute, 22, 24

Hammerstein, Abraham, 4–5

Hammerstein, Abraham Lincoln, 6, 26

Hammerstein, Alice, 40, 50, 54, 57–59, 66, 99, 106, 118–19, 133–34, 137, 145, 158, 171, 177, 212, 217–18, 228, 249, 285–86, 351

Hammerstein, Alice ("Allie") (mother), 3, 9–14, 16–19, 23–24, 27, 40, 60, 118, 359

Hammerstein, Anna ("Mousie"), 3, 12–14, 17–18, 23–25, 27, 34–35, 117–18, 132–33, 171

Hammerstein, Arthur, 6, 8, 14, 26–27, 33–37, 40, 42–52, 54–55, 58–59, 61, 64–66, 83–84, 88, 91, 98–100, 108–9, 113–15, 127, 146, 171, 189n, 205, 286, 308, 325

Hammerstein, Berthe, 4–5

Hammerstein, Dorothy Blanchard (wife), 75–78, 84, 89, 91–93, 96, 98–99, 102–7, 111, 115, 117–19, 124–25, 127, 129–30, 132–34, 138–39, 143–45, 150–51, 153–54, 156, 158, 167, 170, 173–74, 176–78, 183–84, 189, 191, 199–202, 207–8, 210, 212–15, 217, 219, 222, 224, 231, 238, 247–49, 251, 260, 262, 264, 275, 279, 282, 284–89, 291–92, 304–5, 313, 319–20, 330, 332, 337, 340–41, 343–44, 348, 351–60

Hammerstein, Dorothy Dalton, 55, 113, 189n

Hammerstein, Dorothy Underhill, 189n

Hammerstein, Elaine, 47

Hammerstein, Emma Swift, 38

Hammerstein, Harry, 6, 26

Hammerstein, James, 111n, 115, 118, 124, 132–34, 138, 156, 177, 206, 210, 213–15, 217–18, 224, 236, 239–40, 257, 266–67, 285–86, 304, 307–8, 310, 341–42, 345, 354–55, 357, 359

Hammerstein, Maggie, 177, 212

Hammerstein, Malvina Jacobi, 9

Hammerstein, Mary Manners, 212

Hammerstein, Mary Steele, 287

Hammerstein, Myra Finn, 32–34, 39–40, 43, 50, 54, 58–59, 66, 73, 78, 83–84, 89, 92–93, 96, 99, 118, 125, 134, 145, 158, 176, 286

Hammerstein, Oscar, 3–9, 12, 17, 19–22, 25–26, 37–39, 45, 48, 55n, 61, 65, 83, 98, 106, 113, 171, 180, 236, 243, 325

Hammerstein, Oscar II, birth and boyhood, 3, 4, 8–19; cancer operation, 351; courtship with Dorothy Blanchard Jacobson, 75; death of, 359; divorce from Myra Finn, 93;

education, 22–30; living in England, 124–28; living in Hollywood, 102–8, 128–54; marriage to Dorothy Blanchard Jacobson, 98; marriage to Myra Finn, 34; relationship with Richard Rodgers described, 223, 272–76, 343–44; start in the theater, 33; work with Hollywood Anti-Nazi League, 141–43

Hammerstein, Regina, 212n

Hammerstein, Reginald Kent, 3, 12–19, 23–24, 26, 34–35, 58, 83–84, 90, 99–100, 109–10, 127, 132–33, 135–36, 159, 212, 257, 266, 287, 307–8, 324, 340–41

Hammerstein, Rose, 9

Hammerstein, Rose Blau, 5, 6

Hammerstein, Stella, 9–10

Hammerstein, Ted, 189n, 308

Hammerstein, William ("Willie") (father), 3, 6, 8–12, 14, 16–19, 21–27, 31, 33, 48, 50, 55n, 60–61, 109, 118, 150, 152, 243

Hammerstein William ("Billy"), 39, 43, 50, 54, 57–59, 66, 99, 106, 118, 124–25, 130, 133–34, 136, 145, 156–58, 172, 177, 183, 199, 200, 206–9, 212, 266, 285–87, 325, 328, 341, 356, 359

Hammerstein's Nine O'Clock Revue, 52

Hammerstein's Roof Garden, 14

Hammerstein's Theatre, 83, 95, 101, 108

Hammerstein's Victoria Theatre, 8–9, 17, 19, 21–22, 25–26, 36, 61, 109, 152, 243

Hammond, John, Jr., 205

Haney, Carol, 341

Happy Birthday, 250

"Happy Talk," 277

Happy Time, The, 289–90

Harbach, Ella, 106, 170

Harbach, Otto, 33, 46–47, 51–52, 54, 59, 61–62, 64, 66, 83, 91, 106, 114, 152, 154–55, 157, 168, 170

Harding, LeRoy, 19, 23

Hardwicke, Cedric, 90

Harkrider, Joseph, 122

Harlem Opera House, 6–7

Harlow, Jean, 131

Harms & Company, 45

Harris, Margaret, 267

Harris, Sam H., 38, 53, 66

Harris, Sophia, 267

Hart, Lorenz, 24–25, 28–29, 52, 81, 89, 92n, 102, 126n, 138, 145, 148n, 164, 167, 174, 184–86, 191, 194, 231, 235, 304, 348

Hart, Moss, 138, 322

Harwood, John, 94

Hay, Mary, 54, 62

Hayes, Bill, 310

Hayes, Helen, 250

Hay Foot, Straw Foot (see also Gentlemen Unafraid), 157

Haymes, Dick, 217

Hayward, Leland, 259–60, 280–81, 285, 296–97, 300, 307, 344–45

Healey, Ted, 114

Heart Interest, 108

Heart of the Matter, The, 290

Hecht, Ben, 138, 201

Heggen, Thomas, 272

Heggie, O.P., 49

Hein, Silvio, 35

Helburn, Theresa ("Terry"), 184, 190, 194–99, 219–20, 222, 235, 251, 267

Heller, Milton, 40

Heller, Rose, 40

Hellman, Lu, 213

"Hello, Young Lovers," 298–99
Hello Dolly!, 351
Hepburn, Audrey, 344
Herbert, Victor, 23, 33, 46–47
Herz, Ralph, 44
Herzig, Sig, 126n
Heyward, DuBose, 126
Higher and Higher, 274
High Jinks, 47
High Noon, 315
High, Wide and Handsome, 146–49, 151, 153, 194, 319
Hirsch, Louis, 162
Hobson, Valerie, 304
Holiday, Billie, 205
Hollywood Anti-Nazi League, 141–43, 312
Holm, Celeste, 195
Holman, Libby, 89, 94
Holmes, Ralph, 160n
Holtzman, David, 303
Holtzman, Fanny, 291–92, 303
"Home," 298
Home, James, 29–30
"Honey Bun," 269, 276–77
Hopkins, Arthur, 141
Hornblow, Arthur, 56
Hornblow, Arthur, Jr., 140–41, 146, 314–16, 319
Horne, Lena, 217
Hoschna, Karl, 46
Hotel Splendide, 184–85
Houdini, Harry, 22
House Un-American Activities Committee, 313
Howard, Leslie, 54, 73
Howard, Norah, 290
"How Do You Solve a Problem Like Maria?," 346–48
Howell, Nella, 144
Hughes, Elinor, 255, 281
Hunter, Louise, 83

Hutton, Betty, 247
Hyman, Bernie, 152
Hyman, Dr. Harold, 24, 99, 158, 186, 218, 231, 237, 350–51, 355, 359

"I Am Going to Like It Here," 338
"I Cain't Say No," 149n, 287
"I Can't Give You Anything But Love," 145
Iceman Cometh, The, 250
Idiot's Delight, 292
"I Enjoy Being a Girl," 338
"If I Loved You," 224–26
"I Have Been in Love," 298
"I Haven't Got a Worry in the World," 250
"I'll Take Romance," 150
"IloveyouIloveyou," 51
"I'm Alone," 122
"I'm a Yankee Doodle Dandy," 334
"I'm Gonna Wash That Man Right Outa My Hair," 269
"I'm One of God's Children (Who Hasn't Got Wings)," 110–11
"Impossible," 333
"Indian Love Call," 4, 56, 58, 155
"In Egern on the Tegern See," 121
I Remember Mama, 223–24, 234, 247
"It," 68
"It Might As Well Be Spring," 68, 216–17
"It's a Grand Night for Singing," 217
"It's a Grand Old Flag," 334
"It's a Scandal! It's an Outrage!," 194n
"I've Told Ev'ry Little Star," 120, 238
"I Want a Man," 94–95
"I Won't Dance," 127

Jacobs, Morrie, 273, 275

Jacobson, Henry, 75, 84, 96, 105, 134, 286–87, 354
Jacobson, Henry (Dorothy's son), 96, 132–33, 177, 211, 215, 218, 249, 286, 354, 359
Jacobson, Susan, 90, 96, 99, 102, 104–5, 107, 124, 132–34, 156, 177, 206, 215, 218–19, 247–50, 264, 266, 287, 351, 354, 358–59
Jazz Singer, The, 103
Jimmie, 48–49
Joan of Arkansaw (see also *Always You*), 44
John Loves Mary, 250–51
Johnson, Nunnally, 128
Johnson, William, 324
Jolson, Al, 21, 126
Jones, Allan, 140
Jones, Shirley, 234, 317–19, 321
Jubilee, 138
Jumbo, 138
"June Is Busting Out All Over," 228
Junior Miss, 175, 337

Kadison, Milton, 24, 40, 58
Kahn, Gus, 94
Kahn, Otto, 65
Kalman, Emmerich, 83
Kalmar, Bert, 91
"Kansas City," 194n, 321
Karloff, Boris, 171
Katz, Sam, 137, 179–80
Kaufman, Beatrice, 183
Kaufman, George S., 162, 168, 183
Kazan, Elia, 194n
Kean, Dr. Ben, 350–55, 358
Keaton, Buster, 22
Keel, Howard, 247
"Keep It Gay," 310–11
Kellerman, Annette, 21
Kelly, Gene, 147n, 341–42
Kenney, Ed, 340
Kent, Rockwell, 286

Kern, Betty, 89, 97, 144, 237–38
Kern, Eva Leale, 89, 97, 106, 150, 235, 237–38
Kern, Jerome, 42, 44, 46, 50, 59–63, 68, 70–73, 78–79, 82–89, 91, 94, 97–102, 106, 108–9, 114–15, 117, 120–22, 125–28, 130, 137–39, 144–46, 148–52, 154–55, 157, 161–64, 167, 169, 172–74, 178, 184, 194, 208, 217, 223, 235–38, 243, 257n, 278, 307
Kerr, Deborah, 304
Kerr, John, 337
Kerr, Walter, 353
Keyser, Beatrice, 171
Kiepura, Jan, 140
King, Alan, 65n
King and I, The, 126n, 292–304, 309, 319, 323, 328, 335
King, Dennis, 56
Kirk, Lisa, 255
Kiss Me Kate, 282
Klaw, Marc, 38
Klopfer, Donald, 286
Klopfer, Pat, 286
Knapp, Walter, 354
Knickerbocker Holiday, 231
Knights of Song, 157–59
Knopf, Edward, 130, 153
Knopf, Mildred, 130, 153
Koenig, William, 104
Kohinoor, 7
Korjus, Meliza, 152
Korngold, Erich Wolfgang, 140
Kraft, Hy, 130, 313, 358
Krasna, Norman, 250–51
Kreisler, Fritz, 145
Kronenberger, Louis, 233–34, 255

La Boheme, 180
Lady Be Good, 173n
Lady in the Dark, 234, 291–92
Laemmle, Carl, Jr., 139

Lamour, Dorothy, 146
Landon, Margaret, 291, 335
Langner, Armina Marshall, 190, 251
Langner, Lawrence, 190, 194–95, 198, 219–20, 222, 227, 232, 235, 251
Last Time I Saw Paris, The, 172–73, 178
Laurents, Arthur, 329–31
Lawrence, Gertrude, 77–78, 291–92, 299–301, 303–4
Lawrence, T.E., 69
Laye, Evelyn, 175*n*
LeBaron, William, 140–41
Lederer, Charles, 128–29
Lee, C.Y., 337
Le Gallienne, Eva, 220
Lehár, Franz, 140
Lehmann, Lilli, 6
Leigh, Carolyn, 145
Leonowens, Anna H., 291
Lerner, Alan Jay, 89, 203
Lester, Edwin, 262
Levant, Oscar, 211
Levien, Sonya, 315
Levin, Herman, 331
Lewine, Richard, 333
Lewis, Robert, 290
"Liebestraum," 92*n*
Liebling, William, 297
"Life Upon The Wicked Stage," 77
Life with Father, 344
Light, The, 37
Liliom (see also *Carousel*), 220–21, 224, 226–27, 335
Lillie, Beatrice, 77
Major Gordon ("Pawnee Bill") Lillie And William F. ("Buffalo Bill") Cody's Combined Wild West Show, 23, 243
Lindsay, Howard, 159, 211, 333, 344–46
Linn, Bambi, 233, 263, 321

Lion, Harold, 98
Lippmann, Robert, 29
Little Minister, The, 13
Liveright, Horace, 286
Lockhart, Gene, 104
Lockridge, Richard, 167
Loewe, Frederic, 89
Logan, Joshua, 194*n*, 245–46, 250–51, 259–61, 263, 266–69, 272–78, 280–82, 296, 299, 322, 329, 332, 335–37, 357
Logan, Nedda, 264, 266, 272–73
Lombard, Carole, 141
London Opera House, 21
"Lonely Feet," 127, 257*n*
"Lonely Room," 193
Long, Avon, 165*n*
"Look for the Silver Lining," 60
"Looking for a Dear Old Lady," 28
Loos, Anita, 250
Loper, Don, 165*n*
Loring's Rhymers Lexicon, 148*n*
Losee, Harry, 163
"Lost Chord, The," 39
Lottery Bride, The, 108
Louise, 180
Louisiana Purchase, 244
"Lovely to Look At," 145
Love Me Tonight, 194
"Lover, Come Back to Me," 66, 90, 92
Luana, 108
Lubitsch, Ernst, 147
Ludwig, William, 315
Luke, Keye, 340
Lute Song, 297
Lynch, Shawen, 177
Lyrics, 30, 289, 298

MacArthur, Charles, 138
MacDonald, Jeanette, 108, 137
Mackay, Clarence, 21
MacMurray, Fred, 141

Macowan, Norman, 160
MacRae, Gordon, 234, 317, 319
Madame Butterfly, 44, 180, 261
Magna Theatre Corporation, 314–15, 335
Mainbocher, 349
Main, Marjorie, 122
"Make Believe," 80*n*, 83, 88
"Make the Man Love Me," 145
"Make Yourselves at Home," 35
Mama's Bank Account (see also *I Remember Mama*), 219, 223
Mamoulian, Rouben, 146–48, 194, 198, 231, 250
Mandel, Frank, 47, 49–50, 66, 69, 89–90, 109, 115–17, 138, 161
Manhattan Opera House, 7
Manhattan Opera House (second), 8, 19–20
Manhattan Theatre (see also Hammerstein's Theatre), 115–16
Mankiewicz, Herman, 25, 28, 31
Mann, Thomas, 142
Mantle, Burns, 101, 116
"Many a New Day," 194*n*
Marbury, Elisabeth, 162
March, Frederic, 140, 142
Marco Millions, 146
"Maria," 330
Marks, Edward B., 60
Marsh, Howard, 85
Martin, Brooks, 290
Martin, Dean, 336
Martin, Ernest, 324, 332
Martin, Hugh, 160*n*
Martin, Mary, 154–55, 190, 195, 251, 262–68, 276–80, 297, 332, 336, 344–45, 349–51
Marx, Groucho, 195, 332
Mary Jane McKane, 52, 55
Mathias, Melinda, 285
Mathias, Peter, 285
Mathias, Phil, 285

Matthews, Brander, 25
Mayer, Louis B., 196
Maytime, 67
May Wine, 138
McClintic, Guthrie, 290
McCormack, John, 20, 38
McCormick, Myron, 267, 277, 282
McCracken, Joan, 310
McDonald, Grace, 165
Me and Juliet, 308–12, 319
Meek, Donald, 217
Meet Me in St. Louis, 147, 292
Meilhac, Henri, 180
Melba, Nellie, 20, 106
Member of the Wedding, 315, 324
Mence, Len, 100, 300
Meow, 285
Mercer, Frances, 165
Mercer, Johnny, 126*n*, 173*n*
Mercury Theatre, 160
Meredith, Burgess, 220
Merivale, Philip, 73
Merman, Ethel, 242, 246, 330–31
Merriam, Frank, 142
Merrick, David, 322
Messer Marco Polo, 125, 145, 217
Metro-Goldwyn-Mayer, 56, 114, 128, 137, 146–47, 151, 153, 157, 171, 175, 179–80, 183, 196–97, 236, 247, 285, 320, 336
Metropolitan Opera Company, 6, 8, 19–21, 25, 65, 208
Meyner, Governor Robert, 354
Michener, James A., 259–61, 264, 268, 270–71, 284, 335–36
Middleton, Ray, 246
Mielziner, Jo, 231, 253, 267–68, 277–78, 290, 292, 301, 309–10
Miller, Alice Duer, 161
Miller, Henry, 47
Miller, Marilyn, 48, 60, 62
Minnelli, Vincente, 147*n*, 162, 166
Minnevitch, Borrah, 62*n*

Minstrel Show, The, 24
Mr. Ambassador, 262
Mister Roberts, 260, 263, 266, 272, 287
"Mister Snow," 231
Mitchell, James, 321
Mitchell, Ruth, 302
Modern Library, The, 286
Moën, Peter, 156, 177, 203, 206, 228
Moën, Walter, 177
Molnár, Ferenc, 18, 220–21, 224, 226, 231–33
Moore, Grace, 150
Morehouse, Ward, 255
Morgan, Helen, 85, 91, 99–101, 108
Morrison, Hobe, 208, 303, 329, 353
Morrow, Doretta, 300
Motley, 267
Murphy, Dudley, 132
Murphy, Owen, 114
Murrow, Edward R., 332
Musical Stages, 315
Music Corporation of America, 144
Music in the Air, 117, 120–22, 121n, 124, 142, 183, 307–8
Music War Committee, 211
"My Bicycle Girl," 172
"My Defenses Are Down," 246
My Fair Lady, 332
"My Favorite Things," 346, 348
"My Heart Belongs to Daddy," 190
"My Little Redskin," 49
"My Own Little Corner," 333
My Sister Eileen, 175, 337
"Myth That Threatens America, The," 235
Myth That Threatens The World, The, 284
"My Wife," 279

Nathan, George Jean, 208, 233, 308
Nathan, Robert, 126n

Naughty Marietta, 33, 114
NBC (National Broadcasting Company), 165n
Nelson, Ralph, 333
Newman, Paul, 317
New Moon, The, 83, 89–92, 107, 126n, 170
New Toys, 53–54
Nichols, Lewis, 233
Night Is Young, The, 131–32
Nijinsky, 28
Nimmo, James Hunt, 3, 11–12, 18, 115
Nimmo, Janet Smeeton, 3, 11–12, 15, 18
Nixon, Marni, 304
"Nobody Else But Me," 235
Nobody Home, 60
"Nobody Wants Me," 85
No, No, Nanette, 64
"No Other Love," 311
Norton, Elliot, 166, 255, 281, 327, 354
"Now Is the Time," 279
"No Wonder I'm Blue," 110
Nuyen, France, 336–37

Oakland, Ben, 150
Obondorf, Augusta Hammerstein, 171
Obendorf, Clarence, 171, 236
Of Thee I Sing, 231
"Oh, What a Beautiful Mornin'," 186, 188, 198, 241, 316
Oklahoma! (on Broadway), 4, 59, 126n, 147, 186–204, 206–8, 212n, 215, 217, 219, 221, 223–24, 231, 233–35, 242, 244, 247, 256, 262, 267, 282, 287, 303–4, 314, 318, 327–28
Oklahoma! (film), 314–21, 332, 335
"Oklahoma," 197, 199
Oliver, Edna May, 84

"Ol' Man River," 4, 80n, 82–83, 90, 102, 119, 227, 353

Olsen, George, 62

Olympia Theatre, 7–8, 61, 113

"One Alone," 70

"One Foot, Other Foot," 93

O'Neill, Eugene, 48

"One Kiss," 86

"One More Dance," 121

One Night in the Tropics, 157

One Night of Love, 150

One Touch of Venus, 262

"Only Room for One More," 31

On Your Way, 28

Oppenheimer, George, 286–87, 306

Osborn, Paul, 337

"Our Heroine," 261

Our Town, 252, 255

"Out of My Dreams," 194n, 321

"Over There," 334

Pacific Overtures, 242, 302n

Pagan Love Song, 336

Pagliacci, 180

Pagnol, Marcel, 322

Pajama Game, The (London), 290n

Pal Joey, 323

Paramount Pictures, 137, 139–40, 146, 149, 344

Paris Bound, 88

Parker, Dorothy, 128, 130, 142

Patterson, Elizabeth, 146

Peace Pirates, The, 28

"People Will Say We're in Love," 193, 199

Perlberg, William, 149

Person to Person, 332

Peter Pan, 332

Philadelphia Opera House, 8, 21

Pickford, Jack, 28, 62

Pickwick Papers, The, 98

"Pick Yourself Up," 145

Picnic, 337

Pidgeon, Walter, 103–4, 140

Pinza, Ezio, 262, 267, 279, 325, 332, 336

Pipe Dream, 323–29, 331

Platt, Marc, 198

Pop, 49

"*Pore Jud,*" 193, 197

Porgy, 126

Porgy and Bess, 138, 146, 194

Porter, Cole, 81, 138, 164, 186, 281–82

Potash, Shirley, 121n, 264, 273, 305

"Prejudice Is Wrong," 335

Preminger, Otto, 236

Prince, Hal, 302n

Prince, Littler, 247

Princess Theatre, 50, 60, 162

Prinz, LeRoy, 337

"P.T. Boat Song, The" (Steady As You Go), 211

Puccini, Giacomo, 221

Puck, Eva, 85

Pygmalion, 231

Queen O' Hearts, 49–50, 114

Quine, Richard, 165

Rahn, Muriel, 206

Rainbow, 91, 93–95

Random House, 286

Rapf, Harry, 132

Rasch, Albertina, 163

RCA Victor, 311

Reade, Walter, 55

Reckless, 131

Redell, Walter, 176

Reed, Janet, 110–11

Reed, Napoleon, 205

Reinhardt, Gottfried, 152

Reinheimer, Ellie, 40, 106

Reinheimer, Howard, 40, 75, 98, 106, 108, 114, 153, 183, 261, 273–75, 299, 305, 312, 315

Riggs, Lynn, 182, 184, 187, 192–93
Ring in the New, 155
Rio Rita, 72–73, 78
Riskin, Everett, 150
Rittman, Trude, 231, 267, 278, 300
Rizzuto, Phil, 359
Robbins, Jerome, 296, 300, 329–30
RKO-Radio Pictures, 146, 150–52, 196, 249
Roberta, 125, 139, 150
Roberts, Joan, 195, 197
Robeson, Paul, 89–90, 115, 139, 312
Robinson, Edward G., 151, 171
Robinson, Hubbell, 332
Rodeo, 194
Rodgers, Dorothy, 189, 215, 222, 228, 251, 287, 291, 344, 348, 354
Rodgers, Linda, 222
Rodgers, Mary, 222, 233, 343
Rodgers, Mortimer, 29
Rodgers, Richard, 24, 29, 31–32, 40, 44, 52, 89, 92n, 102, 126n, 138, 145–46, 167, 174, 184–92, 194–98, 200, 202, 211, 215–17, 219–23, 226–27, 230–33, 235–36, 242–46n, 250–54, 256–66, 268–70, 273–77, 279–81, 287, 290–93, 295, 297, 299, 302–4, 308–10, 314–15, 318–22, 324–28, 332–33, 335–37, 340, 343–45, 348, 350–51, 354, 358
Rodgers & Hammerstein Pictures, Inc., 315, 336
Rogers, Ginger, 147, 152
Rogers, Will, 9, 22, 215
Romance with Music, 171
Romberg, Lillian, 170
Romberg, Sigmund, 42, 44, 66–70, 83, 86, 90, 92, 102–3, 106, 108–9, 116, 131–32, 138, 161–62, 169, 172, 175, 178, 217
Rome, Harold, 322
Rooney, Mickey, 167, 171
Rosalie, 86

Rose, Billy, 138, 145, 204–6, 212, 218, 263, 304, 307, 328
Rose, Eleanor Holm, 204, 263, 304
Rose-Marie, 54–56, 58–59, 66, 83, 114, 234
Rose-Marie (London), 126n
Rosenberg, Anna Hammerstein, 6, 10, 55n
Rosenberg, Henry, 55n
"Rose's Turn," 331
Rubin, J. Robert, 114
Ruby, Harry, 91, 128–30
Ruggles, Charles, 94–95
Ruskin, Harry, 108–9
Russell, Rosalind, 336
Ruth, Babe, 359
Ryskind, Morrie, 25

St. John, Betta, 263, 267, 277
St. Louis Municipal Opera, 154
Sally, 48, 60, 62, 78
Salome, 20
Saratoga Trunk, 174, 184, 322
Saturday Night, 329
Savage, Archie, 277
Savory, Gerald, 150
Saxon, Luther, 205
Sayonara, 337
Schildkraut, Joseph, 220
Schilling, Margaret, 106
Schurmer, Gus, 318
Schuster, M. Lincoln, 25
Schwab, Laurence, 47, 65, 69, 74, 89, 92, 109, 115–17, 138, 143 152, 154–57, 206, 283, 288
Schwab, Mildred, 288
Schwartz, Arthur, 172
Scott, Randolph, 146, 148
Search, The, 315
Segal, Vivienne, 103
Selznick, David, 24
Selznick, Myron, 24

Seven Lively Arts, 218
Seven Year Itch, The (London), 290n
"Shall We Dance," 301
Shamroy, Leon, 336–37
Sharaff, Irene, 292, 296–97, 301, 309
Shaw, Robert, 206
Shean, Al, 122
Sheean, Vincent, 325
"She Likes You," 194n
Sherman, Hiram ("Chubby"), 165
Sherwood, Robert E., 284
Shiek, The, 68
Short, Hassard, 64, 166, 206, 337
Showalter, Max, 165n
Show Boat, 4, 56, 70–73, 77–78, 81, 84–89, 91, 94, 99, 101, 109, 115, 117, 122, 139, 147, 163, 167, 170, 172, 187, 199, 203, 208, 278, 353
Show Boat (London), 90, 126n
Show Boat (1932 revival), 115, 124
Show Boat (1936 film version), 139, 153
Show Boat (1946 revival), 183, 234–39, 247, 266
Shubert Brothers, 25, 38, 67, 113–14
Shubert, Lee, 114, 206
Simon & Shuster, 289
Simon, Richard L., 25
Simon, Robert A., 114
Sinatra, Frank, 336
Sinclair, Upton, 142
Singin' in the Rain, 147
Sister Gregory, 349–50
"Sixteen Going on Seventeen," 351
Skouras, George, 315
"Small House of Uncle Thomas, The," 296, 300, 305
Smith, Alison, 112
Smith, Cecil, 257
Smith, Kent, 290
Smith, Muriel, 205, 337
Smith, Oliver, 316, 349
"Sober Sue," 22

So Big, 71n
"Softly, as in a Morning Sunrise," 92
"Soliloquy," 66, 220, 228–30
Somebody's Sweetheart, 43
"Some Enchanted Evening," 4, 262
"Someone Will Teach You," 194n
"Something Wonderful," 294–95
Sometime, 36
"Sometimes I'm Happy," 52n
Sondheim, Mrs. Herbert ("Foxy"), 170, 213
Sondheim, Stephen, 79, 89, 171, 213–14, 217, 222, 233, 239–42, 254, 257, 286–87, 305–7, 329–31, 343–44, 357–58
"Song Is You, The," 121
Song of the Flame, 64–65
Song of the West (film version *Rainbow*), 107
Soo, Jack Suzuki, 340
Sothern, Ann, 173n
Sound of Music, The, 102, 122, 344–53
"Sound of Music, The," 4, 345–46
South Pacific, 4, 247, 259–82, 296, 301, 303–4, 318–19, 327–29, 335
South Pacific (film), 335–37, 345
Spiegel, Max, 50
Stage Door Canteen, 183, 242
Stallings, Lawrence, 94
Stanton, Edmund, 6
"Stan' Up an' Fight," 182
State Fair (film), 215, 217, 234, 353, 357
State of the Union, 344
Stay-As-Sweet-As-You-Are-Athletic Club, 130
Steiger, Rod, 317, 321
Stein, Jules C., 144
Steinbeck, Elaine Scott, 287–88, 304, 326
Steinbeck, John, 287, 290, 304, 322–24, 326–29

Steiner, Max, 95
Stewart, Donald Ogden, 142, 184–85, 206
Stewart, John, 290
Stickney, Dorothy, 333, 348
Stong, Phil, 215
Storch, Larry, 340, 342
Story of Vernon and Irene Castle, The, 152
Stothart, Dorothy, 55
Stothart, Herbert, 42–44, 49, 52, 55, 58, 64, 91, 114
Stout, Rex, 211
"Stouthearted Men," 66, 90, 92
Stowe, Harriet Beecher, 300
"Strange Case of Adam Standish Or Psycho-Analysis Strikes Back, The," 165
Strauss, Johann, II, 151
Street Scene, 231
Stronach, Alexander ("Sandy"), 119–20
Stuart, Leslie, 23
Student Prince, The, 67
Styne, Jule, 331
"Suddenly Lucky," 301
Sullavan, Margaret, 287
Sullivan, Arthur, 44, 158–59, 190
Sullivan, Ed, 247, 332
Summer Holiday, 147
Sunny, 59, 61–64, 107, 154
"Sunny," 64
Sunny River, 172, 175, 195, 201, 209
Sunny River (London), 175n
"Surrey with the Fringe on Top, The," 192
Surtees, Robert, 320–21
Suzuki, Pat, 340, 342
Swanson, Gloria, 122
Swarthout, Gladys, 140
Sweet Adeline, 98–99, 101, 114, 139, 172, 353
Sweet Bird of Youth, 339

"Sweetest Sight That I Have Seen," 163–64, 257n
Sweet Thursday (see also *Pipe Dream*), 323–24, 328
Swing High, Swing Low, 141

Tabbert, William, 267, 277
Tales of Hoffman, 20
Tales of the South Pacific (see also *South Pacific*), 259–61, 292
Talmadge, Norma, 143, 163, 170
Tamiroff, Akim, 146
Tandy, Jessica, 160
Taylor, Deems, 206
Taylor, Dwight, 159
Taylor, Elizabeth, 336
Taylor, Laurette, 159
Taylor, Robert, 140
Taylor, Samuel, 289
Teahouse Of The August Moon (London), 290n
Temple, Shirley, 195
Ten for Five, 31
"Ten Minutes Ago," 333
Terrell, St. John, 288
Terris, Norma, 84, 236
Tetrazzini, Luisa, 20
Thalia Theatre, 6
"That's for Me," 217
Theatre Guild, 126, 146, 182, 184, 190, 194–96, 198, 204, 220–21, 231, 255, 287, 314
"There's a Hill Beyond a Hill," 122
"There Is Nothin' Like a Dame," 276
"There's No Business Like Show Business," 244, 247
"They Didn't Believe Me," 59
"They Say It's Wonderful," 244–46
"This Nearly Was Mine," 279
"This Was a Real Nice Clambake," 227
Thompson, Jim, 292, 296
Thomson, Virgil, 182, 208

Three Musketeers, The, 86
Three Sisters, 127, 209, 317
Tickle Me, 46–48, 50
Tiger at the Gates, 324
Till the Clouds Roll By, 236
Tinney, Frank, 46, 48–49
Tiomkin, Dmitri, 152
Tip-Toes, 64
"Tired Business Man, The," 50–51
Titchmarsh, Sarah, 156
"To Alice on Her Birthday," 137
Todd-AO, 314–16, 320, 335
Todd, Michael, 199, 242, 280, 314–15
"Tom," 298
"Tom-Tom," 50
"Tonight," 330
Topper, 287, 306
Tosca, 180
"Totem Tom-Tom," 56
Traubel, Helen, 324, 326, 329
Trentini, Emma, 20, 33
"Twas Not So Long Ago," 102, 353
Twentieth Century-Fox, 215, 217, 234, 236, 249, 304, 335
"Twin Soliloquies," 262, 282
Tyler, Judy, 324

Umeki, Miyoshi, 340, 342
United Artists, 108
United World Federalists, 283
Universal Pictures, 139
Upstage and Down, 31
Urban, Joseph, 122

Valentino, Rudolph, 68
Van Doren, Carl, 25, 28, 33, 36, 284
Van Druten, John, 219, 223 296–97, 300
Van Upp, Virginia, 141
Van Vechten, Carl, 8
Vera-Ellen, 16n
Very Good Eddie, 60n

Very Warm for May, 162, 164–69, 175, 183, 201, 209, 236
Victory at Sea, 332
Viennese Nights, 103, 107–8
Von Trapp, Maria, 349

Wagner, Richard, 121
Walker, Don, 231
Wallace, Mike, 332
Wallach, Eli, 316
Walston, Ray, 310
Walters, Charles, 147n
"Wanting You," 92
Warner Brothers, 65, 69, 102–4, 174, 195
Warner, Jack, 106, 108
Warrior, The, 103
Watanabe, Eleanor ("Doody") Blanchard, 105–7, 177, 183
Watanabe, Jennifer, 177, 183–84
Watanabe, Jerry, 177, 183, 212
Watters, George Manker, 141
Watts, Richard, 167, 353
"Way You Look Tonight, The," 145
"Weaknesses," 31
Webb, Clifton, 54, 62, 137
Weber and Fields, 21, 145
Weingart's Institute (camp), 24, 26 32
Welcome House, 284–85
West, Mae, 36
"Western People Funny," 296
West Side Story, 242, 329
Westmoreland, Elizabeth, 206
"We've Got Something," 48
'We're on Our Way (Infantry Song)," 211
Whale, James, 139–40
What Price Glory?, 94
"What's the Use of Wonderin'," 230
"When I Grow Too Old to Dream," 66, 131–32, 138
When You're in Love, 149

Where Do We Go from Here?, 159–60

Whirl of the World, The, 67

White, Frances, 49

White Horse Inn, 145

White, Miles, 194, 231

White, Sammy, 85

Whiting, Jack, 166

Whiting, Richard A., 44, 116

"Who?," 4, 63–64

"Why Do I Love You?," 80*n*, 87

"Why Oh Why?," 194*n*

"Why Shouldn't We," 56

"Why Was I Born?," 101

Wildflower, 51, 55, 114

Wild Rose, The, 66

Williams, Emlyn, 280

Williams, Jill, 77, 98

Williams, Paul, 144

Williams, Percy, 38

Williams, Tennessee, 339

Williamson Music, Inc., 219

"Will You Marry Me Tomorrow, Maria?," 148

Wilson, Teddy, 205

Winchell, Walter, 83

Windust, Brentagne, 149*n*

Wings Over Europe, 146

Winkle Town, 52

Winninger, Charles, 85, 217

Winsten, Archer, 217

With the Happy Children, 285

Wizard of Oz, The, 133

Wodehouse, P. G., 50, 60, 85

Wood, Grant, 293

Woollcott, Alexander, 51, 53, 71, 130, 304

Woods, Al, 38

Woodward, Joanne, 317

World's Fair Corporation, 172

Worth, Billie, 165*n*

Writers' War Board, 183, 211, 224, 235, 242, 283, 286

Writers' Board For World Government, 211, 283

Wynn, Ed, 36

Yamaguchi, Shirley, 126*n*

Yip Yip Yaphank, 243

YMCA, 108

Yolanda and the Thief, 292

"You Are Love," 80*n*

You Bet Your Life, 332

"You Can't Get a Man with a Gun," 246, 251

You'll Never Know, 31

"You'll Never Walk Alone," 4, 227

Youmans, Vincent, 42, 44, 46, 51–52, 91, 94–95, 162

Young Rida Johnson, 36

"Younger than Springtime," 279

"Your Dream (Is The Same As My Dream)," 157

"You're a Queer One, Julie Jordan," 224

You're in Love, 34

"You've Got to Be Carefully Taught," 269–70

Zanuck, Darryl F., 215

Ziegfeld, Florenz, 60–62, 71–73, 77–78, 83–87, 89, 91, 109, 114–15, 139, 235

Ziegfeld Follies, 48, 77, 292

Zinnemann, Fred, 315–17, 319–21

Zukor, Adolph, 146, 149

About the Author

HUGH FORDIN was born and raised in New York City. After graduating from the School of Speech and Dramatic Art at Syracuse University, he began to produce summer touring shows and road companies of Broadway plays and musicals, one of which was *Flower Drum Song*. Producer of several Edith Piaf concerts in Paris, he had arranged her farewell tour in the United States when she died in 1963. He worked as head of casting for David Merrick before joining Twentieth Century-Fox, where he cast *The Boston Strangler*, and acquired for the studio such properties as *M*A*S*H*, *Play It Again Sam* and *Joanna*. After a stint at screenwriting, in 1973 he wrote his first book, *The World of Entertainment! Hollywood's Greatest Musicals*, about the Arthur Freed Unit at MGM.